WOLPE, Howard. Urban politics in Nigeria; a study of Port Harcourt. California, 1975 (c1974). 314p map tab bibl 73-76115. 16.75. ISBN 0-520-02451-6

Wolpe's account is based on close to two-years' research in Nigeria (1963–65) towards the end of party politics. He offers a detailed account of politics in Port Harcourt since the city's establishment in 1913. From the vantage point of the major port of what used to be Eastern Nigeria and aspired to become Biafra, Wolpe provides an understanding of political processes in the region that is superior to Audrey C. Smock's *Ibo politics* (CHOICE, Jul.–Aug. 1971). This study joins the onslaught on the traditional perspective that dichotomizes "tradition" and "modernity"; it is an African counterpart to the classic by Lloyd I. Rudolph and Susanne Hoever Rudolph, *The modernity of tradition* (CHOICE, Oct. 1968). Wolpe demonstrates "that there is no necessary incompatibility between functioning as a modern economic man, on the one hand, and performing as a communal political actor, on the other." He further shows that communal groups bear little relationships to traditional ethnic groups and that their configurations are constantly in flux. He goes beyond the Rudolphs in his emphasis on how political actors move easily among communal associations, trade unions, and

Continued

WOLPE

religious lobbies. Wolpe has given us a fine case study, accessible to the undergraduate reader, of politics in a plural society that all too many observers continue to analyze in terms of tribalism.

Urban Politics in Nigeria

URBAN POLITICS IN NIGERIA

A Study of Port Harcourt

by Howard Wolpe

University of California Press
Berkeley   Los Angeles   London
1974

University of California Press
Berkeley and Los Angeles, California
University of California Press, Ltd.
London, England
Copyright © 1974 by The Regents of the University of California
ISBN: 0–520–02451–6
Library of Congress Catalog Card Number: 73–76115
Printed in the United States of America

FOR MY SON, MICHAEL.
*May the Nigerian experience help him and his generation
to understand and control the forces
that underpin communal conflict and
violence in all societies.*

Acknowledgments

An accurate recording of the many persons and institutions that have assisted in the preparation of this study, which has spanned a period of ten years, would run several pages. It is possible here to acknowledge the contributions of but a few; the names of many others are scattered through the text itself.

There are three persons to whom particular acknowledgment must be made. Robert Melson of Purdue University, Richard L. Sklar of the University of California, Los Angeles, and my mother, Zelda S. Wolpe, a clinical psychologist, have contributed to every phase of this research enterprise. I have worked so closely with these three scholars over the last several years that it is very difficult to claim unique authorship of the ideas and concepts that are developed in this study of modernization and communal conflict in Eastern Nigeria. I am grateful not only for the intellectual stimulation that their association has provided but also for their encouragement, advice, and friendship.

I wish, too, to express my appreciation to Lucien Pye for his patient and invaluable supervision of the doctoral dissertation that inspired this particular study; to Simon Ottenberg, Frederick Frey, Willard Johnson, and the late William Brown, for their helpful comments and criticism; and to Myron Weiner, John Ballard, G. I. Jones, Archibald Callaway, Ikenna Nzimiro, David Abernethy, James O'Connell, and Marvin Zonis, all of whom have generously contributed of their insights and their data.

In Port Harcourt, Mayor Francis Ihekwoaba and Deputy Mayor Gabriel Akomas made it possible for me to attend both open and executive sessions of the Municipal Council and the local branch of the National Convention of Nigerian Citizens (NCNC); executive officers of the Municipal Council, Town Clerk N. M. Agada and Town Clerk E. O. Ezie, permitted me access to the council archives and gave generously of their time and information; and Mr. T. A. Onyelike and Mr. C. C. Udom made available party records and files. In addition to the above, the following persons were particularly helpful: Hon. Emmanuel Aguma, Mrs. Mercy Alagoa, Mr. Sunday Amadi, Mr. Izuchukwu Areh, Mr. E. I. Bille, Mr. D. S. Brown, Mr. George Chuks-Okonta, Mr. and Mrs. Ralph Davis, Mr. D. Die-Fiberesima, Mr. G. I. Egbunine, Mr. G. E. Hanse, Mr. Apollos Ihemere, Mr. Sam Ijioma, Mr. A. D. W. Jumbo, Mr. A. E. C. Jumbo, Mr. Frank Kennedy, Mr. C. O. Madufuro, Mr. Samuel Mbakwe, Mr. J. U. Mbonu, Mr. Dennis Ndudu, Mr. and Mrs. Nwobodike Nwanodi, Senator Chief Z. C. Obi, Mr. Kalu Ogba, Hon. Michael Ogun, Mr. Daniel Ohaeto, Mr. M. D. Okechukwu, Miss Maureen Olphin, Mr. T. A. Onyelike, Mr. R. O. Osuikpa, Mr. and Mrs. John Salyer, Mr. Luke Ukatu, Hon. John Umolu, and Mr. Xrydz-Eyutchae. A large portion of my interviews were with members of the Port Harcourt Municipal Council; their names appear in the body of the text, and their assistance is gratefully acknowledged.

Officials of the Eastern Nigerian and federal governments and of the Eastern Working Committee of the NCNC helped to place Port Harcourt in regional and federal perspective. In particular, I wish to express my indebtedness to Hon. E. C. Okwu, Dr. the Hon. S. E. Imoke, Hon. Mbazalike Amechi, Dr. G. C. Mbanugo, Mr. E. D. O. Iloanya, Mr. N. U. Akpan, Mr. N. O. Ejiogu, Mr. J. C. Menakaya, Mr. J. O. Munonye and Mr. E Y. I. Ihezue. The assistance of the senior archivist in Enugu, Mrs. R. E. Nwoye, greatly facilitated my search of the National Archives.

My research in Nigeria was supported by the Carnegie Foundation fund of the Center for International Studies at the Massachusetts Institute of Technology and by a supplementary grant of the Institute of African Studies at the University of Ife. Dr. S. O. Biobaku and the Institute of African Studies sponsored my two-year stay in Nigeria (April 1963 to February 1965) and provided living and research facilities during my visits to Ibadan. Dr. Glenn Johnson and Dr. Carl Eicher, both then associated with the Economic Development Institute of the University of Nigeria, similarly provided important assistance in Enugu. The completion and typing of the final manuscript were facilitated by Western Michigan University research grants.

Finally, it is doubtful that this manuscript would have been completed were it not for the support and encouragement that my wife, Nina, lent to the entire venture. This experience has provided many wonderful shared memories, including that notable weekend in which Nina established a personal barrier outside my study until I had completed an especially belabored chapter. For this gentle prodding, and for much more, I am deeply grateful.

Contents

Contents

Contents

xiii

Contents

Urban Politics in Nigeria

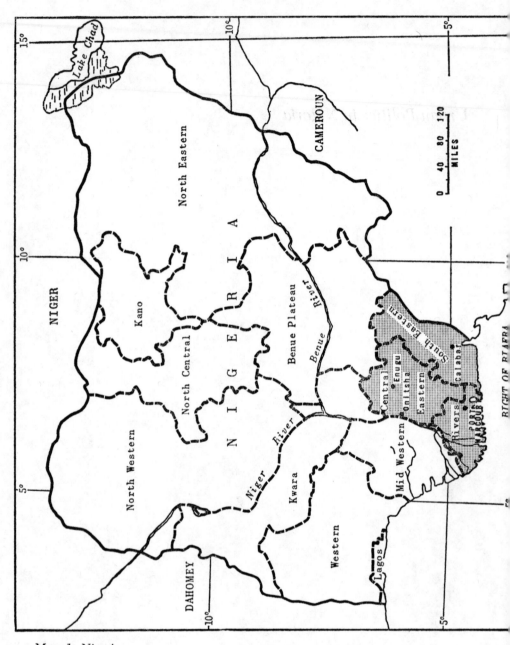

MAP 1. Nigeria.

SOURCE: Eastern Nigeria Ministry of Commerce, *Investment Opportunities in Eastern Nigeria* (Enugu: Government Printer, 1962).

CHAPTER 1
Introduction

It is wisdom to think the people are the city.
It is wisdom to think the city would fall to
pieces and die and be dust in the wind
If the people of the city all move away and
leave no people at all to watch and keep
the city.

—CARL SANDBURG

THE PROBLEM: MODERNIZATION AND COMMUNALISM

This study explores the relationship between modernization and communal conflict through an examination of the changing patterns of social cleavage and community power in the Eastern Nigerian city of Port Harcourt. It has been said that technological and economic development lead ultimately to the decline of communal conflict, and that the emergence of "modern" socioeconomic roles and identities undercuts the organizational bases upon which communal politics rests. This conclusion has resulted from a long-standing sociological perspective that dichotomizes "tradition" and "modernity," that tends to identify communal modes of organization with the "traditional" pole, that sees social change as an evolution from communal to noncommunal forms, and that views communal conflict as the product of cultural diversity and the reassertion of traditional antagonisms.[1] Recently, however, this conventional view has been challenged by several scholars working in culturally plural societies.[2] They have suggested that communalism, far from being a historical anachronism in the modern age may in fact be a persistent feature of social change,

3

and that tradition-modernity models have obscured this theoretical alternative, thereby producing false expectations concerning the direction of change. It is this theoretical issue—the extent to which the forces of modernization tend to erode or to strengthen communalism as a basis for political identification and action—with which this study of urban political development is primarily concerned.

Port Harcourt, prior to the Nigerian/Biafran war a communally heterogeneous urban center in process of rapid growth and industrialization, furnishes an especially appropriate arena for the study of the nature and sources of communal strain. In many respects the prototype of the nontraditional African cities that emerged as a result of the Western impact upon African society, Port Harcourt was established in 1913 as a sea outlet for Nigerian coal deposits just discovered to the north. The city was organized and administered according to European models and by European personnel, but was populated primarily by culturally diverse rural immigrants. And, like so many new cities, Port Harcourt's prewar industrial and commercial expansion—by 1965 the municipality had become the site of Nigeria's second largest harbor, the center of the country's petroleum industry, and the nation's second largest industrial center—was unable to match an extraordinary rate of immigrant-based population growth. Unemployment and overcrowding provided ironic testimony to Port Harcourt's modernity, and established the background of scarcity against which a pattern of communal cleavage and competition unfolded.

A second, related concern of this Port Harcourt study is the exploration of the bases of Ibo organizational adaptability. In his pioneering study of Nigerian nationalism, James Coleman observed that Ibos had played a singular role in Nigeria's postwar political era, dominating both the leadership and the mass membership of the most militant nationalist organizations.[3] However, no less noteworthy was the parallel development among the Ibo of a highly cohesive and organizationally sophisticated ethnic movement. It is this paradoxical blending of "cosmopolitan" and "parochial" orientations which perhaps best defines the modern Ibo political experience and which has attracted the attention of so many observers of the African scene.

4

Port Harcourt has had a role of special significance in the political development of Eastern Nigeria's Ibos. Because it was the only important Ibo-speaking urban center situated on land identified with neither of the major Onitsha and Owerri Ibo subgroups, Port Harcourt was considered "neutral ground" by most Ibos and became, in 1948, the headquarters of the pan-Ibo movement. Moreover, the city's importance as a commercial, industrial, and administrative center yielded an extremely high concentration of Ibo wealth and entrepreneurial and professional skills. Consequently, a study of communalism in Port Harcourt illuminates the factors underlying the much heralded adaptation of the Ibo to urban political life and the modern Nigerian polity.

Finally, this investigation into the politics of communalism in Port Harcourt is intended to shed light on the wider Eastern Nigerian and federal political systems with which the city is linked. No urban community can be divorced from its societal context; to identify and understand patterns of urban conflict and community power is to acquire insight into the politics of the regional and national systems in which cities are embedded. This is especially so in the case of Port Harcourt. On the one hand, prior to the Nigerian/Biafran war, Port Harcourt mirrored more accurately than any other urban community the ethnic and religious makeup of the Nigerian East. As a result, the major sources of strain within the Eastern Region—the conflict between the majority Ibos and minority non-Ibos, the continuous competition among the various Ibo subgroups characterizing most political activity, the persistent hostilities between Catholics and Protestants, and the growing class tension between Eastern Nigeria's "haves" and "have-nots"—were all manifested within the urban community.

On the other hand, the city's economic importance has placed Port Harcourt at the center of both the intraregional and interregional conflicts that have characterized recent Nigerian history. Eastern Nigeria's non-Ibo minorities have long attempted to establish their own state inclusive of Port Harcourt—a goal finally accomplished by the federal victory in the Nigerian/Biafran war—and the city's Ibo majority and non-Ibo minority elements have been centrally involved in the separatist debate. At the national

5

level, the city's economic potential, represented as much by its harbor and industrial facilities as by the adjacent oil fields and petroleum refinery, has made control of Port Harcourt a crucial and continuing concern of the federal government.

"Communalism" in this study[4] refers to the political assertiveness of groups that have three distinguishing characteristics: first, their membership is comprised of persons who share in a common culture and identity and, to use Karl Deutsch's term, a "complementarity of communication";[5] second, they encompass the full range of demographic (age and sex) divisions within the wider society and provide "for a network of groups and institutions extending throughout the individual's entire life cycle";[6] and third, like the wider society in which they exist, they tend to be differentiated by wealth, status, and power. Communal demands and conflict are politically distinctive in that they may reflect a desire for separation and may threaten to alter the political boundaries of the wider society.[7] Commonly such conflicts are labeled "tribalism" and are spoken of as the political expression of "ethnicity." However, communalism is preferred here as a term that has fewer value-laden connotations and that is capable of subsuming, in addition to ethnic conflicts between linguistic/cultural groups, a variety of intergroup conflicts—such as those involving race, religion, and geographic region—which are not always thought of as strictly ethnic in character.

The theoretical perspective that underpins the present study departs in several respects from the dichotomous tradition-modernity models that have often guided empirical research into processes of social and political change. First, communal conflict is seen as being generated neither by traditional factors nor by the simple fact of cultural diversity. Rather, it is viewed as the end product, in a culturally plural society, of competition for the scarce resources of wealth, status, and power. As long as the resources that men seek to acquire are in scarce supply, men will organize themselves for competition and struggle. And, in a context of cultural pluralism, the most effective organizational vehicle is the communal group. In this sense, it is probably more accurate to suggest that conflict produces "tribalism" than to argue, as the conventional wisdom would have it, that "tribalism" is the cause of conflict.

Second, communal groups and boundaries are seen not as fixed, historical entities, but as transformable entities, changing constantly in response to changing social and political exigencies. Indeed, a glance at today's world reveals that much contemporary communal conflict—whether between Hindu and Moslem in India, black and white in the United States, or Ibo and Hausa in Nigeria—is being waged not by traditional entities, but by communities that are the product of technological, economic, social, and political change. Yet, this empirical reality has been obscured by the dichotomous formulation that organizes the developmental process into either/or categories.

Third, modernization is thought of not as a force destructive of communalism (as the dichotomous formulation would suggest), but as one that may well reinforce communal conflict and create the conditions for the formation of entirely new communal groups. In a culturally plural society, modernization has the effect of reorienting formerly separate peoples to a common system of rewards and paths to rewards, thereby generating new patterns of intergroup interaction and competition. Men enter into conflict not because they are different but because they are essentially the same. It is by making men "more alike," in the sense of possessing the same wants, that modernization tends to promote conflict. At the same time, the new patterns of intergroup interaction and competition lead, in turn, to increasing personal insecurity and to a search for individuals and groups that might prove useful allies during intergroup conflict. Eventually, new communal groups emerge through the expansion and internal differentiation of traditional categories.

Last, communal and noncommunal political loyalties are viewed not as incompatible—as tradition-modernity models imply—but as capable of coexisting within the same individual. All persons possess multiple social identities that are of varying salience, depending upon their perception of the situation with which they are faced. In some situations, men may join together in defense of their common religious commitment; in others, they may organize to protect their occupational interests or, at election time, to promote the interests and prestige of their communities of origin. The important point is that since the various identities of any given individual are each triggered by different social situations, seemingly conflicting identities may well be compatible.[8] Social roles may, in effect, be compartmentalized, thereby permitting the individual to respond flexibly to changing social and political circumstances. Thus it is possible for an individual to be both a communal and a noncommunal actor. This suggests, in turn, that the emergence of modern socioeconomic roles and identities need not lead to the destruction of communal modes of organization; communal differentiation and conflict may well persist in the midst of economic modernization.

The relationship between modernization and communalism is complex, and we have attempted here to do no more than sketch the broad contours of a theoretical perspective. A more complete and precise theoretical statement must await a concluding chapter, by which point we will have before us a detailed case study of the politics of communalism in Port Harcourt.

ORGANIZATION OF THE STUDY

The study that follows is divided into four parts. Part I describes Port Harcourt's physical, economic, social, and cultural setting, focusing not only upon the city itself, but also upon the regional backdrop of rural Eastern Nigeria. We then shift, in part II, to an historical overview of Port Harcourt's political development, attempting to highlight—and to explain—the changing character of social cleavage and political competition. Attention is focused, in turn, upon Port Harcourt's formative years (1913–1919), dur-which the colonial government acquired the land upon which the new city was to be developed, and established its European-dominated governmental framework; upon the years of African political coalescence (1920–1943), which saw newly arrived immigrants gathering together to provide mutual protection and assistance in the alien, urban milieu and to confront the local European rulers; and finally, upon the transfer of local government power from European to African hands and the introduction of the franchise (1944–1954). Part III carries the historical narrative forward to the years immediately preceding the Nigerian/Biafran war. Successive chapters explore the nature and significance of communal conflict through case studies of electoral politics, labor/management conflict, religious confrontation, and the struggle between Ibos and non-Ibos over the creation of a separate Ijaw-dominated, Port Harcourt-centered Rivers State. Finally, part IV addresses itself, by way of conclusion, to the theoretical concerns identified in this introduction.

PART I

The Setting

CHAPTER 2
An Introduction to Port Harcourt

> *Who made Port Harcourt what it has evolved to*
> *become today? Many forces were involved in the*
> *building of this town. First of all we must think*
> *of those who surveyed the area; then the workers*
> *who constructed the houses; then we have to think*
> *of those who lived in these houses, as colonial*
> *administrators, civil servants, wage-earning and*
> *salaried employees, traders, teachers, mission-*
> *aries, professionals and the rest. All these ele-*
> *ments collaborated in making Port Harcourt what*
> *it is today.*
> *When the history of this entrepot is accurately*
> *portrayed, the role played by the makers of Port*
> *Harcourt will not be forgotten.*
>
> —DR. NNAMDI AZIKIWE[1]

Urbanism is not new to Africa, the modern city is. Before the
Western intrusion, urbanism in what was to become Nigeria took
two principal forms: the ancient trade centers of the North and
the traditional agriculturally oriented urban centers of the West.
The ancient trade centers, such as the Northern Nigerian towns
of Kano and Katsina, were formed as a result of their location
on major precolonial trade routes and developed into large, administratively sophisticated city-states. Today, new, modern sectors have been grafted onto many of these ancient communities,
but traditional authorities have maintained a prominent position.
   Agriculturally oriented urban centers, exemplified by the Western Nigerian Yoruba towns of Ibadan, Abeokuta, and Oyo, simi-

larly predated European colonialism. Emerging in response to the slave-raiding and political turmoil of the eighteenth and nineteenth centuries, the economy of these urban centers was firmly tied to their surrounding farm lands that were owned and worked by the urban inhabitants. Each town tended to be culturally homogeneous, and kinship was usually the dominant organizing principle of the community. Today, these cities have been strongly affected by the introduction of modern commerce and industry; traditional institutions have been adapted to the requirements of European-style representative government, and the indigenous elements of each town must now contend with large numbers of migrants from other areas. Nevertheless, indigenous social and political institutions still exercise considerable influence within these traditional urban centers.

With the Western impact upon African society, there emerged new kinds of urban centers. Typified by the Eastern Nigerian towns of Enugu, Aba, Umuahia, and Port Harcourt, these new urban centers were founded in direct response to administrative and economic initiatives of the British, or were developed as a result of their favorable location on colonial trade routes.[2] Inspired by European commercial or administrative interests, they were frequently organized and administered in the European image. Even when they were founded at or near the site of an indigenous settlement, as in the case of Onitsha, they quickly became cosmopolitan centers comprised of large, often culturally heterogeneous, immigrant populations. It is these new towns that today are the focal point for most of the administrative, commercial, and industrial activities of the new nations. As a consequence, it is they that most often operate the controlling levers of their national economies and continue to receive the greatest number of urban immigrants; and it is their social and political institutions that are most in a state of flux.

PORT HARCOURT'S PHYSICAL SETTING

Port Harcourt's origins are rooted in the 1909 discovery of coal in Eastern Nigeria's Udi Division.[3] Effective exploitation of the coal fields required the development of a distribution network to enable the coal to be carried to Lagos and other West African ports. The search for a site that would be suitable both as a sea-

14

port and as a railway terminus led to the exploration of the Bonny River and, eventually, to the discovery of the natural harbor that was to become the economic raison d'être of one of Nigeria's most important commercial and industrial centers. The port was subsequently named after Lewis Harcourt (later Viscount Harcourt) who served as secretary of state for the colonies from November 7, 1910, to May 26, 1915.[4]

Lying about forty feet above sea level and a very few degrees above the equator, Port Harcourt has the reputation of being, next to Lagos, the most climatically uncomfortable city in the federation. Daytime temperatures range in the eighties, while the relative humidity averages over seventy-five percent. The rainy season lasts from April to November, but no month is entirely dry. Mean annual rainfall exceeds ninety-eight inches, and in the peak of the rainy season sixteen inches may fall in a single month.

Because of its location on the edge of the Niger Delta's mangrove foreshore, much of Port Harcourt is uninhabitable, consisting in the main of winding creeks and muddy swampland. In the early sixties, the city's population was spread among a number of dry-land residential layouts, ranging from the plush, low density Europeanized sections that accommodated the city's expatriates and Nigerian upper class (senior civil servants, a few professionals, and wealthy businessmen), to the mud and thatch villages of Port Harcourt's small, indigenous settlement. The greatest part of the urban population was concentrated within the medium-to-high density sections known as the "main township" and "Mile 2 Diobu." The latter area, located two miles to the north of the main township, derived its name from the indigenous Ibo-speaking Diobu community that was formerly in control. The division between the main township and Mile 2 Diobu corresponded roughly to the division between the haves and have-nots of the African population. As is so often the case in American towns, railroad tracks marked the socioeconomic boundary.

The main township was comprised of Port Harcourt's original "native location," by the 1960s greatly expanded beyond its original boundaries. The development of this section of town had been orderly, subject to intensive governmental regulation and supervision. Unlike Mile 2 Diobu, the main township consisted

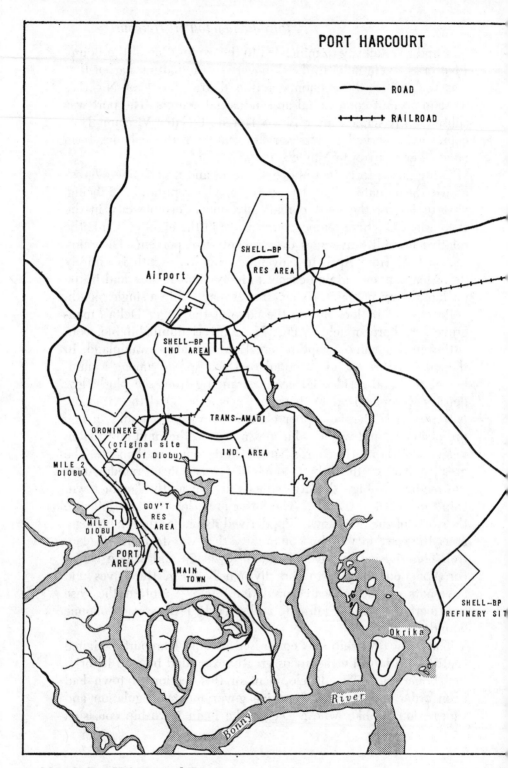

MAP 2. Port Harcourt and Environs.
SOURCE: *Port Harcourt,* published by the Port Harcourt Chamber of Commerce, n.d.

of "Crown land," title to which had been acquired through purchase from the indigenous inhabitants by the British colonial government and then, with Nigerian independence, transferred to the Eastern Nigerian government. Most of the Crown land was leased to private plotholders. Rental agreements were usually long-term, ranging from forty to ninety-nine years, but plotholders were normally required to develop their plots within a specified period of time and in strict accordance with township zoning and construction bylaws.

The main township was distinguished by the size and sturdiness of its residential structures, many of which were imposing multiple-story dwellings housing as many as forty or fifty persons. One section of the main township, referred to as the "Big Man Quarters" by virtue of the large number of prosperous African businessmen and professionals who were located there, consisted almost exclusively of large, three-story dwellings. The greatest number of buildings within the main township and adjacent residential areas, however, were more modest, single-story houses with eight to twelve small rooms; each house could accommodate anywhere from one to twelve independent households. Typically, residential structures—both large and small—were designed in the shape of a "U" or a square, with a large number of rather small rooms encircling an inner courtyard, in much the same way as village huts commonly encircle an open clearing. There were normally one or two bucket latrines for a building's inhabitants, and a single cooking area. There were, of course, variations on this building plan. The newer apartment houses and private homes, and some of the older private residences that were erected by Europeans or by especially prosperous and well-educated Africans, had modern plumbing and kitchen facilities and tended to follow the European architectural style more strictly. In any event, individual households within a building compound typically operated as independent units; communal preparation of food was rare.

Almost all buildings within the main township and adjacent residential layouts were furnished with electricity, but many of the area's residents carried their water from outdoor, public water taps. These public water facilities also served as recreational areas for the township's children. Adults, however, were not quite so appreciative of the inconveniences posed by the absence of indoor running water, and in Mile 2 Diobu even public water taps were in short supply. Periodically, the water tap problem was aired in the letters-to-the-editor columns of the local newspapers.

Another grievance of one group of main township residents hinged on the operation of the city's conservancy service. Most of the population relied upon a bucket latrine system of waste disposal. The Municipal Council's "night soil men" were generally conscientious in their evening collection of the city's buckets; however, they dumped the night soil in the swamp foreshore that bordered one of the city's principal thoroughfares. When the tides were in, the material was washed ashore in an area used frequently as a children's playground.

Almost all streets in the main township were paved, but ever-present potholes made driving hazardous, especially in the wet season. Deep open drains, never quite up to the task of carrying off the heavy rains, ran along the sides of the roads and served as receptacles for both water and human wastes. Port Harcourt streets were acknowledged by Eastern Nigerians as the worst of any of the Region's urban areas. The poor quality of Port Harcourt soil, a lack of foresight on the part of the early engineers, and the heavy volume of the city's commercial and industrial traffic were factors contributing to the city's difficulties. An Israeli engineering firm, commissioned by the Eastern Nigerian government to survey Port Harcourt's road, drainage, and sewerage systems, estimated in 1961 that it would cost over $28,000,000 to provide for the city's present and future requirements.[5] To put this cost estimate in perspective, the total 1962–63 revenue accruing to the Port Harcourt Municipal Council was just over $700,000.[6]

The economic and social hub of the main township was the main market. Nigerians everywhere are by tradition traders, and in Port Harcourt there was scarcely a family that did not have some representation in one of the city's three markets. Competition for market stalls and lock-up shops was fierce in all of them, but nowhere was it as great as in the main market. As was pointed out some years ago by a government commission enquiring into allegations of Town Council corruption, the stakes were high:

Markets have been described as the "life" of Port Harcourt. There are three of them, the main market in the centre of the town, Diobu Market about two miles along the Owerri Road, and the Creek Road Extension market established about 1949, which lies further towards the end of the Port Harcourt peninsula, and not being "on the way to anywhere," has never been popular. Stalls in the other two markets are very much sought after; the scale of rents for Crown plots of land is based on distance from the main market and there is no doubt that sites in or adjacent to this market are the most valuable in Port Harcourt. No figures are available but a fair estimate might be that a trader who had enough capital to stock a stall in the main market could make a profit of £300 a year, and if he could secure and stock a "lock-up" shop he could look forward to a profit of £1,000. The market traders have always been undisciplined and for years their habit of squatting in unauthorized places, of extending their stalls and of keeping half their stock in the public ways, has been a constant source of trouble. In dealing with the allegations against the Council concerning markets it is clear that some sections of traders made a determined and unscrupulous attempt to secure at any cost what they considered to be their rights.

As in most of the urban markets of the Region, anyone who secures a market stall regards it almost as heritable property and there have been numerous actions in the Court against the Council which in pursuance of market improvement schemes attempted to move them.[7]

The excess of demand over supply made the Town Council's power to allocate market stalls and lock-up shops a source of considerable financial reward to opportunistic officeholders. Allegations of corrupt market allocations were among the principal charges that led to the appointment of the 1954 Commission of Enquiry. The commission was critical of the large numbers of councillors' dependents whose names appeared in the market records, and of the councillors' acceptance of "gifts" from market traders.

Mile 2 Diobu, across the railroad tracks, provided a sharp contrast to the main township.[8] Though part of the original 1913 colonial land acquisition, the area of Mile 2 Diobu was subsequently returned to its original Diobu owners and was, therefore, never subject to the same regulation and control exercised by

19

the government over its Crown land holdings. In 1963–1964, over eighty thousand persons were crowded into a space of less than one square mile, and newly arrived immigrants moved into Mile 2 and the surrounding area every day in search of cheap land and accommodations. Monthly room rents began as low as $1.82 and averaged about $4.20 as contrasted with the average main township rent of $5.60.[9]

Comparative statistical data are lacking, but it was evident that the population of Mile 2 Diobu was younger than that of the main township—both in terms of age and in terms of the length of tenure in the urban area. A 1964 housing survey reported that less than 17 percent of the persons in the households covered were over thirty years old, while 42 percent were fourteen years of age or under.[10] Almost all of the 231 adults interviewed (87.3 percent) had lived in Port Harcourt for less than fifteen years; 48.4 percent, in fact, had resided in the city for less than five years. Only two persons had been born within the municipality. As new arrivals, Mile 2 Diobu's male residents tended to move into jobs requiring unskilled or semiskilled labor. Unemployment was an ever-present concern of the employed as well as the jobless.

Many of Mile 2 Diobu's newer buildings, though not of the same construction quality as main township housing, were quite substantial dwellings. According to the housing survey, however, almost 15 percent of Mile 2 Diobu's population lived in mud and thatch huts. Furthermore, the general absence of sewerage and drainage systems, the inadequacy of the area's conservancy service, and the absence of even so much as road traces in some sections, made life in Mile 2 Diobu a constant struggle against mosquitoes, disease, and death. In 1952, the regional senior health officer reported to the Port Harcourt Planning Authority in urgent terms:

> The most pressing health problem in Port Harcourt is African housing. There is an acute housing shortage, and the demands are not being met by the erection of crowded insanitary dwellings in unplanned suburbs . . . there is no control. The whole area (of Mile 2 Diobu) is one vast warren of low, dark, ill-ventilated, small roomed mud and thatch shacks, with an odd permanent or semi-permanent house. There are no roads nor drains. Access is by muddy narrow refuse littered lanes, where

one sidesteps the cesspools and the borrowpits. Refuse lies where it is flung; the only latrines are a few insanitary shallow pits; water is drawn from shallow unprotected wells. . . . The slums of Diobu menace the whole of Port Harcourt.[11]

The year this report was submitted, the population of Mile 2 Diobu was estimated at twelve thousand, and the number of modern-style, permanent houses in the area numbered a hundred.[12] But the migrations of the fifties were already underway. By 1959, only seven years later, the modern housing estimate of the local authorities had increased twentyfold to two thousand, while the population was said to number nearly fifty thousand.[13] Living conditions in 1959 were much the same as they were seven years earlier:

> There are no roads in the area, except for the Regional Trunk Road B, which bisects it, although the house owners have recently made some efforts to clear mud traces and to dig drains designed to carry away the surface water which used to convert Mile 2 into a veritable swamp during the wet season. There is no piped-water supply, the inhabitants being dependent entirely for their water upon insanitary unlined wells dug in their compounds, nor is there any electric light. There are no public buildings, no sanitary structures and the conservancy service, supplied now by a contractor selected by the Ikwerre District Council, is rudimentary. The Ikwerre Council clears refuse stacked at the few points accessible to its tipper lorry, but this service is intermittent, and there are no public dustbins.[14]

In 1959, signs of change in Mile 2 Diobu slowly began to appear. In that year, the Planning Authority formulated plans to begin an attack on the problem of road construction. Then, in 1960, Mile 2 Diobu was brought for the first time under the administrative jurisdiction of the Port Harcourt Municipal Council. It was felt that the Port Harcourt Council was better equipped to handle the typically urban problems presented by Mile 2 Diobu than was the rural-centered Ikwerre District Council, headquartered some forty miles away, but five years later the situation remained desperate. In view of the area's low socioeconomic position, it was not surprising that Mile 2 Diobu had a rowdy and aggressive style of politics of its own, differing substantially from that of the more prosperous and socially secure

main township. Politically, the main township's leaders constituted the city's "establishment"; in their view, Mile 2 Diobu politicians had not yet "arrived."

ECONOMICS OF THE CITY

Port Harcourt's harbor is second in size only to that of Lagos, the
national capital. It serves as the principal distribution point not
only for Eastern Nigerian exports and imports but also for those
of part of the Northern Region. The Eastern Nigeria railway
links the two regions, passing through the rich mineral and
groundnut fields of the North, the coal field of Udi, and the palm
oil plantations of the Ibo hinterland. In 1962–63, roughly one-
quarter of Nigeria's total export and import tonnage (exclusive
of crude oil exports from nearby Bonny) was handled over the
Port Harcourt quays. More significant, however, is the rate of
expansion of the port's shipping operations: between 1930 and
1962–63, the combined deadweight tonnage of general cargo
exports and imports passing through Port Harcourt increased by
almost 1,000 percent.[15]

The harbor and railway, however, provide only one part of the
explanation for Port Harcourt's economic significance. Petroleum
and natural gas round out the economic equation. The search for
oil in Nigeria was begun by the Shell D'Arcy Company (now
Shell–British Petroleum or Shell-BP) in 1937, but it was only in
1956—nineteen years and $42 million later—that the first com-
mercial oil was discovered at Oloibiri, some forty-five miles from
Port Harcourt.[16] By 1963, nine oil and natural gas fields had been
established, eight of these in close proximity to the Eastern Nigerian railway-port. Between 1958 and 1966, crude oil exports
soared from $2.8 million or .8 percent of total exports, to $257.6
million, or 33 percent of total exports. Government oil revenues
from rents, royalties, premiums, profit taxes, and customs duties
rose from $14 million in 1963 to $76 million in 1967.[17] With the
outbreak of the Nigerian/Biafran war in 1967, oil production
temporarily dropped from 580,000 barrels a day to 55,000 barrels,[18] but within a year after the war's conclusion, oil output
reached 1.25 million barrels a day, bringing Nigeria within the
top seven of the world's petroleum producing nations. It is anticipated that by 1973 oil production will reach 2 million barrels a

day, equivalent to nearly 5 percent of total world production.[19] Today, a total of fourteen companies from six countries have concessions for oil exploration, while four companies are actually involved in production. But Shell-BP continues to dominate the industry, accounting for two-thirds of the $1.4 billion total investment, three-fourths of total production, and two-thirds of existing productive capacity.[20] In 1965, Shell-BP joined with the Nigerian federal government to open a $33.6 million oil refinery at Eleme just outside Port Harcourt. It is anticipated that the refinery will be capable of meeting all of Nigeria's domestic requirements for major petroleum products until 1974 or 1975, by which time a second refinery may be in operation. The net foreign exchange benefits of the refinery total in excess of $36 million annually.[21]

The discovery of oil and natural gas laid the foundation for a rapid industrial upsurge in Port Harcourt. In 1958, Shell-BP transferred its administrative and industrial headquarters from Owerri Town in the Ibo hinterland to Umokoroshe, just eight miles outside Port Harcourt's municipal boundaries. This move, prompted by the proximity of the riverain township to the existing oil fields and to both harbor and airport facilities, established the municipality as the petroleum center of the Nigerian federation, and Shell-BP as the leader of the new oil industry. Secondary industries were not long in following. On the one hand, the natural gas found in association with neighboring oil fields (and said to be sufficient to satisfy all projected markets until at least 1990) provided a cheap power source for new industries;[22] on the other, the Eastern Nigerian government gave added incentive to prospective investors by opening the Trans-Amadi Industrial Estate.[23] Industrial plots on this estate were leased by the Eastern Nigerian government to both expatriate and indigenous investors. A tire plant, representing an $8.4 million investment; an aluminum sheet factory ($3.5 million); a glass industry ($2.8 million); a machete factory ($1.25 million); a cement paints industry ($196,000); and an enamelware factory ($280,000) were already in operation in the early sixties. These industries had joined older firms established outside the industrial layout, such as the large Nigerian Tobacco Company, and still other large investments were projected for the near future.[24] Port Harcourt was also characterized by a similar concentration of small industries. A 1961

survey revealed that two-thirds of Eastern Nigeria's small industrial firms, representing investments up to $140,000 were located
in the Region's three largest towns: Onitsha, Aba, and Port Harcourt.[25]

If Port Harcourt played a role of major significance as a national economic center, its role as a *regional* economic center
was even more crucial. Thus, while Port Harcourt contained less
than 2 percent of Eastern Nigeria's population, Port Harcourt's
residents in 1962–63 contributed 18.7 percent of the Region's
total income tax revenues.[26] The heavy tax burden of the municipality stemmed from the city's relatively high wage and salary
levels. In 1961–62, for example, Port Harcourt's industrial operatives were earning average wages of $658.00 per annum, while
the regional average for industrial operatives was only $372.00.
At the same time, the professional, administrative, managerial,
and clerical staff of Port Harcourt's industries were averaging a
$4,570.00 annual income, contrasted with the regional average
of $3,140.00 (and the regional per capita product of $58.80 reported in 1952–53).[27]

THE URBAN POPULATION

It is against this backdrop of extraordinary economic expansion
that Port Harcourt's high rate of population growth—alluded to
in the description of Mile 2 Diobu—becomes understandable.
Drawn by the economic opportunities offered by the expanding
commercial and industrial center, immigrants poured into the
municipality by the hundreds each week. Population statistics,
taken over time, provide some indication of the dimensions of
this migratory flow (table 1). Between 1953 and 1963 alone, the
urban population expanded by over two and a half times.

By far the greatest part of Port Harcourt's prewar population
was composed of short-distance immigrants who had moved into
the railway-port from the Ibo hinterland to the north or, to a
much lesser extent, from the Ijaw-speaking areas adjacent to
Port Harcourt and the Efik-speaking territory to the east. Less
than 7 percent of Port Harcourt's 1963–64 population was indigenous to the area, and relatively few immigrants came from outside Eastern Nigeria.[28] Northern Hausas, Western Yorubas, and
Mid-Western Edos and Ibos all had some representation. In addi-

24

TABLE 1

PORT HARCOURT POPULATION GROWTH

Year	Port Harcourt proper	Mile 2 Diobu	Municipal totals[a]
1921	7,185	—	—
1931	27,000	—	—
1953	59,512	12,788	73,300
1963	95,768	83,795	179,563

[a] Inasmuch as some of the larger industrial establishments lay outside the municipal boundaries, the Port Harcourt urban area technically was larger than the municipality. However, most of those employed even in the outlying industrial plants resided within the municipal boundaries.

SOURCES: (1) The 1921 Census, reported by P. Amaury Talbot, *Peoples of Southern Nigeria* (London: Oxford University Press, 1926), vol. IV, p. 22; (2) *Population Census of the Eastern Region of Nigeria, 1953* (Lagos: Census Superintendent, 1953), pp. 42–47; (3) The 1963 Census Reports for Census Districts Nos. 309301 and 309302 (Lagos, mimeographed); (4) *Annual Report for Port Harcourt District, 1943* (National Archives File OW 5389/7; Riv Prof; 1/29/1101).

tion, there were a small number of Syrian and Indian shopkeepers, and an increasing number of Europeans and Americans had taken up short-term residence in the city.[29] Yet Port Harcourt remained in its immigrant composition essentially an Eastern Nigerian community. The 1953 census figures presented in table 2 illustrate not only the numerical superiority of Eastern Nigerians within the muncipality, but also the extent to which the general distribution of nationalities within Port Harcourt's population paralleled that of the wider Eastern Region. The Ibo-speaking population comprised an overwhelming majority in both cases, with the Ijaws, Efiks, and Ibibios constituting the principal minorities. Though the 1963 census data have not been published in full, it is likely that Ibos accounted for most of Port Harcourt's population growth since 1953. In support of this supposition, the 1964 Mile 2 Diobu housing survey reported that Ibos accounted for 84.8 percent of the total population of this area of newer settlement (as contrasted to the 1953 main township percentage of 77.3 percent).[30] Thus, Port Harcourt was identified not only as an Eastern Nigerian community but also as a predominantly Ibo-speaking community. The preponderance of Ibos in Port Harcourt's urban population was but part of a broader pattern of modern-day Ibo mobility. A "cityless" people traditionally, the Ibo responded enthusiastically to the new economic opportunities

TABLE 2

AFRICAN POPULATION OF PORT HARCOURT AND
EASTERN NIGERIA, BY NATIONALITY (1953)[a]

Eastern nationalities	Port Harcourt		Eastern Nigeria	
Ibo	45,503	77.3%	4,916,734	68.1%
Ibibio	2,022	3.5	737,118	10.2
Ijaw	4,535	7.7	258,962	3.6
Non-Eastern natonalities				
Yoruba	1,935	3.3	11,377	.2
Edo	899	1.5	4,027	.1
Hausa	624	1.1	10,288	.1
Fulani	1	—	757	—
Tiv	10	—	5,121	.1
Nupe	64	.1	2,811	—
Kanuri	16	—	2,151	—
Unclassified Nigerian nationalities[b]				
	2,171	3.7	1,261,614	17.4
Non-Nigerians	1,076	1.8	4,289	.1
Totals	58,846[c]	100.0%	7,215,249	99.9%[d]

[a] The regional totals in this table exclude the census data reported for the Southern Cameroons which was in 1953, but is not now, administered as part of Eastern Nigeria; percentages were computed on the basis of the revised totals. The local Port Harcourt census unit was defined by the 1953 divisional boundaries and thereby excluded Mile 2 Diobu which, until 1960, was administered as part of Ahoada Division. In 1953, Mile 2 Diobu recorded a population of 12,122.

[b] The Efiks of Calabar Division are subsumed under "Unclassified Nigerian Nationalities" in this table. They comprised 1% of the regional population in 1953 and probably a significant proportion of the 2,171 "Unclassified" Port Harcourt residents.

[c] The non-African population of Port Harcourt Division at this time, omitted in the table, numbered 666 persons. This figure may be contrasted with the 3,000–4,000 expatriates resident in the municipality in 1965.

[d] Percentages do not total 100 because of rounding.

SOURCE: *Population Census of the Eastern Region of Nigeria, 1953* (Lagos: Census Superintendent, 1953), pp. 36–37.

offered by the establishment of Western-oriented administrative, commercial, and industrial centers. As late as 1931 there were no Ibo settlements with a population exceeding 20,000, but by 1952 Eastern Nigeria possessed four major cities, each with a population in excess of 50,000; of the total urban population 85 percent was Ibo. Between 1921 and 1952, Eastern Nigeria's urban growth rate (688 percent) far surpassed that of the country's other regions.[31]

As rapid as the pace of Port Harcourt's industrial and commer-

26

cial expansion had been, it still had not been able to match the growth of the town's population.[32] An estimated 11 percent of Port Harcourt's 180,000 residents were unemployed in 1963.[33] Moreover, most of the financial resources of the community were concentrated in very few hands. Thus, while Port Harcourt's *employed* workers were, on the average, better off than their counterparts in other parts of the Region, the town's income distribution was still heavily weighted in the direction of the lowest income categories. Table 3 illustrates this point with reference to the distribution among income categories of those persons who were assessed income tax in 1963–64. Over 90 percent of those persons assessed earned less than £200 ($560) per annum, while only thirteen persons (.1 percent) earned over £2000 ($5,600).

TABLE 3

DISTRIBUTION OF PORT HARCOURT ASSESSED INCOMES (1963/64)[a]

Income ranges (in £'s)	*Persons assessed*	
1– 59	192	.8%
60– 99	14,090	61.3%
100– 199	7,294	31.7%
200– 499	1,156	5.0%
500– 999	187	.8%
1000– 1999	72	.3%
2000–above	13	.1%
Totals	23,003	100.0%

[a] These figures were obtained from the records of the local Internal Revenue Office in Port Harcourt. I wish to express my indebtedness to the Office of the Commissioner of Internal Revenue for authorizing the release of these and related data. Under the Eastern Nigerian taxation system, those persons employed by government departments and large commercial and industrial concerns had their tax deducted from their paychecks; persons independently employed or employed in small firms were "directly assessed." It is the pattern of *direct* assessments that is recorded in this table. Port Harcourt statistics are not available on this point, but regional 1957–58 tax data suggest that the Port Harcourt distribution of Pay-As-You-Earn (P.A.Y.E.) assessments parallels that of the direct assessments. The £100–199 category, however, may include a slightly greater percentage of P.A.Y.E. taxpayers, while the £60–99 category would probably include fewer persons. For the regional data, see the *Annual Report of the Internal Revenue Division, 1957–58* (Enugu: Government Printer, 1960), p. 19.

The pattern of Port Harcourt property ownership paralleled the distribution of Port Harcourt assessed incomes. On the one hand, the vast majority of Port Harcourt's immigrants were rent-paying tenants. The Ostrum survey of Mile 2 Diobu, for example, reported that 93.9 percent of the household heads interviewed paid rent for their lodging. On the other hand, in 1964 the fifty-three largest property owners, representing less than .0003 of the urban population, held 25.1 percent of the total assessed value of all taxable property in the city. Of these fifty-three property owners, eighteen were expatriate industrial and commercial establishments. Only twenty-seven represented Nigerian interests, and of these twenty-seven, three were Nigerian corporate concerns (such as the government-owned Electricity Corporation of Nigeria).[34]

It has already been observed that Port Harcourt neighborhoods possessed a certain degree of socioeconomic homogeneity. A related point that must be made is that aside from the small indigenous Diobu-Ibo community located on the municipality's outskirts, Port Harcourt's residential areas tended to be communally heterogeneous. It is true that Ibos were in the majority in most sections of the municipality; many wards, in fact, were almost exclusively Ibo-speaking, but the Ibo in no sense comprised a homogeneous social or political unit. They had immigrated from over two hundred traditionally autonomous village groups that under the colonial system had been organized into no less than thirteen administrative sections. In Port Harcourt, it was these lower-order traditional and administrative units that constituted the dominant sociopolitical reference points for the Ibo immigrants and around which urban political competition tended to be structured. It becomes politically significant, therefore, that the immigrant Ibo subcommunities were residentially integrated —not only with one another but also with the members of other linguistic groups. Individual rooming houses sometimes contained members of a single Ibo village group, or of one of the minor nationalities. Along a few streets, there were occasional ethnic concentrations—as along the road that borders one of the largest creeks in the area, where a relatively large number of Rivers (Ijaw-speaking) fishing families were found; in the area formerly reserved for junior civil servants, where highly educated Efiks of Calabar Division, Ijaws, and Onitsha divisional Ibos concentrated; and in the block containing the town's only mosque, where Northern Nigerian Moslems congregated. But, with these exceptions, there was generally no such thing as an Ijaw community, or an Efik neighborhood, or an Onitsha Ibo ward.

Given the primacy of communal identities for the vast majority of Port Harcourt residents, the absence of communally segregated residential areas limited the extent to which residentially defined electoral wards developed meaningful political identities. Municipal councillors, though technically serving as ward representatives, were seldom guided in their political behavior by considerations of ward interest. Interest in self and in kinship and wider communities of origin appeared more often to be the dominant points of reference for the local politician as they were for the average citizen. As kinsmen and townspeople were distributed throughout the municipality, political service did not consist of battles for urban amenities (more water taps, better roads, improved conservancy service), for such amenities were "indivisible benefits" that could not be divided among geographically dispersed individuals. Rather, political service normally consisted of the provision of personal patronage in the form of contracts, jobs, and political office.[35] As will be explored in greater depth in another section, the absence of communally segregated residential areas meant, in effect, the absence of a significant neighborhood stimulus to community development.[36]

PORT HARCOURT'S STRANGERS

Writing in 1937, a visitor to the then twenty-five-year-old township pointedly observed:

> Port Harcourt is not, as might be expected, a melting pot where races and speeches, customs and characters will fuse and mingle and out of which a new and stable people will emerge, but rather a railway platform with people coming and going, each family part holding closely together, contemptuous and suspicious of the others, and where nothing of importance to the real life of the family is allowed to happen. No one takes root in Port Harcourt, no one visualizes his future in Port Harcourt, no one hopes to die in Port Harcourt. Men come to make money and have no thought of settling there for good. If they build houses it is only to save rent and to make more money by letting out rooms. The house of their ambition will be built in their own town, within full view of their envious relations.[37]

These words of Sylvia Leith-Ross capture nicely the seeming tenuousness of urban community identity still evident in the Port Harcourt of the 1960s. Much, of course, had changed in the quarter of a century since her visit, and it could no longer be accurately said—if it ever could—that "nothing of importance" was allowed to affect the lives of Port Harcourt's immigrant families. But it did seem that few of Port Harcourt's "strangers" had acquired more than a tangential identification with their community of adoption. In their politics, as in their personal and social lives, they were instrumentally oriented to what the city could offer in the way of material advantages, but they remained expressively oriented to their communities of origin and to their rural-centered kinship ties and institutions. Members of Port Harcourt's Municpal Council expressed their longing for home in varied ways:

> If it were not a question of money, of work, I would not like to live in a township at all. Because there is too much trouble in the township, too much worry, too much noise—radio, gramophone, and other things.
>
> I am liked by my home people. . . . Because of meetings mostly I go home, town meetings, village meetings, church meetings.
>
> If I don't go home, I'll have my village home closed off. . . . In short, I was left as a baby orphan. My mother died when I was sixteen, and my father too died when I was young. I like to return to take care of my family, and as I have a new village home—more spacious than mine in Port Harcourt—I like to return to take care of my house.
>
> I go to see my other sisters and brothers, to know what they need, and to assist them in farming work. And for meeting purposes.
>
> If I have enough money, I would like to live in my home town, where tax is controlled, no water rate, low standard [cost] of living. I am only here because I am looking for some businesses, out of which I hope to make some money.

Port Harcourt, in short, was composed of a transient population, many of whose members were constantly on the move between the city and their home towns. A man might establish a seemingly permanent residence within Port Harcourt itself and, if he could afford to, he would acquire land and build a house. He would send his children to school within the municipality and become an active member of the local church. If members of his family became ill, they would be cared for at Port Harcourt's modern (but tragically overcrowded and understaffed) general hospital. He could even stand for political office within the municipality, seeking a position on the Municipal Council, the regional House of Assembly, or in the federal House of Representatives. But Port Harcourt would seldom acquire the status of a second home; it would remain only his place of business.[38] No matter the distance between his home town and the city, if his earnings and work hours permitted he would return home frequently, as often as three or four times a month.[39] His *first* building would almost invariably be erected in his home town,[40] and he would generally return home for his marriage, for the naming ceremonies of his children, for important comunity meetings, and for his retirement.[41] If he were to pass away while in the city, efforts would be made by his kinsmen to transport his body home for burial in the land of his ancestors. In short, the Port Harcourt resident, despite his apparent urbanity—and Eastern Nigeria's Ibos are renowned for the ease with which they have adapted to urban life—remained closely tied to his rural homeland.

This, then, is the setting of our study: between 1963 and 1965, a rapidly growing, crowded, culturally heterogeneous community of strangers, mostly Ibo rural immigrants who had been drawn to the city by the prospects of trade or by the hopes of wage employment, and who confronted the same kinds of social, economic, and political complexities as those facing new urban dwellers throughout the developing world. But similar complexities do not always yield similar responses. It is true that urban life carries with it certain kinds of organizational imperatives that inevitably transform traditional patterns of behavior. The relatively parochial identities of the traditional order, for example, are often expanded and fused in the wider and more cosmopolitan urban setting; at the same time, new patterns of occupational activity yield new kinds of class differentiation that may or may not cut across communal boundaries. However, at least in the Nigerian context, the urban immigrant's response to the new urban environment, and to other persons within this alien setting, can be understood only in terms of his rural origins and his continuing associations with rural life. It is to the rural heritage of Port Harcourt's immigrant population that we now turn.

31

CHAPTER 3
The Regional Backdrop

The story of Port Harcourt's political development is, in large measure, the story of the Eastern Nigerian's transition from a rural to an urban existence and of his adaptation of rural institutions and perspectives to the new setting. This chapter is concerned with four elements of the rural heritage of Port Harcourt's residents especially crucial to an understanding of the city's political life: first, the pattern of intergroup relationships in precolonial Eastern Nigeria; second, traditional Ibo social and political institutions; third, the differential rates of mobilization that characterized different elements of Eastern Nigerian society; and, fourth, the transformation of communal identities as a result of Western contact.

PRECOLONIAL RELATIONSHIPS

The population of Eastern Nigeria is divided like that of prewar Port Harcourt between a large Ibo-speaking majority and a number of smaller ethnic groups, the most important of which are the Ijaw, Efik, and Ibibio nationalities (see table 2).[1] The Ibo are situated in the Region's forested heartland, while the minority groups are located, for the most part, on the southern, eastern, and northern peripheries of Iboland—the Ijaw along the mangrove creeks of the Niger Delta, the related Efik and Ibibio in the Cross River basin, and a number of smaller peoples in the northeastern Ogoja savannah (map 3).

Perhaps the dominant *political* characteristic of the Eastern Nigerian traditional order was the fragmentation of the countryside. Before 1900 each of the Region's major cultural groups was divided into small, relatively autonomous, political units. Ethnographers have placed the number of independent Ibo societies —or village groups—at over two hundred, ranging in size from several hundred persons to over fifty thousand.[2] The Ijaw, Efik, and Ibibio were similarly divided, though the structure of the local political unit varied across nationalities and even between different cultural sections of the same nationality. The important point is that an Ijaw man identified with his house in much the same way as an Ibibio-speaker identified with his village and an Ibo-speaker identified with his village group.[3] In the Ibo case, for example, each village group had its own name, distinctive historical traditions, and unique linguistic and cultural elements that distinguished it from its neighbors. Seldom did ongoing

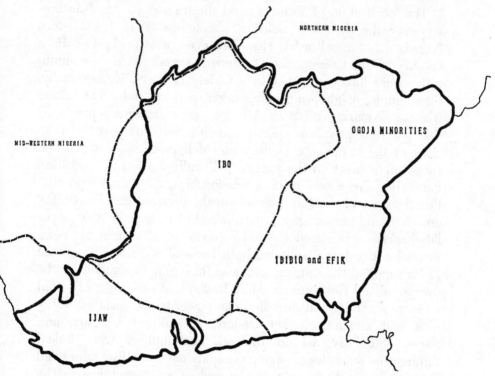

MAP 3. Eastern Nigeria Cultural Zones.
    SOURCE: *Adapted from Report of the Commission Appointed to Enquire into the Fears of the Minorities and the Means of Allaying Them.* Cmnd. 505. London, 1958.

33

political organizations extend beyond the level of the local community, and in no instance was there a precolonial awareness of nationality. "Ibo-ness" and "Ijaw-ness" were as yet unknown qualities. As Simon Ottenberg has observed with respect to the Ibos: "No political superstructure, such as a federation, a confederacy, or a state existed. The Ibo units remained a relatively balanced grouping of independent political structures which never developed into a large formal organization, though some units absorbed or conquered others, some died out, some fragmented, and some changed their characteristics through immigration and emigration." [4] The absence of a political superstructure meant that a fairly high level of tension and insecurity characterized intergroup relationships. While neighboring village groups always maintained social and economic contacts, the average Ibo villager seldom traveled far from his home community.

The localization of identities and the fragmentation of authority were the dominant political characteristics of the Eastern Nigerian traditional order. However, even prior to the twentieth century colonial occupation, Eastern Nigeria's multiple communities were linked together in a variety of ways. Economically, for example, neighboring independent political units maintained trade and market relationships—an economic interdependence that placed a premium upon the maintenance of peaceful relations in the immediate vicinity and demanded at least limited cooperative effort on the part of politically autonomous entities. Paralleling these local trading relationships, the extreme population densities of the Ibo interior—in the prewar years, exceeding one thousand persons per square mile in the most heavily populated areas—stimulated the development of a Regionwide commercial network that spanned both Ibo and non-Ibo sectors: the Delta supplied the salt, protein, and foodstuffs demanded by the overpopulated Ibo country, while Iboland, in exchange, exported its surplus skilled and unskilled manpower in the form of craftsmen and artisans, market traders, agricultural laborers, and slaves.[5] Similarly, within Iboland, communities were linked through the activities of roving occupational specialists who plied their trades in both neighboring and more distant areas. The Nkwerre Ibo (in Orlu Division), for example, became renowned blacksmiths and traders and, according to one account, "played the role of professional spies and diplomatists," as well.[6] Similarly, the Ibo village group of Abiriba (Bende Division) was famous for its blacksmiths and warriors. And, as will be described below, the famed Aro Ibos became Eastern Nigeria's entrepreneurs *par excellence,* dominating the Region's interior slave trade. Each of these groups—the Nkwerres, the Abiribans, and the Aros—were eventually to play important roles in Port Harcourt affairs, and in the politics of Eastern Nigeria.[7]

Diverse social linkages complemented the economic ties binding independent communities. Politically autonomous social units were sometimes linked for religious purposes, as in the sharing of a common religious shrine or in the organization of ritual activities. Politically influential titled and secret societies, too, sometimes cut across family and kinship structures. Marriage between members of different communities provided still another type of linkage, one that facilitated particularly important kinds of economic and social interaction. Men were able to trade with and travel into the social units of their wives, and women (especially among the Ibo) formed societies based upon membership not only in the villages into which they were married, but also in those into which they were born:

> Whereas in their capacity of wives the women look inwards to the village where they are married, in their capacity of daughters they look outward in all directions to the innumerable villages in which they were respectively born. In the first case the unity of the village is emphasized. In the second case—that of the "meetings" between all the women born in the same village but scattered broadcast by marriage among the neighboring villages—it is the links between the villages that are strengthened and institutionalized. . . . The Ibo system of exogamy (women marry into their husband's villages but retain their ties with their communities of birth—and with all other communities into which their female relations have married) works like a cement binding the villages together, or like a consolidating network which has to some extent, among other things, made trading between the village units possible.[8]

In addition to economic and social ties, important linguistic and cultural uniformities transcended political divisions. The persons who lived within each of Eastern Nigeria's major cultural

35

zones shared many important linguistic or other cultural characteristics with other members of their respective ethnic groups
and, in some respects, even with members of different cultural
zones. Ibos, for example, were more like one another than they
were like the Ijaws, Efiks, and Ibibios with whom they had long
interacted. At the same time, in their structural characteristics
and in their social egalitarianism, all four groups were more like
each other than they were like the more hierarchically organized
and ascriptively oriented Yorubas and Hausas of Western and
Northern Nigeria. Though in the precolonial period, these uniformities—both within and across nationalities—had not yet
found their way into the social consciousness of the people, their
existence was of critical significance for Eastern Nigerian political
development. On the one hand, they facilitated the kinds of precolonial economic and social interaction described above; on the
other, they made possible the eventual emergence of the linguistic
and regional identities that were to become crucial points of political reference in the period of colonial occupation.

Finally, notwithstanding the essential fragmentation of authority in the Eastern Nigerian countryside, there were some important instances in which political identities and structures did
transcend the boundaries of village and village group. Large state
structures were absent, but important politically integrative tendencies were present and took various forms. One form of incipient
political integration was that engendered by the system of oracles
found in the eastern and central Ibo areas. The most significant
of these oracle systems was that based in Aro Chuku, an independent village group of nineteen communities situated in Iboland's eastern Cross River sector. The awe and esteem in which
the Aro oracle—known as *Ibini Okpabi* or the "Long Juju"—was
held enabled Aros who were identified with the oracle to travel
along a number of trade routes freely and without fear of attack.
The Aro distributed themselves throughout Iboland to such an
extent that more Aro lived away from their community than in
Aro Chuku. Ottenberg records that wherever they lived, the Aro
"were feared and respected as agents of their oracle." [9] Their
entrepreneurial skills were legendary, and their influence—in
matters both political and economic—was felt in much of Iboland
and even beyond. In some sectors, the settlers assumed control

over the local markets and acquired influence in religious and judicial affairs. The extent of Aro influence is well documented in the "intelligence reports" prepared by British district officers. These reports, excerpts of which follow, make clear the horror and almost paranoid fervor with which colonial officialdom came to view Aro machinations:

> Ozuakoli is in my opinion the worst town in the district . . . they absolutely refuse to give up their guns or prohibit the slave dealing in their market. This is probably due to the overpowering influence of the Aros on the natives, which I find is the same in every District I have been in. They are the curse of the country.[10]
>
> From an economical standpoint the Aro is useless in an up country district, he is not a good producer, and declines to do any manual labour. When they exist in large numbers food rapidly becomes drawn, and labour gets scarcer and dearer, and all kinds of schemes spring into existence.[11]
>
> The Aro immigration is continuing and unless checked will eventually end in the total expropriation of the present Ibo peasant proprietors, a result which has been already achieved at Ndisi-Orgu in Okigwi district and it looks as if the Aros will shortly own and occupy the whole northwest corner of Okigwi district which is partly contiguous to Owerri. . . . The Aro invasion is not a spasmodic effort of the Aro tribe towards natural extension. It has been thought out and carefully worked up for many years. Many years ago the Aro took away the children of certain Ibo chiefs—to Arochuku—imbued them with Aro ideas and ambitions and sent them back to their Native towns to be Aro satraps. . . . The general trend of Aro influence is hostile to the Government, and progress.[12]

The freedom of movement of the Aro agents and settlers enabled the Aro to control the especially profitable interior trade in slaves. Slaves came to the Aro from a number of sources: from large families who were willing to sell their younger children for money and goods, from debtors who sold themselves or their relations into slavery, from physically deformed persons ostracized by their communities, from isolated individuals captured by the Aro or by other Ibos. In addition to these sources, slaves were obtained directly through the judicial activities of the oracle and the military expeditions of the oracle's mercenaries. In Iboland, the oracle acted as a final, supernatural court of appeal. Disputes within or between communities, criminal accusations and allegations of witchcraft, illness or other personal hardships —these and other matters would be brought before the Aro Chuku oracle for decision or diagnosis when it became clear that problems were beyond local solution. In criminal cases, fines— to be paid in slaves—were levied on convicted persons. While it was believed that these slaves were "eaten" by the oracle, they in fact were sold by the Aro to the coastal middlemen.[13]

The influence of the Aro did not depend solely on the prestige of their oracle. In addition, the Aro made effective use of mercenaries, in the person of the famous professional warriors of the Ibo heartland, such as the Abam, the Abiriba, and the Ohafia. These mercenaries not only enhanced the power of the Aro over other Ibo communities but also provided, through their spoils of war, another important source of slaves.

The significance of the Aro and other less influential oracle systems was in their ability to transcend local communal boundaries.[14] The political fragmentation of the countryside was countered in other ways, as well. For example, alliances between neighboring independent communities would be formed and reformed according to the political and military exigencies of the moment. Occasionally, too, as in the case of the hundred thousand–member Ngwa clan in Aba Division, group self-consciousness extended beyond the village or village group.[15] Still another basis of incipient political integration was the emergence of charismatic leaders who were able to extend their personal influence far beyond their immediate community. Their leader-oriented political organizations, however, were transient political phenomena. They were little more than the political extension of exceptionally forceful personalities, and the death of the leader normally signaled the disintegration of the organization.[16]

In summary, the small, autonomous communities of Eastern Nigeria's traditional order shared important economic, social, cultural, and even political ties. The oracle system, spearheaded by Ibini Okpabi, was perhaps the most important integrative agency. By providing a common point of ideological reference for a large body of the politically fragmented Ibo population, and by creating a mobile population—in the form both of slaves and traders

—the Aro-dominated slave commerce helped to lay the foundation for the subsequent regrouping of traditionally small, autonomous communities at higher levels of political organization. As the entrepreneurial middlemen between the Ibo interior and the non-Ibo coast, the Aro also furthered the economic integration of the wider regional area.

Nevertheless, despite the many commonalities characterizing traditional relationships, fragmentation, local autonomy, and social parochialism remained the dominant political facts of precolonial Eastern Nigeria. The foundation of higher-level social and political organization was in place, but the actual construction of the new order was to wait. The social and political universe of most Eastern Nigerians, non-Ibo as well as Ibo, remained the independent local community. Consequently, as an examination of Ibo institutions will indicate, the stability of traditional Eastern Nigerian society was maintained through the balance of roughly equivalent political segments, rather than through the operation of centralized, all-embracing political superstructures.

THE TRADITIONAL MODERNISTS:
A CULTURAL OVERVIEW OF THE IBO

The Ibo depart, in several respects, from the stereotype of traditional societies which has played such an important role in the literature on social and political change. Contrary to the conventional emphasis upon the rigidity and particularism of the traditional social order, for example, the Ibo have long demonstrated their capacity to enter into relationships based upon other than kinship considerations, and to adapt to rapidly changing social and political circumstances. Illustrative of nonkinship-oriented patterns of social and political grouping were the important age-set and age-grade organizations and the secret and titled societies common to much of Iboland.[17] Age organizations, of particular importance in riverain Ibo communities, were generally structured on a village-group basis, but in some cases encompassed related village groups or even genealogically unrelated communities. Their functions were threefold: the performance of public duties, with different age-groups assuming responsibility for different tasks; the provision of mutual help to their membership; and the disciplining of individual members who did not conform

39

to the norms of the group. In some areas, members of the more senior age-sets tended to wield exceptional political authority and to collectively assume a large measure of responsibility for public decision-making.

Secret and titled societies, especially common in and about Onitsha Town, were more exclusive organizations than the age-sets and age-grades, for only the wealthy were able to afford the entrance fees and periodic ceremonial feasts to which each member was expected to contribute. Like the age organizations, however, they too cut across lineal ties and frequently played a crucial role in the making of public policy.[18]

The adaptability of the Ibo to rapidly changing social and political circumstances manifested itself in a variety of ways. We have already taken note, for example, of the incorporation of strangers into host communities, notwithstanding the deep-seated Ibo suspicion of communal outsiders. Typified in the absorption of Aro elements by non-Aro communities, this traditional flexibility anticipated, and perhaps facilitated, the later Ibo receptivity to elements of European culture.[19]

Ibo adaptability was reflected, also, in a pattern of constantly shifting political alignments and lines of conflict. Each level of Ibo society was comprised of an implicitly unstable federation of segments: village groups were divided into villages, villages into extended families, extended families into still smaller segments. The political relationships among the components of any given unit were in constant flux, moving toward but never quite attaining a point of stable equilibrium. In the face of threats to the integrity of the larger political system, the various sections of any subordinate unit could adapt themselves quickly and effectively (albeit only temporarily) to the requirement for larger-scale organization. In short, the stability of the Ibo political system lay in "*ad hoc*, ever-shifting alignments at different levels of the society rather than in hierarchical, continuously functioning structures and institutions." [20]

Ibo culture emphasized individualized achievement, especially as expressed through independent economic activity, as the path to social status and political influence. Status and influence were not inheritable, but were determined by individual initiative and performance. Seniority alone, while it yielded formal status and commanded both respect and affection, did not necessarily confer political influence. Rather, effective power rested with men who attained their influence through their personal qualities of leadership and their financial prominence. As G. I. Jones has noted, the Ibo leader functioned in a manner not unlike that of the American political boss: "Ibo leaders were not war leaders, but rather first class negotiators, judges and party organizers." [21] As in the urban communities of Boston, New Haven, and New York, political survival in an Ibo community hinged, fundamentally, on the leader's ability to mould and to maintain a cohesive personal following by using the political system to the advantage of his constituents.

In the Ibo context, as in the American, the politician was first and foremost a broker of conflicting interests and personalities. His political success was, in large measure, a function of his ability to resolve disputes both within his own community and between persons from his and neighboring communities. Because of the always-threatening political environment, the leader's "foreign relations" effectiveness was of particular importance. Cases involving people in different communities were difficult to resolve, for different political jurisdictions were involved. Community leaders, however, were persons whose networks of political contacts often extended beyond their own communities: "The more influence a man could exert inside his own town, the more he was valued and respected by leaders in other towns." [22]

But political influence depended not only on an individual's abilities as a negotiator and mediator; also important were the material resources the aspirant leader was able to command. Wealth was an important political resource from three standpoints. First, in the Ibo perspective the acquisition of wealth was taken as the most tangible evidence of personal achievement. Second, wealth was a requirement for admission into the secret and titled societies that, in some communities, played a critical role. Exclusion from these bodies would sometimes mean the frustration of one's political ambitions. Third, and most important, wealth could be used directly to extend a person's network of political contacts. On the one hand, a wealthy individual could supply the armaments required for raiding and protection. On the other, in a society that placed great emphasis upon the individual's

41

obligations to his family and lineage, a man's influence was largely a function of his generosity. Indebtedness to the donor accompanied the donation, and indebtedness was the stuff out of which political influence was made.[23]

Associated with the achievement orientation of the Ibo was a highly egalitarian political ethos. A contemporary saying, "The Ibos have no chiefs," while not strictly accurate, expresses the traditional, and still continuing, Ibo opposition to persons who would seek to exercise an inordinate degree of personal power:

> The community . . . is not prepared to surrender its legislative authority to any chiefs, elders, or other traditional office holders. The members of a village section may be prepared to allow certain of their more influential men to represent them and to act for the section, but they retain the right to relieve them of this duty and replace them by others should they act contrary to their wishes. . . .[24]

> In Afikpo government a formal system of checks and balances against the exploitation of power . . . is not needed. Individual leaders retain their power only as long as they represent the opinion of the majority, for Afikpo are too self-assertive to allow themselves to be dominated by someone with whom they do not agree.[25]

The public business of an Ibo community was typically organized and conducted by village and village-group councils of elders.[26] The powers of these councils, however, were severely limited. No segment within the political unit was bound by decisions in which it did not participate or approve; hence, all decisions, if they were to be effective, had to be based upon unanimous consent. Moreover, all adult males from the segments represented in the council had the right to attend council meetings and to air their views.[27] In short, rule by fiat played no part in the Ibo system of government by consensus.

If we were to conclude this cultural overview of the Ibo on the note of individualism and egalitarianism we would be omitting a critical dimension of the Ibo experience. For what is significant about the Ibo is not simply their emphasis upon individualized achievement, but the fact that this individualism was closely tied to the maintenance of strong communal ties and institutions. Individuals identified closely with their various lineage, age-grade, and other communal units; and the success of their entrepreneurial and political initiatives often depended upon both moral and material group support. The values of "the group," of an individual's social obligations to his community of origin, of consensual decision-making, of communal ownership of land—these were no less a part of traditional Ibo culture than the emphases upon achieved status and individual performance. This point bears emphasis because it raises some question as to the validity of those dichotomies, outlined in the introductory chapter, which associate tradition with the behavioral attribute of communalism, and modernity with that of individualism.

This discussion of Ibo culture has taken us somewhat afield of our central concern with the relationship between modernization and communal conflict. However, while our intention is to develop theoretical propositions that have applicability across societies, we cannot ignore the cultural dimension entirely. Moreover, it seems not unlikely that certain of the political characteristics of Port Harcourt's Ibo-speaking residents described in later chapters—their organizational flexibility, the apparent ease with which they moved between communal and noncommunal institutional structures, the pragmatism of their political style—are traceable, at least in part, to the traditional modernity that was their cultural heritage. In addition, as we have suggested in passing, cultural predispositions may well have played a role in establising the very rapid rate with which Ibos (and other Eastern Nigerians) were mobilized into the new kinds of occupational and economic activity induced by Western contact.[28]

DIFFERENTIAL MOBILIZATION

The term "social mobilization" was coined by Karl Deutsch to refer to "the process in which major clusters of old social, economic and psychological commitments are eroded or broken and people become available for new patterns of socialization and behavior." [29] The linked processes of change subsumed within the concept of social mobilization—such as urbanization, the introduction of mass education, the diffusion of the mass media, the development of increasingly efficient and productive commercial networks—have the collective effect of generating new patterns of intergroup interaction and competition among peoples who, prior to their mobilization, were operating within relatively parochial, separate environments. Mobilization means the reorientation of a large number of citizens to a new system of rewards and paths to rewards in all spheres of society. People's aspirations and expectations change as they are mobilized into the modernizing economy and polity. They come to want, and to demand, more— more goods, more recognition, more power. Significantly, too, the orientation of the mobilized to a common set of rewards and paths to rewards means, in effect, that many people come to desire precisely the same things. It is by making men more alike, in the sense of possessing the same wants, that mobilization tends to promote conflict.

The various communal groups that comprise a culturally plural society are seldom mobilized at the same rate. Varying cultural predispositions; variations in the kinds of environmental opportunities available to different communities; and variations in the timing, intensity, and character of Western contact—all work to create intergroup differentials in the developmental process. The consequence of these differentials is that some peoples gain a head start in the competition for the scarce rewards of modernity. New socioeconomic categories, therefore, tend to coincide with, rather than intersect, communal boundaries, with the result that the modern status system comes to be organized along communal lines. There is, consequently, little to ameliorate the intensity of communal confrontations. The fewer the cross-cutting socioeconomic linkages, the more naked such confrontations and the greater the likelihood of movements of communal nationalism.

In Eastern Nigeria, differential mobilization had the effect of widening the sociopolitical cleavages not only between the region's majority and minority nationalities, but also between subgroups of the dominant nationality. Thus, differential rates of educational expansion and economic growth heightened the always latent division between the landlocked Owerri Ibo interior, on the one hand, and the more advantaged marginal Ibo (Onitsha, Aro) riverain groups and non-Ibo (Ijaw, Ibibio, Efik) coastal communities, on the other. Those communities that were so situated as to control access to the interior, or that were at the center of the developing riverain trade routes, were simply in a better position to take advantage of the new commercial and educational opportunities brought by the European traders and missionaries.

Within Iboland, it was Aro Chuku and Onitsha Town that assumed positions of commercial—and hence political—preeminence with respect to their Ibo-speaking neighbors in the heartland. We have already noted the broad influence of the Aro oracle and the prominent role played by the Aro Ibo in the interior slave trade. With the trade's abolition in the late nineteenth century, the fortunes of the Aro and of other African middlemen declined abruptly. As Coleman has pointed out, African slave traders were as much affected by the cessation of the slave trade as were the white slave dealers. "The first Nigerian middle class was liquidated by the abolition of the external slave trade." [30] It was not long, however, before the Aro and their Ibo allies moved into new lines of endeavor. Sklar cites the interesting statistic that the Ibo-speaking Ohaffia group, a military ally of the Aros, produced five Ph.D.'s in the two decades following World War II.[31] Aros, similarly, assumed important roles within the commercial, educational, and political life of Eastern Nigeria.

Culturally distinctive from the peoples occupying the Ibo heartland, the Onitsha townspeople and those from adjacent and related communities are considered by many non-Onitsha people to be only marginally Ibo, despite the fact that the symbols of modern-day Ibo unity, Dr. Nnamdi Azikiwe and Colonel Odumegwu Ojukwu, are from Onitsha Town. Nevertheless, the Onitshans have long occupied prominent positions within the Region's economic, social, and political life. As G. I. Jones has commented, "Onitsha was in the right geographical position to become the focus for the political, economic, and cultural development of the Ibo." [32] Located on the trade routes linking the Northern, Central, and Southern Ibo with the Niger and, by extension, with Northern and Western Nigeria, Onitsha Town was established as the colonial administrative headquarters for one of Iboland's two main provinces and as a major educational center.

The educational advantage of the Onitshans was quickly translated into occupational advantage, thereby greatly enhancing Onitsha Town's traditional stature. Onitsha townspeople and persons from neighboring communities within Onitsha Division who had access to Onitsha schools became the first African teachers of children in outlying Ibo and non-Ibo areas. Onitshans similarly moved into the highest clerical and administrative positions occupied by Ibo-speakers within Eastern Nigeria's European mercantile firms and the civil service. The establishment of an Anglican industrial mission in Onitsha Division for the teaching of carpentry, masonry, and similar skills also gave Onitshans a headstart in the competition for skilled and technical employment. The extent to which the education and skills of the Onitshans were in demand outside of Onitsha Town is indicated by the extremely high mobility of the Onitshan population: it is estimated that between 1857 and 1931 the indigenous population of Onitsha Town declined from 13,000 to 3,271.[33] It was not long before many of these "Onitshans abroad" were to come to positions of national as well as regional prominence. And it was largely as a consequence of this Onitshan preeminence that the most fundamental communal cleavage within Iboland, as within the city of Port Harcourt, became that dividing the Onitsha Ibo (variously defined, depending upon the social context, as Onitsha Town, Onitsha Division, or Onitsha Province) and the main body of non-Onitsha or Owerri Ibo (also variously defined as Owerri Town, Owerri Division, or Owerri Province).[34]

Outside Iboland, it was the Ijaw, Efik, and Ibibio peoples who prospered as a result of their control of the riverain ports. On the one hand, it was they who received the Ibo slaves from the Aro traders and other middlemen and who handled the final transactions with the Europeon slave dealers. The slave trade thus had the effect of placing the Ibo of the interior in a subordinant social position vis-à-vis the non-Ibo slave owners and traders of the coast. Of course, with Westernization and the subsequent introduction of the franchise, the historical tables were to be suddenly turned: the formerly disadvantaged but always numerically superior Ibo were to emerge as Eastern Nigeria's dominant group. Significantly, "It was among the Ibos, formerly despised by the people of Calabar as a source of slaves and as a backward people of the interior, now feared and disliked as energetic and well-educated, that the first political party was formed." [35]

On the other hand, the Ijaw, Efik, and Ibibio benefited not only by their control of the riverain slave trade but also by the subsequent concentration of the first European mission schools in their relatively accessible communities. As in the case of Onitsha Town, their early educational advantage gave these communities a significant lead in the regional competition for occupational and social position. Calabar's Hope Waddell Institute, for example, was for thirty years Eastern Nigeria's only secondary school. Established in 1895, at a time when few Ibos (especially those of Owerri Province) had yet received primary education, the Hope Waddell student body was originally composed primarily of Efiks and Ibibios from the lower Cross River and of other non-Ibo elements from Yorubaland, Sierra Leone, and Ghana.[36] By 1940, the proportion of Ibos within the student body had increased substantially, and other secondary schools had been established within Iboland itself; by this time, however, the earlier Efik and other non-Ibo graduates had consolidated their position within the senior ranks of Nigeria's occupational hierarchy and had acquired a well-developed sense of their educational and social superiority. Moreover, because of the community's reservoir of educated talent and because of its long exposure to the Western world, Calabar was designated by colonial officialdom as the governmental center for the ethnically heterogeneous Cross River basin; for a time, in fact, Calabar served as the administrative headquarters for the entire Eastern Province.

In much the same way, the educationally advantaged Ijaw riverain towns of Bonny and Degema became the administrative points of entry into Ijaw and southern Ibo (i.e., Owerri) areas. When the administrative advance into Owerri country was launched in the last decades of the nineteenth century, not a single school had been established within this southern Ibo territory. (The Owerri provincial urban center of Port Harcourt had not yet come into existence.) By contrast, missionary schools were operating in Onitsha Town as early as 1857 and in the Ijaw-speaking areas adjacent to southern Iboland as early as 1865.

In 1917, even though the headquarters of the vast Owerri Province had been shifted from Ijaw country to the Ibo heartland's Owerri Town several years earlier, Ijaws were still the most numerous ethnic group within the provincial administration, accounting for at least 40 percent of the province's seventy clerks and interpreters.[37] Of even greater significance, perhaps, Ijaws in combination with other non-Ibo elements controlled the most senior posts within the civil service. As table 4 illustrates, non-

TABLE 4

ETHNIC COMPOSITION OF AFRICAN STAFF, OWERRI PROVINCE (1917)

Nationality	1st class and 2nd class clerks	3rd class clerks and unqualified interpreters	Total staff
Ibo	3.4%	34.1%	21.4%
Non-Ibo	89.7%	48.9%	65.7%
Unknown	6.9%	17.1%	12.9%
	100.0%	100.1%ᵃ	100.0%
	(N = 29)	(N = 41)	(N = 70)

ᵃ Percentages do not total 100 because of rounding.
SOURCE: Owerri Provincial Estimates, 1917 (National Archives File OW 274/16; Riv Prof; 1/14/240). Mr. G. I. Jones assisted the writer in identifying ethnic origins by examination of the names contained within the staff estimates.

Ibos accounted for 65.7 percent of the province's total African staff and 89.7 percent of the most senior positions. (Twenty-eight of the forty-six non-Ibos comprising these percentages were Ijaw; the remainder included five Efiks; six persons of Sierra Leonian, Yoruba, or Ghanaian extraction; and seven non-Ibos whose nationality cannot be positively identified.) This non-Ibo preeminence may be expressed in another way: of twelve Ibo clerks employed in 1917, only one had risen above third class rank; by contrast, sixteen of the twenty Ijaw clerks employed in the same year had attained first class or second class rank.

COMMUNAL TRANSFORMATION: THE EMERGENCE
OF NEW CLEAVAGES

The Western impact upon Eastern Nigeria not only reenforced the previously latent cleavage between the landlocked Ibo interior and the riverain Ibo and non-Ibo area; it also stimulated the emergence of entirely new social, economic, and religious bases of political alignment. In some instances, as in the emergence of new occupational and class identities and in the adoption of Christian sectarian labels (e.g., Catholic and Anglican), the new bases of alignment transcended existing communal partitions. In other instances, however, the new bases of alignment perpetuated

communal modes of organization. Sectarian religious boundaries, for example, at the same time that they transcended some communal divisions coincided with and reenforced others. Similarly, new administrative boundaries, rather than undermining the organizational bases of the communal order, had the effect of providing a foundation for broader-based and more politically effective communal units. Thus, the new administrative units of native court area, division, and province incorporated traditionally autonomous communities within a common structural framework and, in the process, generated new political interests and identities that were related to, but transcended, the village and village-group boundaries of the traditional system.

Significantly, the new administrative units were essentially artificial units representing additions to, rather than substitutions for, traditional social units. The British administrative structure wid-

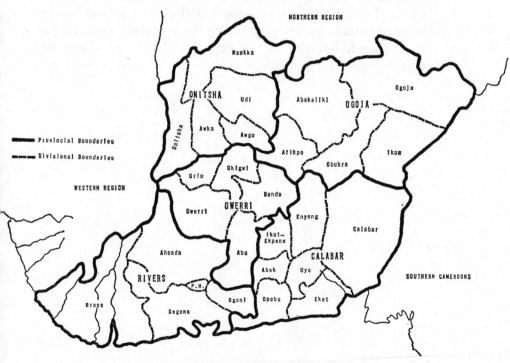

MAP 4. Pre-1959 Eastern Nigeria Administrative Boundaries.
SOURCE: *Adapted from Report of the Commission Appointed to Enquire into the Fears of the Minorities and the Means of Alaying Them.* Cmnd. 505. London, 1958.

ened the circumference of traditional social interaction without destroying the indigenous social structure or undermining the communal modes of organization upon which the traditional system rested. New and wider concentric circles of authority were simply superimposed upon the traditional circles of village and village group. Moreover, though the British administrative partitions were often arbitrarily placed, at the widest, provincial level the boundaries did correspond with the Region's major linguistic divisions, thus making Eastern Nigeria's five provinces critical rallying points for the cultural-linguistic political movements of a later era. In 1959, these five provinces—Ogoja (linguistically mixed), Calabar (Efik and Ibibio-speaking), Rivers (Ijaw-speaking primarily), and Owerri and Onitsha (both Ibo-speaking)— were divided into twelve smaller and more culturally homogeneous provincial units. Nevertheless, Port Harcourt's Eastern Nigerian inhabitants still identified themselves (in 1963–1965), socially and politically, by reference to the older provincial and divisional boundaries (map 4). Even the especially artificial partition between Ibo-speaking Owerri and Onitsha provinces had retained its political significance.[38]

PART II
Changing Patterns of Community Power

CHAPTER 4

The Formative Years: Land Acquisition and the Colonial Presence (1913–1919)

Over the six-decade span of the municipality's history, Port Harcourt has passed through four distinct historical periods, each characterized by a structurally distinctive political system and the political ascendancy of a different segment of the growing immigrant population.[1] This historical pattern is strikingly similar to that of the immigrant community of New Haven, as described by Robert Dahl;[2] and a comparison with the New Haven experience illuminates the dynamics of political change in Port Harcourt. In both cases, the changing social characteristics of public officials—with leadership passing, to use Dahl's terminology, from the "patricians" to the "entrepreneurs" and thence to the "ex-plebes"—reflected profound alterations in the structures and criteria of political recruitment. To quote Dahl's characterization of political change in New Haven:

> In the first period (1784–1842), public office was almost the exclusive prerogative of the patrician families. In the second period (1842–1900), the new self-made men of business, the entrepreneurs, took over. Since then, the "ex-plebes" rising out of working-class or lower middle-class families of immigrant origins have predominated. These transformations reflected profound alterations in the community, in the course of which important resources of obtaining influence were fragmented and dispersed. Wealth was separated from social position by the rise of industry, and public office went to the wealthy. Later,

popularity was divorced from both wealth and social position
by the influx of immigrants, and public office went to the ex-
plebes, who lacked wealth and social position but had the advantage of numbers.[3]

As the following historical narrative will indicate, in Port Harcourt the sequence of immigrant-group ascendancy corresponded
roughly to the sequence in which the home communities of the
urban immigrants were exposed to the Western educational and
acculturative impact; changing patterns of leadership were thus
a direct reflection of the differential mobilization of the various
elements comprising Port Harcourt's population.

GOVERNMENT AND THE DIOBUS

A review of Port Harcourt's formative years (1913–1919) affirms
Kenneth Little's important observation that "the modern African
town is mostly a product of forces external not only to itself but
to African society in general. . . . It has grown up mainly in response to the market economy introduced by European colonialism. . . . It exists, therefore, not in its own right but because it
serves a variety of administrative, commercial and industrial purposes whose origin lies in a national and international system of
politics and economics." [4] Port Harcourt was established to serve
the needs of Europeans, and the city, from its earliest days, was
in many respects as much a European as an African town.

   The original land acquisition negotiated by the colonial government with the indigenous owners of Port Harcourt covered
an area of twenty-five square miles. The acquisition involved six
separate transactions and the chiefs of seven communities, all of
whom laid claim to some portion of the land the government required. The two communities that figured most prominently in
these negotiations, by virtue of their claim to the greatest part of
the land area in question, were Okrika and Diobu.

   The Ijaw-speaking Okrikans, by culture and history, were part
of the Bonny-centered political and economic empire. Primarily
an island people, the Okrikans maintained fishing settlements and
markets along the creeks surrounding the Port Harcourt peninsula. The precise boundaries of original Okrikan hegemony remain uncertain and were, in 1963–1965, the subject of still pending litigation. The British negotiators of 1913 accepted the Okri-

kan claim to the ownership of the largest acreage, but it is quite possible (as contemporary Diobu residents emphatically argued) that the Okrikan success in these early land negotiations was due to the higher status the Okrikans occupied in the eyes of the British administrators. Exposed at an earlier date to contact with European traders and missionaries, the Okrikans by 1913 were already very much involved with the British, both economically and administratively. The more parochial, less educated Diobu farmers were therefore at a considerable disadvantage. The colonial government's appointment of an Okrikan to supervise the removal of the town of Diobu to a new site was indicative of this imbalance.[5] Against this background, the continuing Diobu feeling that "What the Okrikans took was out of cleverness rather than out of right," becomes understandable. Significantly, perhaps, the Okrikans made no effort to resist the 1913 government acquisition, and whatever identification they may have had with Port Harcourt land prior to that time was effectively terminated by their acceptance of £3,000 compensation.[6]

By language and culture, the Diobus comprise a section of the Ikwerre tribe, an Ibo-speaking people situated to the south of the Owerri-Onitsha Ibo heartland. Historically, however, the Diobus maintained close ties with their Ijaw-speaking Okrikan neighbors. They were originally linked to the Okrikans by trade and by intermarriage, and the postcolonial Anglicization of both Okrika and Diobu furthered the bond between the two communities. As a result of the Anglican Church's earlier penetration into Ijaw country, Ijaw missionaries and educators (some of Okrikan origin) became the Diobus' first ministers and teachers. The Diobus and Okrikans were also linked by the contempt both groups held for the Ibo from the Owerri hinterland to the north. This attitude of contempt stemmed from the identification of Owerri Ibos as slaves or, in the years following the cessation of the slave trade, as casual laborers who traveled south to work on the increasingly profitable Ikwerre palm plantations. To the Ikwerres, as to the Ijaw, the Owerri Ibos were "bush," to be scorned as social inferiors.

Unlike the Okrikans and the other communities that were party to the 1913 land acquisition, the Diobus violently objected to the expropriation of their land by the colonial authorities. Nor did they take enthusiastically to their proposed resettlement in an area nearby. In fact, the presence of a British Man O'War had been required to effect even nominal acceptance of the colonial occupation of Diobu. The subsequent land expropriation and proposed Diobu resettlement only increased the resistance of the indigenes. Thus, on November 5, 1913, the commissioner for the Eastern Provinces wired the colonial secretary: "Attitude of Diobu people up to present have been satisfactory though they do not in my opinion intend to make any move unless compelled to do so. If wholesale removal is intended consider Police detachment of at least 20 men. Men and Sergeant necessary to safeguard against any possible friction." [7] The commissioner urged the colonial secretary to assure the Diobus that a policy of resettlement would be implemented only where necessary and that the government, in any event, would proceed gradually. The Diobu response was to accept £500 compensation for a tiny portion of their land, but to reject the £2,000 offered in 1913 as compensation for the remainder of the proposed government acquisition. But the Diobu rejection was ignored, and construction of the new railway port was begun. The disputed land area was declared Crown land, subject to government control, allocation, and development. [8]

RAILWAY CONSTRUCTION AND THE FIRST IMMIGRATION

Chiefs and people of Owerri, . . .

Under the beneficent rule of His Excellency the Governor General in whose person His Majesty the King has been pleased to place the Government of your country you will enjoy many blessings. Justice, as hitherto, will be administered impartially and trade, the mainspring of this wonderfully rich country, will be fostered so that it may continually increase thus enabling you to amass money. . . . If it were not for the white man, who so often sacrifices his life in a climate unsuited to him, you would not be enjoying the necessities and luxuries of life you are enjoying at the present moment. Both White and Black are necessary to each other, you can easily understand. You require articles the white man produces and the white man requires the produce of your country so therefore we should be able to work side by side for our mutual gain as without him the wealth of the country cannot be developed.

I am glad to note that you have so readily responded to the call for labour for the "great iron road" which is under course of construction. . . . You will . . . quickly understand its utility when you see it completed. . . .[9]

From its inception, Port Harcourt felt the full weight of colonial authority. The land acquisition concluded (at least to the government's satisfaction), work commenced immediately on the erection of the wharves and the construction of the railway. Lord Lugard, the governor-general, was determined that these projects should move forward swiftly. A compulsory labor force was therefore organized to complement whatever volunteer labor was forthcoming.

The recruitment of "political" labor, as distinguished from volunteer "casual" labor, proved a constant source of irritation to the local colonial administrators. In frequent government memoranda directed to the Port Harcourt District Office and to their provincial commissioners, these officials voiced their objections:

June 24, 1914

Sir,

In reference to Port Harcourt labourers for this District, I have the honour to state that another 127 left here this morning.

I do not wish you to think they go willingly, they have been practically forced to go and under Escort.

I understand that 17 have run away from previous batches after being at work a few days.

I attach the complaints of three headmen who have again returned to Port Harcourt for a third term of service today.

I have the honour to be,
Sir,
Your Obedient Servant
(sgd)
District Officer, Ikot-Ekpene[10]

One district officer, writing to the Port Harcourt District Office a few days later, observed that it took nearly two months, "visiting centers and holding frequent meetings of Chiefs and Headmen, before I could persuade the Chiefs to give labourers for the first party (only a small one of 119 men)." [11] Citing the hardships that the prospective laborers faced on their journey to Port Harcourt, he admonished the township officials: "I do not think the difficulties of recruiting labour for the Railway and the amount of extra work that it entails, if conscientiously done by District Officers, such as travelling, holding meetings, registering (each man is given a separate number chit with full particulars), mustering, checking names and numbers with lists, despatching, dealing with complaints, runaways and correspondence, are sufficiently appreciated at Port Harcourt." [12] Conditions were no more pleasant along the railway line itself. Wages were poor (varying between nine pence and one shilling per day for ordinary laborers, slightly higher for headmen); living arrangements were crowded; and during the wet season, disease was prevalent.

It was not long before Port Harcourt's political laborers were joined by a considerable number of voluntary immigrants who were attracted, primarily, by the prospects of salaried and wage employment and, secondarily, following the completion of the Enugu–Port Harcourt railway line in 1916, by the prospects of lucrative trading opportunities. Then, as later, these immigrants came from many places, both from within and without Nigeria, but the Ibos outnumbered all the other groups combined. Table 5 presents a detailed breakdown of the township's ethnic composition in 1921, five years after the completion of the Eastern Nigeria Railway line.

From the standpoint of subsequent political developments, it is significant that the largest part of the earliest specifically Ibo migrations to Port Harcourt originated in Owerri rather than in Onitsha Province. Bende, Aba, and Owerri Divisions were especially well represented in both the political labor gangs and in the ranks of the voluntary immigrants. On the one hand, heavy population densities and consequent land shortages within much of Owerri Province encouraged the development of a mobile population; on the other, Port Harcourt's proximity to the Owerri area made the new port a logical destination for Owerri traders and job seekers. To the north, Onitsha Town performed much the same function for would-be immigrants from the rural hinterland of Onitsha Province. Thus, while Owerris gravitated toward Port Harcourt, the majority of Ibos from Onitsha Province tended to be drawn toward Onitsha Town. In later years, the long-standing numerical superiority of the Owerri Provincial Ibos in Port

TABLE 5

PORT HARCOURT'S POPULATION,
BY ETHNIC GROUP AND REGION OF ORIGIN (1921)

Nigerian Africans	Population	Percentage
Ibos	4,493	62.1
Yorubas	745	10.3
Hausas	312	4.3
Ijaws	262	3.6
Efiks	237	3.3
Ibibios	207	2.9
Others	308	4.3
Non-Nigerian Africans	511*	7.1
Europeans	158**	2.2
Totals	7,233***	100.1****

* All but 30 of the 511 non-Nigerian Africans came from three countries: the Gold Coast, Sierra Leone, and Liberia.
** Only 12 members of the European population came from non-British areas.
*** The census officer noted that his figures may have underestimated the total population by as much as 10%, due to the temporary absence of some residents and the resistance of others to being counted.
**** Figures do not total 100 because of rounding.
SOURCE: 1921 Census Report, submitted by the Port Harcourt Station Magistrate (and District Officer).

Harcourt was to contribute to their resentment of Onitsha domination of the town's key political, administrative, and other managerial posts.

PLANNING AND DEVELOPMENT

"It is important to remember," writes a former secretary of the Port Harcourt-Obia Planning Authority, "that the port was from the first a *railway* port, as indeed, the coal mine was a railway mine. It was railway engineers who built the port, the railway, and the city of Port Harcourt." [13] Before 1918, the administration of the township was entrusted exclusively to the railway department, and it was during these years of exclusive railway department rule that the basic lines of Port Harcourt's urban development were drawn. As a consequence, this Eastern Nigerian municipality today has the distinction of being one of West Africa's few planned communities.

The early planners left little to chance. Residential areas were

59

marked out, one for Europeans and one for Africans, and these were separated from the prospective industrial and commercial areas. Streets were mapped with some semblance of order. Residential, commercial, and industrial plots were carefully demarcated and then allocated on a rental basis. Market construction was supervised by the Local Authority who also controlled the allocation of market stalls. Regulations to govern private building construction were formulated, and a drainage and sewage system was begun. A housing program for the African employees of the government departments and commercial firms was initiated, with the employees residentially grouped according to their occupation. Significantly, this latter policy prevented the development of ethnically homogeneous residential areas, such as are found in other West African cities.

Progress was swift. Dr. Laurie, a government sanitary officer, obviously impressed with the speed of Port Harcourt's development, reported on his March 1916 inspection of the new township:

> Port Harcourt, although in a state of transition at present has, for a new town, made more rapid progress in development than I had anticipated. Most of the European town has been laid out and temporary or semi-permanent buildings put up. . . . Conservancy and scavenging is done by contract. The drainage is carried out scientifically and well. Water is derived from wells, some of which are 40 feet in depth. There is an excellent mineral water factory and the price is so low that the whole of the Europeans in the town and along the line need not, if they choose, prepare or drink anything but soda water. A good temporary Cold Storage was established at the end of last year. . . .
>
> The same consideration that is extended to the European for the purpose of keeping him in good health and increasing his happiness is also shown towards the native who enjoys many privileges hitherto unknown at such an early stage of the development of any place. The town looks well with its regular layout, and its wide streets and open spaces. Rapid progress is being made with road making and drainage under the direction of Mr. Powell, the District Engineer. The clerks inhabit corrugated iron houses beyond the Artisans quarters. Carpenters and bricklayers live in rows of huts between the traffic section and the traders and beyond the traders and nearer the swamp the labour-

ers live in bush huts or corrugated iron rooms which are constructed back to back. All these buildings are temporary and cost Government £150 per month to maintain. . . . I must record that it was a great pleasure to me to go round the town and its surroundings. . . . Indeed everybody seemed to be deeply interested in the development of Port Harcourt. One is deeply thankful for all that has been done in Port Harcourt.[14]

Certain problems, however, remained beyond the grasp of the early planners. First, as a result of the planning priority given the European Location, the planners never effectively confronted the problem of road, sewage, and drainage systems within the Native Location. The wide streets to which Dr. Laurie referred, for example, were shortly to become the town's principal issue of controversy. The wider the street, it seemed, the more numerous and treacherous the potholes.

Second, the authority of Port Harcourt's local officialdom was not effective beyond the main township and the residential layouts immediately adjacent. Mile 1 Diobu, an indigenously owned area included within the administrative boundaries of the new city, was physically isolated from the center of the urban area and tended to be ignored by Port Harcourt's planners. Neighboring Mile 2 Diobu, similarly, was until 1960 beyond the administrative jurisdiction of the Port Harcourt Township and therefore not subject to the township's building regulations and other local bylaws. In consequence, both Mile 1 and Mile 2 steadily deteriorated into what one administrative officer described as "squallid slum of wattle framework with mud slapped on." [15]

Third, even in terms of the main township's development, the early plans were not without their technical flaws. Prepared by railway engineers, these plans quite naturally were geared to the requirements of the railway and the port. These requirements, however, did not always coincide with the long-term interests of a rapidly expanding urban area:

> One of the permanent planning problems of Port Harcourt is presented by its geography. Built on a long narrow peninsula Port Harcourt has always been a natural bottleneck. This problem has not been made easier by the way the railway has been brought down to the Port. It has always seemed odd that the main evacuation route from the Port (which soon became known

as Factory Road) should pass *between* the line of factories and the railway sidings which serve them. As early as 1921 the Public Works Department complained of the damage done to this road by spining oil drums in loading and unloading produce between the stores and the railway yards. One supposes that the builders of the town, being railwaymen, gave little thought to the problem of future road development.[16]

Finally, despite the generally impressive accomplishments of Port Harcourt's early planners and the township's extremely rapid physical development, little emphasis appears to have been placed upon aesthetic considerations. Perhaps industrial and commercial centers everywhere are subject to much the same fate—buildings are profitable enterprises, scenic landscapes are less so—but Port Harcourt somehow seems drearier than most. In 1937, Sylvia Leith-Ross described the township in these terms:

> The Europeans live in a well-kept but unattractive reservation separated from the native town by a stretch of dismal no-man's land. The township is even more depressing though it has nothing like the slum quarter which existed in Lagos until a few years ago. Roads are broad but unshaded, houses are according to official specifications but have not one single feature of comfort or of beauty, standpipes and latrines and incinerators are installed but only emphasize the unkempt, inhospitable look. The township has not the squalor of poverty so much as the squalor of alien ugliness. . . . All round lie the swamps, black mud and sucking water, walled by the stilt-like roots of the mangroves.[17]

In later years, the situation improved substantially, but Leith-Ross' 1937 description of the railway-port still held meaning in the 1960s.

THE EUROPEAN PATRICIANS

During Port Harcourt's formative years, the available political resources were monopolized by the local European minority. Ultimate power resided in the hands of the British Local Authority, and his Township Advisory Board was comprised entirely of European officials, and representatives of European mercantile firms. Like New Haven's patricians, the members of Port Harcourt's first colonial elite "had all the political resources they needed: wealth, social position, education, and a monopoly of public office; everything, in fact, except numbers—and popularity with the rank and file." [18] And, as in New Haven, what these men lacked in popularity was more than compensated by the sense of legitimacy with which their claim to govern was endowed, not only by themselves but by their African subjects.

From the start, there was little pretense concerning the directness of local British rule. Confronted by the ethnic heterogeneity and transiency of the urban population, and by the absence of viable local political institutions that could incorporate the disparate immigrant elements, the British chose to ignore the pattern of native administration established in the rural areas and to rule the township directly, without resort to African intermediaries. It is interesting to note, however, that in the first two years of the township's existence, a move was in fact made to establish a "Native Court . . . to deal with offences committed by the local labourers engaged for Railway Construction." [19] But the inauguration of the court was delayed, and a short time later the local authorities were advised to defer the court's establishment indefinitely.

The station magistrate was the central governmental figure of these early years. He was both the senior railway department official and the local representative (i.e., district officer) of the administration. His responsibilities were both administrative and judicial, and within the township, his authority was supreme. He was the individual upon whom all local political pressures impinged, the local official to whom all requests and all grievances were directed, the principal intermediary between the local community and the higher reaches of the far-flung colonial apparatus. He was, in short, to use the administrative vernacular of the period, the Local Authority.

For five years, the Local Authority was Port Harcourt's only effective institution of local government. Then, in 1917, Port Harcourt's Township Advisory Board was established as part of the implementation of the Nigeria Townships Ordinance passed in that year. This legislation appears to have been as much a response to the demands made by the European mercantile interests for a greater voice in urban affairs, as it was an expression of the British commitment to democratization. As early as 1916 (and possibly at an earlier date) the British mercantile houses in Port Harcourt were organized into the Traders Committee, which, in that year, made representations to the government in connection with proposed rents on Port Harcourt plots.[20] The establishment of a Township Advisory Board was a means of formalizing the link between the mercantile interests and the colonial government.

At the inaugural meeting of March 6, 1918, the board's membership was divided evenly between representatives of the government and representatives of mercantile interests. In subsequent years, the Township Advisory Board was to be increasingly dominated by official (i.e., government) members, but the traders and financiers were to retain a strong voice in the board's deliberations, and there were few instances when the board knowingly placed recommendations that violated the interests of Port Harcourt's expatriate business community. That is not to say, however, that the Europeans comprised a totally united community. European missionaries, for example, were in many respects a group apart. Moreover, official and mercantile interests were not always coterminous. The Colonial Office had to concern itself with a wide range of problems that often had little to do with the requirements of the business community, as in 1916, when the financial exigencies of the government overrode the demand of the Traders Committee for lower rents on Port Harcourt plots.[21] In later years, government concessions to the nationalist movement similarly represented a divergence between European official and European commercial interests.

The Township Advisory Board, like the Local Authority to whom its advice was directed, concerned itself with an extraordinary variety of issues. Minutes of meetings held in 1918 and 1919 suggest something of the wide scope of the board's advisory responsibilities, as well as something of the limited nature of the township's local financial resouces. Recommendations of the board during the first two years of its existence included the following:

1. The appointment of a Market Master at £18 per annum (contrasted to the appointment, in 1963, of four Municipal Council market masters at a combined salary of just under £640 per annum).

2. Provisions of £25 for the construction of an animal enclosure and for the payment of overtime fees to Sanitary Inspectors.

3. The allocation of £55 for the construction of a Laundry and well.

4. The adoption of bylaws to govern the market.

5. A request to Government to post a permanent labor force to the Local Authority to maintain the Township roads.

6. A request for Crown land allocation for the purpose of erecting a tennis court for the European clerks of the Mercantile Firms.

7. Provision of £80 for drainage of the Native Location.

8. The erection, by Government (or the Township), of several rows of labourers' quarters to remedy the drastic housing situation in the Native Location. A small rent to be charged.

9. Provision of funds for the construction of a golf course: "It was . . . decided to put in £100 towards the construction of the course next year. The Board desired to draw attention to the immense improvement that will be effected in the Township by the establishment of the golf course, enabling Europeans to take healthful exercise after their work, as well as materially improving the Residential area in the vicinity."

10. The inauguration of a letter delivery system.

11. The approval of an application by one J. C. Benjamin for a piece of land to use as a pen for cattle to be imported from Calabar for slaughter in the Township.

12. The institution of an evening curfew for those without lamps, as protection against burglaries.[22]

The list could be greatly expanded, but for present purposes it is sufficient to call attention to four points. First, Simon Ottenberg's observation that a characteristic feature of African urban government "is that its development has generally been guided from above . . . ,"[23] is directly applicable to Port Harcourt's experience. Port Harcourt was ruled from on high, and local officials were carefully circumscribed in their discretionary power. The Township Advisory Board, for example, was empowered only to request and to recommend, not to decide. On more than one occasion, in fact, the board was forcefully reminded of its limited responsibilities. In October of 1918 Lord Lugard complained to the Owerri Provincial Resident: "I note that it is stated that the

Council [the Township Advisory Board] "authorized" the Legal Adviser to do certain things. Until Port Harcourt becomes a 1st Class [Township] and the Advisory Council becomes the Local Authority [as a Town Council] it cannot authorize anything or anybody. It is merely advisory. It will be well to point this out to Mr. Lynch (the Station Magistrate)." [24] Six years later, the board was again reprimanded by the Resident for usurping the powers of the commissioner of lands in processing applications for leases of Crown land: "Please note this. It is not the first occasion Government has drawn attention to what it considers an encroachment by the Board on its prerogatives. As I understand the matter, the Board has nothing to do with any leases, neither does the allocation of plots [outside the Native Town] concern it." [25]

Even the station magistrate who was, far and away, the single most authoritative figure within the local community, found his powers to be severely limited. Indeed, it is likely that his rural administrative counterparts, operating in areas of less vital economic and administrative significance to the Colonial Office, were permitted a much freer hand in the administration of their districts.[26] Few matters could pass through the station magistrate's office without being called to the attention of his administrative superordinates, and approval of the magistrate's recommendations was by no means automatic.

This centralization of power under the colonial system is of more than historical interest. No feature of that system was held onto more tenaciously in the postindependence period than the centralized administration of the earlier era. The point has often been made that, partly as a consequence of this administrative precedent and partly because of other economic and technical factors, local government in the African setting often means little more than local ratification of decisions made by a central administration.

Second, despite the diversity of the subjects covered in the deliberations of the board, the scale of advisory board operations in this early period was very small indeed, especially when contrasted forty-five years later to the relatively elaborate bureaucracy of Port Harcourt's Municipal Council. Township estimates for 1918–1919 called for expenditures totaling, in 1964's dollar equivalent, $2,355, as compared to the Municipal Council's estimated expenditure for 1963–64 of $940,226.[27] Similarly, Port Harcourt's entire local government staff in 1921 totaled only fourteen persons.[28] The staff of the Municipal Council in 1964–1965 numbered 205 persons,[29] and if the staffs of the District Office and the Planning Authority were added to the 1964–1965 council figure, this number would substantially increase. These comparisons, we may note parenthetically, are suggestive of the growing pains Port Harcourt was to experience as a result of its rapid development. Within a period of less than fifty years, the city's public services (as measured by budgetary allotments) were to expand almost forty thousandfold, while the demand for these services was to grow even more rapidly.

Third, African interests were totally subordinated to those of Port Harcourt's European community. This point is rendered emphatically by the order of priorities established by the board: £80 for the drainage of the entire Native Location (which, from its inception, was known for its propensity to flood during the wet season) and £100 for the European golf course. Even when the full severity of the drainage problem in the Native Location was finally recognized by the board members, the rationale for corrective action remained that of the furtherance of European interests: "Mr. Wilson [the President of the Chamber of Commerce] raised the question of the drainage of the Native Town and stated that great inconvenience was being caused to the firms, by the continual absence of their Native Clerical Staff, who complained of having to wade to their work after rain." [30]

Finally, local community power was effectively monopolized by the European community. Until 1926, no African sat on the Township Advisory Board and African access to the board remained informal and indirect. In November 1919, when a Hausa man petitioned the board for permission to open a subsidiary market at the waterside, the board decided to sound out African opinion on the subject by having individual board members consult their respective African employees.[31] During Port Harcourt's formative years, the communications linkages between the city's European governors and its African governed were tenuous at best.

CHAPTER 5

The Political Coalescence of the African Community (1920–1943)

The recruitment of political labor, together with the commercial attractions of the new railway-port brought together Africans of diverse cultural backgrounds and politically autonomous traditions, involved them in new forms of impersonal and often intensely competitive interaction, and subjected them to the authority of an alien colonial power. This chapter examines the response of Port Harcourt's immigrants to their new urban milieu, focusing, in turn, upon four key dimensions of social and political change: first, the transformation of communal categories in response to the exigencies of urban life; second, the emergence of new organizational forms; third, the early African response to local European domination; and last, the developing patterns of leadership within the African community.

COMMUNAL TRANSFORMATION IN THE CITY

Frequently it is said that communal categories and identities are the givens of social life. One can change one's occupation, but one cannot change one's communal group as readily. Recently, however, scholars have pointed out that under conditions of social mobilization and intergroup conflict, communal boundaries are indeed transformable. Two principal forms of communal transformation have been distinguished: expansion and differentiation.

Communal Expansion

A number of observers have noted the emergence within non-Western urban areas of communal identities and groupings that

68

are considerably wider in their embrace than the communities of the traditional order: "A reductive process takes place in the town: the intricate mosaic of the countryside becomes simplified to a manageable number of ethnic categories. A sense of membership in a group significantly expanded in scale from the clan and lineage system of the very localized rural 'tribal' community develops."[1] Illustrating this point, Crawford Young describes the emergence of the Congolese "Bangala" identity as an example of "artificial ethnicity" produced by intergroup competition in Kinshasha, in which disparate groups from the "up-river" area joined together to confront the indigenous Bakongo.[2] Similarly, addressing themselves to the Indian case, the Rudolphs describe the process whereby Indian *jatis* (popularly known as castes) of unequal status join to form political and economic alliances against their competitors. It is the exigencies of modern competition that provide the impetus to such alliances: "The higher castes need numerical strength to sustain their power and status; the lower ones need access to resources and opportunities that support of the higher ones can yield."[3] The Rudolphs observe that such alliances raise the ritual status of the lower castes and thus transform their traditional identities.

It is important to note that the expansion of communal boundaries need not mean the destruction of old communal identities and loyalties. It may mean simply the superimposition upon the traditional reference points of wider concentric circles of communalism. The old identities, typically, coexist with the new, and continue to play an important role in structuring social relationships and shaping political affiliations. Moreover, it is the traditional groupings that serve as the principal channels of recruitment into the wider systems of social and political interaction. In short, the primary effect of communal expansion is not to eliminate traditional identities but to multiply the communal points of reference available to urban residents.

Turning to Port Harcourt, communal expansion in the city produced no less than four new levels of socially and politically significant communal identity. First, at the highest level, was a growing racial consciousness inclusive of all Africans or all blacks. Closely fused with the political status of "colonial subject," this racial identity was a direct response to the common subordination of all Africans to a class of racially distinct Europeans. Growing racial consciousness expressed itself in a variety of ways, as in this excerpt from the minutes of a 1932 meeting of a local communal association: "The question of a black medical officer at Owerri Hospital was raised. It was reported that some group of Owerri people had written a protest against the taking over of Owerri Hospital by a black doctor. This action was much lamented by the Union. Mr. D. suggested a publication in the local paper against the measure which has thus been taken. This was not thought a very suitable step to take but the Patron instructed the Secretary to write to Owerri Union, Aba, asking why they allowed such a protest to pass." [4] It expressed itself, too, in this gentle political warning contained in the editorial column of a local newspaper: "The black man should . . . co-operate heartily with the white man but the former must always remember that he is not to remain an automatic machine forever." [5] It expressed itself, finally, in the formation of the African Community League, a federation of local communal association (known popularly as tribal unions or improvement associations) organized in 1935 to give political voice to the aspirations of the African community.

At a second level, communal expansion expressed itself in the emergence of new, affect-laden identities of nationality, identities that reflected a modern consciousness of cultural and linguistic unities of which traditional man was largely unaware. Like the development of the new racial consciousness, so the emergence of identities of nationality—based on a new sense of Ibo-ness or Ijaw-ness—reflected new patterns of social interaction and competition to which Port Harcourt's early dwellers were exposed.

The emergence of a united and politically assertive Ibo community provides an especially clear illustration of the dynamics of nationality in the new urban setting. The first instance in which Port Harcourt's Ibos acted upon an awareness of their common nationality occurred in 1933, and was occasioned by the return from overseas of Dr. S. E. Onwu, Iboland's first medical doctor. On the initiative of a few educated Ibos, arrangements were made to accord Dr. Onwu a Port Harcourt reception. For the first time, Ibos holding diverse communal allegiances acted collectively on the basis of their widest linguistic unity. Money was raised from several Ibo communal associations and a reception was held in the schoolroom in the center of the township. The success of this venture prompted the decision to transform the reception committee into an "Ibo Union," a permanent organization embracing all Ibo elements in Port Harcourt.[6]

While Dr. Onwu's reception provided the immediate stimulus for the formation of the Ibo Union, the organizational initiative reflected, at base, a new political assertiveness generated largely by increasing Ibo resentment at their local subordination to the more advantaged non-Ibo minorities. As one of the Ibo Union's foundation members recalls, "At that time, the people holding senior posts were from Sierra Leone, Yorubaland, and Calabar. Ibos were regarded as infidels."

The social and political superiority enjoyed by members of Port Harcourt's minority groups, a reflection primarily of their earlier exposure to Western education, had several manifestations. Non-Ibo Sierra Leonians, Gold Coast emigrants, Yorubas, Efiks, and Ijaws dominated the African strata of the local government departments and European mercantile firms.[7] Similarly, Port Harcourt's first African social elite, as defined by membership in the prestigious Port Harcourt Grand Native Club (formed in 1920, and later renamed the African Club), contained disproportionate numbers of these well-educated and highly positioned non-Ibo elements. In 1935, despite the fact that the Ibos had begun to advance, members of the non-Ibo minorities still accounted for eleven of the club's twenty-one officers and executive members (table 6). Between 1920 and 1940, the presidency of the club was shared by a Gambian, an Ijaw, and Efik, and a Yoruba. No Ibo appears to have served as president until the late 1940s.[8]

Also underlying the movement toward Ibo political integration was Ibo annoyance at the absence of any meaningful representation on the Township Advisory Board. The first African appointment to the board did not come until 1926, and as late as 1936 the African community was granted but two seats. Of equal concern, the Africans had no voice in the selection of their representatives. Consequently, government-appointed members— I. B. Johnson, a Gambian businessman and retired civil servant, and S. T. Ikiroma-Owiye, an Ijaw-speaking Kalabari trader and retired civil servant—lacked the support of the very persons

71

TABLE 6

AFRICAN CLUB EXECUTIVE COMMITTEE, BY NATIONALITY (1935)

Nationality	Number
Ibo	10
Onitsha Province (5)	
Mid-West (3)	
Section not known (2)	
Non-Ibo	11
Efik (4)	
Yoruba (5)	
Ijaw (2)	
	N = 21

SOURCES: The membership of the Executive Committee was recorded in the *Nigerian Observer*, February 1935. I am indebted to Ikenna Nzimiro and G. I. Jones for assistance in the identification of the members' nationalities.

whose interests they were supposed to be representing. The Ibos resented their political dependence upon men who not only were not Ibo but who were, in a sense, more European than African. Ibo discontent with this state of affairs, shared by other non-Ibo elements of Port Harcourt's African community, prompted the search for some means whereby the district officer could more directly communicate with Port Harcourt's black citizenry. As one of the Ibo Union's organizers put it, "We wanted the white man to send messages directly from the District Officer to us." The Ibo Union was but the first step toward the creation of a viable African Community League, representative of all of the township's major nationalities, and capable of serving as the formal intermediary between the colonial government and the African population.

Non-Ibo dominance and Ibo underrepresentation were especially resented by the better-educated Ibos. Significantly, the first officers of the new Ibo Union were almost all school certificate holders. The president, vice-president, and secretary were, respectively, a government education officer, the chief clerk in the local Treasury Department, and the chief clerk for the regional manager of the United Africa Company—all men who moved either within or just below non-Ibo circles and who, therefore, were particularly sensitive to the relatively low esteem in which

Ibos were held by the dominant non-Ibo elements. Although these educated Ibos commanded greater status and financial resources than were available to the Ibo rank and file, they felt relatively more deprived vis-à-vis the high positioned non-Ibos with whom they compared themselves. It was this sense of relative deprivation that underlay the rising Ibo self-consciousness and the formation of Port Harcourt's Ibo Union. In effect, it was the competitiveness of the modern urban milieu, rather than the assertion of traditional antagonisms, which gave rise to the consciousness of nationality. Tribalism, in Port Harcourt, was the product of modernity and the educated middle class rather than of tradition and illiteracy.

The process of communal expansion which produced the new sense of racial group membership and the new identities of nationality generated still a third set of communal reference points: new "geo-ethnic" identities that corresponded to the artificial administrative units in which the immigrants' traditional communities of origin were located.[9] Port Harcourt residents, especially if they were of the Ibo-speaking majority, tended to identify themselves to new acquaintances by reference neither to their village or village group nor to their nationality, but rather to the intermediate geo-ethnic communities of clan court area, division, and province.

Nontraditional geo-ethnic identities assumed importance because they comprised the lowest level of social grouping at which Port Harcourt's Ibo immigrants were sufficiently numerous to make an impact upon the wider urban community. In some cases, traditional groupings did not yield enough persons even to form an improvement union. Thus, an elder from the Ibo-speaking community of Akpulu recalled that by 1929, the date of his arrival in Port Harcourt, only two other Akpuiu men had taken up residence in the township. Unable to form their own organization, these three Akpulu immigrants were admitted to the fifteen-member Akokwa Town Union, organized in 1933. Akokwa and Akpulu were politically autonomous but neighboring village groups in Orlu Division; and in the impersonal and competitive environment of the new city, their rural proximity and common cultural heritage took precedence over their traditional political separation. Then three years later, when the Mbanesa Clan Union (corresponding to the artificial Mbanesa Clan Court Area in which both Akokwa and Akpulu were situated) was organized, the Akpulu members promptly withdrew from the Akokwa Union and turned their attention exclusively to the larger geo-ethnic clan union. Subsequently, in 1938, the growing Akpulu community in Port Harcourt launched its own Akpulu Town Union with a foundation membership of eleven or twelve men.

Just as the competitiveness of the urban milieu contributed to the stratification and increasing self-consciousness of Ibo and non-Ibo nationality groups, so did it play into the interaction between the various geo-ethnic segments of the large Ibo community. The more highly educated immigrants from Onitsha Province, for example, were the first of the Ibos to move into clerical and administrative posts and into skilled and technical occupations. This occupational and educational superiority translated itself into membership in the African Club (of the eight Ibo executive members of the club in 1935 whose areas of origin are known, five were from Onitsha Province while the remaining three were from culturally related Ibo areas of Mid-Western Nigeria; none were from Eastern Nigeria's Owerri Province), into membership on the Township Advisory Board (the first two Ibo members were from Onitsha Province), and into leadership of Port Harcourt's Ibo community (the first vice-president and secretary of Port Harcourt's Ibo Union were both from Onitsha Division and Z. C. Obi, the union's first branch secretary, subsequently became president of the national Ibo State Union).

Intra-Ibo differentiation occurred even at the level of administrative divisions and traditional village groups. Certain communities within Orlu, Bende, and Owerri Divisions of Owerri Province, for example, were long renowned for the aggressiveness and shrewdness of their traders, and it was the men from these towns, notably Nkwerre (Orlu Division), Abiriba (Bende Division), and Oguta (Owerri Division), who tended to assume the city's indigenous commercial leadership. These and other immigrant groups were accorded prestige in the larger community commensurate with the commercial success of their leading traders.

The continuity of the educational and occupational patterns established in the 1920s and 1930s is highlighted by an examination of the social composition of the 1964 executive committees of three of Port Harcourt's most important communal associations: the Onitsha Divisional Union (Onitsha Province), the Orlu Divisional Union (Owerri Province), and the Mbaise Federated Union (Owerri Division, Owerri Province).[10] Thus, as table 7

TABLE 7

EXECUTIVE COMMITTEE MEMBERS OF THREE
COMMUNAL ASSOCIATIONS, BY EDUCATION (1964)[a]

Education	Onitsha Divisional Union	Orlu Divisional Union	Mbaise Federated Union
No education	9.8%	26.3%	26.7%
1–3 years	—	5.3	—
4–8 years	19.5	—	10.0
Elementary school certificate	39.0	31.6	36.7
Postprimary[b] education	4.9	5.3	6.7
Secondary school[c] certificate	19.5	10.5	6.7
Postsecondary academic or technical training	2.4	—	—
University or professional degree	—	—	—
Unknown	4.9	21.1	10.0
Totals	100.0% (N = 41)	100.1%[d] (N = 19)	100.1%[d] (N = 30)

ᵃ These data and those presented in table 9 were obtained through interviews with leading officers of the three unions. I wish to express my particular indebtedness to Senator Chief Z. C. Obi, and to Messrs. Luke Ukatu, Daniel Ohaeto, and C. O. Madufuro who provided invaluable assistance on this and other aspects of this study. An explanatory note on the educational categories employed is contained in appendix 1.
ᵇ Includes Teacher Training Colleges, postprimary correspondence courses, and postprimary technical training.
ᶜ Either the West African School Certificate (W.A.S.C.) or the General Certificate of Education.
ᵈ Percentages do not total 100 because of rounding.

illustrates, the Onitsha executive body in 1964 was composed of a smaller proportion of persons who had received no schooling (9.8 percent, as contrasted with 26.3 percent of Orlu executive members and 26.7 percent of Mbaise executive members), and a higher proportion who had studied beyond the primary school certificate (26.8 percent compared with 15.8 percent [Orlu] and 13.4 percent [Mbaise]). Occupationally (table 8), 36.6 percent of

TABLE 8

EXECUTIVE COMMITTEE MEMBERS OF THREE
COMMUNAL ASSOCIATIONS, BY OCCUPATION (1964)

Occupation	Onitsha Divisional Union	Orlu Divisional Union	Mbaise Federated Union
Managers	—	—	6.7%
Clerks	36.6%	10.5%	23.3
Educators	—	5.3	3.3
Businessmen and big traders	9.8	31.6	6.7
Petty traders and contractors	26.8	42.1	26.7
Artisans	12.2	5.3	6.7
Skilled and unskilled laborers	2.4	—	6.7
Domestics, washermen, custodians	2.4	—	10.0
Other	4.9	—	6.7
Unknown	4.9	5.3	3.3
Totals	100.0% (N = 41)	100.1%[a] (N = 19)	100.1%[a] (N = 30)

[a] Percentages do not total 100 because of rounding.

the Onitshans occupied clerical posts, compared with 10.5 percent of the Orlus and 23.3 percent of the Mbaises. The Orlu commercial prominence was indicated by the high proportion of the Orlu executive members (73.7 percent) who were either businessmen or petty traders and contractors; the comparable Onitsha and Mbaise figures were 36.6 percent and 33.4 percent, respectively.[11]

Further evidence of the differentiation of Owerri and Onitsha Ibos by occupation is provided by the geo-ethnic composition of Port Harcourt's African business elite in the early sixties. Of the twenty-five Africans identified by the writer as Port Harcourt's economic notables, nineteen were traders and businessmen.[12] Of these nineteen entrepreneurs, twelve or 63.2 percent were from Owerri Province, primarily from Orlu and Owerri Divisions, while only three (15.8 percent) were from Onitsha Province. The remaining four (21.1 percent) included two Ijaws, one Yoruba, and one Mid-Westerner. In short, while Port Harcourt's Onitshans came to occupy the prestigious African posts within the civil service and European mercantile firms, it was the relatively less-educated Owerris who assumed the leadership of Port Harcourt's African commercial sector.[13]

Thus far, we have identified three layers of communal identity in Port Harcourt: race, nationality, and geo-ethnicity all emerged as new points of social and political reference for the city's immigrant population. But communal expansion in Port Harcourt was expressed on yet a fourth level in the distinction that emerged between the Diobu native community and the numerically preponderant stranger elements. This division between the indigenes and the strangers did not have the same political significance as in many other African urban centers, inasmuch as the indigenous community was too small to compete on equal terms with the immigrants. Nevertheless, as will be indicated in later chapters, the interaction between the natives and the strangers comprised an important part of the urban political scene. We have already noted the historical contempt in which the interior Ibo immigrants were held by the Diobu Ikwerres. The alienation of Diobu lands, first to the government, and then to immigrant Ibo land speculators, only served to intensify Diobu hostility toward the strangers in their midst. The important point, for present purposes, is that the communal category of stranger joined otherwise disparate immigrant elements within a common frame of reference.

Communal Differentiation

The new patterns of social interaction and competition facing Port Harcourt's early immigrants led not only to the expansion of communal categories, but also to the increasing internal differentiation of the members of both traditional and new communal groupings by religion, by occupation, and by social status. Such differentiation has been cited by some scholars as evidence of the deterioration of communal identities and institutions. This conclusion appears to follow from those dichotomous models that suggest that communally particularistic and socioeconomically universalistic roles and identities lie at opposite ends of a single social continuum, the emergence of the latter heralding the disappearance of the former. This formulation, however, is not borne out by the Port Harcourt experience. The emergence of new identities that differentiated the members of communal groups meant the multiplication of points of social reference

77

rather than the substitution of the new for the old. An individual could be a railway worker and also an Owerri Ibo; his acquisition of a new socioeconomic identity did not mean the elimination of his communal identities. Consequently, while socioeconomic identities often cross-cut communal boundaries and—in some situations—superseded the political salience of communal identities, class formation in Port Harcourt did not mean the deterioration of communal perspectives and institutions. This point will become clearer when we consider, in later chapters, the complex political interrelationships between communal and noncommunal identities.

Communal differentiation in Port Harcourt was manifested, first, in the proliferation of new religious identities. Through the 1920s and 1930s, religious sects and church meetings multiplied rapidly. "In one street alone," Sylvia Leith-Ross could write in 1937,

> the inquirer finds the Methodists, the Niger Delta branch of the Church Missionary Society, the Roman Catholics, the Faith Tabernacle, the Baptists, the African Church, the Salvation Army, the African Methodist Episcopals (Zion branch), the African Methodist Episcopals (Bethel branch), the New Church (Swedenborg), the Apostolic Mission, the Seventh Day Adventists, the First Century Gospel (an offshoot of the Faith Tabernacle), and up a side street, a Mohammedan mosque. Other sects come and go, showering badly printed pamphlets as they pass, generally produced in the United States or in South Africa.[14]

The new religious identities cut two ways. On the one hand, they signaled the creation of new cleavages within ethnic and geo-ethnic categories: Christian converts were set off from traditional religious adherents, Catholics from Protestants, Methodists from Anglicans. As a general rule, all Christian converts within a village or village group joined the same denomination, so that the new religious affiliations reenforced traditional communal identities. Beyond the local level, however, religious divisions developed within the emerging geo-ethnic and nationality groups. In later years, the cleavage between the region's Catholic and Protestant populations was to assume particular significance.

On the other hand, these same religious identities frequently joined together individuals from groups that were historically or culturally separate. Thus, Port Harcourt's high status St. Cyprian's Anglican Church, which conducted its services in English, was composed of ethnically diverse, but educationally and religiously homogeneous Sierra Leonians, Lagos Yorubas, Ijaws, and Onitsha Ibos. Similarly, Port Harcourt's first Catholic Church contained within its congregation a large number of historically distinct Ibo subgroups joined by their common religious faith; likewise, the local Methodist Church grouped together Ibos from Bende Division with the normally Presbyterian Ibibios and Efiks from Uyo and Calabar.[15]

During the 1920s and 1930s, the years of political coalescence in Port Harcourt, it was the integrative aspects of the new religious identities which were especially important. The churches were the only ongoing purposive institutions involving the mass of the urban community which were clearly "above tribe," effectively amalgamating a vast number of traditionally autonomous peoples. But the churches did more than simply set a precedent for collective action. They also produced two men—Rev. E. K. Williams and Rev. L. R. Potts-Johnson, both Sierra Leonians and both Methodist pastors—who, drawing upon the immense prestige associated with their religious calling, were able to provide the necessary leadership for the movement toward African political integration. Their role in Port Harcourt's political development will be taken up when we turn to the early African response to European domination.

A second source of communal differentiation in Port Harcourt was the emergence of new occupational roles that produced new patterns of internal cleavage within communal groups and also new patterns of social and political grouping which cut across communal lines. Men began to organize on the basis of their occupational interests as well as on the basis of their communal identities. In 1921, for example, the multiethnic township staff collectively petitioned the government for increased salaries and improvements in their conditions of service. On another occasion in these early years, African employees of the European mercantile houses petitioned the Township Advisory Board on the subjects of drainage and water supply in the Native Town. Likewise, an organization calling itself the African Progress Union vented the economic grievances shared by a communally diverse group of traders and petty landlords.[16]

Lastly, communal groups were also internally differentiated by the emergence of new patterns of social stratification which anticipated the subsequent development, in the years following World War II, of a sharp cleavage between an increasingly privileged Nigerian political class and an antiestablishment coalition of youth, radical trade unionists, and intellectuals. Individuals, like communal groups, were stratified according to their occupational and educational characteristics. Within each of Port Harcourt's ethnic and geo-ethnic communities, a class of men emerged which was set apart from the communal rank and file by their exposure to Western education and by their relatively high position within the township's occupational hierarchy. It was these men who assumed the leadership of their communal organizations and gave direction to the movement for self-improvement both in the city and in their communities of origin. Most remained tied to their communal groups—occupation seldom superseded "community" in the urban ordering of social priorities—but their prestige and influence differentiated them from the mass of their fellow townsmen. Moreover, the social standing of some of these men transcended the boundaries of their own communal groups and they acted, in certain situations, as the members of a self-conscious elite group. The members of the African Club were part of this emergent class, and so were the African clerics who played such an important role in giving direction to the movement for African political unity. These men were all well educated and all performed prestigious occupational roles in the Church, in government departments, or in the European commercial firms. And, though few possessed the wealth characteristic of the entrepreneurial "big men" of contemporary times, most were, by the standards of the day, well-to-do. Nevertheless, despite their transcendent social status and the awareness of their elitist positions, the primary allegiance of all but a few (the exceptions included the leading clergymen) remained to their communities of origin.

THE FORMATION OF COMMUNAL ASSOCIATIONS

Immigrants to Port Harcourt in the first decades of the twentieth century were entering a strange social, economic, and political environment. For many, the trip to Port Harcourt represented their first departure from their communities of origin, their first separation from their kinsmen, and their first experience of life in a communally heterogeneous and functionally specialized urban setting. As Kenneth Little has observed,

> urban life is characterized *inter alia* by a specialization of function. Instead of being carried on by the kin group and the tribe, activities of the town are divided among a larger number of institutions. There are mines, factories, shops and offices to organize economic production and conduct business, schools to undertake education and the training of the young; churches and mosques have charge of religion; law and order are the responsibility of magistrates and of the police; and with the new emphasis on individualism the trend is towards the small elementary family.[17]

For the new arrival, a number of age-old problems were in need of new solutions. To whom could he turn in time of financial crisis? How would disputes with his fellow urban residents, of the same or of a different town, be resolved? Who would assist him in the performance of traditional marriage, child-naming, and burial rites? How were his new occupational interests to be protected? In Port Harcourt, as in other of Nigeria's new urban communities during the interwar period, the formation of "voluntary associations" seemed the answer to these many problems. These associations provided the mechanism by which traditional institutions and loyalties could be adapted to the exigencies of urban life.[18]

The new associations, expressing the complexity of urban social differentiation and the multiplicity of new social, economic, and religious interests, took many forms. Of greatest significance, however, both from the standpoint of the individual immigrant and from that of the urban social system, were the "communal associations." Described popularly, and in the literature on West African voluntary associations, as "tribal unions," communal associations were actually organized at all levels of the developing African social structure. Thus, some communal associations were family, village or village group (town) meetings, while others were organized around the artificial administrative units of clan court area, division, and province;[19] still others, such as the Ibo

State Union and the Ibibio State Union, embraced entire nationalities. Such communal associations were, in Kenneth Little's
phrase, "peculiarly the result of migration":

> Basically, they represent the newly arrived migrant's response
> to urban conditions. Belonging, in his rural home, to a compact
> group of kinsmen and neighbours, he has been used to a highly
> personal set of relationships. He knows of no other way of com-
> munal living than this and so to organize similar practices of
> mutuality is for him a spontaneous adjustment to his environ-
> ment. Nor in view of the strangeness of his suroundings is it
> surprising that the migrant often prefers to remain as far as
> possible in the company of previous associates. The result is that
> instead of weakening tribal consciousness, life in the new urban
> environment tends in some respects to make it stronger.[20]

Taken collectively, the communal associations had a dual social
and political significance. Socially, their effect was to substantially
reduce what William Kornhauser has termed the "discontinuities
in community" resulting from a rapid increase in the rate of social
change.[21] They, in effect, served as surrogate kinship institutions
for Port Harcourt's immigrant population, easing the adjustment
of new arrivals to the strange urban milieu and providing social
support during their stay in the city.

Politically, since the greatest part of Port Harcourt's adult male
citizenry was linked to one or another of the city's innumerable
"improvement unions," these communal associations became the
organizational medium for the political integration of the African
community. They simply provided the most natural and efficient
means for mobilizing the urban population. Ethnicity and geo-
ethnicity were the dominant social facts of the urban milieu, and
these unions were the focal points around which Port Harcourt's
communally oriented social life revolved. No other African institutions possessed comparable moral force or organizational
sophistication. Ironically, in later years, when self-government
was on the horizon and the requirements for African political
unity no longer appeared so urgent, these same associations and
the communal parochialism which they also reflected were to
contribute to the refragmentation of the African community.

Among the different nationality groups present in the city,

variations in numerical strength produced variations in the pattern of organizational development. Among the smallest groups, attempts to organize family, village, and town meetings were seldom successful, and for some minorities—such as the Sierra Leonian and Yoruba communities—nationality associations were the only viable organizational form.

Larger immigrant communities formed associations at each level of their highly segmented social order. Among these populous groups, such as the Ibo communities from Owerri and Onitsha Divisions, multiple associational membership became the norm rather than the exception. A man could easily be a triple dues-paying member of a family, village, and town union, and might even represent his town union in a clan or divisional association. Survey data concerning patterns of organizational membership in these early years are, of course, lacking, but data obtained for forty of forty-six Port Harcourt municipal councillors who were in office during the early 1960s are suggestive. Thirty-five of these forty councillors were strangers to Port Harcourt, and all but one were Ibo. Of these thirty-five, three (8.6%) belonged to at least one communal association, thirteen (37.1%) belonged to two, and nineteen (54.3%) belonged to three or more. It is, of course, likely that politicians had a higher rate of organizational participation than the community at large. It was the writer's impression, however, in the absence of other statistical data, that virtually every adult Ibo male in Port Harcourt was a registered member of some communal association, and that many (perhaps a majority) belonged to more than one. If a man were unemployed and could not afford the required dues payments, it was not unusual for his dues to be paid by a well-to-do relation, or for the union to grant him special consideration. Indeed, the failure to register with one's family or village meeting was, in some instances, met with social ostracism.

The various levels of the Ibo associational structure were only loosely coordinated, but as a general rule, the smaller family, village, and town unions assumed primary (though never exclusive) responsibility for meeting urban needs (such as the provision of burial, illness, marriage, and emergency loan benefits), while larger unions (including clan, town, and sometimes village associations) raised funds not only for local welfare assistance but also for scholarships and civic projects in their homelands. The wider divisional unions, of which the Owerri Progressive Union was an example, gradually became transformed into federated bodies composed of representatives of the lower-order town and clan unions. As such, they concerned themselves less with social welfare and recreation and more with the arbitration of internal disputes, with the enhancement of the image and prestige of their division within the city, with the political advancement of their "sons," and with the mediation of communications from the highest echelons of the Port Harcourt and national Ibo bureaucracies to the urban town, village, and family unions. In the 1950s, when the major struggle for local self-government had been won and the franchise had established the Ibos as the pre-eminent political power within the community, it was the Ibo divisional unions that became the primary nonparty vehicles for local political action. Finally, at the pinnacle of the local Ibo associational structure was the all-embracing Ibo Union, composed of representatives of the divisional unions and concerned primarily with advancing the interests of the Ibo community vis-à-vis the colonial administration and Port Harcourt's other nationality groups.

In closing this discussion of communal associations, it is well to note that in Port Harcourt, as in urban communities throughout Nigeria, the organizational initiatives of the Ibos extended beyond their immediate place of residence. Thus, many of the city's Ibo communal associations were joined with their counterparts in Nigeria's other urban areas in federations of "all branches abroad." Port Harcourt's Nnewi Patriotic Union, for example, combined with its Nnewi counterparts in other cities to form a single federated organization, thereby establishing regular channels of communication between all Nnewi men who had traveled out of their home town. Moreover, as part of a Nigeria-wide urban initiative, the Port Harcourt unions encouraged the formation of "home branches" within their rural communities of origin and the integration of these branches with their respective urban federations. The ties of rural Iboland with Nigeria's urban centers were thus formalized, and Ibos "abroad" were able to exercise increasing influence on developments at home.[22]

THE AFRICAN RESPONSE TO EUROPEAN DOMINATION

Communal transformation, together with the emergence of new organizational forms, laid the foundations for the political integration of Port Harcourt's immigrant community. Communal expansion produced wider and more organizationally effective communal units. Western education and a new occupational structure gave rise to a new elite increasingly impatient with colonial domination, and to leaders able to transcend the various communal divisions of the African community; and the development of a network of communal associations provided the necessary organizational medium to mobilize the African population. An ideological impetus to the movement toward integration and the actual creation of a comprehensive political organization inclusive of the entire African community were all that were lacking. In the 1930s, these were provided by the publication of the township's first newspaper, the *Nigerian Observer*,[23] and by the inauguration of the African Community League.

Potts-Johnson and the Nigerian Observer

With a proud masthead, "A weekly Periodical devoted to the interests of Education, Religion, Commerce, Race Problems and various other problems affecting British West Africa," and the motto, "For God, Our Country and Our Race," the *Nigerian Observer* made its appearance. Introduced on January 4, 1930, the paper was largely the handiwork of one extraordinary individual, the Reverend L. R. Potts-Johnson. This man, more than any other single person, was responsible for awakening in Port Harcourt's African community a supratribal political consciousness and an awareness of the community's organized political potential. No man had a more dramatic impact upon Port Harcourt's political life. On January 5, 1944, the *Nigerian Eastern Mail* declared: "The Rev. L. R. Potts-Johnson, if an election were to take place, would score the highest votes. He has always shown very keen interest in the affairs of Port Harcourt, he is easily accessible and any poor man or woman can see him at any time. He is always prepared to take up the people's case." In the 1960s, Potts-Johnson was still remembered as "the central figure in Port Harcourt during his lifetime . . . a very good man . . . often the foundation of the Port Harcourt Municipality is credited to him." "He was the only man after E. K. Williams (a fellow Methodist pastor) who could meet the Resident and speak freely without shivering. A tall, huge man with attractive personality. Much respected." [24]

Rev. Potts-Johnson was one of several thousand Africans who came to Nigeria from Sierra Leone between the latter part of the eighteenth and the early twentieth centuries. Many of these emigres were the descendants of freed slaves who had been carried, originally, from Western Nigeria. Whether or not Potts-Johnson himself was of Yoruba descent, however, is not known. In any event, Potts-Johnson first arrived in Nigeria in 1911. He secured employment in the civil service, first as a clerk in the Nigerian Secretariat and then as a tutor in the renowned King's College, Lagos. He was subsequently persuaded to join the Wesleyan Methodist Church as a tutor in the Wesleyan Boys High School and was accepted as a candidate for the ministry. In 1916, following missionary tours in Calabar and Ogoni, Potts-Johnson opened the Wesleyan Methodist Church in the new township of Port Harcourt. His ordination followed shortly thereafter and, in 1921, he traveled to England to begin a three-year course of study in science and education. His return to Nigeria was marked by tours of duty, as pastor and as tutor, in Lagos and Calabar.[25]

In 1924 Potts-Johnson reestablished residence in Port Harcourt. He resigned from the Methodist ministry at this point but remained active as a preacher, offering his services to any church that requested his participation. In 1930, he launched his newspaper and two years later, on May 2, 1932, he founded the Enitonna High School, one of the first and most ambitious educational projects undertaken by a Nigerian African. The success of both of these projects quickly brought Potts-Johnson to the attention of both the African and the European publics. Even before the African Community League was formally launched and Potts-Johnson had assumed the league's presidency, he had established himself through the voice of his newspaper as the African community's unofficial spokesman. In later years, he was to become not only the president of the African Community

League (a post he was to hold for ten years in succession), but also a member of the Township Advisory Board, the president of the Sierra Leone Union, the president of the Port Harcourt Win-the-War-Fund Committee, the chairman of the Ex-Servicemen's Welfare Association, and the first Port Harcourt member of the Eastern House of Assembly (1946–1949). In his capacity as regional assembly member, he was appointed in 1948 to the Select Committee of the Eastern Regional House of Assembly established to review the existing system of local government in the eastern provinces. In 1949, just prior to his death in that year, the popular community leader was officially honored as a member of the British Empire.

The *Nigerian Observer* espoused an ideology of African self-help, not of anticolonialism. Its editor-publisher, in fact, went to great lengths to insure the paper's acceptance by the local colonial authorities and, perhaps for ideological reasons of his own, avoided a frontal attack upon the colonial system. Potts-Johnson's opening editorial established the paper's conservative credentials:

> the "Nigerian Observer" is out to deal with Commerce, Religion, Education and other problems affecting British West Africa. As will be observed we have left out Politics. In our opinion, Politics in West Africa have been so muddled that it is like a muddy pool and none can drink of it with safety. We fear cholera which very often follows indiscriminate indulgence of the stream. Our attitude however must not be interpreted as an utter disregard of the subject; what we mean is that at our present stage of development we ought to concentrate our energy, talent and time to commerce, religion and education and pay less attention to politics, but when the Political sky is clear and the atmosphere less humid we shall come out for occasional airings.[26]

Three months later, joining the ideological debate then raging among African intellectuals between supporters of J. E. K. Aggrey, an American-trained African who espoused cooperation between white and black, and the followers of Marcus Garvey, a militant Jamaican black who urged the doctrines of non-cooperation and African irredentism, Potts-Johnson came out squarely in support of Aggreyism:

Without cooperation of White and Black there can be very little or no progress in Africa. It is true that the white man possesses all the capital, training and experience necessary for the development of the Black man's country, but the white man for climatic and other reasons cannot do all the work alone, the black man too must contribute something however poor. But in the stupendous work of co-operation, the Black man is not to be satisfied with the menial work which usually comes his way. He should endeavor so to improve himself as will compel the white man to offer him a honourable role. At the same time the black man must not attempt to do all by himself what for centuries to come he cannot reasonably be fit to do, he should not adopt the impossible attitude of "Africa for the Africans" and he should steer clear of Gandhi's shoals and sandbanks of non-co-operation.[27]

The paper's basic commitment to working within the colonial system notwithstanding, the *Nigerian Observer* served as a significant medium of both social and political expression. Local affairs were discussed and local grievances aired. Its pages registered editorial and citizen complaints concerning the inadequacy of the water supply in the Native Location, the odor of the public latrine, the absence of street names, the overcrowding in the Native Hospital, the poor state of the roads, and the too-frequent transfers of Port Harcourt's station magistrates. Church news often occupied a number of columns, and not infrequently, entire sermons were printed and discussed. The social activities of the elite figures to whom the paper was primarily addressed were similarly reported in detail.

Also voiced within the *Observer*'s pages were the concerns of the township's educated residents respecting developments within their rural communities of origin. Both Ibos and non-Ibos used Potts-Johnson's newspaper to criticize the colonial authorities for not moving more quickly to develop the rural hinterland, and to debate such diverse subjects as the effectiveness of the Eastern Nigerian Native Court system, the kingship succession in an Ijaw community, and the siting of a secondary school to serve Ijawland.

In addition, the *Nigerian Observer* concerned itself with developments elsewhere in Nigeria and Africa, and with news of world significance. Potts-Johnson's particular concern with the

Nigerian educational system manifested itself in a number of editorials urging the establishment of a secondary school in Port Harcourt and attacking rumored educational reforms as motivated by the British desire to forestall African advancement. Other issues of broad scope which were highlighted in the *Observer*'s editorial columns were the limited nature of the franchise available to Lagos residents and the slow pace of Africanization within the Nigerian civil service. Regarding international news, the paper regularly carried a column entitled, "The World," which in a single issue included such diverse items as the "Jewish Wailing Wall," "Anti-God Campaign in Russia," "Germany's Motor Vehicles," "Bolshevism in Siam," "Unrest in Afghanistan," and the "Congo Native Mutiny." [28] The political ferment in India was one subject that attracted particular attention in 1930 and inspired an editorial, "India: a Lesson to British West Africa": "The Indians who clamour for complete independence are either very ignorant of the conditions obtaining in their own country or must be men who have not the best interests of their country at heart. They seem to forget that once British Raj is withdrawn the Hindus and Muhammedans who are traditional antagonists will jump at one another's throats and that nothing short of civil wars, or riots, and general anarchy will reign supreme." [29]

Lastly, the *Nigerian Observer* served as Potts-Johnson's medium to mobilize the African community on behalf of the goals of self-improvement and political unity. He used his editorial columns constantly to goad the African community to take action on its own behalf. Thus, in a January 25, 1930, editorial entitled, "Nigeria: Her commerce and the African," Potts-Johnson chastised his readers:

> Now, what is the position of the Africans in the Commercial activities of Nigeria? Without mincing matters we must say at once that it is that of hewers of wood and drawers of water. But who is to blame? The African, of course. . . .
> If the African feels that he is being unfairly treated he should act in a way that will command the respect of the White Man. Our Anglo-Saxon friends are always too ready to bow to merit whenever they can detect it. The fact that they have recently elected Mr. Peter J. C. Thomas the well known Negro Merchant

of Lagos as President of the Lagos Chamber of Commerce is evidence of this fact.

The African is unwilling to cooperate with his fellow countrymen. . . .

As a people the Africans are not individualistic, but superficial contact with Western ideas has produced a race of men entirely different from the Native African and certainly not in any way like the accomplished European. Each Westernised African prefers to distrust his neighbors and carries on his trade single-handed. As long as this continues the African must continue to suffer commercially.

Again, in an editorial a month later, he called upon the members of the African community to band together to protest the condition of the streets in the Native Location.[30] Then, on March 15, 1930, Potts-Johnson, in bold-face type, editorialized on "The Necessity for Co-operation in Port Harcourt." It was in this editorial that the proposal to establish an African organization comprised of the representatives of each of Port Harcourt's nationalities was first publicly ventured:

As a result of conversations had with various members of the Community we have had to learn and unlearn various things. We have discovered to our surprise, that some are of the opinion that whenever Government desire to carry out a particular policy they must have their way whatever we may say or do. Others there are who think that each should make its representations separately to Government; whilst there are those who hold the view that each tribe should form its own association and a Central Committee set up to be composed of representatives appointed by the association of each tribe.

The last view is the only one that has been engaging our serious attention and it seems the one that we can confidently recommend to the public for their consideration because we find in it the germs of true progress and genuine desire for co-operation. Briefly, the idea is that the Jekris, Ibos, Efiks, Yorubas, Fantees and Sierra Leonians etc. should have separate associations of their own; and then there could be formed a Central Committee of the various tribes. The members of the Jekri association will appoint their own representatives to represent them on the Central Committee, the Ibos and the other tribes too, will do the same. Whenever occasion arises for the discussion of any matter of public importance and interest, the association of each tribe will first meet and consider it in every detail. After this the Central Committee will meet, and if need be, make representations to proper quarters. Such representations, having the support of the entire community, cannot fail eventually, if not immediately to produce good results. . . .

Will not the Leaders of each tribe seriously take the matter to heart and summon a meeting of their people? . . . The position of the Gold Coast people in West Africa of today affords an interesting and enviable example of what cooperation can achieve. Why should we not in our little world of Port Harcourt practise principles of co-operation and self-help?

Potts-Johnson's proposals, it will be noted, predated even the formation of the Ibo Union in 1933. Potts-Johnson was ahead of his time—the African Community League would not be formed until 1935—but there is little doubt that his newspaper and editorial comment were instrumental in furthering the process of political integration. By providing a communications medium linking all of Port Harcourt's literate citizens, by establishing an ideological framework for political action, and by offering instruction in the techniques of political organization, the *Nigerian Observer* took the first concrete step toward the goal of a politically united African community.

The African Community League

The presentation of the constitution of the newly formed Port Harcourt African Community League to the Local Authority on October 1, 1935 marked a major turning point in Port Harcourt's political development. The league was formally convened by the Reverend E. K. Williams, like Potts-Johnson a Sierra Leonian and a Methodist pastor. Its inauguration represented the culmination of a long personal campaign waged by both Potts-Johnson and by Williams. The success of their campaign, however, appears to have been due as much to the depression-oriented economic grievances of this period—high market stall, land, and house rents comprised major subjects of complaint in 1935 and 1936—as it was to their own persuasiveness. Sylvia Leith-Ross, in Port Harcourt during the depression's worst phase, was struck by the gloominess of the town's economic mood: "Though the boom years after the war brought great prosperity, the depression that followed was correspondingly acute and Port Harcourt shares that specially desolate air which seems to surround any place of which the growth has been suddenly arrested." [31] The economic situation gave new urgency to the plea for political unity made by the two Methodist pastors.

Under the terms of its 1935 constitution, the African Community League consisted of the representatives of nine of the township's cultural/linguistic groups. The Ibo, Delta (Ijaw), and Yoruba communities were each accorded ten representatives, while the smaller Benin, Calabar, Gold Coast, Togoland, Hausa, Sierra Leone/Gambia, and Warri communities were each alloted six.[32] The formation of the league inspired the organization of additional communal associations, and new unions (such as the Urhobo and Isoko Unions) were soon added to the list of Community League members. A decade after its inauguration, the league's principle of communal representation was itself modified to permit the inclusion of the ethnically mixed Plot-Holders and Market Traders Associations.

The extent to which the league was representative of the African population at large was a matter of continuing concern to both the members of the new organization and to the Local Authority. When, in September and October of 1936, the league sought recognition as "the sole medium between Government and the Community" and requested official representation on the Advisory Board,[33] the Local Authority expressed "grave doubts as to whether the African Community League really voiced public opinion in Port Harcourt as the Ibo representation on the League Council did not appear to be in fair proportion to the population of Port Harcourt. . . . I see no reason for increasing the present African members from two to six though I think that the membership might in time be increased to four on condition that at least two of the members are Ibos." [34] The Ibo Union subsequently met privately with the Resident and the Local Authority to voice its own request for increased Ibo representation on the Township Advisory Board.[35] In the end, however, only one of four new 1937 appointees was Ibo. It was not until 1944–1945 that the composition of the league was revised to conform more closely with the actual distribution of national-

ities—under a new constitution the Ibo Union's twenty representatives comprised the league's largest voting bloc—and that
Ibo representation on the Advisory Board was increased to two
members.

The African Community League was the product of an independent political effort, ideologically and organizationally distinct
from the subsequent revolutionary movement for Nigerian national independence. The league's political objectives were local
and limited:

> The League . . . in principle holds no political outlook but
> mainly to watch the municipal interest of Port Harcourt Com-
> munity, that is to say: all that affect land rents, water and lighting
> supplies, tax payers affairs, Township and Health improvement,
> protection from pestilence and robbers, and other possible relief
> to the community; to cooperate for the furtherance of any pro-
> gramme in respect of occasional loyal tributes such as would be
> expected from British subjects and protected persons.
>
> Any misunderstandings between two or more tribes or sections,
> provided such misunderstandings have no criminal tendency, may
> be brought to the League for settlement if parties concerned so
> wish it. . . .
>
> In brief, the League is out to cooperate with the Local Au-
> thorities in every way possible to make the township worth living
> for the ultimate elevation of the community, the welfare of local
> market and maintenance of sincere loyalty to the British Govern-
> ment.[36]

The new organization, in short, was accommodationist. It
sought no confrontation and no test of strength with European
officialdom. As one of the league's central figures recalled, "There
was nothing very eventful in those days in Port Harcourt. . . .
[We would] only get together when dignitaries were coming to
Port Harcourt, to welcome them . . . and when issues arose we
felt were not sufficiently covered we would make representations." That is not to say that all league proposals were acceptable to the Local Authority. The 1936 league request, for example,
that six additional African representatives be appointed to the
Advisory Board was answered by the appointment of only four
new African members. The important point is that during the
1930s and early 1940s, the Local Authority and African Com-

munity League never entered into serious conflict. At one point, in fact, when the Resident overrode league demands for certain rent reductions in 1937, the league not only accepted the Resident's decision but used Potts-Johnson's newspaper to mobilize support for the existing law.

The new organization's accommodationist orientation can perhaps be explained in terms of the composition of the league's membership. First, the communal leaders who comprised that membership were preoccupied, as were their counterparts in other Nigerian cities during these years, with the task of strengthening their respective ethnic and geo-ethnic organizations. Their political energy and economic resources were directed primarily to their family, town, and divisional unions, which commanded their first attention and political loyalty as the urban expressions of their cultural and linguistic heritage.

Second, a large proportion of the league's more influential members were prosperous traders and otherwise well-to-do individuals who had a direct interest in the maintenance of local political stability and who were at least as concerned with the protection of their own economic position as with the representation of the interests of the African rank and file. The power wielded by these commercial interests manifested itself in the repeated league representations on such matters as the high cost of electric light bills, the rents charged for Crown land allocations, and the allegedly unjust enforcement of local building by-laws. The remark of an unfriendly Local Authority that the league appeared to represent the property owners rather than the people of Port Harcourt was not entirely without foundation. Independent traders who owed their commercial success to the patronage of expatriate mercantile firms (most notably, the United Africa Company), were seldom inclined—whatever their distaste for the economic and political power exercised by the European establishment—to risk their favored economic positions by overt and provocative political activity.

Finally, the league derived its ideological inspiration and motive force from the gradualist leadership of Potts-Johnson and E. K. Williams, two highly Westernized, non-Nigerian Africans whose political thought tended to be framed in terms of race rather than of territorial nationalism.[37] The colonial premises of Western cultural superiority and the derivative "right to govern"

were implicitly accepted in Potts-Johnson's doctrine of cooperation: "the black man," Potts-Johnson cautioned his readers, "must
not attempt to do all by himself what for centuries to come he cannot reasonably be fit to do, he should not adopt the impossible
attitude of 'Africa for the Africans' and he should steer clear of
Ghandi's shoals and sandbanks of non-co-operation." The time
would eventually come, in Potts-Johnson's view, when Africans
would assume responsibility for their own political destiny, but
that privilege would have to be earned by "cooperation and self-
help."

A LEADERSHIP OF ACCESS: THE NON-IBO PATRICIANS

During these years of political coalescence in Port Harcourt, the
leadership of the African community rested primarily in the hands
of highly Westernized non-Ibos. These non-Ibo "patricians" were
at the center of Port Harcourt's African political life until the
middle 1940s and maintained a powerful voice in local affairs
until their ballot-inspired exclusion in 1949. Their dominance
manifested itself, as we have seen, in the origins and control of
the local press—while the *Nigerian Observer* was open to contributions from and news about all groups within the city, it
inevitably became primarily identified as a non-Ibo organ—and
in their control of the African Community League, which was
never headed by an Ibo despite the group's overwhelming numbers. But nowhere was non-Ibo hegemony more evident than in
the African membership of Port Harcourt's Township Advisory
Board.

Of the twelve Africans who served between the board's inauguration in 1918 and its demise in 1949, only four were Ibo
(table 9). No Ibo was appointed to the board until 1937, almost
twenty years after the board's inception and eleven years after
the appointment of the first African members. The eight non-Ibo
members included three Ijaws, two Sierra Leonians, two Yorubas,
and one Gambian. These eight held in common the social attributes of education, high occupational status, and secure financial position: they included four retired civil servants; two professionals; one pastor; and one man who performed simultaneously
the roles of pastor, secondary school proprietor, and newspaper
editor-publisher.

In short, the Township Advisory Board's non-Ibo members

TABLE 9

AFRICAN MEMBERSHIP OF THE TOWNSHIP ADVISORY BOARD

Years served	Member	Nationality	Occupation
1926–1937	S. T. Ikiroma-Owiye	Ijaw	Retired 1st-class customs clerk, trader
1926–1949	I. B. Johnson	Gambian, with links to Sierra Leone	Retired treasury department clerk, contractor, auctioneer, cinema proprietor, photographer
1937	E. K. Williams	Sierra Leonian	Pastor
1937–1940	S. N. Obi	Ibo (Onitsha Division)	Assistant chief clerk, treasury department
1937–1941	F. O. Lucas	Yoruba	Barrister
1937–1949	L. R. Potts-Johnson	Sierra Leonian	Pastor, secondary school proprietor and principal, printing press proprietor, newspaper editor and publisher
1937–1949	George F. Spiff	Ijaw	Retired supervisor of customs, building contractor
1940–1945	Z. C. Obi	Ibo (Onitsha Division)	Chief clerk for U.A.C. regional manager, promoted to U.A.C. junior manager in 1945, subsequently a private trader and contractor
1941–1948	O. Ajibade	Yoruba	Medical doctor
1944–1949	E. U. Eronini	Ibo (Owerri Division)	Retired government hospital dispenser, private druggist and produce trader
1945–1949	R. O. Nzimiro	Ibo (Owerri Division)	Retired chief clerk, U.A.C.; trader
1948–1949	W. B. Dublin-Green	Ijaw	Retired government hospital dispenser, private druggist

all belonged to the upper echelons of the African community's social hierarchy. (Three of these men—I. B. Johnson, O. Ajibade, and W. B. Dublin-Green—held the presidency of the African Club.) Education, occupation, and wealth gained for these non-Ibo patricians admission to the township's African social elite and, more importantly from the standpoint of their political influence, *access* to the world of European officialdom. Education, occupation, and wealth were valued not in themselves but, rather, for the influence and prestige that they garnered in official circles. The writing and submission of petitions, the ability to conduct oneself with confidence during board deliberations or during other English-speaking confrontations with Europeans, the requisite knowledge and accoutrements of European civilization—all these things were dependent upon the education, occupational skills, and financial resources that these men possessed.

Not only did men such as Potts-Johnson and Williams possess the requisite political resources, but given the colonial context, which placed a premium upon racial political unity, their very minority status located Port Harcourt's non-Ibos in a singularly advantageous position to provide effective leadership. On the one hand, non-Ibo leaders were neutral vis-à-vis the large and competitive Ibo subcommunities. On the other, they did not pose the same political threat to non-Ibo minority groups that might have been the result of Ibo leadership. In this respect, the communal identity of Port Harcourt's non-Ibo patricians was inseparable from their other social characteristics; and their political position derived, in large measure, from the very ethnicity of the urban political milieu. Communal identities comprised the most convenient mode of social and political categorization in the new urban community, and the primary points of social and political reference for the newly urban citizens. From this perspective, Port Harcourt politics were from the outset ethnic politics; and Port Harcourt's non-Ibo patricians, no less than their Onitsha Ibo and Owerri Ibo successors, were ethnic political actors.

COALESCENCE AND ACCOMMODATION

Through the years of political coalescence, the premises of the colonial system were generally accepted by the African community, and no overt hostility was expressed by Africans toward their European rulers. The African community was turned in upon itself, its attention concentrated upon the tasks of internal integration and organization. Port Harcourt was a new community possessed of young and transient urban immigrants. Most carried with them to the city a tradition of popular participation in the affairs of the community, and the urban improvement unions that proliferated during this period provided an invaluable training ground in the norms and techniques of Western-style democratic participation. But time was still required to develop the organizational base and political self-confidence necessary for a direct confrontation with the colonial system. The next chapter tells the story of that confrontation and of the eventual transfer of power from Europeans to Africans which was its result.

CHAPTER 6
The Transfer of Power (1944–1954)

Four elements were central to the transfer of local power from European to African hands. First, an increasingly militant and assertive African Community League dared at last to confront the official establishment head on and to assert the right of local self-determination. Our discussion begins with a description of what I have called the "Palmer Affair," the township's first major political controversy in which an aroused and united African community successfully pressed the colonial government to restrain an overly zealous Local Authority. This 1944 confrontation is examined in the context of other manifestations of the increasing militancy of the African Community League, most notably, the revision of the league's manifesto to incorporate explicitly political objectives and the presentation of new demands directed for the first time toward the acquisition of governmental power. The discussions within the African community and between league officials and colonial administrators, which these demands for local self-determination provoked, throw light upon both African and British political perspectives during this period, and provide interesting data on the practical problems involved in the transfer of power at the local level.

A second significant element in the transfer of local power was the introduction of the franchise. With the resulting democratization of the political system, patterns of leadership and conflict within the African community were significantly altered. On the one hand, numerical strength became an independently important political resource, leading to the political exclusion of the numerically weak non-Ibo patricians and the rise of a new class of Ibo entrepreneurs and young professionals. However, testifying to the still continuing importance of the political attributes of wealth and social status, most of the "new men" were from the more educationally and occupationally advantaged sections of Iboland —Onitsha Province and culturally related areas in Mid-Western Nigeria. On the other hand, the competitiveness of the new electoral system had the effect of intensifying intra-African political divisions. As the transfer of power accelerated at both the national and local levels, the confrontation with the colonial establishment was increasingly subordinated in Port Harcourt to the local struggle for political position, and Port Harcourt politics came increasingly to focus upon the subcultural competition between Owerri and Onitsha Ibos. Thus, democratization in Port Harcourt meant the intensification of communal conflict.

The third crucial element in the transfer of power in Port Harcourt was the city's "nationalist awakening," and the simultaneous bifurcation of the leadership of the local African community— the "locals" on one side, the Zikists and other nationalist "cosmopolitans" on the other.[1] Whereas the former tended to focus on strictly local affairs, especially as they related to the African Community League and later to the newly created Port Harcourt Town Council, the nationalists tended to look beyond the city to the broader confrontation between the colonialists and the Azikiwe-led NCNC. As will be indicated, the council-oriented politicians and the nationalists were not really opposed groupings; they simply operated in different political spheres and symbolized different political issues.

Finally, the emergence of the NCNC—the Eastern-based and Ibo-dominated political party—as the focal point of African political power in the local community was the fourth key element in the transfer of power in Port Harcourt from European to African hands. This consolidation of party power in Port Harcourt was but the local manifestation of the development of a single-party regime in Nigeria's Eastern Region. From this point on, intergroup conflict in the urban area, as in Eastern Nigeria, became essentially a matter of intraparty struggle. The intensity and social bases of local political rivalry were not appreciably changed by the consolidation of party power; the institutional context within which that competition was waged, however, was substantially altered.

The Palmer Affair

In November 1943, the Palmer Affair terminated Port Harcourt's era of political tranquility. C. H. S. R. Palmer, Port Harcourt's then incumbent Local Authority, had acquired a reputation for arrogance and administrative rigidity, neither quality especially admirable to highly egalitarian Eastern Nigerians. The full import of Palmer's appointment to Port Harcourt was brought home to the African community when, toward the end of the year, Palmer launched an intensive campaign to "clean up" the city and to insure the strict enforcement of township building bylaws.

Overcrowding had become a critical problem. Modern housing construction simply could not keep pace with the flow of immigrants, and squatter and slum settlements were threatening to erase the progress that had been made toward the planned development of the urban area. In his annual report, the medical officer of health warned: "In the past the Township Building Inspectors have been slack and many buildings are now in occupation which do not even comply with old building rules. It is unfortunate that for the most part, Port Harcourt consists of large houses of 10 to 14 rooms; each room is let out and occupied by whole families. Tenement SLUMS are being created, the town is being overcrowded and a race of absentee landlords is arising. . . . More building was done in Port Harcourt during 1943 than for some years past." [2]

Palmer would brook no opposition in his determination to set things right. Landlords were warned that henceforth no contraventions of the building bylaws would be permitted, and that breaches of covenants to develop their plots would result in forfeiture of their Crown leases. Then, overriding the league's objections that war conditions made his policy both inexpedient and unjust, Palmer set out to demolish all buildings considered "dilapidated and dangerous and insanitary." [3] "While we were talking," an African participant in the Palmer Affair recalled, "this man would get his laborers, and go around and pull down the houses

. . . the matter was acute. . . . The Township Advisory Board
told him to go softly, that they were poor people who were willing
to build new homes but that notice should be given. . . . He was
a man who argued with nobody. His argument was action." Out-
lining his position in a letter to the Provincial Resident, Palmer
rejected all pleas for administrative leniency:

> The population of Port Harcourt has grown from some 20,000 to
> an estimated figure of 27,000 in the last four years. Many hun-
> dreds, I would almost say thousands, of them have no bonafide
> business or employment in Port Harcourt. They were not forced
> to come here. I have said, and still maintain, that people who
> wish to live in Port Harcourt must be prepared to comply with
> the Township and Public Health Ordinances, Rules and Regula-
> tions. If they cannot do so, they have no "right" to live in Port
> Harcourt. They should not expect the law to be waived in their
> own interests or to occupy dangerous or insanitary buildings.
> I am continually astonished at the lack of civic spirit shown by
> the leaders of Port Harcourt society. They seem to allow hard
> cases to blind them to the public interest. I believe these agita-
> tions are engineered by the property-holders.[4]

But the organized political opposition of the league could not
be easily dismissed, and early in 1944 a delegation of the league
was granted a personal audience with the chief commissioner for
the eastern provinces. At this meeting, a reconciliation was finally
effected between the league and Local Authority Palmer, but not
until a number of concessions had been made to the African
petitioners. It was agreed that lease forfeitures would henceforth
be the business of the courts and not of the Local Authority, that
the Local Authority would no longer assume jurisdiction over
any litigation involving Crown land, and that the Local Authority
would no longer delay the approval of building plans that con-
formed to government regulations but failed to meet his own
exacting standards. In response to these concessions, the league
delegation dropped its complaints concerning "more personal"
matters, indicating that "they were entirely satisfied and did not
wish to proceed." [5]

The Palmer Affair was closed, but the new political era of confrontation that the affair symbolized was just opening. The problems of internal fragmentation that had dominated the African

political scene in the 1920s and 1930s had been resolved, and the political potential of a united African community was slowly being recognized. This new political awareness and assertiveness manifested itself not only in the league's opposition to the policies of the township's Local Authority but also, and more importantly, in new demands that Port Harcourt be accorded representation in the Nigerian Legislative Council, and that the city be elevated to the administrative status of a first class township, with an elected and fully responsible Town Council.

By 1943, Lagos and Calabar were the only two Nigerian townships in which Africans could directly elect representatives to the Legislative Council. Lagos possessed a modified form of local self-government, but nominated members were still in the majority on the Lagos Council.[6] Thus, the demands of Port Harcourt's African Community League for elected representation in the Legislative Council and for a Town Council with an elected majority were, by the political standards of the day, radical proposals of national as well as local significance.

R. K. *Floyer and the Floyer Report*

The African Community League's proposals for local self-government were placed before the township's new Local Authority, R. K. Floyer, in March 1945.[7] In sharp contrast to many other British officials, Floyer was in sympathy with African aspirations. He felt that the colonial government had made some grievous errors in retarding local political development, and he was not adverse to addressing his written criticisms of colonial policy to his administrative superiors. It is one of the ironies of Port Harcourt's political history that the official who played the most significant role in making local self-government a reality should, on the eve of the Town Council's inauguration in 1949, so antagonize the African community that the Community League resolved to oppose his assumption of the council presidency. Not privy to the dialogue Floyer had waged relentlessly with colonial officialdom, the league interpreted Floyer's last minute words of caution as the expression of an insulting paternalism.[8]

The league's initial proposals for elevating Port Harcourt's administrative status were an intriguing combination of both daring and moderation. On the one hand, the league declared as its ultimate objective none other than a "full-fledged municipality," in which an elected Town Council would have executive powers and would assume responsibility not only for those subjects within the Township Advisory Board's jurisdiction, but also for a number of social welfare and other administrative services outside the board's local purview.

On the other hand, it was felt that full self-government could not be rushed into without preparation, and that inadequate financial resources and a shortage of African technical staff necessitated the acceptance of "an intermediate stage not exceeding five years, between the present which is advisory and the proposed full fledged municipality." [9] During this intermediate stage, the council's functions were to be limited to those exercised by the Advisory Board, but the council—unlike the Advisory Board —would be empowered to raise revenue for essential projects. In this transitional stage the council would maintain a ratio of elected to nominated members of eight to four or ten to four. Executive officers of the central government would serve the council in supervisory and advisory capacities, and the council's first president would be a colonial official. For purposes of the elections, the town would be divided into wards and the electoral franchise restricted to those persons twenty-one years and above who were either householders or had a minimum annual income of £50 ($140.00). There was to be no sex discrimination.

Early in 1946, following the presentation of the league proposals, Local Authority Floyer traveled to Lagos to study the structure and operation of the Lagos Town Council. This trip was followed by the preparation of a remarkable document, subsequently known as the Floyer Report, which offered a set of philosophical and technical guidelines for the projected experiment in local self-government. The Lagos Town Council served as Floyer's model, but a number of far-reaching modifications of the Lagos scheme were suggested. Because of the report's controversial character, its publication was initially suppressed by the commissioner for the eastern provinces. However, a revised version of the report, excerpts of which appear in appendix 6 to this study, was subsequently made public.[10]

The Floyer Report served as a working manuscript rather than as a definitive statement of policy. Its principal contribution was to give structure to the debate, to crystallize the kinds of decisions that both the African community and the colonial authorities would have to make before local self-government could become a political reality. Five issues commanded particular attention in the community dialogue that followed Floyer's return from Lagos: (1) the powers and responsibilities of local government institutions, (2) potential sources of local government revenue, (3) the ownership of Port Harcourt Crown land, (4) the type of franchise desired, and (5) the composition of the projected Town Council.

(1) *Powers and Responsibilities.* What powers and responsibilities were to be accorded Port Harcourt's institutions of local government? What was "local government" to mean for the township's citizens? In view of Port Harcourt's economic significance to the entire nation, would not a considerable portion of the township's affairs continue to be managed by central authorities? As the Local Authority observed in an early communication to the Owerri Provincial Resident,

> . . . Port Harcourt . . . cannot be politically considered either as independent of Nigeria as a whole or as likely to become so in the future . . . its importance is as a gateway to the Eastern Provinces and the North, and as a rail head for produce and tin. Its position therefore is directly dependent upon Nigeria as a whole. The central government have spent large sums of money in buildings, plant and equipment for this reason—that Port Harcourt serves a large portion of Nigeria. In the future, with post war development as an immediate possibility, the importance of the Port, the railway and the aerodrome will increase, and Port Harcourt will even more than now, play a vital part in the development of the country as a whole and the Eastern Provinces in particular. It can be safely assumed that further improvements to the Port, railway and especially the aerodrome will be carried out by the Central Government. The question must be asked therefore, is Government actually contemplating giving "local Government" to Port Harcourt and how can this be done when the Central Government has such large interests already established and likely to increase. Local Government cannot be anything but a name if there is no control of local enterprises and activities, and I submit that this point is made clear before any real progress can be envisaged.[11]

Two distinct but related questions were involved: the functions of the projected Town Council, and the relationship between the council and the central authorities. With respect to the first of these questions, a consensus quickly emerged. It was agreed, by both the league and the government, that the port, railway, and postal facilities, and the control of the police force, were to remain the responsibilities of the colonial government. Municipal responsibilities were to include markets, sanitation (including building control and conservancy service), traffic, roads (the construction and maintenance of which would be assisted by central government funds), schools, welfare services, and the purchase of the township's water and electricity for resale to urban consumers. (When it was learned that the regional water works were no longer operating at a profit, a Community League proposal that the Town Council should take over the urban water supply was abandoned.)

The relationship between the projected Town Council and the national government was inherently a more controversial subject, one which even by the 1960s had not been finally resolved. The Port Harcourt Town Council was, in theory, to be patterned after the English model, and Port Harcourt was to have all the freedoms and all the obligations of English municipalities. This condition meant that the township, as in England, would remain subordinate to the national government. All council estimates and bylaws would require government approval.[12] The object of these controls, a government circular indicated, was "to ensure that the money collected from the public in the form of rates is not wasted and that the local legislation is well considered and not oppressive." [13] Within its own sphere of operations, however, the Town Council would have executive as well as legislative authority. Thus, the council could prosecute rates defaulters and bylaws offenders and would have control over its own administrative staff.

(2) *Local Government Finance.* A second and equally crucial subject was how the services to be provided by the Town Council were to be financed. The league proposed that the council be made the recipient of the Crown land rents then being collected by the government. The government, however, rejected the league proposal, arguing that Crown land revenue should be reserved

for "developments and improvements" of the areas from which the rental income derived and that such development programs would be the responsibility of a newly constituted Planning Authority and not the Town Council. With regard to its own activities, the council would receive some government assistance, but would also be required to raise new local revenues in the form of water or property taxes.

No feature of the plan for local self-government provoked more heated controversy than that calling for the introduction of new rates. Port Harcourt's landlords were fearful that the principal tax-paying burden would fall on their shoulders, and they raised their collective voice in loud protest. Under their guidance, the newly inaugurated Plot Holders Union and the Ibo Union each passed resolutions against the proposed property tax of two shillings of each pound of a building's assessed value.[14] The Plot Holders Union went so far as to issue a press release calling for the postponment of the municipality for ten years on the grounds of cost.[15] Even the African Community League itself suddenly reversed course and urged that the speed with which the township was moving toward local self-government be slowed. The issue finally came to a head in September 1947 when, at a special session of the Township Advisory Board, the Reverend Potts-Johnson proposed on behalf of the Community League that the two shilling rate be lowered, if it could not be abolished, and that increases in conservancy fees and vehicle license fees be considered as supplementary sources of income.[16] At this point the board's chairman, Local Authority Floyer, joined the argument: "The Chairman said that whilst it was true that Government had indulged townships with free amenities, it must be appreciated that Port Harcourt had asked to "take over" many of these services. It was obvious that they could not be carried on without paying the cost. If the control of their own affairs was too expensive at 2/-, it could be suggested to Government that in view of the state of public opinion, that only half-control should be granted for a year or two. This meant a non-elected majority and half the necessary rates." [17] Then, at a second special session of the Advisory Board held one week later the Community League's and the Ibo Federal Union's objections to the proposed two shilling rate were withdrawn. The resistance of Port Harcourt's propertied interests to any and all taxation schemes, however, persisted. In this resistance, of course, Port Harcourt's landlords held much in common with landlords everywhere.

(3) *The Land Question.* The legal status of the Crown land on which the bulk of Port Harcourt rested was an issue directly relevant to the finance question, because Crown land rents were an attractive source of potential revenue for the prospective first class township. It was therefore proposed by the Community League that the Crown's interest in the land be vested in the Town Council or, alternatively, that the government hand over to the council a grant equivalent to the rents collected. The Floyer Report argued that this request was not entirely unreasonable: while the government had invested capital in the land, the amount it received in rents over the twenty-seven-year period of Port Harcourt's occupation approached a three hundred percent rate of profit. Moreover, no rent had been paid by the government on land occupied by its own buildings and, continued Floyer, "it might perhaps be admitted that in the past Government has been somewhat backward in developing its property, in respect of which it has the special obligation towards the community of an owner as well as the general one of a Government. . . . It is a fact that owing to previous inaction, the Native Location is at present so over-crowded that development on a scale which no local body can undertake unaided has become an urgent political necessity." [18]

On another occasion, Floyer noted that psychological as well as financial reasons underlay the league's proposal that the Crown's interest in Port Harcourt land be vested in the Town Council: "they wish to 'own themselves,' and there is no doubt that the vesting of those lands in the Council would enhance civic pride, perhaps the most potent influence towards responsibility and self-respect." [19] He warned: "in the African, the desire to own the land he lives on is exceptionally strong . . . and it should not be undervalued if it is desired that the Municipality should be successful." [20]

In the end, Floyer's advice went unheeded. Local representatives were permitted to advise on the allocation of Crown land plots, but the ownership of the land remained with the government, and the rents deriving from Crown land leases accrued to the Planning Authority rather than to the democratically elected Town Council. Floyer's emphasis upon the significance of the land issue, however, was well placed. The lack of commitment on the part of Port Harcourt's settlers to their community of residence could be attributed, in large measure, to their tenant status. Still, it is doubtful that the mere vesting of ownership rights in the Town Council would have significantly altered the sense of tenancy experienced by most of Port Harcourt's immigrants or modified their primary orientation to their communities (and lands) of origin.

(4) *The Franchise.* One especially controversial issue concerned the nature of the proposed local franchise. The Community League's initial suggestion of a limited property franchise was designed to exclude what were viewed as irresponsible elements from the governmental process: only house owners and persons with £50 gross annual income were to be eligible to vote. This property qualification, which in 1949 would have produced an electorate numbering between two and three thousand persons in a population exceeding forty thousand, was rejected by the government. The colonial authorities, however, accepted the implicit league premise that very few members of the African community were equipped to participate in local self-government. Floyer's optimism concerning the ultimate success of the proposed political experiment was not shared by his administrative superiors. The secretary for the eastern provinces expressed this official skepticism in a note to the commissioner:

> One matter on which Mr. Floyer's opinion would have been valuable is whether elections are likely to produce as many as eight citizens of the necessary ability who will devote to their duties the time that will be required. It is one thing to be a vocal member of the T.A.B. without any responsibility and it is quite another to have to attend the various Council and Committee meetings which municipal Government will require and to give to their proceedings the thought which a proper discharge of responsibility demands. Mr. Floyer impliedly deplores the caution which would start with an elected minority but I visualize

elections in which, although two or three of the successful candidates will be men of worth, the remainder will be "politicians" of very poor calibre who have got in only because the more substantial citizens are too busy with their own private affairs to be willing to stand for election.[21]

Floyer himself was not unguarded in his optimism. He too supported a limited franchise, observing that "the citizen should contribute in proportion to his wealth sufficient to ensure that he exercises his vote with due responsibility."[22] To the Township Advisory Board, he declared: "The reason for the property qualification is that those who pay the rates should decide how much they should be and how they should be spent. If those who do not pay rates are given the power to vote, they are apt to vote for expensive amenities and correspondingly high rates, secure in the knowledge that they will not have to pay them."[23] And, in his report, the Diobu indigenes were excluded entirely from the franchise on the grounds that "I am unable to recommend anyone with sufficient education and goodwill who will be a natural representative."[24] The central thrust of Floyer's argument, however, was that Port Harcourt's citizens would rise to the challenge and that, in any event, an apathetic electorate would not necessarily invalidate the experiment in local self-government:

While the danger undoubtedly exists that the electorate will confine itself to grumbling and fail to vote, and that this must if it occurs be regarded as a comparative failure as an experiment in democratic local government, so long as there is a reasonably strong [executive] staff little actual damage is like to result. In England a poll of 50% of the electorate is quite usual, and where there is a hotly contested election this is far more frequently the result of political or ideological reasons than any other. Apart from this it may even be argued that an apathetic electorate is evidence of reasonable contentment with the existing administration, and it also results where in any particular ward there is an outstanding candidate for whom there is no adequate opponent. Particularly where there are two candidates in each ward, the system is likely to serve the needs of the people without controversy. It is admitted that the community will require education in electioneering, and it is interesting to note that ideas to this end are already forthcoming from the people themselves. . . . From the interest already shown I have no fear that there will be a shortage of candidates.[25]

While acceptable to the league and to the propertied interests that the league represented, a property taxpayers franchise was strongly opposed by two organized elements of the African community, neither of which felt their interests to be adequately represented by the league: the trade unionists, who feared they would have little voice on a council elected by property taxpayers, and the politically radical Zikists, Port Harcourt's first nationalists who were ideologically committed to the doctrine of universal or near-universal adult suffrage. Inasmuch as the government remained committed to a limited franchise, the debate focused upon the level at which the taxpaying qualification should be set. After considerable discussion, the Township Advisory Board endorsed a compromise position that restricted the franchise to persons over twenty-one years of age who paid a minimum of £8 in annual taxes or rents.[26] As Floyer observed, the £8 qualification, which yielded a potential electorate of some eight thousand persons,[27] was "designed to admit to the franchise everyone who pays rent for one good room. It was pointed out that most of the lowest class of the population (and some others) live several in a room; and there was, I think, a feeling that anyone who pays the rent now charged for even one room in Port Harcourt deserves a vote if only as a consolation." [28] Another complication was that the £8 rate was considerably lower than the Lagos rate of £15, and some officials expressed concern about political repercussions that might result from the implementation of the Port Harcourt scheme. Floyer, however, successfully urged that the Lagos precedent be ignored.

(5) *Composition of the Town Council.* The composition of the projected Town Council was in many respects the most critical of the issues requiring resolution before local self-government could become a reality. The African Community League's advocacy of a precedent-setting elected majority was vigorously defended by Local Authority Floyer who argued, on principle, that political development in Nigeria's urban areas was proceeding at too slow a pace. Floyer's specific proposal called for a council composed of eight elected members and six nominated members,

the latter to include three government officials (district officer, medical officer of health, and provincial engineer), two unofficial European commercial representatives, and an unofficial African member representing disenfranchised persons.

The league accepted the principle of nominated representation, but when the order activating the new council was issued, the government did not exercise its right to nominate unofficial members. Only the three government officials were appointed to the council—one of these, the district officer, was designated the council's first president—and the number of elected members was increased to twelve, two members for each of six electoral wards.[29] Elected members were thus in a controlling majority.

African opinion was divided on the question of how the electoral system should be structured. The league was firm in its commitment to the organization of electoral wards on a geographical basis, but some elements of the community advocated communal rather than territorial representation. Anticipating what a strictly popular franchise would mean for their own political future, non-Ibos reasoned that their interests would be better protected if the council were to be composed of representatives elected by each of the township's nationality groups. In the end, however, communal representation was rejected by the Township Advisory Board "as a retrograde step," and by other elements of the community on grounds of impracticability. Proposals put forward by European members of the Advisory Board calling for special railway representation were similarly rejected.[30]

One interesting sidelight of the debate surrounding the proposed electoral system was the request of the African community that the Government Residential Area (GRA), occupied almost entirely by Europeans, be constituted a ward whose representatives were to be elected in the same manner as in other wards. Local Authority Floyer enthusiastically concurred in this request: "The fact that a European was 'standing' for election on the same basis as Africans is of political importance and good propaganda in favour of inter-racial confidence." [31] When the first Town Council election was held, however, it was an African woman, the well-educated wife of a prominent Yoruba magistrate, who was chosen to represent the GRA. A second GRA seat went uncontested, the vacancy subsequently being filled by the appointment

111

of the Chamber of Commerce president and local U.A.C. manager, a European popular with the African community.

Also involved in the discussion of the Town Council's composition was the subject of the council's executive staff. The African Community League originally tended to deemphasize the importance of the staffing problem, arguing that the engineering and sanitary services of the town should continue to be administered by already existing agencies. Floyer, in rebuttal, emphasized that unless the council had its own staff (European or African), the political situation would not differ substantially from that which existed under the Township Advisory Board. On this issue, as on others, Floyer was in the anomalous position of prodding a cautious African community: "if the Council is to have real responsibility, even over a limited field, it must have an Executive of its own who has no other loyalty, and though the Supervising Government Official may preside at its deliberations, his functions must be those of adviser and not of an employee." [32]

The league eventually saw Floyer's point, and it was agreed that the key posts of town clerk, town engineer and medical officer of health would be filled by Africans, if at all possible. If Europeans were required, they were to be fully qualified for their posts (a point urged by Port Harcourt's Zikists) and were to be hired only on a limited basis. The original league proposal for an "intermediate stage" of partial local autonomy was abandoned.

THE IMPACT OF THE FRANCHISE:
POLITICIANS AND COMMUNALISM

On June 15, 1949, the Port Harcourt Town Council—Nigeria's first governmental institution to have an elected African majority —was formally inaugurated. Few persons had participated directly in Port Harcourt's first experiment with Western-style elections. Of the township's estimated population of forty-five thousand, less than eight thousand persons were qualified to vote under the terms of the restricted taxpayers franchise. Of this number only twenty-three hundred persons actually registered and, on a day of heavy rain, only 1,051 ballots (representing less than fifteen percent of the total qualified electorate) were cast in the four two-member wards in which elections were contested. [33] In the two remaining two-member wards, three candidates were returned unopposed. As noted previously, one seat in the Government Residential Area remained vacant until the appointment of the European president of the local Chamber of Commerce.

The low level of voter participation notwithstanding, Port Harcourt's elevation to the status of a first class township with an elected and fully responsible Town Council precipitated a number of major alterations within the structure of power then prevailing within the local community. First, the introduction of the franchise heralded the transfer of a significant measure of power to the township's African majority. Before 1949, as we have seen, Port Harcourt was administered by the district officer acting as Local Authority. A Township Advisory Board, consisting of appointees representing official, mercantile, and African interests, was consulted by the Local Authority, but the board had no real responsibility and the Local Authority was not bound to accept the board's advice. Moreover, Africans on the board were in a permanent minority. In contrast, the Town Council was organized on the basis of an elected African majority—only four Europeans, three of whom were government officials and technicians, were appointed to the first Town Council—and was assigned major decision-making responsibilities. The Town Council, in effect, became the township's new Local Authority.

By creating a competitive political system with sufficiently attractive political stakes, the introduction of the franchise in Port Harcourt had the second major effect of refragmenting the township's African community and intensifying intra-African communal conflict. With the elevation of Port Harcourt's administrative status, the local center of political gravity immediately shifted from the African Community League to the Town Council. Public office was no longer a function of League sanction and recommendation, but rather of one's popularity at the polls. The premium that had been placed upon racial unity and the maintenance of a common political front dissolved upon the attainment of the league's principal objective of local self-government, and the men and groups that comprised the league entered into open competition for the rewards of political office. Thus, the Ibo Union intervened directly in the Town Council elections of 1949. The restraints under which the union had operated during the era of the Township Advisory Board were no longer applicable, and the union attempted to maximize Ibo victories in the council elections by allocating interested Ibo candidates among the various wards in such a way as to reduce the likelihood of self-defeating electoral competition between Ibos. Similarly, political strategies of individual candidates often took Port Harcourt's diverse communal associations as their organizational point of departure.

Candidates did not restrict their appeals to their own communities of origin—the forming of electoral alliances of expediency between unrelated immigrant communities was to become a distinguishing characteristic of Port Harcourt's political pragmatism—but almost invariably their respective communal associations provided the core of their political strength. The important point is that most candidates attempted to manipulate ethnic and geo-ethnic loyalties in the interest of their own political advancement. At the initiative of a prospective Onitsha candidate, for example, the Onitsha Divisional Union called an emergency meeting on the eve of the 1949 Town Council elections to explain to its membership the mechanics of voting registration and balloting, and to urge bloc voting on behalf of all Onitsha men. Earlier, toward the end of 1947, grievances of some members of the Onitsha Divisional Union with respect to the allocation of market stalls and land plots had led the same individual to suggest the formation of a political alliance with other elements of Onitsha Province (i.e., Awka, Enugu, Awgu, and Nsukka Divisions). Now, he argued, a massive Onitsha turnout was necessary to bring an end to Onitsha victimization at the hands of the more numerous Owerris. Members of the divisional union were asked to carry the registration and voting campaign to their town and family meetings.

Third, by adding numerical strength to the critical political resources of occupational standing, wealth, education, and social position, the introduction of the local franchise led to the emergence of a new Ibo-speaking urban political elite. Democratization in Port Harcourt had begun before 1949: it evidenced itself during the early 1940s in the increasing assertiveness of the Ibo bloc within the African Community League, in the revision of the league Constitution to permit greater Ibo representation, and in the appointment of additional Ibo members to the Township Advisory Board. It was not until the introduction of the franchise, however, that the full import of the community's redistribution of political resources was realized in the virtual exclusion from public office of those non-Ibo minority members who earlier had played a leading role in the African community. Between 1949 and 1954, twenty-eight Africans served on the Town Council (tables 10 and 11). Of this number, all but five were Ibo-speaking, and three of the five non-Ibo councillors were appointed rather than elected members. The one non-Ibo who had been certain to play a dominant political role even in the era of the franchise, the Reverend Potts-Johnson, had been disqualified from election to the first council because his nomination papers were filed after the prescribed deadline. (By contrast, in the prefranchise era, eight of the twelve Africans who had served on the Township Advisory Board were non-Ibo; similarly, as has been noted, all African Community League presidents were non-Ibo.) Even more significantly, Ibos controlled the key positions within the council itself.[34]

The new politicians represented most sections of Iboland, but Ibos from those areas that had received the earliest exposure to Western culture and education (notably, Eastern Nigeria's Onitsha Province) assumed commanding roles. Thus, barrister G. C. Nonyelu (Awka Division, Onitsha Province) and petty trader V. K. Onyeri (Aro-Ibo, Awka Division, Onitsha Province) became president and vice-president, respectively, upon the retirement of the council's first European president. Following the second council general election of July, 1952, Nonyelu and Onyeri were succeeded by two more Onitsha Ibos: shopkeeper M. D. Okechukwu (Onitsha Division, Onitsha Province) and retired U.A.C. junior manager and trader/contractor Z. C. Obi (Onitsha Division, Onitsha Province).[35] When the second council was dissolved in 1954 (following charges of corruption and maladministration), still another Onitsha Ibo, businessman G. C. Ikokwu (Onitsha Division, Onitsha Province) became president of the appointed Caretaker Council.

This Onitsha preeminence, which was simply the political counterpart of Onitsha superiority within both the educational and occupational hierarchies of the local Ibo community, was maintained despite the Onitsha minority position within the population at large. Owerri immigrants were in the majority in Port Harcourt,

TABLE 10

AFRICAN MEMBERSHIP OF THE TOWN COUNCIL (1949–1952)[a]

1. *Mrs. E. Adesigbin:* Yoruba; Western Nigeria; Protestant; trader/importer and the wife of a prominent Yoruba magistrate.
2. *A. O. Akwuike:* Ibo; Owerri Division, Owerri Province; Protestant; trader.
3. *M. I. Asinobi:* Ibo; Mbieri, Owerri Division, Owerri Province; Protestant; trader; president, Owerri Divisional Union; president, Ibo Union (Port Harcourt Branch).
4. *A. P. Asisi-Abbey:*[b] Ijaw; Bonny, Degema Division, Rivers Province; Protestant; trader.
5. *C. U. Dibia:* Ibo; Mbaise, Owerri Division, Owerri Province; Protestant; trader.
6. *B. O. N. Eluwa:* Ibo; Bende Division, Owerri Province; Protestant; administrative secretary, Ibo State Union.
7. *G. C. Ikokwu:*[b] Ibo; Oba, Onitsha Division, Onitsha Province; Protestant; transporter (businessman).
8. *S. Mac Ebuh:* Ibo; Asa, Aba Division, Owerri Province; Protestant; journalist and letter writer; founder, Market Traders Association; secretary, African Community League; Town Council's first African vice-president but disqualified as a councillor shortly after his election.
9. *R. O. Madueme:* Ibo; Nnobi, Onitsha Division, Onitsha Province; Protestant; retired school teacher and trader.
10. *G. C. Nonyelu:* Ibo; Amobia, Awka Division, Onitsha Province; Protestant; barrister; appointed member, Eastern House of Assembly; first African president of the Town Council.
11. *A. C. Nwapa:*[b] Ibo; Oguta, Owerri Division, Owerri Province; Protestant; barrister; resigned following election to the Eastern House of Assembly (1951) and appointment as central minister of commerce and industry; 1st vice-president, Ibo State Union.
12. *N. O. Okaro:*[b] Ibo; Ogidi, Onitsha Division, Onitsha Province; Catholic; retired public works department carpenter and petty contractor; president, Ogidi Improvement Union; Executive Committee member, Onitsha Divisional Union.
13. *M. D. Okechukwu:* Ibo; Ukpor, Onitsha Division, Onitsha Province; Catholic; shopkeeper; president, Ukpor Improvement Union; vice-president, Onitsha Divisional Union; vice-president, Ibo Union (Port Harcourt Branch).
14. *P. Okirigwe:* Ibo; Okigwi Division; Owerri Province; Catholic; trader.
15. *V. K. Onyeri:* Aro-Ibo; Ajalli, Awka Division, Onitsha Province; Catholic; trader; chief political intelligence officer, Zikist Movement; financial secretary/treasurer, African Community League; financial secretary, Ibo Union (Port Harcourt Branch); president-general, Aro Improvement Union; Town Council's second African vice-president.

[a] The first Town Council general election, organized on the basis of a limited ratepayers franchise, was held on June 15, 1949. Councillors were elected to serve three-year terms.

[b] Asisi-Abbey, Okokwu, Nwapa, and Okaro entered the council through by-elections following the disqualification (on a registration technicality) of Dibia, Mac Ebuh, and Eluwa, and the death of A. O. Akwuike.

SOURCES: Personal interviews, newspaper accounts, and Town Council Minutes. National Archives File RP 5744/7; Riv Prof; 1/46/122.

TABLE 11

Elected Councillors

1. *G. E. Asikogu:* Ibo; Owerri Division, Owerri Province; Catholic; teacher.
2. *M. I. Asinobi* (reelected): Ibo; Mbieri, Owerri Division, Owerri Province; Protestant; trader; president, Owerri Divisional Union; president, Ibo Union (Port Harcourt Branch).
3. *J. O. Ihekwoaba:* Ibo; Nkwerre, Orlu Division, Owerri Province; Protestant; transporter and trader.
4. *Z. C. Obi:*[b] Ibo; Nnewi, Onitsha Division, Onitsha Province; Protestant; retired U.A.C. junior manager and trader/contractor; vice-president, Onitsha Divisional Union; founder and patron, Ibo Union (Port Harcourt Branch); president, Ibo State Union; Town Council vice-president.
5. *M. C. Okechukwu* (reelected): Ibo; Ukpor, Onitsha Division, Onitsha Province; Catholic; shopkeeper; president, Ukpor Improvement Union; treasurer, Onitsha Divisional Union; vice-president, Ibo Union (Port Harcourt Branch).
6. *W. D. M. Okpala:* Ibo; Uga, Awka Division, Onitsha Province; Protestant; trader.
7. *R. O. Madueme* (reelected): Ibo; Nnobi, Onitsha Division, Onitsha Province; Protestant; retired school teacher and trader.
8. *G. C. Nonyelu* (reelected): Ibo; Amobia, Awka Division, Onitsha Province; Protestant; barrister; former appointed member, Eastern House of Assembly; former Town Council president.
9. *R. O. Nzimiro:*[b] Ibo; Oguta, Owerri Division, Owerri Province; Protestant; retired chief clerk, U.A.C. and trader; wife's trading business was one of the largest in Nigeria, and she was a prominent leader of Port Harcourt's market women.
10. *T. O. Ugwa:* Ibo; Ovim, Okigwi Division, Owerri Province; Protestant; trader.

Appointed Councillors[c]

11. *W. B. Dublin-Green:*[b] Ijaw; Bonny, Degema Division, River Province; Protestant; retired government dispensary storekeeper.
12. *U. C. Onwunyi:* Ibo; Ogidi, Onitsha Division, Onitsha Province; Protestant; barrister.
13. *A. Opia:* Ibo; Aboh Division, Mid-Western Nigeria; Protestant; retired civil servant (Marketing Board) and trader.
14. *G. N. Mordi:* Ibo; Asaba Division, Mid-Western Nigeria; Catholic; U.A.C.
15. *G. B. Somiari:* Ijaw; Okrika, Degema Division, Rivers Province; Protestant; barrister.
16. *J. O. Ugochukwu:* Ibo; Nkwerre, Orlu Division, Owerri Province; Protestant; trader/contractor.
17. *C. A. Williams:* Yoruba; Western Nigeria; Protestant; retired pharmacist.

[a] The second Town Council was elected on June 14, 1952. On June 29, 1954 this council was dissolved by order of the Eastern Regional government and a Caretaker Council appointed in its place. A commission was appointed "To inquire into the workings of the Port Harcourt Town Council prior to its dissolution," and the commission investigated numerous allegations of wrongdoing by both the 1952 council and its predecessor. The report of this commission is discussed at greater length below.

[b] Obi, Nzimiro, and Dublin-Green were former members of the Township Advisory Board.

[c] Dublin-Green, Onwunyi, Opia, Ugochukwu and Williams were appointed to the council by the governor when it was found that twelve councillors were insufficient to man the necessary committees. Mordi and Somiari were appointed to replace Nzimiro and Onwunyi when the latter two resigned just prior to the council's dissolution in 1954.

but because of their relatively limited educational resources, were seldom able to provide an effective challenge to their Onitsha Ibo competitors. The sudden political ascendancy of non-Onitsha barrister A. C. Nwapa (Oguta Town, Owerri Division, Owerri Province) in 1951 was, in a sense, the exception that proves the rule. Oguta, a riverain community and important oil palm produce center as early as 1885, was one of the few towns within Owerri Province that had received a commercial and acculturative impact comparable to that experienced by the Onitsha area. Oguta's history, in short, was more like that of Onitsha than of Owerri communities.[36]

The franchise-based Ibo politicians differed from their non-Ibo patrician predecessors in several respects. Whereas the members of the Township Advisory Board consisted, in the main, of professionals and prominent businessmen (many of whom were, in addition, retired civil servants), the new town councillors tended to be drawn from less prestigious and less prosperous elements of the population. They included, for example, several petty traders and contractors, and even the lawyers among them were but junior members of their profession. Only two of the councillors elected in 1949 approached the financial stature of the Township Advisory Board's propertied members. Also in sharp contrast to the membership of the Township Advisory Board, four of the council's first fifteen members had less than eight years of elementary education.

Many of the new councillors were, in short, "men on the make," individuals hopeful of converting their newly obtained political position into social and economic gain. It is not surprising, therefore, that one of the first issues to command the council's attention concerned the allocation of highly prized Crown land plots. In 1948, prior to the inauguration of the Town Council, a Plot Allocation Committee had been organized by the government to advise the Resident with respect to this sensitive policy area. To the democratically elected councillors of 1949, this committee—whose membership was drawn from the now defunct Township Advisory Board—seemed a political anachronism. As District Officer and Council President H. N. Harcourt observed in a report on the council's early deliberations, "This [Plot Allocation] Committee at once became a target for the Council's criticism and was condemned for its composition of nominated members, several of whom were rich landlords and unsuitable, in the eyes of the reforming Councillors, for the performance of delicate tasks such as the selection of the most deserving out of 500 applicants for only 10 plots." [37] In point of fact, the council's opposition to the Plot Allocation Committee did not appear to be completely disinterested. When the Resident finally agreed—at the council's insistence—to disband the committee and to receive advice on plot allocation from a committee of the Town Council, recommendations were immediately made to award plots to each of the committee's five African members, to the committee chairman's wife for the purpose of establishing a maternity home, and to two other members of the council. "This sample of the Council's work," noted President Harcourt, "incurred derision within the Township and was not calculated to inspire confidence in the Councillor's spirit of selfless service." [38]

As a preamble to the description of Port Harcourt's belated nationalist awakening, to which we now turn, it should be noted that the political assertiveness of Port Harcourt's new councillors seldom extended beyond a concern with the distribution of local patronage. As a group, the men who served on the Port Harcourt Town Council between 1949 and 1954 were distinguished by their noninvolvement in the nationalist agitation characteristic of this period; in fact, only three of the eleven councillors elected in 1949 were active members of local nationalist organizations. Virtually all of the councillors held high positions within their respective ethnic and geo-ethnic communal associations, and it was to their immigrant subcommunities that the township's local politicians were fundamentally oriented. These associations provided the organizational base and the moral support for their political activity. The "national community" comprised but a secondary point of reference for Port Harcourt's first elected officeholders.

PORT HARCOURT'S NATIONALIST AWAKENING

The campaign waged by Port Harcourt's African Community League for local self-government was distinguished by its moderation. Elsewhere in Nigeria, especially in the cosmopolitan seaport and administrative center of Lagos, the 1940s marked the beginning of an era of militant Nigerian nationalism. August of

1944 witnessed the Lagos formation of the National Council of Nigeria and the Cameroons (NCNC), the nation's first effective mass political organization. In June of the following year, Nigeria's first nationwide general strike marked the political emergence of the country's young labor movement. And in 1946 a triumphal eight-month NCNC tour of the provinces raised £ 13,000 to finance a nationalist delegation to the Colonial Secretary in London.[39] Yet, through all of this social and political ferment, Port Harcourt barely stirred. It was not until late in 1946 that an attempt was made to form a Port Harcourt branch of the NCNC, and it was not until 1951 that this attempt met with some political success. Nationalist sympathizers were many, but nationalist organizers few.

In part, Port Harcourt's political passivity can be explained in terms of an organizational failure at the center. Until May 1951, membership in the NCNC was restricted to organizations that retained their autonomy vis-à-vis the nationalist congress. As Sklar remarks, the NCNC's leader, Nnamdi Azikiwe, was "a less than dedicated organizer," and made relatively little effort "to create a disciplined and cohesive organization."[40] Between 1948 and 1951, to quote Coleman, "the NCNC, as an organization, was virtually moribund."[41]

Local factors were also responsible for the township's comparative lack of organizational initiative. In contrast to Lagos, Port Harcourt in the 1940s was more strictly a commercial center. Whereas the influential and progressive Lagos Ibo Union included large numbers of government clerks and technicians and house servants to Europeans, the Port Harcourt Ibo Union consisted mainly of independent traders and entrepreneurs.[42] The more prosperous of these men, who were by and large more conservatively oriented than the younger and better-educated Lagos civil servants, exercised considerable influence not only within the African Community League but also within their nationality and respective subnationality village, town, clan, and divisional unions. The "big men" attracted to the city both near and distant kinsmen, and a large proportion of their commercial earnings was devoted to maintaining the new urban arrivals. Their generosity was repaid in the form of personal allegiance by their dependents, and it was on the basis of the resulting allegiance networks that their influence at all levels of the associational hierarchy rested. One of

Port Harcourt's early nationalist leaders recalls: "The Asinobis, Abechetas, Nwadikes—the 'City Fathers'—you could trace power back to them. Nothing you could do without getting their support in the background. . . . They were the people with money and influence."

Asinobi, Abecheta, Nwadike—these were three of Port Harcourt's more prominent Ibo traders, members of the new Ibo commercial class that emerged during the 1940s. All three fell within that elite group referred to colloquially as the "City Fathers" or "town elders," by virtue of their age, the length of their residence in the township, and their financial achievement. Like other of Port Harcourt's "big men," they had prospered during the wartime period of scarcity, during which time the expatriate commercial houses channeled the bulk of their imports through selected African traders who were termed "agents" or "registered customers." These registered customers held a virtual retail monopoly on all European imports. Not only were they guaranteed a certain percentage of their monthly turnover, but in many instances they were free to set their own retail prices. Profits were naturally high, and a minimal capital investment very quickly yielded extraordinary dividends.[43]

The United Africa Company played an especially important role in Port Harcourt as in other Nigerian cities—not only through the opportunities afforded its registered customers, but also through loans given to Nigerian entrepreneurs for the establishment of businesses and for the purchase of palm produce in the interior intended for resale to the U.A.C. As a U.A.C. manager commented, probably with only slight overstatement, "there is not a single wealthy (Port Harcourt) trader that did not get his start from U.A.C." When it is noted that many prominent Nigerian businessmen with U.A.C. connections have for long been active in Nigerian public life, the question of U.A.C. influence on Nigerian government policy becomes of more than passing interest. For present purposes, it is sufficient to note the dependence of several of Port Harcourt's more influential traders and entrepreneurs upon the expatriate commercial firms.[44]

The conservative bent of Port Harcourt's commercially oriented power structure notwithstanding, the new township could not remain indefinitely outside the national political arena. The same social and economic forces underlying Lagosian militancy were at work in Port Harcourt and it was only a matter of time before the Eastern Nigerian commercial entrepôt would be drawn into the nationalist spectrum.

Nnamdi Azikiwe and Port Harcourt

On November 22, 1937, the *West African Pilot* was launched with the proud and messianic masthead, "Show the light and the people will find the way." The paper was an immediate success. Its racialist and militant viewpoint represented a sharp departure from the moderate and frequently accommodationist-oriented press of an earlier era, and its Ibo editor-publisher, Nnamdi Azikiwe, was propelled into the center of the nationalist stage. Smaller Azikiwe provincial papers, supplementing the *Pilot*'s national circulation, were soon established in the major Nigerian townships of Lagos, Ibadan, Onitsha, Kano, and, in 1940, Port Harcourt. This highly successful journalistic effort served the dual function of advancing Azikiwe's own political (and financial) position and of bringing formerly isolated communities within a single communications frame. As James Coleman has noted, Azikiwe's "combative and provocative journalism was the principal source of his fame and power, and the most crucial single precipitant of the Nigerian awakening. . . . Nigerian political activity was still Lagos-centered, but Nigerians throughout the country were for the first time permitted the stimulation of vicarious participation." [45]

For Ibos everywhere, Nnamdi Azikiwe's sudden national prominence held special significance. The last of the major Nigerian nationality groups to be "pacified," the industrious Ibo were engaged in a determined effort to achieve economic, social, and political parity with the relatively more Westernized Yoruba. In 1921, 40.3 percent of the Yoruba inhabitants of Southern Nigerian townships but only 11.0 percent of the Ibo inhabitants were educated. Of twenty-seven Nigerian barristers in the early 1920s, twenty were Yoruba and seven were African foreigners. [46] Dr. S. E. Onwu, Nigeria's first Ibo doctor, returned to his country only in 1933; Louis Mbanefo, the first Ibo lawyer and later chief justice of Eastern Nigeria, returned four years later. In Port Harcourt, similarly, the township's first African doctor to establish residence (in 1939) was a Yoruba, and it was not until 1947 that Port Harcourt received its first Ibo barrister in the person of A. C. Nwapa. It is in the light of these data that the interest of Ibos everywhere in Nnamdi Azikiwe becomes understandable. Azikiwe symbolized Ibo aspirations. In Richard Sklar's words, "Azikiwe was the first great Ibo leader of the twentieth century. Notwithstanding his constant affirmation of non-tribal African values, he could not be unmindful of the fact that he was identified by his people (the Ibo) with their own national pride. His career typified their growing assertiveness in Nigerian affairs." [47]

Primarily because of Azikiwe's participation, the Lagos-originated NCNC was dominated by Ibos; and subnationality Ibo communal associations, structurally linked with their counterparts in Port Harcourt and other of Nigeria's urban areas, comprised the bulk of the NCNC's affiliated organizations. During the NCNC's 1946 tour, Ibo Unions in Port Harcourt and other of Eastern Nigeria's urban centers coordinated local fund-raising campaigns and arranged to receive the touring delegation. In Port Harcourt, one guinea minimum contributions were mandatory of all Ibo residents who could afford this sum, and the divisional unions were made responsible for the actual collection. In addition, the African Community League and other non-Ibo communal associations made independent contributions.

The NCNC was a national, not a tribal party: its leadership was firmly committed to a pan-Nigerian ideal and its membership embraced many Yorubas and members of other nationality groups. The predominance of Ibo elements within both the organization's leadership and rank and file, however, was an undeniable fact. The subsequent identification of the pan-Ibo cultural and educational movement with the pan-Nigerian NCNC political movement "alarmed the leaders of other nationalities, who saw what they suspected to be a growing threat of Ibo domination." [48] Once Yoruba-Ibo conflict erupted in Lagos, these fears became, in effect, a self-fulfilling prophecy: the Ibo State Union was converted into a political instrument designed to further Ibo political fortunes through the medium of the NCNC.[49]

The Local Zikists

The formation of a Port Harcourt branch of the Zikist movement in 1946 marked the first significant organizational effort of the township's local nationalists. The national Zikist movement had its genesis in Nigeria's first nationwide general strike. In June of 1945, seventeen unions embracing thirty thousand public workers went out on strike over demands for higher wages and cost of living allowances. The strike lasted thirty-seven days and its political impact was enormous: "the strike shocked both Europeans and Africans into the realization that Nigerians, when organized, had great power, that they could defy the white bureaucracy, that they could virtually control strategic centers throughout the country, and that through force or the threat of force they could compel the government to grant concessions." [50]

The strike's political significance was not lost on Azikiwe whose papers supported the striking workers despite a threatened government ban on publication. Then, on July 8, 1945, Azikiwe's two Lagos dailies, the *West African Pilot* and the *Daily Comet,* were closed down. Charging that government officials were seeking to assassinate him, Azikiwe issued a dramatic "last testament," and went into hiding in his home town of Onitsha.

The net effect of Azikiwe's allegations was a sharp increase in his political stature and popularity, especially among his Ibo followers. Azikiwe's political opponents, however, attempting to turn the "incident" against him, charged that a gross fraud had been perpetrated upon the Nigerian public. It was to counter these criticisms and, at the same time, to create a new and more militant instrument of "positive action" that the Zikist movement was launched. Deriving its ideological impetus from the African irredentist philosophy of A. A. Nwafor Orizu,[51] the organization was founded in Lagos by four young Nigerian journalists. Branches were soon formed in urban centers throughout Nigeria, and the Zikist movement was quickly transformed into a nationwide, NCNC-affiliated organization of radical youth.

The Port Harcourt branch of the Zikist movement was formed largely on the initiative of John Umolu who, in 1946, was a young Edo storekeeper for the United Africa Company and a trade unionist. In Port Harcourt, as elsewhere, most of the Zikists were young, educated men of little to moderate means. The more prominent of the early Port Harcourt members included seven clerical functionaries (one storekeeper, one customs officer, four clerks, one stenographer), one teacher, one petty trader, and two second-

ary school students. In testimony to Azikiwe's supratribal appeal,
they comprised five Ibos, two non-Ibo Mid-Westerners, two Efiks,
one Gold Coast immigrant, and one Cameroonian.

The Port Harcourt Zikists strenuously objected to the domination of the African Community League by Port Harcourt's wealthy
bourgeoisie, and Zikist opposition to the league's endorsement of
a property taxpayers franchise constituted the township's first
overt expression of class hostility. Significantly, however, relationships between the African Community League and the more radically inclined Zikist movement remained otherwise cordial. For
one thing, some Zikists were actively involved in the league as
well as in the communal associations from which the league
derived its membership. John Umolu, for example, represented his
Mid-Western Afenmai Union in the Edo Union and attended the
Community League as a representative of the latter. V. K. Onyeri,
like Umolu destined to become a member of the Eastern House
of Assembly, served not only as a prominent Zikist officer but also
as the president-general of the Aro Improvement Union, as the
financial secretary of the Port Harcourt Ibo Union, and as financial
secretary and treasurer of the African Community League. Also
contributing to the cordiality of relationships between the league
and the Zikists was the fact that they each had rather specialized
concerns: the former with local and the latter with national affairs.

Nationally, the Zikist movement was short-lived. In 1948 leaders
of the movement devised an ingenious stratagem intended to in-
still a new revolutionary fervor within a then lifeless NCNC. The
Zikist plan was to provoke the British into imprisoning a martyred
Nnamdi Azikiwe. Unfortunately, the plan failed. Azikiwe was not
informed of the Zikist program—it was anticipated that he would
not willingly consent to become the movement's martyr—and,
while Azikiwe defended the right of the Zikist movement to its
views and its policies, he dissociated himself in no uncertain terms
from the movement's program of revolutionary action. The Zikist
"call for revolution" was issued, but instead of Azikiwe it was the
Zikists themselves who were brought to trial and convicted on
charges of sedition.[52] Port Harcourt Zikists were not involved in
the sedition trials, but some months later a death blow was dealt
the entire national organization. In February 1950, a young Zikist
attempted to assassinate the chief secretary to the government, Sir

Hugh Foot. Almost immediately the Zikist movement was proclaimed an unlawful society, and more of its members were imprisoned.

Through the 1940s, the political impact of Port Harcourt's young radicals was minimal. Their mere existence, however, was evidence of important developments that were taking place beneath Port Harcourt's political surface. The Zikist movement was but part of a wider nationalist awakening manifesting itself, for example, in new organizational activity on the local trade union front. Thus, John Umolu, the founder of the Port Harcourt branch of the Zikist movement, also took the initiative in forming an unsuccessful Mercantile Workers Union, and subsequently, the Port Harcourt branch of the Amalgamated Union of the United Africa Company African Workers (UNAMAG). In August 1950, UNAMAG went out on strike and succeeded in obtaining a substantial increase in the cost-of-living allowance for U.A.C. workers. In Port Harcourt, as in Lagos, the success of this strike garnered political capital for the union's leadership. But only four months later a second strike of mercantile workers was called. This time UNAMAG and the Nigerian Labor Congress, of which UNAMAG was a member, were unprepared and suffered a sharp defeat.[53] In Port Harcourt, John Umolu, while increasing his political stature in the African community, was dismissed from the U.A.C. and blacklisted by the local mercantile firms. Two years later, however, Umolu received new employment as one of Port Harcourt's two members in the Eastern House of Assembly. Umolu was the first —and until 1965 the only—Port Harcourt political figure to come to public attention through the labor movement.

Port Harcourt's nationalist awakening manifested itself also in an increased community concern with events outside Port Harcourt. Thus, the infamous November 18, 1949, "Enugu shooting," which saw the police slaying of twenty-one coal miners and the wounding of fifty-one others, led, a week later, to riots in the township. The Port Harcourt riots lasted for several days and resulted in at least two deaths and eighty-three arrests.[54] In the Commission of Enquiry that followed the Enugu incident, G. C. Nonyelu, a Port Harcourt barrister who was serving simultaneously as a town councillor and as Port Harcourt's representative in the Eastern House of Assembly, joined several other prominent

Nigerian barristers in representing the Colliery workers. The response of Port Harcourt's African community to the Enugu shooting provided dramatic testimony to the township's final entry into the national political arena.

The Bifurcation of Local Leadership

Concurrent with Port Harcourt's nationalist awakening was the emergence of two relatively distinct leadership groups: one placing relatively greater emphasis upon matters of local concern, the other more closely linked ideologically and organizationally with the Nigerian nationalist movement; one was oriented primarily to the African Community League and the Port Harcourt Town Council, the other primarily to the Zikist movement and the NCNC. These groupings were not mutually exclusive and were not in direct conflict. No town councillor expressed opposition to the nationalist movement, and some councillors were very much a part of political developments outside Port Harcourt; conversely, some nationalists were very much involved in the struggle for local political position. But the groupings did express divergent ideological perspectives and political styles.

The bifurcation between the locals and cosmopolitans expressed itself most sharply in a continuing cleavage between the local branch of the NCNC and Port Harcourt's public officeholders. Thus, at a time when non-Ibos continued to be excluded from the Town Council, two non-Ibos—Dr. Ajibade, the prestigious Yoruba doctor, and John Umolu, the popular Edo trade unionist and former Zikist—took over the leadership of the local party branch from two Ibos. Party leaders evidently were recruited on a different basis during this period than were the franchise-based town councillors. On the one hand, local nationalists were ideologically committed to attempting to transcend communal divisions within their community and to avoid tribalism. On the other, NCNC leaders were sensitive to the charges of Ibo domination leveled at their party by their political opponents.

Similar factors appear to have generated the subsequent nomination and election of non-Ibo Umolu to the Regional House of Assembly in 1953. To some extent, Umolu's election (and re-election in 1957) testified to his stature as a nationalist leader in good standing with the Ibo rank and file. But, as Umolu's later repudiation by Port Harcourt's Ibo establishment was to verify, his prominence within NCNC circles and his electoral successes of the 1950s were made possible only by the short-term determination of the NCNC leadership to present a picture of pan-tribal party solidarity. A policy of "ethnic arithmetic" was dictated by immediate political circumstances—Nigerian independence was not to be formally achieved until 1960—and was of particular importance to the regional and national party executive committees and governmental establishments. In effect, there were two distinct sets of criteria operative in political recruitment to local and regional-national offices. It is this variation—or bifurcation—which explains the apparent paradox of non-Ibo exclusion within the city government occurring simultaneously with the election to the Regional House of Assembly of non-Ibo (but nationalist hero) John Umolu. This phase, however, was but a transitional one. The removal of the nationalist, anticolonial dynamic in 1960 undermined an important element of Umolu's local political base, and in 1961 he was cast aside by the Port Harcourt NCNC party Executive.[55]

THE CONSOLIDATION OF PARTY POWER

During the early 1950s, the NCNC was preoccupied with the ways and means of the consolidation of power at both regional and local levels. Whatever the party's obvious structural weaknesses, the NCNC retained an enthusiastic grass-roots following throughout Eastern Nigeria and through much of the Western Region as well. For Ibos especially, the party of "Zik" had come to acquire almost mystical significance, becoming in effect an extension of the traditional order. Opposition to local party candidates was a frequent occurrence, but opposition to the party *per se*—within Iboland—was virtually unknown. Yet the NCNC in 1951 still lacked the political teeth of power and patronage. The process by which these were acquired in Port Harcourt is the subject to which we now turn. It is useful to consider this final consolidation of local party power in terms of four critical events: first, a structural reorganization of the party machinery; second, the suppression of the Nwapa-initiated party rebellion of 1953; third, the 1954 dissolution of the Town Council by the Eastern Nigerian government; and fourth, the clash between the national NCNC establishment, and the leadership of the Port Harcourt-based Ibo State Union.

Party Reorganization

The Town Council elections of 1949, in combination with the 1951 elections to the Regional House of Assembly, pointed up the organizational impotence of Port Harcourt's local party branch. Candidates in the 1949 election stood as individuals rather than as party nominees; the party exercised no control over their nominations, their campaigns, or, if they were successful, their subsequent activities as councillors; and, as we have seen, few councillors identified themselves with the militant nationalist goals of the NCNC.

Similarly, in 1951, when A. C. Nwapa, the Oguta Ibo barrister only recently returned from his studies overseas, and Dr. O. Ajibade, the Yoruba doctor who had provided distinguished service on the defunct Township Advisory Board, were selected as the NCNC nominees to stand election to the Regional Assembly, the local organization had no means of discouraging a rash of independent candidacies. The party simply lacked the necessary political leverage to insure obedience and discipline on the part of its supporters, a number of whom—by virtue of the introduction of the franchise in 1949—had already established independent political bases. In the end, A. C. Nwapa, the NCNC candidate and Port Harcourt "favorite son," and V. K. Onyeri, vice-president of the Town Council, former Zikist, and an independent candidate, were elected. Nwapa's election was clearly a personal rather than a party victory, and received wide support within the African community.[56] Ajibade's defeat and Onyeri's victory, however, produced numerous allegations of tribalism, oath swearing, and corrupt practices.[57] In any event, the elections of 1951 highlighted the disunity and political ineffectiveness of the local NCNC. Personality and community, rather than party, remained dominant themes of local political activity.

In the aftermath of the 1951 elections, local NCNC activists turned once again to the problems of party organization and recruitment. Following a new policy directive, the local branch was reorganized on the basis of individual rather than organizational membership. With the resulting elimination of structural units (in particular, the communal associations) intervening between the party and the individual, new blood was brought into the organ-

ization (table 12), and party membership acquired more personal
significance.

TABLE 12

PORT HARCOURT NCNC PROFILE, 1951[a]

(all figures in percentages, N = 30)

Nationality		Area of origin		Occupation	
Ibo	80.0	Owerri Province	46.7	Administrators and	
Ijaw	10.0	Owerri Division	(23.3)	clerical functionaries	36.7
		Orlu Division	(6.7)	Firm Manager	(6.7)
Yoruba	3.3	Okigwi Division	(3.3)	Agent of Cultural	
Itsekiri	3.3	Bende Division	(13.3)	Association	(3.3)
				Clerk	(26.7)
Togoland	3.3	Onitsha Province	26.7		
				Learned arts and skills	20.0
		Onitsha Division	(20.0)	Professional	(6.7)
		Awka Division	(6.7)	Educator	(10.0)
		Rivers Province	13.3	Journalist	(3.3)
		Ahoada Division	(3.3)		
		Degema Division	(10.0)	Private enterprise	40.0
				Businessman or	
		Mid-Western Region	6.7	big trader	(6.7)
				Petty trader or	
		Western Region	3.3	petty contractor	(33.3)
		Togoland	3.3		

[a] The data upon which this table is based were drawn from personal interviews.
Thirty members of the executive were identified on the basis of these interviews, but
the total membership may have exceeded this number.

Concurrently, the structural reorganization also reduced the
party's dependence upon the Ibo economic notables who had exercised a generally conservative influence upon the NCNC through
their respective communal organizations. These notables remained
an important factor in the general political process. In providing
important symbolic support to the unity and stability of the African community, they in effect served as the urban counterpart of
the rural elders. It was still important, for example, to seek the
informal sanction of the City Fathers (non-Ibo as well as Ibo) on
important matters, and they continued to be called upon to resolve
party disputes or render needed financial assistance. But the political initiative was no longer in their hands. As two party informants
put it, "The Big Men—you use them to support a decision which
has been taken, one way or the other. . . . We made most of
them patrons to make them big men and collect their money, but

we ran the party." Not all of the City Fathers willingly acquiesced to their reduced position, but there was little they could do. In the words of one party patron, "They make us patron. And they don't even know the meaning. We are supposed to be retired, not supposed to be bothered to attend meetings. They call us when they need financial assistance. Then they ask us to sit in and decide when there is a conflict. And when we advise, then they don't listen."

A. C. Nwapa and the Sit-Tight Crisis of 1953

The 1951 elections resulted in a major victory for the NCNC in the Eastern Region. Those candidates (such as V. K. Onyeri) who had stood as independents were quickly accepted into the party's fold, and when the Assembly was convened, the NCNC held sixty-five of sixty-nine seats. The party was therefore in a position to designate the eastern assemblymen who, under the terms of the 1951 Macpherson Constitution, were to join their Western and Northern counterparts as members of the Central House. Port Harcourt's barrister-assemblyman, A. C. Nwapa, was one of the men designated to move to the center; subsequently, Nwapa accepted the portfolio of central minister of commerce and industry.

In Western Nigeria, where NCNC President Nnamdi Azikiwe himself stood and won election, the party fared less well. The newly formed Action Group, organized by a section of the Yoruba nationality hostile to Azikiwe and his Ibo-dominated NCNC, emerged with a controlling majority in the Western House of Assembly. As a result, Azikiwe, who had intended to move into the Central Legislature from his position in the Western House of Assembly, found himself instead as the unofficial leader of the Western opposition.

Azikiwe and other national leaders of the NCNC had been opposed to the Macpherson Constitution from the outset. Their only goal in contesting the 1951 elections, in fact, "was an NCNC majority in the regional and central legislatures that would act to 'paralyze the machinery of government' and lead to a reformulation of the Constitution." [58] Now, with their leader barred from the center, NCNC militants increased their resolve to bring down the Constitution. When, in contradiction to Azikiwe's declaration

131

of opposition, rebellious parliamentarians under A. C. Nwapa's leadership resolved to give the Constitution "a fair trial," the stage was set for a brutal struggle between the ministerial and the extra-parliamentary elements of the party.

The story of this struggle has been told elsewhere, and need only be sketched briefly.[59] In defiance of their party's directive, Nwapa and two other NCNC central ministers and six NCNC eastern ministers refused to resign their offices and were expelled from the party. The NCNC eastern assemblymen then proceeded to block all legislation before the House, thereby compelling the lieutenant governor to use his reserve powers to enact a critical appropriations bill and eventually forcing the dissolution of the Eastern House of Assembly.

In the regional elections that followed in 1953, the NCNC was returned to power once again and the former dissident ministers found themselves in a numerically insignificant opposition. Similarly, the promulgation of a new Constitution in 1954 forced the dissolution of the federal House and the holding of new federal elections, in which the NCNC emerged with thirty-two of the forty-two seats allocated to the Eastern Region and a majority of the seats allocated to the Western Region. The results of both the regional and the federal elections provided a clear demonstration of the party's strength in Southern Nigeria and, more particularly, of the inefficacy of opposition to the NCNC in its Ibo stronghold.

The 1953–1954 election results also testified to an increasing regionalization of power, a trend that was substantially furthered by the federal Constitution of 1954. Under the new Constitution, the central government relinquished its right to review proposed regional legislation. The central or federal government's powers were clearly specified and all residual powers rested with the regional governments. Federal revenue was now to be allocated on the basis of regional derivation as well as regional need, and regional public services and judiciaries were to be established. Most importantly, perhaps, the national marketing boards were to be regionalized, and provision was to be made for the establishment of statutory corporations to allocate investment and loan funds. Thus, within each region the party in power assumed control of highly powerful instruments of commercial and political patronage.[60]

132

Throughout the 1953 crisis, the Port Harcourt branch of the NCNC remained loyal to Azikiwe and the party's national leadership. By 1953, the local party had come under the influence of the more radically oriented NCNC Youth Association, a successor of the outlawed Zikist movement,[61] and firmly supported disciplinary actions against the rebellious sit-tight ministers. In fact, the party branch treasurer, G. C. N. Akomas, destined in later years to become local NCNC president and Port Harcourt deputy mayor, was suspended for his failure to sign a resolution demanding A. C. Nwapa's resignation.

On one issue, however, the Port Harcourt branch was diametrically opposed to its national leadership. Inasmuch as the dissolution of the Eastern House of Assembly in 1953 had been made possible by the cooperation of NCNC parliamentarians, the party's Central Working Committee decided that all the incumbent NCNC assemblymen who had abided by party discipline should be responsored by their local branches in the elections to the new assembly. But the Port Harcourt NCNC was only slightly less opposed to its second assemblyman, V. K. Onyeri, than it was to the rebellious Nwapa. Only after high-level NCNC leaders personally interceded did the local branch agree to accept the Central Working Committee's directive.[62] In the end, Onyeri and John Umolu, who had been nominated to stand in the place of A. C. Nwapa, were both successful as the NCNC candidates for the Eastern House of Assembly.

The Party vs. the Town Council

NCNC electoral victories in Port Harcourt during the early 1950s were a tribute to the personal charisma of Nnamdi Azikiwe rather than to the organizational strength of the local party branch. This much was clear from the failure of the NCNC to gain control over the Town Council, the most critical source of local governmental power and political patronage. The Town Council remained the key to the consolidation of party power in the township.

The tradition of council political autonomy established in the elections of 1949 was continued in the general council elections of July 1952. When the ballots were counted, only four NCNC-sponsored candidates had won council seats. Four of the six successful independent candidates declared for the NCNC immediately after their election, and a party caucus designated the man to be elected council president, but this postelection facade of NCNC control did not alter the essential fact of the political independence of the new councillors.

Following the example of its predecessor, the second Town Council rapidly acquired a reputation for inefficiency and corruption. Allegations made against the council were several and, as the eventual public enquiry indicated, not without foundation.[63] The council's administration of the three township markets was easily the most politically volatile subject, giving rise to the most vociferous complaints. The allocation of market stalls and lock-up shops often seemed to be contingent upon the payment of bribe or upon family connections with the councillors. Moreover, it was evident that councillors were but little interested in curbing market racketeering. Most market stalls, for example, were hired from the council by speculators who sublet what was an extremely scarce and precious product at much higher rates. A survey of fifteen sheds in the main market revealed that of a total of 364 stalls no more than 142 were occupied by the council's official tenants.[64] Another survey disclosed the names of several councillors and their relations among the market stall allottees. On one occasion, a councillor's construction firm was awarded more than half the work of a £24,000 contract to build a market extension.[65]

It was to provide a check on these and other improprieties that the Port Harcourt branch of the NCNC proposed, in March 1953, to form a Parliamentary Committee, comprised of both NCNC Executive members and NCNC councillors, whose function it would be to determine council policy.[66] Despite an initially enthusiastic response on the part of the councillors, the Parliamentary or Municipal Committee, as it came to be known, proved unable to control council deliberations. When the NCNC Executive attempted to impose its will, as in a resolution calling upon the Town Council to dissociate itself from ceremonies honoring the coronation of Queen Elizabeth II, the NCNC councillors proclaimed their opposition to "outside interference." [67] Attempts to curb council abuses met with even greater resistance, and the Municipal Committee soon ceased functioning.

The failure of the NCNC Executive to gain control over the Town

Council forced the local party branch into direct and open opposition to the township government. Through a newly formed "front" organization, the Rate Payers and Voters Association, the NCNC Executive moved to bring pressure on the Eastern Nigerian government to dissolve the council. Toward the end of September 1953, Azikiwe and other national party leaders themselves intervened (unsuccessfully) in a controversy over the allocation of market stalls.[68] Police investigations into council activities were launched, and received the support and assistance of local party leaders. Then, in October, the Rate Payers and Voters Association petitioned the Resident for the immediate establishment of a Commission of Enquiry. The petition was followed by demonstrations and counter-demonstrations before the council and the Resident; they were organized by the Rate Payers and Voters Association and by councillors at whom much of the agitation was directed.[69]

The government still made no move, and pressure was intensified. Earlier, the NCNC Executive had called upon all NCNC councillors to resign their seats and thereby dissociate themselves from the malpractices in which the council was engaged. When all but one councillor refused, the Executive moved to expel the remaining NCNC councillors from the party. Then, in February 1954, V. K. Onyeri and John Umolu were mandated by the local NCNC Executive to move on the floor of the Eastern House of Assembly for the appointment of a Commission of Enquiry into the Port Harcourt Town Council. In his motion, Eastern Assemblyman (and former Councillor) Onyeri "alleged that as constituted, the council was a den of iniquity and he charged it with organised bribery and corruption, partiality over the award of contracts, nepotism, favouritism, administrative inability, victimisation and the mis-use of the council's funds." [70]

Government action on the Onyeri-Umolu motion was delayed pending the conclusion of court cases in which councillors were involved. In the interim, an internal dispute within the council further undermined the council's public stature. Council President M. D. Okechukwu and Vice-President Z. C. Obi, both of whom hailed from Onitsha Division and were officers of the Onitsha Divisional Union, had been at odds for a long period; a committee of the union, in fact, had been appointed to reconcile their differences. The reconciliation was unsuccessful, however, and the feud intensified, dividing the council into two antagonistic factions.

Late in 1952, the council, at the suggestion of the medical officer of health, initiated plans for a vast public housing project valued at over £575,000.[71] When it subsequently developed that the president's faction had secretly committed the council to a contract with a German construction firm (in which one of the members of this faction had a financial interest), the vice-president's faction held its own meeting and dissociated itself from the agreement already signed. By now, the debate had become public and the permanent secretary of the ministry of local government was sent to Port Harcourt to enquire into the contract situation. On June 29, 1954, the entire council met in regular session: the president refused to permit the filing of a violently worded motion demanding his censure, and the meeting was eventually adjourned without having transacted any business. The same day, the council was reconvened by the Senior Resident "and informed that it had been dissolved by the Lieutenant-Governor by Order in Council for the reason that its administration was wasteful and inefficient." [72]

The appointment of a five-person Caretaker Council and of a Commission of Enquiry into the workings of the Port Harcourt Town Council marked further steps in the consolidation of party power in the township. On the one hand, the commission's findings served to publicly discredit those councillors who had refused to abide by the directives of the local NCNC Executive Committee; on the other, the composition of the Caretaker Council operated to insure that this appointed body would be more amenable to party direction (table 13). Four of the five caretaker councillors were party members in good standing—they included D. K. Onwenu, the local NCNC Chairman—and the fifth was a politically independent Ijaw barrister from Okrika who was destined to become Eastern Nigeria's solicitor general. Furthermore, Onwenu's position on the Caretaker Council enabled the local NCNC Executive Committee to monitor council deliberations. A new Municipal Committee was established to advise the council and, early in 1955, a special committee of the Executive was appointed to assist the council in the selection of a new town clerk.[73]

The selection of G. C. Ikokwu, an Onitsha businessman and

TABLE 13

MEMBERSHIP OF THE CARETAKER COUNCIL (1954–1955)

1. *G. C. Ikokwu* (president): Ibo; Oba, Onitsha Division, Onitsha Province; Protestant; transporter (businessman); executive member, Onitsha Divisional Union; NCNC.
2. *J. J. Ogbuehi:* Ibo; Ibeku-Umuahia, Bende Division, Owerri Province; Protestant; petty trader and ex-clerk; NCNC.
3. *Mrs. G. Okoye:* Ibo; Ogidi, Onitsha Division, Onitsha Province; Protestant; petty trader; president, Port Harcourt's Women's Wing of the NCNC.
4. *Hon. D. K. Onwenu:* Ibo; Aro-Ndizuogu, Orlu Division, Owerri Province; Protestant; vice-principal and tutor, Baptist and Enitonna High Schools; president, Port Harcourt NCNC; member, federal House of Representatives.
5. *G. B. Somiari:* Ijaw; Okrika, Degema Division, Rivers Province; Protestant; barrister; independent.

former town councillor, as the Caretaker Council's president was greeted with little enthusiasm by local party leaders. Despite his official credentials, Ikokwu had never actively participated in party affairs. Consequently, when, after twelve months in office, Ikokwu and other council members began to lobby with the Eastern Nigerian government for a still further extension of their original six-month term of office, Port Harcourt NCNC officials— including Councillor and branch president Onwenu—launched an active and ultimately successful campaign to unseat the Caretaker Council and to hold fresh elections. This campaign, detailed in chapter 7, was related to an important struggle between rival cliques within the NCNC for control of the council and of the party's Executive Committee. For present purposes it is sufficient to note that the campaign's success gave added political leverage to the local party branch. In the elections that followed, the NCNC emerged with seventeen of twenty-two council seats, and the party's Executive was finally in a position to insure discipline among its elected representatives. Significantly, former Council President Okechukwu and Council Vice-President Obi, who had been expelled from the Port Harcourt branch of the NCNC for their failure to resign their seats in line with the party's directive, were unsuccessful in their bid for reelection as independent candidates.

The consolidation of party power in Port Harcourt was but one phase in the development of a single-party regime in Nigeria's Eastern Region. It was, in effect, the local manifestation of the regionalization of power that decisively shaped the country's political life in the late 1950s. In the December 1953 elections to the Eastern House of Assembly, the NCNC secured seventy-two of eighty-four seats and control of the regional government.[74] An extensive administrative apparatus was put at the disposal of the party, and the NCNC made the most of its opportunity. An elaborate patronage system was developed—by 1956, twelve boards and statutory corporations manned by over a hundred political appointees had been established—and the party used its newly acquired control over jobs and contracts to reward its supporters and punish its detractors.[75] From the standpoint of Port Harcourt's important commercial interests, of particular significance was the NCNC's control of the all-important Regional Marketing Board, Finance Corporation, Development Corporation, and the African Continental Bank. Party domination transformed the licensing and loan-giving functions of these agencies into highly effective instruments of political control. No less important, as the dissolution of the Port Harcourt Town Council dramatically demonstrated, was the NCNC's control of the government ministry responsible for overseeing the Region's local councils.

Locally, too, new reward and punishment dispensing opportunities emerged. Thus in Port Harcourt, council contracts for the supply of building materials and the construction of public facilities (e.g., market stalls, council schools) were channeled to the party faithful who, in return for this patronage, were expected to contribute five percent of the value of their contract awards to the party coffers. Similarly, nomination by the local Executive Committee—which was now tantamount to actual election—became a much valued form of political patronage. Officeholders also enjoyed additional perquisites, such as easier access to commercial firms (for jobs and contracts) and government departments (for jobs, contracts, plots, and the like). All of these developments, it should be noted, in Port Harcourt and elsewhere in Eastern Nigeria, took place against a backdrop of almost total commitment of the Region's Ibo-speaking majority to "the party." The strength of the NCNC derived fundamentally from this consensus and only secondarily from its control of the governmental machinery.

The NCNC *and the Ibo State Union*

The postwar transfer of power in Port Harcourt, we have seen, involved the transfer of political and administrative responsibility not only from British to African authorities, but also from the township's non-Ibo minorities to its Ibo-speaking majority. By the late 1940s, the prosperous and rapidly expanding railway-port had become an Ibo city in political as well as social fact. Moreover, for several reasons previously considered—the township's proximity to central Iboland; its "neutrality" as between the major Owerri and Onitsha Ibo subgroups; the cosmopolitan character of its Ibo population; its high concentration of wealth, skills, and rural-oriented influentials—Port Harcourt was an Ibo city with special significance for the movement toward pan-Ibo social and political integration. Appropriately, therefore, Port Harcourt, in 1948, replaced Lagos as the administrative headquarters of the premier Ibo organization, the Ibo State Union. As a consequence, several of Port Harcourt's leading personalities were drawn into the complicated sphere of pan-Ibo politics and, in the process, local politics became inextricably linked with regional and national Ibo affairs.

The Ibo State Union (known as the Ibo Federal Union prior to its transfer from Lagos) was the organizational embodiment of the movement toward pan-Ibo integration begun almost two decades earlier.[76] Originally concerned solely with the educational and material development of Iboland, the I.S.U. was sharply politicized during the postwar years by the outbreak of Yoruba-Ibo conflict in Lagos. It was not long, however, before the close identification of the Ibo State Union with the NCNC—for a short period, NCNC President Nnamdi Azikiwe had himself assumed the presidency of the Ibo State Union—became detrimental to the party's own interests and, in 1953, the leadership of the I.S.U. passed into the hands of less activist social and economic notables. Z. C. Obi, a town councillor and former U.A.C. clerk-turned-businessman, one of the best-educated of Port Harcourt's older generation, assumed the union's presidency, while V. C. I. Anene, also a local businessman, became the union's administrative secretary. With the introduction of leading members of the host Port

Harcourt Ibo Union into the Executive Committee of the Ibo State Union, the latter body became increasingly identified as a Port Harcourt institution.

A detailed examination of the Ibo State Union lies beyond the scope of the present study. We will only observe, briefly, that with the ascendancy of Obi and Anene, the Ibo State Union entered a period of sharp and continuous national political decline and, at different points in time, actually emerged as a center of latent, ineffective opposition to Azikiwe and the NCNC. This opposition appears to have been related to two distinct developments. First, inasmuch as the NCNC and the Ibo State Union were the only two nongovernmental institutions inclusive of all Ibo-speaking elements and purporting to speak with authority for Ibos, persons who, for one reason or another, felt aggrieved by actions of the NCNC turned to the Ibo State Union for support. As a result, the I.S.U. became a logical platform for the venting of a myriad of local anti-NCNC Ibo grievances.[77] Second, the leadership of the Ibo State Union—as evidenced by its dominant Port Harcourt component—tended to be drawn from among Iboland's prosperous city-based elders who resented their political subordination to a rising class of party activists. The Ibo State Union, in effect, served as a vehicle for the political self-assertion of this group. In sum, the cleavage between the Ibo State Union and the national leadership of the NCNC was part of the generational and neo-class conflict separating Port Harcourt's prestigious City Fathers from the local party branch. In point of fact, most of the men designated as City Fathers were leading members of either the Ibo State Union or the Port Harcourt Ibo Union.

To place this NCNC–Ibo State Union cleavage in proper perspective, it should be emphasized that the lines of opposition were seldom sharply drawn. For one thing, the I.S.U. hierarchy was divided by the same communal cleavages that plagued the NCNC: communities of origin were more normally the dominant points of political reference for Ibo State Union Executive members as they were for party leaders.

More crucially, the lower levels of the Ibo governing apparatus were generally unaffected by the high level conflict. As Sklar observes, "While the Ibo State Executive has not been amenable to facile manipulation by the NCNC leadership, the lower echelons of the Union—i.e., the town, village, district, and clan unions—work virtually without direction to identify the NCNC with the cause of Ibo welfare. In many instances, town and clan unions affiliated with the Ibo State Union have made up for the organizational failings of the official party organization." [78] Indeed, the political impotency of the Ibo State Union leadership was but a reminder of the extent to which the NCNC had in fact consolidated its position within Port Harcourt as within the rest of Iboland.

Moreover, Ibo State Union opposition to the NCNC was usually couched in moderate terms. As the patrons and representatives of their respective subnationality associations, the members of the Ibo State Executive were constrained to avoid an open break with the party. Besides, many of these members had an enormous financial stake in the maintenance of party and government goodwill. This latter point was rendered emphatically in 1961 when several Port Harcourt businessmen who were supporting an antiparty candidate for the Eastern House of Assembly were reminded that their government bank loans and political appointments were subject to immediate recall.

Finally, in the late fifties and early sixties the persistent threats of Northern domination of the federal government, and of the secession of non-Ibo elements from Nigeria's Eastern Region, served as major supports to the cohesion of the Ibo political system, significantly moderating the latent divisions between party and Ibo State Union leadership. In fact, during the 1964–1965 period of national political turmoil, NCNC leaders used the Ibo State Union as a cover for their own tribally oriented political propaganda. Pamphlets attacking alleged Northern oppression were drafted by committees of civil servants and leading politicians, and after presentation to the Ibo State Union's Executive Committee, published under the union's auspices. [79]

The Incorporation of Conflict

The consolidation of party power in Port Harcourt did *not* mean an end to political conflict within the township. To the contrary, as the transfer of power from European to African hands was completed, the political stakes were increased and the competition

141

for local political position intensified. Politicians still aspired to power and the demand for political status continued to exceed the supply of available offices.

Nor did the institutional changes of the 1940s and 1950s alter the social bases of political cleavage in the community. Men continued to be differentiated according to their communities of origin, their educational and occupational attainments, and their religious commitments; and they continued to organize in response to their perception of their interests in given situations. Now, however, in contrast to the earlier era, political factionalism was for the most part contained within a single controlling political party

PART III

*Community Power in Prewar
Port Harcourt (1955–1965)*

CHAPTER 7

Democracy, Opportunism, and Geo-Ethnicity

With the restoration of elected local government in December 1955, Port Harcourt entered a new political phase, one that in many ways was analogous to New Haven's years of plebeian democracy. In Port Harcourt, as in New Haven, "popularity was divorced from both wealth and social position by the influx of immigrants, and public office went to the ex-plebes, who lacked wealth and social position but had the advantage of numbers."[1] The communalization of politics was intensified, and political leadership passed from the hands of the minority Onitshan Ibos into those of the less advantaged but always more numerous Owerris. This and the next three chapters analyze the years of Owerri dominance from several perspectives. In this chapter, we are concerned with how the Owerri ascendancy was achieved and with the impact of geo-ethnicity upon local electoral politics. We later explore, in chapters 8, 9, and 10, the political significance of other lines of social division—involving class, religion and nationality—which either cut across or transcended the geo-ethnic cleavages around which the electoral process was organized.

THE OWERRI ASCENDANCY

From the township's inception, Ibos from Owerri Province greatly outnumbered Ibos from the more distant Onitsha Province. But successful communal politics required more than numbers. It required, also, the introduction of the franchise—accomplished in 1949—and the emergence of leaders possessing the political sophistication to recognize the potential of geo-ethnic political strategies and the political skills needed to translate that potential

145

into public office. Between 1949 and 1955, it was the Onitsha Ibos, who had received an earlier and more intensive exposure to Western education and who were more prominent within the local occupational and social hierarchies, who provided the most effective political strategists and leaders. As a result, the Onitsha representation on the Town Council during these years almost equaled that of the Owerri, despite the fact that there were fewer Onitshans within the population at large.[2] More importantly, Onitshans controlled the highest offices within the Town Council: between 1949 and 1955 all five of the town councillors who served as council president or vice-president were from Onitsha Province. Within the NCNC, similarly, two rival youth wings—the NCNC Youth Association and a later-organized Zikist National Vanguard —were both led by Onitsha men. If we turn to the Ibo State Union, the same pattern of Onitsha preeminence was manifest, with both the president and the administrative secretary hailing from Onitsha Division. Finally, even the editor of the local *Eastern Nigerian Guardian* during much of this period was from Onitisha Province.

But with the appointment of Port Harcourt's Caretaker Council in July 1954, the days of Onitsha preeminence were numbered. Like its two predecessors, this council was dominated by immigrants from Onitsha Province, its chairman and the one female member both hailing from Onitsha Division. Only one of the five members could claim bona fide Owerri provincial connections, and this individual was at the time a political unknown. D. K. Onwenu, another member and the local NCNC president, was technically also of Owerri Province (Aro-Ndizuogu, Orlu Division), but his Aro identity placed him, for purposes of communal arithmetic, in a somewhat special category. Thus, from the standpoint of the Owerris, the Caretaker Council's composition only perpetuated their subordination vis-à-vis the Onitshans. More seriously, rumors were rampant that the Caretaker Council had discriminated against a member of the council's administrative staff because of his Owerri origins, and that two Owerri candidates for the position of town clerk had been passed over in favor of an Onitshan. The accuracy of these charges is unimportant: Port Harcourt's citizenry tended to view most matters of patronage and job placement through a communal prism, with the consequence that allegations of tribalism and nepotism were always effective weapons in the hands of the politically ambitious. What is important is that these charges became the basis in 1955 for the first concerted effort by Owerri politicians to mobilize political support on the basis of a geo-ethnic appeal to provincial pride.

The organizational vehicle of the new Owerri movement was a newly established Owerri Provincial Union. The actual initiative for the formation of the O.P.U. appears to have come from a group of Owerri women who, in the words of an early male participant, "invited the men to wake up and help organize." Plans were quickly mapped for an Owerri take-over of Port Harcourt's key political positions, beginning with the local branch of the NCNC:

> It was in this Union that we decided Owerri people, not being very dynamic in everything, should participate in everything in town . . . with a view of capturing the NCNC Divisional Executive. A committee was set up . . . asked to undertake and make sure that Owerri captured the major offices in the Executive.
>
> The Owerri people are complacent . . . [they] don't attach a great importance to anything. The Onitsha people attach great importance to everything; it happened they were more interested in attending meetings, and so on. The Owerri people needed to be awakened. . . . Even the people who were unable to pay their dues, we dig into our pockets so they pay their dues and can become financial members of the party.[3]

It should be noted that the Owerris were not alone in their opposition to the Caretaker Council. Several months earlier, both Onitsha and Owerri members of the politically hungry NCNC Executive had met with the Provincial Resident to urge dissolution of the Caretaker Council and had petitioned the minister of internal affairs for new elections. Still other politicians, notably the Onitsha members of the dissolved Town Council of 1951–1954 who had been accused of corruption by the Floyer Commission of Enquiry and were anxious to make a political comeback, had personal reasons for wanting a restoration of elected local government.

At last, the Eastern Nigerian government agreed not only to the dissolution of the Caretaker Council and the holding of new elections, but also to the raising of the township's administrative status to that of a municipality. Port Harcourt was now to have a salaried mayor, chosen from among and by the newly elected councillors, and the council was to have more discretionary authority with respect to staff appointments and the award of contracts than that permitted councils of lesser status. In short, the stakes of local political competition were to be significantly raised.

Owerris and the Municipal Council

With the Municipal Council elections of December 15, 1955, the Owerri political ascendancy was confirmed. Forty-three candidates vied for the twenty-two council seats and, as table 14 indicates, the election outcome signaled the beginning of a sharp and continuing increase in the percentage of council seats occupied by Ibos from Owerri Province and an equally precipitous decline in relative Onitsha strength. Thus, the percentage of total Owerri seats climbed from 46.8 percent and 35.3 percent in 1949 and 1952 to 56.5 percent, 62.0 percent, and 65.2 percent in the three council terms following the caretaker period. Simultaneously, relative Onitsha strength declined from 40.0 percent and 35.3 percent of total council membership in 1949 and 1952 to 13.0 percent, 9.5 percent, and 19.6 percent in the post-Caretaker Councils.

Immediately following the council election, the NCNC Executive Committee designated as the party's nominees for mayor and deputy mayor, respectively, Richard O. Nzimiro, a prominent Oguta-Owerri businessman who was supported by the Owerri Provincial Union, and A. E. Alagoa, a prestigious barrister who was the son of an important Ijaw paramount chief and an Ibo woman from Okigwi Division (Owerri Province), and when the newly elected Municipal Council convened, Nzimiro and Alagoa were duly elected to their designated posts. At the time of their appointments, neither man was a member of the NCNC Executive Committee or active in party affairs, but they both were held in great personal esteem by the community at large, and party leaders were anxious to restore public confidence in the Municipal Council.[4]

148

Owerris and the NCNC *Executive*

The post-1955 pattern of steadily increasing Owerri representation within the Municipal Council was paralleled within the
NCNC divisional Executive. In 1956, the new Executive Committee
elections were held, and local NCNC President D. K. Onwenu
was replaced by W. K. Anufuro, the Owerri vice-principal of a
Catholic secondary school who had come to political prominence
through his role in the Owerri-led campaign for the dissolution of
the Caretaker Council. At the same time, the ratio of Owerris to
Onitshans within the Executive rose sharply from 46.7/26.7 in
1951 to 62.5/12.5 in 1956 (table 15).[5] In succeeding years, the
Onitshan representation on the Executive Committee increased
somewhat (as it did in the 1961 council), but not sufficiently to
offset the extreme Owerri advantage. It would appear significant
that after 1955 few Onitsha men were successful in obtaining
NCNC nomination for public office. Onitsha politicians continued
to occupy seats on the Municipal Council, but none represented
Port Harcourt in the Eastern Nigerian House of Assembly or the
federal House of Reresentatives, or held the important posts of
mayor, deputy mayor or NCNC president.

Ironically, the architect of Onwenu's defeat and Anufuro's
victory within the local NCNC Executive was from Onitsha Division: Youth Association President J. U. Mbonu. During the late
1950s, control of the Executive rested largely in the hands of this
Nnewi-born sales manager and contractor. An excellent organizer
and one of Port Harcourt's more eloquent nationalists, Mbonu had
placed little reliance upon Onitsha support, and his personal following spanned the city's communal divisions. On the one hand,
Mbonu recognized that the success of an Onitsha politician in
Port Harcourt depended upon his ability to draw support from the
more numerous Owerris, and that he could scarcely appeal to an
Owerri man on the basis of Onitsha self-interest. On the other,
Mbonu was schooled in the antitribal, one-Nigeria rhetoric of the
postwar Zikist movement, and many of his coleaders within the
Youth Association were themselves former Zikists. As Sklar has
observed, most Youth Association leaders "believed strongly in
the radical principle of a unitary state, and they were bitterly dis-

TABLE 14

Town Council Profiles, 1949–1965
(all figures in percentages)[b]

	1949 Council (N = 15)[a]	1952 Council (N = 17)	1954 Caretaker Council (N = 5)	1955 Council (N = 23)	1958 Council (N = 42)[c]	1961 Council (N = 46)
Ethnic Group:						
Ibo	86.7	82.4	80.0	82.6	88.1	97.8
Ijaw	6.7	11.8	20.0	13.0	7.1	2.2
Efik	—	—	—	—	2.4	—
Yoruba	6.7	5.9	—	4.3	—	—
Nupe	—	—	—	4.3	2.4	—
Area of Origin:						
Owerri Province	46.8	35.3	40.0	56.5	62.0	65.2
Owerri Division	(26.7)	(17.6)	(—)	(17.4)	(14.3)	(19.6)
Orlu Division	(—)	(11.8)	(20.0)	(13.0)	(14.3)	(17.4)
Okigwi Division	(6.7)	(5.9)	(—)	(8.7)	(14.3)	(13.0)
Bende Division	(6.7)	(—)	(20.0)	(17.4)	(14.3)	(15.2)
Aba Division	(6.7)	(—)	(—)	(—)	(4.8)	(—)
Onitsha Province	40.0	35.3	40.0	13.0	9.5	19.6
Onitsha Division	(26.7)	(23.5)	(40.0)	(8.7)	(7.1)	(15.2)
Awka Division	(13.3)	(11.8)	(—)	(4.3)	(—)	(2.2)
Udi Division	(—)	(—)	(—)	(—)	(—)	(2.2)
Rivers Province	6.7	11.8	20.0	21.7	21.5	13.1
Port Harcourt Division	(—)	(—)	(—)	(8.7)	(14.3)	(10.9)
Degema Division	(6.7)	(11.8)	(20.0)	(8.7)	(4.8)	(2.2)
Brass Division	(—)	(—)	(—)	(4.3)	(2.4)	(—)
Calabar Province	—	—	—	—	2.4	—
Mid-Western Region	—	11.8	—	4.3	2.4	2.2
Other	6.7	5.9	—	4.3	2.4	—

	1	2	3	4	5	6
Occupation:						
Administrators and clerical functionaries	6.7	11.8	—	4.3	16.7	13.1
Firm Manager	(—)	(5.9)	(—)	(4.3)	(2.4)	(2.2)
Agent of Cultural Association	(6.7)	(—)	(—)	(—)	(—)	(—)
Clerk	(—)	(5.9)	(—)	(—)	(14.3)	(10.9)
Learned arts and skills	20.0	29.4	40.0	13.0	9.6	6.5
Professional	(13.3)	(23.5)	(20.0)	(4.3)	(2.4)	(—)
Educator	(—)	(—)	(20.0)	(8.7)	(4.8)	(6.5)
Journalist	(6.7)	(5.9)	(—)	(—)	(2.4)	(—)
Private Enterprise	66.7	58.8	60.0	73.8	64.3	65.3
Businessman or big trader	(20.0)	(29.4)	(20.0)	(30.4)	(21.4)	(19.6)
Petty trader or petty contractor	(46.7)	(29.4)	(40.0)	(39.1)	(42.9)	(45.7)
Farmer	(—)	(—)	(—)	(4.3)	(—)	(—)
Artisans	6.7	—	—	8.7	4.8	10.9
Other	—	—	—	—	4.8	4.3
Religion:						
Protestant	80.0	82.4	100.0	73.9	69.0	58.7
Catholic	20.0	17.6	—	13.0	23.8	37.0
National Church	—	—	—	8.7	4.8	4.3
Moslem	—	—	—	4.3	2.4	—
Education:						
Less than elementary (Standard VI) certificate	26.7	17.7	20.0	34.7	23.8	28.2
Standard VI certificate	46.7	58.8	40.0	30.4	40.5	41.3
Postelementary education	26.6	23.5	40.0	34.8	35.7	28.2

a Tabulations include appointed African councillors and councillors elected at special by-elections, but exclude Europeans who were appointed to the 1949 council.

b Percentages do not always total 100 because of rounding.

c The 1958 Council is inclusive of those persons elected for one-year terms in 1960, following the merger of Mile 2 Diobu with the municipality.

Sources: Personal interviews.

TABLE 15

NCNC Executive Profiles, 1951–1964[a]
(all figures in percentages)[b]

Attribute	Elected 1951 (N = 30)	Elected June 1956 (N = 40)	Elected Sept. 1957 (N = 37)	Elected March 1959 (N = 44)	Elected Feb. 1962 (N = 90)
Ethnic Group:					
Ibo	80.0	92.5	97.3	93.2	95.8
Ijaw	10.0	2.5	—	2.3	2.1
Yoruba	3.3	—	—	—	—
Itsekiri	3.3	2.5	—	2.3	1.0
Nupe	—	2.5	2.7	2.3	—
Edo	—	2.5	—	—	1.0
Togoland	3.3	—	—	—	—
Areas of Origin:					
Owerri Province	46.7	62.5	64.8	63.4	63.6
Owerri Division[c]	(23.3)	(25.0)	(29.7)	(27.3)	(31.3)
Orlu Division	(6.7)	(17.5)	(13.5)	(11.4)	(12.5)
Okigwi Division	(3.3)	(5.0)	(2.7)	(2.3)	(6.3)
Bende Division	(13.3)	(12.5)	(16.2)	(20.1)	(13.5)
Aba Division	(—)	(2.5)	(2.7)	(2.3)	(—)
Onitsha Province	26.7	12.5	16.2	16.0	21.9
Onitsha Division	(20.0)	(10.0)	(13.5)	(11.4)	(16.7)
Awka Division	(6.7)	(—)	(—)	(2.3)	(4.2)
Udi Division	(—)	(2.5)	(2.7)	(2.3)	(1.0)
Rivers Province	13.3	10.0	5.4	11.4	10.4
Port Harcourt Division	(—)	(5.0)	(2.7)	(6.8)	(8.3)
Ahoada Division	(3.3)	(2.5)	(2.7)	(2.3)	(—)
Degema Division	(10.0)	(2.5)	(—)	(—)	(2.1)
Brass Division	(—)	(—)	(—)	(2.3)	(—)

	13.3	7.5	13.5	9.1	4.2
Other	13.3	7.5	13.5	9.1	4.2
Not Ascertained	—	7.5	—	—	—
Occupation:					
Administrators and clerical functionaries	36.7	15.0	21.6	18.2	10.4
Firm manager	(6.7)	(2.5)	(5.4)	(6.8)	(1.0)
Agent of Cultural Association	(3.3)	(—)	(—)	(—)	(—)
Clerk	(26.7)	(12.5)	(16.2)	(11.4)	(9.4)
Learned arts and skills	20.0	7.5	10.8	9.1	3.1
Professional	(6.7)	(2.5)	(2.7)	(2.3)	(1.0)
Educator	(10.0)	(5.0)	(8.1)	(6.8)	(—)
Journalist	(3.3)	(—)	(—)	(—)	(—)
Private enterprise	40.0	65.0	56.7	68.1	75.1
Businessman or big trader	(6.7)	(27.5)	(13.5)	(38.6)	(31.3)
Petty trader or petty contractor	(33.3)	(37.5)	(43.2)	(29.5)	(43.8)
Artisans	3.3	2.5	8.1	2.3	5.2
Other	—	2.5	2.7	2.3	6.3
Not Ascertained	—	7.5	—	—	—
Religion:					
Protestant	—	47.5	48.6	56.8	61.5
Catholic	—	22.5	35.4	25.0	30.2
National Church	—	15.0	13.5	15.9	6.3
Moslem	—	2.5	2.7	2.3	—
Animist	—	—	—	—	1.0
Not Ascertained	100.0	12.5	—	—	1.0
Education:					
Less than elementary (Standard VI Certificate)	—	22.5	21.6	11.4	36.1
Standard VI certificate	—	30.0	40.5	36.4	42.6
Postelementary education	—	30.0	35.4	38.6	21.3
Not ascertained	100.0	17.5	2.7	13.6	—

TABLE 15—*continued*

[a] The D. K. Onwenu Executive, which served from November 1952 to June 1956, is excluded from this table because of insufficient data. The membership of the 1951 Ajibade Executive was determined on the basis of personal interviews with participants, and coverage may be incomplete. Minutes of the NCNC Executive Committee and NCNC Youth Association records contained the membership lists of the later Executive Committees. Social background data were drawn from interviews with leading members of each committee. Tabulations for the Executive Committee elected September 1957 exclude the party patrons. This omission explains the apparent decline in the proportion of entrepreneurs serving on the committee during this period.

[b] Percentages do not always total 100 because of rounding.

[c] In 1959 and 1962, the largest part of Owerri Divisional representation was drawn from the single community of Mbaise. Mbaises comprised 18.2% and 18.8% of the 1959 and 1962 Executives, respectively.

appointed when the party leadership agreed to the 'regionalist' constitutional departure of 1954." [6] For these men, political appeals to divisional and provincial loyalties were no different from appeals to linguistic group and region: both were viewed as destructive of Nigerian unity.

But Mbonu's position of leadership within the NCNC Executive did not go unchallenged, and as the Owerri strength within the Executive Committee increased, his position became increasingly tenuous. Finally, in 1959, Mbonu was ousted from the Executive. The Onitsha decline and Owerri ascendancy were complete.[7]

The Dualism of Political Life

This discussion of the Owerri ascendancy would be incomplete without mention of those few non-Owerri personalities who somehow survived the Owerri onslaught. In some cases, considerations of ethnic arithmetic and national party image were responsible. Thus, to counter the image of the NCNC as a "southern" party, Mallam Abu, a Nupe member of the Port Harcourt branch of the Northern Elements Progressive Union (NEPU), was given a seat on both the NCNC Executive and the Municipal Council during the 1950s. Similar calculations were involved in the support given by Eastern Nigerian party leaders to Mid-Westerner John Umolu and to the later assembly candidacy of Diobu indigene Emmanuel Aguma.

There were also a few minority figures who prevailed simply by virtue of their personalities and abilities. Perhaps the most notable example was an Ijaw businessman, Municipal Councillor A. D. W. Jumbo, who had access to the upper echelons of both party and government. A personal friend and long-time political associate of Premier Dr. Michael Okpara and of the chairman of the party's Eastern Working Committee, Jumbo in 1964 was serving simultaneously as deputy chairman of the Eastern Nigerian Development Corporation, member of the board of directors of the African Continental Bank, member of the National Executive Committee of the NCNC, and regional chairman of the reorganized Zikist movement. Locally, he was one of the most popular and influential members of the Municipal Council. He had previously served one year as deputy mayor and, in 1964, was serving as chairman of the council's Education, Library, and Welfare Committee. Significantly, however, despite his personal popularity, his participation in high-level party deliberations, and his prominence within the Municipal Council, Jumbo was repeatedly denied the local party's nomination for office as mayor. In this respect, Jumbo was the exception that proved the rule of the communalization of Port Harcourt's party machinery.

The apparent incongruity between Jumbo's prominence within the walls of the council chamber, on the one hand, and his political impotence within the local party executive, on the other, sheds light on a significant dualism inherent in Port Harcourt political life. For communalism in Port Harcourt impinged only upon issues of political *recruitment and patronage*—issues upon which the prestige and recognition of immigrant groups depended —and did not affect routine council deliberations on such matters as finance, road and market maintenance, school construction, and the like. These latter subjects did not involve the communal interests of Port Harcourt's citizens. On these and related matters, councillors and party members either divided themselves according to their *residential* interests (as when amenities, such as paved roads and electric lighting, were to be allocated among Port Harcourt's communally heterogeneous neighborhoods) or followed the direction of the council's informal leaders. Within the council, at least when the distribution of contracts and jobs was not at issue, an individual's soundness of judgment, reputation for personal integrity, and oratorical skills were the principal requisites of political leadership, and his communal origins were irrelevant. Thus, Jumbo could be immensely influential in local affairs and still not be able to translate this influence into the kind of communal backing required in contests for higher office. There was, then, no contradiction between Jumbo's commanding position within the council, a body that did not usually involve itself with matters affecting the communal interests of its membership, and his failure to capture his party's nomination as mayor.

In terms of urban development, Port Harcourt's political dualism cut two ways. From one perspective, the crisscrossing of residential and communal interests limited the range of political issues that activated communal identities and hence communal conflict. As the experience of countless other urban centers suggests, where residential interests coincide with communal interests, almost any public decision becomes the occasion for communal confrontation. This was not the case in Port Harcourt. The other side of the "communal coin," however, is that the *absence* of communally defined and segregated residential areas in Port Harcourt limited the extent to which residentially defined electoral wards developed meaningful political identities. A significant neighborhood stimulus to community development was therefore lacking.[8]

GEO-ETHNICITY AND POLITICAL RECRUITMENT

The Owerri ascendancy in Port Harcourt reflected the development and manipulation of a new set of geo-ethnic identities. The new identities, as we have seen, bore little relationship to the traditional order; they were, rather, a response to the social and political exigencies of urban life. Ibos in Port Harcourt typically identified themselves to new acquaintances by reference neither to their nationality nor to their traditional community of origin, but to the administrative division and province in which that community was located. Their Ibo nationality was, from the standpoint of the local community, seldom a useful reference point, for the vast majority of the urban population was Ibo-speaking; on the other hand, traditional communities of origin were typically so small as to have little meaning for strangers. It was only at the intermediate levels of nontraditional social grouping—clan court area, division, and province—that Ibos were sufficiently numerous in Port Harcourt to establish a viable communal identity and political base. We want now, through the medium of two case studies of electoral competition, to explore more fully the dynamics and political significance of geo-ethnic conflict in Port Harcourt.

Geo-ethnicity I: The Federal Election of 1964–1965

In July 1964, Port Harcourt's politicians began preparations for the then-pending federal elections. No date for the elections had yet been announced, but numerous dates in September and October were rumored. (The elections were finally scheduled for December, then cancelled in the East when the federal prime minister refused to postpone the elections despite reported widespread campaign irregularities in Northern and Western Nigeria, and finally held in Eastern Nigeria on March 18, 1965.)[9] Five persons commenced active campaigns for the NCNC nominations; two others announced their candidacies late and did not have any impact on the final outcome (table 16). The strategic problems and responses of the major candidates varied; here we attempt to highlight only a few of the more distinctive elements of their respective campaigns.

TABLE 16

CANDIDATES FOR THE PORT HARCOURT NCNC NOMINATION IN
THE 1964 FEDERAL ELECTIONS

1. *Miss Margaret Aguta:* Mbieri, Owerri Division; U.K.; trained barrister; Protestant.
2. *Mr. V. C. I. Anene:* Oba, Onitsha Division; businessman with a British diploma in business administration; former president, Zikist National Vanguard (Port Harcourt Branch); secretary, Ibo State Union; *Guardian* columnist; NCNC Executive member; Protestant.
3. *Mr. Samuel Mbakwe:* Obowo, Okigwi Division; U.K.; trained barrister; NCNC Executive member and legal advisor; member, NCNC Eastern Working Committee; Board member, Nigerian Broadcasting Corporation; Protestant.
4. *Mr. J. U. Mbonu:* Nnewi, Onitsha Division; contractor; former municipal councillor; former president of Port Harcourt NCNC Youth Association and newly elected president of the Port Harcourt Zikist movement; NCNC Executive member; member, NCNC Eastern Working Committee and NCNC National Executive Committee; former board member, Nigerian Broadcasting Corporation; Catholic.
5. *Mr. G. C. Nonyelu:* Awka Division; barrister and former federal director of public prosecutions; former president, Town Council; Protestant.
6. *Mr. C. C. Obienu:* Nnewi, Onitsha Division; businessman (palm produce licensed buying agent); NCNC patron and Executive member; Protestant.
7. *Hon. D. D. Okay:* Mbaise, Owerri Division; contractor and former market trader; incumbent member, federal House of Representatives; former municipal councillor; NCNC Executive officer; National Church.

It was clear from the outset that the man to beat was the incumbent member of the federal Parliament, Hon. D. D. Okay, and the campaigns of each of the other candidates were accordingly directed to mobilizing opposition to Okay's renomination. It was D. D. Okay, a market trader and former municipal councillor, who had led the move, in 1959, to oust Onitshan J. U. Mbonu from his position in the NCNC Executive. Okay hailed from Mbaise, that economically impoverished section of Owerri Division which, since 1954, had aspired to independent divisional status. Long active in party affairs, Okay had been selected by the local Executive to stand election in 1957 to the Eastern House of Assembly. But when the party's National Executive Committee insisted that all incumbents be renominated, Okay relented, agreeing to step down for the incumbent (albeit highly unpopular) V. K. Onyeri.[10] However, Okay was shortly compensated for his sacrifice when, a short time after the regional elections, Port Harcourt's member in the federal House of Representatives was killed in an automobile accident and Okay was selected as the party's nominee in an easily won by-election. Then, in 1959, Okay was easily reelected to his seat in the federal Parliament.

As the 1964 elections approached, incumbent Okay faced two principal strategic problems in his bid for reelection. First, the party's Central Working Committee decided in August to expand the size of the local nominating committees throughout the Region so as to reduce the traditional temptation of candidates to attempt to buy their nominations. The only issues unresolved by mid-August (and not settled finally until nomination eve in mid-October) were the size and mode of composition of the selection committees. These factors were subjects of vital concern not only to D. D. Okay, of course, but to all the candidates: since the incumbent was known to control a majority on the local NCNC Executive Committee, it followed that any expansion of that committee or a decision to substitute an entirely different electoral body, would work to the advantage of Okay's opposition. Several candidates, consequently, engaged in private lobbying sessions with members of the party's Central Working Committee. The C.W.C. directed, finally, that the selection committees in urban areas be comprised of party members elected directly from the constituency's various wards. Though an apparent defeat for Okay, the additional requirement that only dues-paying party members in good standing might participate in the selection process vitiated most of the apparent advantage Okay's opposition had obtained. The attempt by other candidates to hurriedly register and pay the dues of their party supporters within each ward simply could not match Okay's comparable five-year organizational effort.[11]

Okay's second principal problem concerned opposition to his candidacy from within his own Mbaise Federal Union. It was considered a local political truism that "You can never win election in Port Harcourt without your clan union support—because Port Harcourt is an immigrant society. . . . Everyone owes his own loyalty to his own group—and it will be very difficult to choose the most suitable candidate for anything. Rather, it is the man who has the best organization among his own people." [12] In the past, D. D. Okay had heeded this truism well, but his support within the Mbaise community had slipped noticeably in recent years. Some Mbaises voiced their concerns openly, claiming that Okay had not shown sufficient gratitude for their earlier efforts on his behalf and was little concerned with the welfare of his own people. As one Mbaise leader put it, "He is a Port Harcourt man. . . . He belongs to no cultural organizations; he simply registers his name." Another added, "The only reason for the annoyance is D. D. Okay's ignoring Mbaise, and his non-attendance at meetings."

Feeling against Okay ran so deeply in some Mbaise circles that one executive member of the Mbaise Federal Union, who hailed from the same section of the same clan within Mbaise as Okay, had contemplated standing against his townsman in the federal elections. He was dissuaded from doing so only by the persistent entreaties of other Mbaises and by the persuasion of the mayor, Francis Ihekwoaba (Nkwerre, Orlu Division, Owerri Province), who was politically indebted to Okay for supporting his reelection as mayor in 1963.

In late August, an emergency meeting of the executive committee of the Mbaise Federal Union was convened by Chief F. U. Anyanwu, one of Port Harcourt's wealthiest Nigerian businessmen and a patron both of the NCNC and the Mbaise Federal Union, for the purpose of rallying Mbaise support behind Okay's candidacy.[13] In recognition of the personal feeling against Okay, the appeal of Chief Anyanwu of other Mbaise leaders was phrased in terms of Mbaise prestige and the battle that Onitsha elements were waging against the Mbaise members of the federal Parliament. That the appeal was successful was indicated by the subsequent comment of one of Okay's Mbaise critics: "If it is a case of Nnewi [in Onitsha Division] saying, 'It is our right [to send a man to the Federal Parliament],' then I will say, 'No!' Mbaise has had this right, and we are not going to relinquish this." Port Harcourt's Mbaise immigrants closed ranks after this meeting and actively supported D. D. Okay's candidacy.

The three Onitsha candidates for the nomination—former

Youth Association leader J. U. Mbonu, Ibo State Union Secretary
V. C. I. Anene, and prosperous businessman and party patron
C. C. Obienu (a Nnewi townsman of Mbonu's)—shared similar
strategic problems: first, they were the members of a geo-ethnic
minority; second, they faced the prospect of a split Onitsha vote;
third, with the possible exception of Mbonu, they lacked a viable
organizational base.

The first move was made by Obienu, who invited both Mbonu
and Anene to join him in meeting with over twenty prominent
Onitshans resident in Port Harcourt.[14] Two such sessions were
held, but they failed in their object of persuading two of the
Onitsha candidates to step down in favor of a third, and Mbonu,
Anene, and Obienu proceeded with their individual campaigns.
However, the day before the Nominations Committee was to
meet, V. C. I. Anene suddenly withdrew from the contest in favor
of J. U. Mbonu. Obienu, whose personal following was thought to
be limited in any event, stayed in the race.

To counter the liabilities of Onitsha minority status and a divided Onitsha community, all three candidates adopted an explicitly supratribal approach, couching at least the public aspects of
their campaigns in the rhetoric of "good government." One candidate attempted to highlight his superior educational qualifications
by giving a series of public lectures (published in the local newspapers) on "the parliamentary form of democracy." Another candidate organized two separate campaign committees, one composed exclusively of Onitsha men and the other exclusively of non-
Onitsha men. The candidates arranged meetings with the leaders
of the indigenous Diobu community to solicit their support, and
ward agents of the candidates attempted to register new party
members irrespective of their geo-ethnic origin. Finally, when the
Zikist movement president fell ill, J. U. Mbonu reassumed the
chairmanship of the youth wing he once headed and attempted
to mobilize its largely non-Onitsha membership behind his candidacy.

The fifth principal candidate, Okigwi-born barrister S. O.
Mbakwe, was confronted by the dual problems of the recency of
his entry into Port Harcourt politics and the loyalty of a large
number of NCNC party workers from Owerri Province to either
D. D. Okay or Okay-supporter, Orlu-born Mayor Francis Ihek-

161

woaba. The people of Okigwi and Orlu share many cultural and linguistic characteristics and, until 1948, were administered as a single division. In Port Harcourt, consequently, Okigwi and Orlu immigrants comprised a fairly cohesive geo-ethnic community, as indicated by the often-heard comment, "An Orlu man thinks of himself as the same as an Okigwi man." Yet, in 1964, that cohesiveness was undermined by the political indebtedness of Francis Ihekwoaba to D. D. Okay for the latter's assistance when the mayor was standing for reelection in 1963. In that year, Ihekwoaba faced challenges to his position from the Bende-born deputy mayor, G. C. N. Akomas, and the popular Ijaw councillor, A. D. W. Jumbo. The Orlu Divisional Union rallied to Ihekwoaba's defense by delegating representatives, including both Orlu elders and politicians, to meet with representatives of the Bende Divisional Union to persuade Chief Akomas to withdraw from the contest. Before this meeting had reached a conclusion, D. D. Okay returned from a trip to Enugu with a memorandum, under the letterhead of the premier's office, implying the premier and NCNC President Michael Okpara wanted Ihekwoaba and Akomas returned to the posts they currently held. The premier's office subsequently disclaimed any knowledge of the endorsement, but not before the local Executive had voted to instruct the NCNC municipal councillors to reelect Ihekwoaba and Akomas as mayor and deputy mayor, respectively.[15]

Ihekwoaba's debt to D. D. Okay had now come due—and Samuel Mbakwe's candidacy was affected accordingly. Okigwi and Orlu people were not that numerous in the main township to begin with, and Mbakwe could ill afford significant defections from his "home base." Thus, it was a serious blow to his campaign when Ihekwoaba declared for Okay and carried a large part of the Orlu vote that might otherwise have gone to Mbakwe. Mbakwe did have the active campaign assistance of the leaders of Port Harcourt's Okigwi and Orlu Youths' Association and the support of party members of other geo-ethnic groups. The lack of secure communal backing, however, fatally weakened his political position.

The final vote of the Selection Committee toward the end of October surprised few: D. D. Okay received forty-seven of the ninety-two valid ballots; Mbonu was second with twenty, Mbakwe polled nineteen, and Obienu had six; neither barrister Margaret Aguta nor barrister G. C. Nonyelu, the late entries, received a vote. Okay had lacked the financial resources and educational qualifications of several of the candidates; was opposed by the two local newspapers; and, as a back-bencher, controlled little governmental patronage. But Okay was an astute politician who recognized the fragility and impermanence of political alignments in Ibo-speaking Port Harcourt and who had made the task of political organization a full-time concern. The assistance he had provided in finding jobs and contracts for some, or in furthering the political ambitions of others, yielded a substantial reserve of political capital he could draw upon when needed. In point is the remark of a Diobu leader and Okay supporter that "Okay keeps in touch with the people all the time, even comes to some village events—whereas the other contenders are only now trying to come down to the level of the people because they want something." Finally, not to be forgotten was the fact of Okay's membership in an exceptionally well organized, well financed, and politically cohesive geo-ethnic community. Opposition estimates of Mbaise strength in the Selection Committee ranged between thirty and forty; though these may have been an exaggeration, Mbaise strength was clearly substantial and a major factor in Okay's decisive victory.

The outcome of the delayed federal elections, held finally on March 19, 1965, was never in doubt. The only challenges to D. D. Okay's reelection came from an Ibo trade union leader standing on the platform of a party allied with the Northern People's Congress and from a Yoruba trade unionist standing as a Socialist Workers and Farmers party candidate.[16] Okay's victory was overwhelming, with eighty percent of the ballots cast going to the NCNC candidate. Significantly, however, the vote turnout was exceptionally light even by Port Harcourt standards. Perhaps because of the certainty of the outcome, perhaps because of the NCNC electorate's general lack of warmth for the NCNC candidate, only 6,019 Port Harcourt voters, representing approximately fifteen percent of the eligible electorate, chose to participate in the election of March 19.[17]

Geo-ethnicity II: Electoral Politics in Mile 2 Diobu

Electoral politics in the Mile 2 Diobu of the 1960s can only be understood in terms of the area's historical pattern of stranger settlement and long-standing administrative isolation. Mile 2 Diobu, originally part of the Port Harcourt land acquisition, was returned to the Diobu indigenes in 1928. Not long thereafter, Ibo immigrants, primarily from the Owerri hinterland, began to settle in Mile 2 and, after World War II, to buy and sell extensive parcels of Diobu land and to erect numerous slum tenements to accommodate the steady inpouring of new urban dwellers. Administrative shortsightedness placed this sector of exploding population outside the jurisdiction of the Port Harcourt Township. Mile 2 Diobu was administered from the Ahoada District Office, over forty-seven miles away, and (until 1960) the government's presence in Mile 2 was maintained by little more than the occasional visits of the district officer.[18]

The earliest of the stranger-landlords in Mile 2 Diobu were from the culturally related and, until 1948, administratively united Orlu and Okigwi Divisions of Owerri Province. A few of these Orlu and Okigwi immigrants rapidly acquired immense personal fortunes through their speculative land activity and considerable political influence within their local domain. In recognition of their personal prominence and prestige in the area, they were appointed by the Ahoada District Office to serve as Mile 2 Diobu's "tax collectors," and their political influence was thereby vastly extended. Also contributing to their mystique and political control was the formation of a landowner-controlled "Cabinet," which, in the absence of other institutionalized authority, came to operate as a de facto local government for the stranger population of Mile 2 Diobu.[19] The extent of the Cabinet's influence is suggested by this partially paraphrased comment of a Mile 2 Diobu informant:

> [The Cabinet consisted of the first strangers to the area. If you came in subsequently, and] wanted to come and live there, you had to get their permission. If you had the intention of getting a property, you must tell them. They would tell you to bring wine or money or goats—or to perform certain rites—for them to approve it. If one purchased land from the natives

164

without their permission, they would go and negotiate with the natives for the same piece of land and the natives would return the money [to the previous buyers]. . . . They were the immediate government. They collected the taxes. . . . They also came together for the improvement of the area. . . . When the D. O. came here, they were the people he would meet.

But as a formal institution the Cabinet was short-lived. In 1952, a number of Mile 2 Diobu's younger men, including the junior townsmen and relations of the Orlu and Okigwi landlords and also members of the expanding immigrant communities from Owerri and Bende Divisions organized a Stranger Elements Association in an attempt to check the power of the Cabinet. In the words of one of the association's founders,

> When we saw they [the Cabinet members] were creating a lot of atrocities, we formed a force to tackle the association. We formed, in 1952, the Stranger Elements Association . . . a platform to tell them what they were doing was bad. Because if you told them by yourself you would be jailed.
>
> We tried very much to stop some of the bad things these people were doing, to educate [the residents of Diobu] properly, to make them know their civil rights. And when the D. O. was · scheduled to visit Mile 2, we would all be there to meet with him. He would send notice to the Cabinet informing them he was coming to talk to members of Mile 2 Diobu. He would come very often—twice a month—and we would discuss the matters he would present.
>
> [At the meeting, members of the Stranger Elements Association would provide chairs for the Cabinet members], because, after all, we are junior to them. [But] after they felt our weight, they came and joined our side so we would not molest them.

The Stranger Elements Association provided the nucleus of the Mile 2 Diobu branch of the NCNC, formally inaugurated in 1953 by G. I. Elugwaornu, an Mbaise immigrant who at the time was a trader and member of the Port Harcourt NCNC Executive. Between 1953 and 1957, the Elugwaornu-led Mile 2 Diobu NCNC embraced the representatives of most of Mile 2 Diobu's immigrant groups and dominated the area's political life. Officials of the party acted as the principal intermediaries between the colonial government and the local population, and controlled elections to the Mile 2 Diobu Local Council. But self-government had yet to come to Mile 2 Diobu. The Mile 2 Diobu Local Council was a body without revenue, staff, or power. Representatives of the Mile 2 Council did sit on the superordinate bodies of Eastern Nigeria's three-tiered system—the Ikwerre Rural District Council and the Ahoada County Council—but in these latter agencies they were outnumbered by the indigenous Ikwerre people to whom the urban problems of Mile 2 Diobu were of little interest.[20]

Perhaps because the stakes of political competition were relatively unimportant, the first years of NCNC domination of Mile 2 Diobu political life were relatively quiescent. The only subject that produced periodic flurries of political activity was the persistent but always unavailing effort of the colonial authorities in Ahoada and Port Harcourt to control the activities of Mile 2's real estate speculators and to introduce some semblance of order into Mile 2 Diobu development.[21] But the regional election of 1957 destroyed Mile 2 Diobu's political stability by introducing the kind of geo-ethnic conflict that had long characterized the political life of the main township. However, as a 1964 comparison of Mile 1 and 2 Diobu municipal councillors and NCNC executive members with their main township counterparts indicates (table 17), the Diobu area of stranger settlement had a relatively higher concentration of Owerri immigrants. Consequently, the most salient line of political cleavage was drawn *within* Owerri Province rather than between Onitsha and Owerri Provinces as in the main township. More specifically, Mile 2 political life after 1957 focused upon the cleavage between the Orlu-Okigwi landowners and their relations, on the one side, and the more recently arrived settlers from other sections of Owerri Province (most notably, Bende Division and the Mbaise section of Owerri Division), on the other.[22]

The struggle between these geo-ethnically dissimilar groups was actually precipitated by a personal rivalry between two men who were of the same division (Okigwi) and town (Okwelle): Chief J. I. Emenike and Chief J. R. Echue. Both were former policemen, members of the Cabinet, and among Mile 2 Diobu's wealthiest inhabitants. In 1957, they, together with the local NCNC president, G. I. Elugwaornu, decided to contest with the Ikwerre natives for the NCNC nomination in the Ahoada con-

TABLE 17

MUNICIPAL COUNCILLORS AND NCNC EXECUTIVE MEMBERS,
BY URBAN RESIDENCE AND AREA OF ORIGIN (1961–1964)[a]
(all figures in percentages)[b]

Area of origin	Municipal councillors		NCNC *Executive members*	
	Main township	*Miles 1–2 Diobu*	*Main township*	*Miles 1–2 Diobu*
Owerri Province	66.8	78.2	63.8	75.6
Owerri Division	(16.7)	(26.1)	(23.4)	(46.3)
Orlu Division	(16.7)	(21.7)	(12.8)	(14.6)
Okigwi Division	(5.6)	(21.7)	(8.5)	(4.9)
Bende Division	(27.8)	(8.7)	(19.1)	(9.8)
Onitsha Province	27.8	17.3	25.6	22.0
Onitsha Division	(22.2)	(13.0)	(21.3)	(14.7)
Awka Division	(5.6)	(—)	(4.3)	(4.9)
Udi Division	(—)	(4.3)	(—)	(2.4)
Rivers Province	5.6	—	4.3	—
Degema Division	(5.6)	(—)	(4.3)	(—)
Mid-Western Nigeria	—	4.3	6.4	2.4
	100.2	99.8	100.1	100.0
	(N = 18)	(N = 23)	(N = 47)	(N = 41)

[a] Tabulations include those municipal councillors who served between 1961 and 1965 and those NCNC Executive members elected in February 1962. Tabulations do not include the five councillors and eight Executive members who were of Port Harcourt's indigenous Diobu community.

[b] Percentages do not always total 100 because of rounding.

SOURCES: Minutes of the NCNC Executive Committee and personal interviews.

stituency. But the strangers could not agree on a candidate, and the official NCNC nomination went to the indigenous Ikwerre candidate. The Mile 2 Diobu branch then decided to stand an independent candidate against the Ikwerre native. Still the branch could not agree on their candidate. Chief Emenike won in the initial balloting within the local Executive, but the branch president, G. I. Elugwaornu, encouraged Emenike's townsman and personal rival, Chief Echue, to also contest the election.

Chief Echue later withdrew from the 1957 race, in obedience to a directive from the NCNC,[23] but the lines of opposition were fixed, and subsequent attempts to resolve the differences between what came to be known as the Emenike and Elugwaornu factions of the party were repeatedly rebuffed. In 1960, the party's Eastern Working Committee appointed R. B. K. Okafor, a federal parliamentary secretary and popular nationalist figure, to investigate and attempt to resolve the factional conflict within the Mile

2 Diobu branch. Okafor's efforts paved the way for the merger of
the Mile 2 Diobu NCNC with the Port Harcourt Executive Committee but did not eliminate the divisions within the Mile 2
Diobu branch. Commenting upon the reciprocal charges of tribal
politics made by the two sides, Okafor observed:

> In most cases, they [the leaders of the Elugwaornu and Emenike
> wings] are the leaders of the unions and consequently wield tre-
> mondous influence in the unions. . . . Orlu and Okigwi people
> came in large numbers and settled at Diobu perhaps through the
> goodwill of elder brothers like Chiefs Emenike and Echue. The
> fact that these people came in large numbers into politics does
> not, in my opinion, imply domination. The fact that they can use
> their numerical strength to carry away the decisions of the local
> branch is equally not domination. It is government by propor-
> tional representation which is admissible in a democracy. Our
> new party constitution has guaranteed this system. My finding,
> therefore, is that both factions appeal to tribal sentiments when
> it suited them to do so. The more of your tribesmen you can regis-
> ter in the NCNC the better position you stand in winning party
> offices. This malady is common in all branches of the NCNC,
> especially in urban areas.[24]

But Mile 2 Diobu's geo-ethnic cleavage reflected more than a
clash between personalities and cultural subgroups. It reflected
also a very sharp socioeconomic division—the landlords and first
settlers vis-à-vis the landless and the economically disadvantaged.
One member of the Elugwaornu wing of the party captured the
"class" aspect of the intraparty rivalry in his comment, "The
early settlers here are Emenike people, they bought most of the
land. They are the richest, and they think that they will lead in
politics as well, not knowing that the knowledge of politics and
that of riches differs. . . . They are naturally greedy people . . .
who want to snap up everything." In respect of its socioeconomic
underpinning, geo-ethnic conflict in Mile 2 Diobu closely re-
sembled the cleavage between the relatively better educated
Onitshans and the less advantaged Owerris in the main township.

Factionalism in Mile 2 Diobu was a persistent phenomenon,
the division between the Orlu-Okigwi and Bende-Mbaise wings
of the party again leading in 1961 to the nomination and election
of an Ikwerre native. This second defeat, however, drove home

to the members of both Diobu factions that, despite their differences, they were united by their common bonds of strangerness in an electoral constituency inhabited primarily by natives. At last, in the 1964–65 federal elections, the two factions joined to support a single candidate, NCNC President G. I. Elugwaornu, so as to control a majority in the Ahoada Central Constituency Executive. This time, however, it was the natives' turn to stand an independent candidate against the official NCNC nominee. In a close election marked by numerous allegations of irregularities and voting fraud from both sides, Elugwaornu was defeated by a prominent Diobu indigene, barrister Nwobodike Nwanodi.[25]

In addition to their common bonds of strangerness, most Mile 2 Diobu residents were tied together by their common relative deprivation vis-à-vis the more prosperous main township. Especially after 1960, when Mile 2 Diobu was administratively merged with Port Harcourt and acquired representation on the Port Harcourt Municipal Council, did the economic ghettoization of Mile 2 Diobu assume political significance. On the one hand, aside from a few notable exceptions, Mile 2 Diobu's political activists tended to be less well-off economically and less well educated than main township politicians (tables 18 and 19), and they were sensitive to the social contempt in which they were held by Port Harcourt's social and political establishment. On the other hand, Mile 2 Diobu leaders were united in their resentment of the history of administrative neglect that their

TABLE 18

MUNICIPAL COUNCILLORS, BY URBAN RESIDENCE AND INCOME (1961–1964)
(all figures in percentages)[a]

Income	Main Township	Indigenous Diobu	Miles 1 and 2 Diobu
Less than £200	—	20.0	17.4
£201–£500	38.9	60.0	26.1
£501–£1,000	16.7	20.0	26.1
£1,001–£3,000	22.2	—	—
£3,001–£5,000	5.6	—	13.0
More than £5,000	5.6	—	8.7
Not ascertained	11.1	—	8.7
	100.1	100.0	100.0
	(N = 18)	(N = 5)	(N = 23)

[a] Percentages do not always total 100 because of rounding.
SOURCES: Personal interviews.

TABLE 19

Municipal Councillors and ncnc Executive Members,
by Urban Residence and Education (1961–1964)[a]
(all figures in percentages)[b]

Education	Municipal Councillors		ncnc Executive Members	
	Main Township	*Miles 1–2 Diobu*	*Main Township*	*Miles 1–2 Diobu*
Less than elementary (Standard VI certificate)	22.2	30.4	27.6	48.8
Standard VI certificate	33.3	47.8	38.3	43.9
Postelementary education	44.5	21.7	29.8	7.3
Not ascertained	—	—	4.3	—
	100.0 (N = 18)	99.9 (N = 23)	100.0 (N = 47)	100.0 (N = 41)

[a] Tabulations include those municipal councillors who served between 1961 and 1965 and those ncnc Executive members elected in February 1962. Tabulations do not include the five councillors and eight ncnc Executive members who were of Port Harcourt's indigenous Diobu community.

[b] Percentages do not always total 100 because of rounding.

Sources: Minutes of the ncnc Executive Committee and personal interviews.

area had experienced, and in their determination after the 1960 merger to see that Mile 2 Diobu would henceforth receive its fair share of urban amenities. When it came to the distribution of such amenities (roads, electricity, water taps, conservancy service, and the like), their communal divisions were promptly superseded by their shared concern with the development of Mile 2 Diobu.

Geo-ethnicity: A Political Assessment

A number of propositions can now be advanced concerning the nature and political significance of geo-ethnicity in Port Harcourt:

(1) *Geo-ethnic Pragmatism.* Geo-ethnic political competition had a distinctively pragmatic quality. The geo-ethnic units of clan court area, division, and province were essentially artificial entities, commanding relatively little affect on the part of their members. It was as a consequence of this artificiality that geo-ethnic blocs were extremely unstable. The successful politician was one who, by a skillful trading of promises and favors, could forge an alliance of geo-ethnic community leaders. He was, in short, the ethnic ward heeler of American renown.

This analysis of geo-ethnic pragmatism, it should be noted, applies with equal force to regional as to urban politics. The fact that the politically relevant administrative units of Iboland were of no traditional significance may help to explain the essentially pacific nature of intra-Ibo competition and the ability of Ibos to pull together in the face of an outside threat. By contrast, where the colonial administrative units coincided with traditional entities, as in Yorubaland and Hausaland, intranationality competition had an especially volatile character. This fact suggests that the "secret" of Ibo organizational adaptability is to be found, at least in part, in the political realities of a highly fragmented social order.

(2) *The Socioeconomic Roots of Communalism.* Geo-ethnic conflicts in Port Harcourt were invariably associated with socioeconomic inequalities and competition. The differential rates at which the various elements of Port Harcourt's immigrant society had been mobilized into the modern sector of the developing Nigerian economy had placed some groups at a distinct competitive advantage vis-à-vis others. Consequently, geo-ethnic conflict was as much a class as a communal phenomenon; basically it reflected the competition between differentially advantaged individuals for the very scarce resources of wealth, status, and power.

(3) *Geo-ethnicity as a Political Weapon.* The politicalization of geo-ethnic identities in Port Harcourt was at least partially attributable to the self-interested machinations of aspirant politicians. The operation of a democratic franchise in Port Harcourt meant that political leaders required some degree of mass support in order to maintain themselves in power. In the culturally plural milieu in which they were operating, aspirant politicians were thus encouraged to make appeals to the most easily mobilized communal loyalties, and to define themselves primarily as the representatives of communal interests.

(4) *Geo-ethnicity and Commercialization.* The emergence of geo-ethnic politics in Port Harcourt was closely associated with the commercialization of the entire political realm. On the one hand, local business interests came to play an increasingly significant role within the party establishment. As wealth and numbers became important political assets in their own right, men who lacked occupational and social standing but were in a posi-

tion to assist the party financially, or were simply members of large and well-organized geo-ethnic communities, were permitted entry to the political arena. The wealthy businessman and traders became party patrons, the petty traders and contractors, party workers. Thus, the proportion of Executive members engaged in private enterprise rose from 40.0 percent in 1951 to 75.1 percent in 1962–1964 (table 15).[26] Simultaneously, the proportion of administrators and clerical functionaries, and of professionals, educators, and journalists, declined.

On the other hand, politics came increasingly to be viewed as a commercial venture in its own right. As Kenneth Post has observed, "Many of [the leaders of southern political parties] . . . were also people who had careers to make socially and politically, people who had seen that politics was a new way by which they could improve or maintain their economic and social positions. Often party loyalty was regarded as an investment and standing for election as a business venture." [27]

For petty traders and small contractors, in particular, public office was a means of obtaining social recognition. In their own words,

> It gives me an honor: I can go to any office and will be admitted to see whoever may be the boss of any office without hesitation. Not minding my being a small man. You know, I am a small man. I have no personality. But if I say I am Councillor N., they will let me in. . . . I can attend parties by invitation with V.I.P. men.
>
> Only to popularize my name. There is no office I can't enter today where I won't be regarded as somebody. And had I not been a Councillor, my townspeople could not have asked me to be in their almanac. Even in dreams I play a noble role.
>
> Councillors are given honor—and when you go to functions, they give you separate chairs.

And for both the rich man and the poor, public office and the party were business as well as political enterprises. An indication of the economic rewards anticipated by some of these men is provided by the sums expended on political campaigns. Six NCNC municipal councillors, for example, who were unlucky enough to be involved in contested elections, reported spending sums ranging from £50 to £400—for positions that (officially) paid only a monthly sitting allowance of £4 ($11.20) over a three-year term.[28]

Once elected, councillors vied with one another for appointment to the "lucrative" committees responsible for the award of contracts or the appointment of staff and teachers.[29] The unofficial activities of some commissioners, even in the post-Caretaker Council years, were too blatant to escape official notice. Between 1962 and 1964, five councillors were suspended, three for allegedly accepting bribes in connection with the award of a contract for conservancy service, and two for allegedly accepting bribes in connection with the allocation of market stalls. The first three lost their seats following a guilty verdict by the courts; the two accused of market corruption resigned at the request of the NCNC Executive Committee.[30]

Several municipal councillors were also registered with the council as contractors and often received preferential treatment in the award of small council contracts for the supply of building materials. In addition, in 1964 some councillors were silent partners in a construction firm awarded a major £15,357 contract. (The noncouncillor members of this company identified by the writer were all members of the NCNC Executive Committee.)

An especially notable instance in which party workers joined to promote their business interests occurred in 1964, when several of Port Harcourt's property owners, who were also party members, used the platform provided by the NCNC Executive Committee to protest against an Eastern Nigerian government plan to develop a government residential estate for expatriate businessmen. Local property owners feared that the government plan would undermine their own real estate investment. The matter first came before the NCNC Executive Committee in the form of a letter from a newly inaugurated Port Harcourt Landlords and Businessman's Association, an ad hoc organization formed for the specific purpose of protesting the government plan. Its chairman was V. C. I. Anene, the administrative secretary of the Ibo State Union and a member of the NCNC Executive; its secretary was a prominent local barrister and party supporter. Its membership included several members of the NCNC Executive.

An emergency meeting of the NCNC Executive was called to consider the Landlords Association letter, and the debate that ensued was, in the Ibo style, both vociferous and lengthy. A leading NCNC officer observed that his own apartment building intended for expatriate occupancy was lying vacant, and contended that the government had no business "competing with private investors." [31] However, some members objected to NCNC involvement in the property owners' dispute with the government, on the grounds that "We would be fighting ourselves" in permitting the local NCNC to argue against the NCNC government. Another objection was raised, to the effect that "the landlords are becoming Shylocks." The latter speaker was promptly reminded that "If you haven't got today, tomorrow you'll have your own," and that in the interest of his own prospective real estate investment he had best support the landlords of the moment. In the end, the business view prevailed. A subcommittee was appointed to investigate and take action; shortly thereafter, a delegation was sent to Enugu to consult with the minister of commerce and industry.

(5) *The Alienation of the Intelligentsia.* Closely related to the communalization of political competition and the commercialization of political life was the virtual disappearance from local public life of Port Harcourt's professionals and other intelligentsia. In 1964, but one of Port Harcourt's fifty-odd barristers held membership in the NCNC Executive; and, after Mayor Alagoa's resignation in 1961, no barrister or other professional sat on the Municipal Council.

After independence, few professionals made any effort to involve themselves politically in the local community. The formation of the Port Harcourt Welfare Society in 1960 represented the only effort of local professionals to join together for the purpose of giving "intellectual guidance to Governmental authorities in their efforts to raise the living standards of the people socially, economically, industrially, and in other fields." [32] The society met regularly for over a year; put forward a number of policy proposals, ranging from slum clearance to an investigation of a £60,000 contract that the Municipal Council had awarded for the building of a new town hall; and received delegations of complaining citizens. The society and its chairman, Dr. N. T. C.

Agulefo, a Canadian-trained medical practitioner, rapidly acquired a sizable personal following. The society's momentum, however, was quickly dissipated in 1961, when Agulefo attempted to convert the popular support that he enjoyed into a seat in the regional House of Assembly. A combination of NCNC pressure and internal bickering within the Society led to the organization's quiet dissolution. Defeated in his bid for the NCNC nomination for the Assembly seat, Agulefo stood against the party as an independent and failed.

To some extent the noninvolvement of Port Harcourt's professionals in local political activity reflected the long-standing bifurcation between the city's locals and cosmopolitans. Most professionals tended to be far more cosmopolitan in their tastes and interests than less-educated residents, and those that were politically concerned tended frequently to be more attracted by the lure of regional power than by the struggle for local political position.

To an even greater extent, however, the noninvolvement of these professionals reflected the hostility with which they were commonly met by the local party establishment. Party members of long standing resented the intrusion of men who were overseas when the nationalist struggle was being fought and won; and the more poorly educated of the party workers were threatened by the educational credentials of the city's intelligentsia.

More significantly, perhaps, the members of this intelligentsia —most notably the professionals and the civil servants—comprised an increasingly alienated segment of the urban society. The absence of survey data precludes the statistical validation of this sense of alienation, but the impressionistic evidence was overwhelming. A well-known Port Harcourt barrister spoke for many of his professional colleagues when he observed:

> Many barristers hold membership in the NCNC but don't attend meetings. . . . It would not look very nice to get yourself involved in local politics. It would put yourself in an embarrassing position with regard to your clients. You would become identified with one section of the community.
>
> And the local people seem to regard politics as a means of acquiring a living. If you're in politics you get government patronage—contracts, appointments to boards, et cetera—and they feel,

"You lawyers have a way of living. Why come to take that away from us?"

It is very difficult to become active in local politics. You become enemies of a section of the people, and they will misrepresent you politically.

Another barrister spoke contemptuously of the NCNC Executive members as "idiots" and "illiterates," most of whom had "never been to school. Hardly anyone there can speak a whole English sentence correctly, and they would prefer to speak in the vernacular." A Port Harcourt journalist commented even more forcefully: "The local NCNC is dominated by idiots, numb-skulls, people who never went to school, jobless people who live on politics, who go into the Council just to take bribes." A well-to-do business manager who was himself a former NCNC official compared the Port Harcourt political situation in 1964 with his recollections of an earlier day:

> Any kind of broadmindedness then has disappeared now. Everyone is looking at it in terms of "is my brother there?" "What can I get out of it?" The missionary spirit is gone.
>
> It is difficult to know on what basis some of the present members of the Council were chosen. The people included those who normally would not have passed in the olden days, people who in the normal community would not even pass as respectable. . . . I could not sponsor them at any club. When people ask, "Who is he? What does he do?," what can you say? . . . Is politics a little rougher, a little cruder? I don't know.

CHAPTER 8

Proletarian Protest

We shift now from an examination of the operation of geo-ethnicity to an analysis of the role and political significance of other lines of social division in Port Harcourt which either cut across or transcended the geo-ethnic cleavages around which the electoral process was organized. This and the next two chapters consist mainly of case studies of political conflict involving different kinds of interest groups. We begin with the general strike of June 1964, involving a massive confrontation, not only in Port Harcourt but nationwide, between workers and employers. Succeeding chapters consider, in turn, the conflict between Catholics and Protestants over educational policy and the continuing struggle between Ibos and non-Ibos over the creation of a separate Ijaw-dominated Rivers State with Port Harcourt as its administrative capital. In each instance our purpose is to identify the factors generating these antagonisms, to assess the impact of different kinds of interest groups upon the structure of local community power, and to explore the interrelationships between communal and noncommunal political identities.

THE GENERAL STRIKE OF JUNE 1964: PROTEST OR REVOLUTION?

Between June 1 and June 15, 1964, the members of over fifty commercial, industrial, and government trade unions in Port Harcourt joined an estimated eight hundred thousand workers across the nation in a two-week general strike, Nigeria's first nationwide labor protest since 1945.[1] The strike's political impact was enormous; and many Nigerians professed to see the birth of a new age in which tribalism would be no more, and the politicians would heed the will of a national citizenry that had transcended tribal and linguistic divisions and would no longer accept the corruption and drift that had come to characterize Nigerian political life.

The strike *was* a highly significant political initiative; of this fact there can be little doubt. As William Friedland has commented,

> The organizational forms of African trade unions are often misleading because they appear so weak and so chaotic by the standards of industrial societies. They should be evaluated, however, within the framework of their own societies, which have as yet few well-organized voluntary groups outside the tribal and familial system and which often lack effective administrative structures and systems for the maintenance of public order to cope with labor protests. In this context, trade unions loom much larger, and their ability to gain sudden great political potential as national protest movements becomes less surprising.[2]

A distinction must be drawn, however, between a "national protest movement," which represents a momentary upsurge of public revulsion, and a "revolutionary movement," which seeks to overturn the organizational bases of a political system; similarly, there is a distinction to be made between an economic interest group, which seeks to influence government policy, and a political party, which attempts to elect men to public office.

The following analysis of the general strike and its political aftermath in Port Harcourt suggests that the strike's leaders were performing like the leaders of a socioeconomic protest, not like those of a revolutionary political party, and that the strike's political success was due precisely to the fact that it did not constitute a threat to the organizational bases of Nigeria's political system. Support for the strike in Port Harcourt did cut across communal lines, but we will argue that this meant not the erosion of communal identities but, rather, their temporary displacement. When it came to questions of the pocketbook—to questions of salary and conditions of service—Port Harcourt's workers held much in common irrespective of their diverse communal attachments. During the strike it was the socioeconomic identities of these men which were in the foreground: in the confrontation with employers, their communal points of reference held little salience, and labor unity was possible. However, when the strike had concluded and preparations were begun for the pending federal parliamentary elections, communal identities were triggered once again and the workers acted upon their communal loyalties.

Labor Unrest and the Morgan Commission

In Nigeria, as in so many other developing areas, the greatest part of the wage-earning labor force is employed by public authorities. Consequently, Nigerian trade union agitation has often been aimed directly at the federal and regional governments. And so it was in 1963.

It had been four years since Nigeria's federal government employees had received their last wage increases. Repeated trade union demands for wage hikes, improved job security, and new negotiating machinery had fallen on deaf ears. The federal government, having little to fear from a divided and financially bankrupt labor movement, rejected all trade union initiatives. Nigeria's cost of living, however, continued to rise; increasing numbers of unemployed kinsmen continued to drain the financial resources of the employed worker, and Nigerians found it increasingly difficult to reconcile the government's plea for national austerity with the grand manner in which their politicians and senior civil servants lived. As Friedland has remarked, the government preached economy but "would do nothing to rectify the inequities of the governmental wage system, the exorbitant fringe benefits for senior officials, and the high salaries of the public corporation executives." [3] In Port Harcourt and throughout the country, the "postindependence disillusionment" had set in, and calls for higher wages, on the one hand, and for an austerity program for the political establishment, on the other, struck a responsive chord in the urban body politic.

Because the greatest part of Nigeria's commercial and industrial development was centered in the South, and because the coalition government ruling the federation was dominated by the Northern Peoples' Congress, trade union agitation in 1963 and 1964 inevitably coincided with the widening conflict between

North and South which, in 1967, was to plunge Nigeria into a catastrophic civil war. It would be incorrect, however, to interpret the labor protest simply as a manifestation of this regional conflict. On the contrary, the leaders of the abortive strike of 1963 and the general strike of 1964 were inspired by motives that were clearly supraregional: their appeals and their oratory were directed at the reform of the political establishment in its regional as well as its federal aspects.

In 1963, the country's warring trade union federations finally succeeded in closing ranks to form a Joint Action Committee of Nigerian Trade Union Organizations (known as the J.A.C.), and the federal government could no longer ignore what was at last a united labor front. J.A.C. leaders threatened to launch a general strike to coincide with Nigeria's Republic Day of October 1, and the month of September witnessed work stoppages on the railway and at the wharf, both in Lagos and Port Harcourt. The government relented, recognized the J.A.C., and agreed to appoint a commission "to investigate the existing wage structure, remuneration and conditions of service in wage-earning employments in the country and to make recommendations concerning a suitable new structure, as well as adequate machinery for a wages review on a continuing basis." [4] Importantly, the commission's terms of reference embraced not only federal employees but also those of the regional governments and private establishments.

The Morgan Commission, named for its chairman, Justice Adeyinka Morgan, heard testimony for over six months and submitted its report to the federal prime minister on April 30, 1964. The report, which was reported to contain recommendations for the overhaul of Nigeria's entire wage structure and the creation of new negotiating machinery, was not immediately made public, and a J.A.C. suspicious of the government's intent pressed for its release. Again, on May 8, a general strike threat was issued. In response, Minister of Establishments Jacob Obande, the only major official to whom labor leaders had access during these days of heightening tension, promised publication on May 25. On May 27 the Morgan Report was finally released but with no indication of the government's response to the commission's recommendations, and a final seventy-two–hour ultimatum was issued by the J.A.C. At midnight on May 31 (after the workers had received their monthly paychecks), the ultimatum expired, and the national strike call was issued.

The government's long-awaited white paper was finally published three days later. In it, the Morgan Commission's recommendations were rejected as too costly. It was argued that in adopting the unorthodox principle of a "living-wage," the Morgan Commission "has increased the existing minimum wage by 58 percent in some cases, and in some cases by 100 percent, whereas the pattern in the cost of living index would have produced an increase of say 15 to 20 percent." [5] Alternatively, more moderate wage increases were proposed. Where the Morgan Commission called for a monthly minimum wage of £12 for Lagos and Port Harcourt (with an existing wage rate of £8/15/3), the government offered a £9/2/- minmum for Lagos alone; and where the Morgan Commission proposed a £10 monthly minimum for Eastern Nigeria's other urban areas and for its rural sector, the government countered with £6/10 monthly minimum for the whole of the Eastern Region. Minority reports that were made by some members of the Morgan Commission and that proposed major cuts in allowances and other perquisites of senior civil servants and politicians were ignored altogether. And, as Abernethy has observed, "The fact that the public share of the Morgan Commission's proposals could have been financed by abolishing the automobile allowance was conveniently overlooked." [6] Not unexpectedly, the government's offer proved unacceptable to the leadership of the Joint Action Committee. The strike continued.

Port Harcourt's Labor Leadership: The Reemergence of Non-Ibos

Between 1959 and 1964, Port Harcourt's trade union leadership had been subject to the same divisions as were characteristic of Nigeria's Lagos-centered national labor movement. Local unions that were branch affiliates of nationwide organizations headquartered in Lagos naturally identified themselves with the factional sympathies of their central unions, while unions headquartered in Port Harcourt formed their own affiliations with one or another of the rival trade union federations: the ICFTU-affiliated United Labor Congress (ULC), the Nigerian Trades Union Congress (NTUC), and after 1962, the neutral (as between the

ULC and the NTUC) Labor Unity Front (LUF). Repeated attempts had been made to organize a united Port Harcourt Council of Labor to coordinate local trade union activity, but these organizational efforts (in 1955, 1958, and 1961) were short lived. Failures of leadership and, especially in 1958 and 1961, the continuing struggle between the left and right wings of the labor movement over the issue of affiliation with the Western-oriented International Christian Federation of Trade Unions, had frustrated attempts to achieve local unity.

Renewed activity on the national labor front in 1963 was paralleled in Port Harcourt. In August, the presidents and secretaries of approximately thirty local unions met to establish an eight-man "strategic committee" to organize Port Harcourt workers for anticipated strike action the following month. Significantly, the committee's membership comprised representatives of all the major factions and of some of Port Harcourt's largest unions. But when the September strike action commenced, the strategic committee succeeded in pulling out only the workers on the Nigerian Ports Authority and the Nigerian Railways.

Port Harcourt's trade union leaders resolved not to suffer a second defeat and immediately began preparation for the expected general strike in 1964. In March, the Port Harcourt Council of Labor was formally reinaugurated (for the fourth time). Representatives from over forty unions participated in the election of the ten officers who, together with one representative from each union, formed the Labor Council's Executive Committee. While policy-making responsibilities were theoretically lodged in this committee, once the general strike was under way, the ten officers were constituted into a self-styled management or strategic committee, and the larger Executive Committee was formally convened only twice during the two-week period.

The composition of the management committee, depicted in table 20, provides an interesting contrast to that of the local NCNC hierarchy described in the previous chapter. As trade unionists and salaried employees, the officers of the Council of Labor, of course, differed occupationally from the members of the trader-dominated NCNC Executive and Municipal Council. But perhaps the most striking dissimilarity between the composition of the

TABLE 20

MEMBERSHIP OF THE STRIKE MANAGEMENT COMMITTEE
OF THE PORT HARCOURT COUNCIL OF LABOR, 1964[a]

1. *President E. I. Bille:* Ijaw; Degema Division; Supervisory clerical position, A. G. Leventis Co.; former NCNC member and founding member of a rejuvenated branch of the Dynamic party in 1961; 2nd vice-president of the national A. G. Leventis Union and secretary of the union's Port Harcourt branch. National union affiliation: ULC.
2. *Secretary Jones Alajo:* Yoruba; Lagos; full-time trade unionist and former apprentice shipwright for the Nigerian Ports Authority; former NCNC member and secretary of the Port Harcourt branch of the Socialist Farmers and Workers party; former vice-president of the NTUC and secretary of the Port Harcourt branch of the Railway and Ports Workers Union. National union affiliation: LUF.
3. *Vice-President Watson Gabriel:* Ijaw; Degema Division; clerk in the Palm Line Agency; president of the Port Harcourt branch of the U.A.C. and Associated Companies African Workers Union. National union affiliation: LUF.
4. *Assistant Secretary Emmanuel Ohiri:* Ibo; Owerri Division; Electrician; former NCNC member and the assistant secretary of the Port Harcourt branch of the Dynamic party; municipal councillor; former professional trade unionist with the Independent United Labor Congress (IULC) but holding no union affiliation in 1964.
5. *Treasurer L. S. Akele:* Edo; Benin City, Mid-Western Nigeria.
6. *Financial Secretary Nwabueze:* Ibo-Asaba, Mid-Western Nigeria; Barclays bank employee.
7. *Assistant Financial Secretary Effiong:* Efik; Calabar Division; Barclays bank employee.
8. *Publicity Secretary J. E. Ojimadu:* Ibo-Mbaise; Owerri Division; former Shell-BP clerk and full-time trade unionist; secretary of three Port Harcourt unions: Michelin Tyre Company Union; Sir Lindsay Parkinson Company Union; African Metal Workers Union. National union affiliation: ULC.
9. *Auditor Chukwuma:* Ibo; Onitsha Division; employee of the inland waterways department.
10. *Auditor S. M. C. Bello:* Yoruba; Western Nigeria; cashier in the Vivian, Younger and Bond Company; president of the Vivian, Younger and Bond Company Union.

[a] The designated national union affiliations do not necessarily reflect the personal sympathies of the individual trade unionist. In some instances, local Port Harcourt branch unions had little control over national union policies formulated in Lagos.

SOURCES: Personal interview with leading members of the Port Harcourt Council of Labor.

NCNC hierarchy and that of the trade union management committee was the significant non-Ibo component of the latter. Six of its ten members, including the three most senior officials, were non-Ibo. Its chairman, E. I. Bille, was from the Ijaw-speaking community of Old Bakana; its secretary, J. Alajo, was a Yoruba-speaking Lagosian; its vice-president, Watson Gabriel, was an

Ijaw-speaking Kalabari; and its treasurer, financial secretary, and auditor were, respectively, from Benin City, Calabar, and Western Nigeria.

At least two questions immediately present themselves. Why were non-Ibos disproportionately attracted to positions of trade union leadership? And why was a predominantly Ibo rank and file receptive to non-Ibo trade union leadership?

That non-Ibos were attracted to the trade union movement may have been due, in part, to their exclusion from the NCNC establishment. We have seen that in Port Hartcourt, public office and political patronage were the virtual monopolies of those holding the proper ethnic credentials. In the eyes of non-Ibos both within and without Port Harcourt, the NCNC and the Eastern Nigerian government were communal institutions to which they had little access and for which they (together with some young Ibo radicals) had little political sympathy. From this perspective, then, non-Ibo participation in the labor movement was a political act, an expression of antiestablishment sentiments rooted as much in the Eastern Nigerian communal order as in the socioeconomic conditions of urban life.

In this light, it is not surprising to find that several of the non-Ibo Council of Labor's management committeemen had either previously been involved or were currently involved in complementary political activity. The Ijaw chairman, E. I. Bille, for example, had held a prominent position in the NCNC in an earlier day but had long since left the party. Jones Alajo, the Labor Council's Yoruba secretary was also the secretary of the Port Harcourt branch of the Socialist Workers and Farmers party (SWAFP). Still another leading non-Ibo member of the Council of Labor, Sonny Yellowe (an Ijaw from Bakana and former president-general of the Shell-BP Union), was the SWAFP vice-president. And the Ibo members of the management committee were similarly on the outside of the local NCNC establishment. Like E. I. Bille, the Ibo assistant secretary, Emmanuel Ohiri, had earlier been very active in NCNC affairs. He had broken with the party, however, and in 1961 had successfully stood election to the Municipal Council on the platform of the dissident Dynamic party.[7] Likewise, Ojimadu, the management committee's Ibo publicity secretary, was assistant secretary of the local SWAFP branch.

For non-Ibos, then, as well as for Ibo radicals, trade unionism had become an organizational vehicle to protest their exclusion from the political establishment and to express their opposition to the Ibo-dominated Eastern Nigerian political regime. But while this fact may explain the non-Ibo (and radical Ibo) attraction to trade unionism, we have yet to account for the acceptance by a predominantly Ibo rank and file of a non-Ibo-led strike management committee.

Perhaps the explanation of this latter phenomenon lies in a consideration of the organizational prerequisites of effective trade unionism. It would appear that trade union leadership aspirants (together with their rank and file) had little to gain from communally based political strategies.[8] Unlike a politician whose position could be used to benefit his own communal supporters to the exclusion of his competitors, the rewards that an effective trade union leader had to distribute—concessions from management in the form of higher wages, job security, fringe benefits, and the like—had to be divided equally among all union members performing similar jobs—irrespective of their communal origins. Of course, if communal groups were rigidly stratified by occupational rank or segregated by occupational role, then communal considerations might very well play a significant role not only in the selection of trade union leaders but also in the establishment by such leaders of their bargaining priorities and in their allocation of rewards among the trade union rank and file. This situation, however, was not the one confronting Port Harcourt's communally heterogeneous and highly fluid labor force.

But the noncommunal character of the trade union leadership struggle was due to more than the simple irrelevance of communal factors. Unlike the NCNC whose electoral position was so secure in Port Harcourt that it could survive continuous internal factionalism, a trade union's organizational effectiveness was wholly dependent upon the unity and discipline of its membership. The introduction of communal strategies in the struggle for leadership simply insured that all would be losers in the all-important confrontation with the employer. Trade unions were never entirely free of communal rivalries and conflicts, and the introduction by aspirant leaders of such communal factionalism almost invariably destroyed whatever organizational strength a trade union had been able to develop.

From this perspective, then, it is perhaps wiser to ask why non-Ibo trade union leaders should *not* have been accepted by an Ibo rank and file. Non-Ibos tended, as we have seen, to be relatively better educated as compared with the Ibo population at large; and those with leadership potential tended frequently, because of their exclusion from Ibo-dominated political structures, to have longer experience in the trade union movement. Even more important, non-Ibo leadership helped to minimize the potential of intratrade union communal conflict that might have been engendered by leadership struggles among Ibos. Communal strife, as has been suggested, had to be avoided at all costs, and non-Ibos were, by definition, removed from the Ibo communal rivalries that characterized Port Harcourt political life. In effect, the non-Ibo trade unionists in 1964 may have been playing much the same unifying role as the non-Ibo patricians had played during the early years of Port Harcourt's political coalescence. Finally, non-Ibos were in a far better position than their Ibo trade union brethren to lead a public protest against a political establishment that was, after all, largely Ibo in composition. Not constrained by ties of blood and community, or by considerations of vested interest, non-Ibos were freer to lead and to speak out on matters of common concern to both Ibo and non-Ibo workers.

Port Harcourt's Employers and Shell-BP

The employers' counterpart of the Port Harcourt Council of Labor was the Port Harcourt branch of the Nigerian Employers Consultative Association (NECA). Comprised of the representatives of over fifty (mostly expatriate) commercial and industrial concerns, the local branch of NECA functioned, as did the Council of Labor, to coordinate the activities of its members and to mediate communications between Lagos and Port Harcourt. It met on several occasions while the strike was in progress and maintained close contact with the Eastern Nigerian government representatives in Port Harcourt, the provincial commissioner and the provincial secretary.[9] At no time, however, did NECA negotiate bilaterally with the Council of Labor. Meetings of representatives of NECA and the Council of Labor were arranged by the provincial secretary to discuss problems pertaining to public safety, but aside from informal discussions between individual managements and their company unions, the strike issues themselves were never negotiated locally.

There was no exact business counterpart of the Labor Council's management committee, but the always visible and highly professional Shell-BP Petroleum Development Company of Nigeria, Ltd., Port Harcourt's largest private employer and capital investor, played a major role in employer deliberations both in Port Harcourt and in Lagos.[10] In testimony to Shell-BP's national influence, not only within the business community but upon the Nigerian government, a key participant in the Lagos deliberations reported that when negotiations between the J.A.C. and the federal government were about to commence, Shell-BP was asked by the Nigerian negotiators to submit a memorandum on negotiating strategy and to make rough calculations on the labor costs involved not only in the Morgan Commission recommendations but also in those of the already-published (but apparently never researched) government white paper.[11]

Shell-BP's domination of these proceedings was somewhat less than enthusiastically received by many expatriate employers, both in Port Harcourt and in Lagos. One expatriate business manager expressed what was in fact a very common concern:

> Shell-BP is able to exert too much influence for the good of industries out here. . . . The tie-up with the federal government is so close at the moment and they are so dependent on maintaining their cordial relationships that if their interests are not so badly at stake, they may concede a point—and force the smaller concerns to do the same. Shell won't be affected by the Morgan Report because Shell is so high already. . . . We have laid ourselves open to NECA's interest being subordinated to Shell-BP.

On at least two occasions, the Port Harcourt branch of NECA actually refused to follow Shell-BP's lead. The first of these occasions occurred on the strike's third day, when NECA ignored Shell-BP's recommendation and accepted the Council of Labor's request that the striking workers be allowed to remain in their shops (and hence off the streets). Then, in the strike's second week, the issuance of a NECA-sponsored employer ultimatum to the striking workers was a sharp repudiation of the counsel that Shell-BP had provided. In the second instance, but not the first, Shell-BP management reluctantly agreed to accept NECA's decision.[12]

The General Strike: Port Harcourt Highlights

Perhaps the most significant feature of the general strike in Port Harcourt was its organizational effectiveness, as measured by both the completeness of the local work stoppage and by the avoidance of violence. The first to be affected by the J.A.C. strike order were Port Harcourt's major mercantile firms, most notably the various subsidiaries of the United Africa Company, and the railway terminal. On the strike's second day, employees of the postal and telegraph services joined in, and more commercial and industrial firms were closed. By the third day, the work stoppage in Port Harcourt was virtually complete. Shell-BP and other industrial firms in the Trans-Amadi Industrial Estate which had not yet closed their doors were besieged by striking workers and forced to shut down. The Municipal Council offices, the provincial secretariat, the banks, and the schools were all closed, either at the initiative of their employees or on the threat of violence by demonstrators. Only the African market, small commercial establishments, and the offices of the provincial secretary and commissioner were left (by design) largely undisturbed.[13]

From the strike's onset, Port Harcourt's trade union leaders were determined to keep their labor protest peaceful. Almost daily mass rallies were held to inform the workers of the day's happenings, to rally the strikers' morale, and to urge nonviolence. Until the employers' ultimatum at the end of the second week, trade union leaders assiduously avoided public attacks on the expatriate firms. At their mass rallies they repeatedly emphasized that the foreign businessman was actually on the side of the workers, that he recognized that the quarrel of the workers was not with the European but with their own government, and that as long as the workers behaved responsibly, they would continue to enjoy the support of their employers. The Council of Labor's "inspection teams," which roamed the city each day to make certain that workers stayed off their jobs (strike vote or no strike vote) and to insure they were not intimidated by their employers, relied upon the threat of, but never the actuality of, violence.

On the fourth day of the strike, a meeting of labor leaders with NECA and the heads of government departments resulted in further measures to minimize the potential for violence or public disorder. Many expatriate concerns undertook to permit their workers to enter their firms and "sit-down," as the labor leaders had requested, and the Labor Council representatives on their part agreed to attempt to curb vandalism and rioting, to obtain police permits for all public meetings, and to ask the township's conservancy workers (i.e., the night soil men) to heed the public warning of the senior medical officer that the public health was being critically endangered by their work stoppage. That these measures were successful is indicated by the fact that during the entire two-week period there was not a single instance of mob violence in Port Harcourt. Intimidation did occur: early in the strike a few African drivers of expatriates were forcibly removed from their cars, and African cooks and stewards in European residential areas were occasionally confronted by hostile strikers. But no loss of life resulted, destruction of property was virtually nil, and looting was nonexistent.

Nevertheless, there were many Port Harcourt residents, especially in the expatriate community, who anticipated serious violence and who took precautionary measures. Shell-BP, possibly overreacting because of the company's exposed position in the luxurious Shell Compound on the municipality's outskirts, went so far as to direct that all their employee's wives remain indoors and that their house servants be released. During the same period, word was passed through the expatriate community that planes were standing by to evacuate the city's European population if that should become necessary. This initial panic reaction quickly subsided as it became clear that the strike was directed solely at the government and that the trade union leaders were working to maintain law and order.

This record of nonviolence is somewhat ironic, in that one of the historical myths to survive the general strike is that Port Harcourt was the single Nigerian city to experience major violence. The origins of this myth apparently were national press accounts that reported police resorting to tear gas and riot sticks to quell mob action in the main township. The writer was present

during the alleged instance of mob violence. What in fact tran-
spired was that the police, for reasons that are obscure, felt that
a labor rally that was assembling on a public field threatened
the public safety. Tear gas bombs were thrown to disperse the
gathering, with the result that the members of what had been a
carefully controlled and entirely peaceful assembly were forced
into the streets and away from the supervision of their trade
union leaders. Admittedly, the sight of thousands of persons running or cycling through the streets carrying palm branches (which
had become the symbol of unity with the striking workers) did
little to relieve what had become a very tense situation. Nevertheless, no subsequent incidents were reported. The afternoon labor
rally held the same day—this time with no police interference—
was preoccupied with the prevention of violence, and the labor
leaders renewed their plea that the workers ignore police or
other provocations.[14]

The general strike in Port Harcourt was distinguished not only
by its organizational effectiveness, but also by the organizational
autonomy of the local strike leadership—a result of a disruption
of communications with Lagos. Early in the first week, phone
communications between the Port Harcourt Council of Labor
and the Lagos J.A.C. failed completely, and neither the government-owned radio nor a crippled national press could be relied
upon for accurate coverage. The only recourse available to the
Council of Labor was to send a personal representative by automobile to the capital city. On June 5, the council's assistant
secretary departed for Lagos; and it was not until June 9 that
Port Harcourt's labor leaders received, by means of his return,
their first reliable information about J.A.C. policy and the state
of affairs in Lagos. In the interim, the Port Harcourt Council of
Labor acted independently of the Lagos leadership.

Another notable feature of the strike action in Port Harcourt
was the tendency, as the strike continued into its second week,
for the bread-and-butter issues that initially had commanded the
greatest attention to be fused with a general attack upon the
Nigerian political establishment. In the mass rallies, trade union
impatience at the federal government's intransigence manifested
itself in increasingly aggressive attacks upon corruption and the
privileges enjoyed by the political establishment, and in more

frequent references to the need for a labor party. Significantly, however, little criticism was aimed directly at the Eastern Nigerian government or the NCNC. Non-Ibo attacks on the NCNC would probably not have been well received by the Ibo rank and file. Moreover, word had come from Enugu that the NCNC was now officially behind the labor leaders. If true, this development was surprising, inasmuch as the Eastern Nigerian premier (who was also the national NCNC president) had originally joined with the other regional premiers and the prime minister in endorsing the federal government's white paper.[15] Whatever the veracity of the report, it had the effect of uplifting the workers' sagging morale. The Port Harcourt strike held firm.

A further distinguishing characteristic of the Port Harcourt strike experience was the general reluctance of local politicians to become involved with the labor crisis. During the first week of the strike, the mayor, together with one or two other municipal councillors with business interests, had been present at the meetings of the firms and government departments convened by the provincial secretary, but had had little to say. When, early in the second week, the mayor called the Municipal Council into emergency session to consider a request from the commissioner of police that the council pass a resolution banning all processions and public meetings, the politicians adopted a hands-off policy: the police were asked to first exhaust the powers that constitutionally were theirs and that, in the view of the councillors, they had not exercised. The council did resolve to seek the cooperation of the labor leaders in reopening the schools. This initiative, however, failed, with the Council of Labor taking the position that it was the teachers themselves who had decided to strike and that the matter was, therefore, out of the hands of the labor leadership.

Lastly, the Port Harcourt experience was distinguished by the bitter opposition of the local labor leadership to the J.A.C. decision, at the end of the second week, to call off the general strike and go back to the bargaining table with the federal government. Before this decision was reached, word had come from Lagos that the NECA-sponsored employer ultimatum to the striking workers—calling upon workers to return to their jobs within forty-eight hours or face dismissal—had had the intended effect, and men were returning to their jobs. A Port Harcourt delegation quickly departed for Lagos. There, in concert with other Eastern Nigerian labor leaders, the Port Harcourt delegates pressed the Joint Action Committee for the strike's continuation, but were overruled. In sharp contrast to the still-total work stoppage in Eastern Nigeria, the strike had collapsed in the Northern Region and was continuing in name only in Lagos; and the always latent divisions within the J.A.C. leadership were once again threatening to undermine the unity of the labor front. Moreover, the federal government, for reasons of its own, was suddenly indicating a willingness to negotiate the strike issues if the workers returned to their jobs.[16] Consequently, to the Lagos leadership it appeared that the labor movement had more to gain than to lose by the strike's termination. But to a disgruntled Port Harcourt leadership, the subsequently announced agreement between the J.A.C. and the federal government to end the strike and commence negotiations "on the basis of the Morgan Commission report" was little more than a face-saving move designed to conceal the fact that certain Lagos labor leaders had been unable to control their rank and file.[17]

On June 15, the strike was officially called off, and negotiations between the J.A.C. and representatives of the federal and regional governments were commenced. Two weeks later, the results of the negotiations were announced: government wage and salary levels were to be substantially raised (though not nearly to the extent recommended by the Morgan Commission); minimum wages were to be established for each of seven economic zones into which the country had been divided; wage and salary increases were to be backdated to January; and the workers were to be paid for the period they were on strike.

There was little jubilation in trade union circles in Port Harcourt. It was noted that the agreement contained no reference to the fundamental inequities in Nigeria's wage and salary structure, to the extravagant allowances and fringe benefits enjoyed by the ministers and senior civil servants, and to the corruption that was such an established part of Nigerian political life.

As for the employers, they felt completely betrayed by a weak and incompetent federal government. The government's capitulation of June 13, which came at the very moment when it appeared the strike might be breaking, was incomprehensible to many businessmen. The expatriate business community was all the more dismayed when, subsequently, the government negotiators insisted that the Nigerian Employers Consultative Association—which technically had no authority to commit its membership to any course of action whatsoever—sign the June 29 Memorandum of Agreement.

The Political Sequel: Trade Unionists as Politicians

With the general strike concluded Nigerians shifted their attention to the pending federal elections, scheduled somewhat indefinitely to be held toward the end of the year. An analysis of the national implications of this election and of the Constitutional crisis that it engendered lies beyond the scope of the present study. It is sufficient to note that the election took the form of a head-on clash between North and South, that the Joint Action Committee officially endorsed the southern-based United Progressive Grand Alliance (UPGA), that the unity of the national labor front dissolved after the general strike, and that radical trade unionists in both Lagos and Port Harcourt attempted—unsuccessfully—to convert the popular support they enjoyed during the general strike into political backing for workers' candidates outside the framework of the NCNC-dominated southern political alliance.

Thus, in Port Harcourt, two members of the general strike's management committee stood election for Port Harcourt's single seat in the federal House of Representatives. Jones Alajo, the Council of Labor's Yoruba secretary, stood as the candidate of the Socialist Workers and Farmers party while Emmanuel Ohiri, an Ibo municipal councillor and the Labor Council's assistant secretary, stood on the platform of the Dynamic party. The Dynamic party, it should be noted, was a member of the northern-dominated Nigerian National Alliance (NNA), a fact that did not endear its Ibo candidate to Port Harcourt's Ibo electorate. As for the SWAFP candidate, the NCNC never took seriously the candidacy of the Yoruba trade unionist. When the much delayed Eastern Nigerian election was finally held on March 18, 1965, the NCNC candidate and incumbent member of the federal House, D. D. U. Okay, secured 4,851 of the 6,019 votes cast, and both Alajo and

Ohiri lost their deposits. The loss of Councillor Ohiri's deposit is especially noteworthy, in that he was a member of Port Harcourt's populous Owerri community.

These election results are no doubt subject to varying interpretations, but one conclusion seems inescapable: the same trade unionists who had enjoyed the solid support of Port Harcourt's predominantly Ibo rank and file during the general strike were deserted when they transformed themselves from leaders of a protest movement into parliamentary candidates of political parties that were in opposition to the NCNC. The moment the strike had concluded, the lines of political cleavage within the urban community were redrawn. The socioeconomic identities that Port Harcourt's Ibo workers shared with workers in all of Nigeria's urban centers and that for two weeks had shaped the political life of a nation were once again subordinated to the communal identities of region and nationality. Concurrently, the alternative fused leadership structure of regional party (NCNC) and ethnic community (Ibo), a structure quite distinct from that which had guided Nigeria's politics of socioeconomic protest, was reactivated. In short, the general strike had left undisturbed the communal foundations of the urban political system.

CHAPTER 9
Church and School in the City:
The Politics of Religion

In 1956, the adoption by the Eastern Nigerian government of a new educational policy placing a ceiling upon the further expansion of voluntary agency (i.e., mission) schools sparked a major political clash between the Region's rapidly growing Roman Catholic Mission and the ruling NCNC, and fanned the embers of the long-standing and bitter rivalry between the Catholic and Protestant churches. Religious tension persisted into the early sixties, when the 1956 decision again became a matter of public dispute and Port Harcourt emerged as a major center of religious politics. This chapter examines the historical bases of religious conflict in Eastern Nigeria and explores the impact of religion upon Port Harcourt political life.

In terms of our theoretical concerns, religious politics in Port Harcourt offers some striking parallels with the politics of militant trade unionism described previously. We will find, for example, that the division between the city's Protestants and Catholics, like that between Port Harcourt's employers and employees, reflected, at base, a broad socioeconomic cleavage between differentially advantaged populations. Moreover, religious conflict in Port Harcourt—like labor conflict—was issue-specific. Religious identities were activated by issues of educational policy; when these were not in the political foreground, the salience of religious loyalties and the effectiveness of religious protest activity were sharply reduced. Consequently, religious politics in Port Harcourt posed no more a threat to the dominant party establishment than did the politics of labor protest.

The educational policy enunciated in 1956, which declared that henceforth all new Eastern Nigerian primary schools were to be under the control of local governmental bodies and that only such local authority schools would be eligible for government building grants, departed sharply from the government's traditional encouragement of mission educational expansion. The earliest British colonial officials had opted to subsidize and regulate already-operative voluntary agency schools rather than to enter into a major program of direct governmental sponsorship and administration. As David Abernethy records, the grant-in-aid system that evolved was justified largely on the grounds of economy and administrative efficiency:

> . . . the missionaries had the advantage of a head start in educational work, and considerable effort would have been required to control their activities with care; certainly it would have been difficult to replace them. The grant-in-aid system represented, moreover, a considerable saving of scarce administrative talent and of government money, for if the government assumed control of the mission schools it would have incurred the expenses of the whole apparatus of inspection, administration, and teacher training that each mission was financing with its own resources. A further saving was in teachers' salaries. Whereas teachers directly employed by the government were paid civil service salaries according to the amount of training they had received, the government insisted that it was not responsible for ensuring equivalent salaries for voluntary agency teachers, although it might subsidize them through grants-in-aid. As a result, mission teachers invariably received less than government teachers, and the government benefited from the former's services at little cost to itself.[1]

From the perspective of the voluntary agencies, similarly, church control of secular education made administrative—and political—sense. From their first involvement in Eastern Nigeria, European missionaries had stressed the importance of secular education, not only as a means to the evangelical end of mastery of the written Bible, but also as a tactical necessity in the competition for religious converts. Closely linked in the eyes of Africans with the administrative and commercial agents of European imperialism, the missionaries found that a purely evangelical approach held little appeal. Education, however, very quickly became a much valued commodity, offering to the African a means by which he could begin to cope with the European presence and an avenue for the achievement of new goals and aspirations. In short, the missionaries "discovered that often people who rejected their teaching were willing to risk having their children indoctrinated in return for an instruction in reading, writing and arithmetic." [2]

A number of factors prompted the abrupt 1956 reversal of the long-standing policy of encouragement to voluntary agencies. Perhaps the most crucial was the concern of the NCNC leadership with the social, economic, and educational costs of continued interdenominational conflict over the control of schools. Just after the turn of the century, the various Protestant missions active in Eastern Nigeria agreed to the creation of exclusive territorial jurisdictions for each denomination.[3] The Catholics, however, were not party to these comity agreements and refused to acknowledge any territorial limitations to their own activities. Moreover, the resulting religious competition was exacerbated by the historical circumstance that the leading missionary representatives of the two religious traditions were also identified with conflicting European nationalities: the Protestant missionaries were primarily English and Scotch, the Catholic missionaries, French and Irish. The stage was set for a violent religious confrontation, especially in the Ibo provinces where Catholic and Protestant mission groups were both well-represented, and what began as a conflict on the clerical level was quickly transformed into a battle of the laity.

Interdenominational rivalry proved costly to Eastern Nigeria, in human as well as in money terms. Competition between mission bodies to establish or control new schools and churches within local communities intensified traditional divisions or created communal conflict where none had existed previously. At the same time, the competition for school children—and the insistence by the voluntary agencies that children attend schools only of their denomination—often produced a needless duplication of educational facilities and an unnecessarily harsh burden upon a community's financial resources. The more the government sought to encourage educational expansion, the more intense became the religious rivalry, for voluntary agencies were encouraged to widen their operations and to compete for increased government grants-in-aid. This point seemed especially crucial in 1956, for the government was just embarking upon a program of universal primary education. In the eyes of many NCNC leaders, the only way to reduce the social and economic costs of interdenominational rivalry was to narrow the educational role of the voluntary agencies by insisting that all new primary schools be exclusively state-controlled.

A second factor possibly motivating the new policy of secularization was Protestant concern with an increasingly aggressive and successful Catholic church. Despite a head start in Eastern Nigeria's evangelical competition, the Region's various Protestant denominations had rapidly lost ground to a persistent Ibo-centered Catholic drive for school children and converts. By the 1940s, the Catholics were the largest single denomination. By the mid-1950s, Catholics were operating almost half of the Region's primary schools, were moving rapidly into the secondary school and teacher-training fields, and were even talking of establishing a Catholic university.[4] These Catholic advances were viewed with dismay by the Region's Protestant forces, who were more threatened by the possibility of Catholic domination than by the secularization of Eastern Nigeria's school system. The Protestants recognized that a ceiling placed on all voluntary agency expansion would be a relatively greater hardship to the more rapidly expanding Catholic mission, and many therefore gave either tacit or active support to the declaration of state control.

Protestant acceptance of an expanded government role (and Catholic opposition to that same role) may have been due, in part, to the recognition that the upper echelons of both the party and the civil service were Protestant-dominated—a reflection of the earlier and relatively more intensive involvement of Protestant missions in the development of secondary schools. Thus, only one member of the Executive Council (Cabinet) in 1957 was Catholic. As late as 1964, the permanent secretary of the ministry of education and all five of the ministry's senior education inspectors were Protestant, as were the minister of education and the Eastern Nigerian premier.

Yet another factor that may have motivated the 1956 ban on voluntary agency expansion was the feeling shared by NCNC policy-makers that, in principle, the state should play the dominant role in educational and economic development, and that the historical dependence of the government upon the voluntary agencies compromised the nationalistic aspirations and independence of Nigerians. Not only had the missions been closely identified with the colonial regime, but the Roman Catholic Mission still remained largely in the hands of an expatriate (primarily Irish) clergy. Aside from this question, however, it did not seem unreasonable for the government to insist upon control of a program of educational expansion that was in fact to be largely financed by public revenue.[5]

Whatever the intent of the policy-makers, the new assertion of state control was greeted with little enthusiasm by the voluntary agencies. The Catholic response was especially swift and hostile. Political action groups were formed; petitions were drafted; mass protest rallies were held (in Port Harcourt as well as in other cities); and in the 1957 Regional elections, Catholic politicians stood, in a few constituencies, as independent candidates in opposition to the NCNC. The intensity of religious conflict varied from community to community, but in at least one town, the introduction of the religious question led to "a spectacular realignment of political groups . . . ; overnight the formerly intense ethnic conflict between the Onitsha indigenes and the non-Onitsha Ibo settlers was eclipsed by an interdenominational row between Catholics and Protestants that persisted well beyond the 1957 elections." [6] Only one independent Catholic candidate was actually successful in the March election but the Catholic insurgency was not without political impact: "organized Catholic action appears to have made an impression on the NCNC leadership. The right of parents to choose a school for their children on the basis of religious preference was acknowledged and the proportion of Catholic ministers in the new government was increased to about 50 percent." [7]

The ban on voluntary agency expansion, however, remained intact—and in dispute. The policy was adjusted to enable voluntary agencies to execute already-planned-for expansion programs and during the politically tense 1956–1957 period, a number of additional administrative concessions were made to placate the Catholic leadership. But the Ministry of Education refused to compromise on the principle of state-controlled education. In 1960, in fact, the ban on voluntary agency school construction was extended to include even private schools that received no government subsidy. As a memorandum from the chief inspector of primary schools explained: "Any new Primary School (even though it be Private) should be recommended only where it is absolutely necessary; and there are possibly only a few areas in the Region where any new schools are necessary. . . . What we really need is to build up and consolidate on the rapid expansion of the last two years, and not new and superfluous schools aimed at mere prestige or to disturb existing schools." [8] Catholic petitions and protests continued to be ignored. As Protestants, the ministry's officials were less than sympathetic with Catholic militancy. One high-ranking official put it this way: "It is my own view that the Catholics care more about religious indoctrination than they do about education. For them, education is only a means to an end." And, as educators, they were determined to put an end to what they viewed as senseless (and alien) interdenominational wrangling. In the words of another ministry official,

> This region is a relatively happy one—except for this denominationalism. . . . If the State would run their schools, I would prefer it. Let them live all day on Sunday in the Churches . . . it is never really our people. Left to our people there would not be these demonstrations. We feel these demonstrations are inspired by missionaries who have a stake. I don't think Africans themselves had come to these un-Christian views about religion. I don't think our people understand what these quarrels are about . . . the Minister wants one [religious] syllabus for all schools. If they are really Christians, they should be able to get together and join up.

RELIGIOUS POLITICS: A CASE STUDY

Toward the end of 1963 and into 1964, Catholic opposition to the government's education policy was renewed on a regionwide basis, with Port Harcourt serving as the principal battlefield for much of the conflict. Three separate issues were involved: first, the government's decision to shorten the system of primary instruction to six years (from what was, until 1961, an eight-year program commencing at age five); second, a continuing debate over the proposed imposition of a common religious syllabus for both council and voluntary agency schools; and third, the government's refusal to lift its ban on the expansion of voluntary agency primary schools. It was this latter issue that became the central rallying cry of organized Catholic political action in 1963–1964.

Universal primary education had had a stormy beginning—on the financial and educational as well as on the religious front. As originally conceived, U.P.E. was to be an entirely "fee-free" program of primary education, to be paid for out of increased regional taxes. However, when the program was finally launched in 1957, it quickly became evident that the government had drastically overextended its financial and educational capabilities. A detailed analysis of the administrative and political trials and tribulations of U.P.E. has been presented elsewhere;[9] here we only want to catalogue the major problems confronting Port Harcourt's U.P.E. or Municipal Council schools in the early sixties.

First, Port Harcourt's Municipal Council schools faced a serious shortage of qualified personnel. On the one hand, the management of these schools was assigned to the town clerk who, like the members of the council's Education Committee who had responsibility for the appointment of teachers (subject to the approval of the Provincial Education Office), had no particular expertise in the field of school administration and had other, equally pressing, responsibilities. On the other hand, qualified teachers were in short supply. In 1964, twenty percent of the 187 teachers employed by the municipality had had no training whatsoever and another thirty-nine percent held only the lowest grade teacher's certificate.[10] In this regard, Port Harcourt's experience was similar to that of other local authority schools. In fact, it had been government policy to post trained teachers only to schools that had earned government grants prior to the introduction of U.P.E. in 1956; trained teachers were to be assigned to the local authority schools only after a certain proportion of trained staff had been attained in the previously grant-earning institutions. As Abernethy notes, "In light of the government's commitment to expansion through schools controlled by local authorities, such a policy seemed self-defeating, and indeed it was one of the principal reasons why the local government schools did not win public confidence when they were opened. But some distinction between school categories was deemed necessary to 'avoid an unchecked dilution and a general lowering of standards all over the Region.' " [11]

Second, the Municipal Council's reputation for corruption undermined public confidence in the quality of education received through council schools. In this respect, too, the Municipal Council's stature was not unlike that of local councils throughout the Region. A not uncommon charge was that teaching positions were purchasable by the highest bidder. In any event, voluntary agency schools, especially the still largely expatriate-operated Catholic schools, enjoyed a reputation for greater administrative integrity and higher educational standards.

Third, the Municipal Council schools were both overcrowded and underequipped. In October 1960, before the Municipal Council had assumed the additional burden of Mile 2 Diobu U.P.E. schools, the provincial education officer for the Ministry of Education reported to the town clerk that fifty-seven additional classrooms would be required to meet the expanded school population in 1961.[12] He warned that unless these classrooms were constructed, council schools would not be permitted to raise their grade level (as had been planned) beyond Standard III.[13] Four months later, the Provincial Education Office again pleaded with the council to take remedial action:

> Equipment in the M.C. Schools: Apart from the Works Road school all the other Municipal Council schools are very poorly equipped. In almost all of these there are no screens to separate classes; in some, 2 classes share ONE blackboard (horrible thing); teachers have no school books of their own, no separate tables for them nor seats. All the Council schools had no attendance registers up to Monday January 30.
> Accommodation: . . . There is shocking congestion in the Council schools and this is not conducive to efficient learning or good results.
> I hope, Sir, that you will please look into the above complaints. This Ministry is very sad about the position of things in the Port

Harcourt Municipal Schools. There is (in several cases) utter dis-
regard of advice and instructions from the Ministry. There is in-
discipline and slackness among staff of these schools, and there is
an impression created (too noticeable by the public) by the
teachers and management of the Municipal Council Schools of
being above Education law and regulations. . . . Unless the
management co-operates sincerely with this office further com-
plications are bound to arise.[14]

Finally, the Municipal Council was in dire financial straits; its
revenue simply could not match the rapidly spiraling demand for
urban services. A principal reason for the council's financial difficulty was its consistent failure to collect the local taxes upon
which its estimates had been based. In 1964, the council was an
estimated £90,000 in arrears on its collection of taxes, the bulk
of which was owed by a relatively few, quite wealthy property
owners.[15] Consequently, when the council requested Ministry of
Local Government approval of a supplementary £10,000 estimate
for emergency school construction, it was turned down on the
grounds that the council was too far in arrears on its collection of
taxes. It was only after an emergency tax drive by the Municipal
Council and the intercession of the provincial secretary and the
local inspector of education that the Ministry of Local Government partially relented, permitting the council to spend an additional £6,000 to build three new classroom blocks.[16]

When the January 1964 school year opened, overcrowding in
council schools had reached crisis proportions, notwithstanding
the Ministry of Local Government's approval of the additional
£6,000 expenditure. Over one thousand children still had no
classroom accommodation. The voluntary agency schools had
filled their quotas and were barred by law from expanding their
facilities further, and the Municipal Council did not have sufficient funds to erect classrooms to handle the overflow. The stage
was set for a demonstration before the provincial commissioner's
office by Roman Catholic women protesting the lack of classroom
space for their children and the ban on voluntary agency expansion.[17]

Organizationally, the women's demonstration of February 12,
1964, had its origins in the October 1956 formation of the Eastern
Nigeria Catholic Council (ENCC), an action group of politically

203

militant Catholic laymen formed for the express purpose of combating the government's educational policy: "The ENCC viewed government policy as a conspiracy against the Catholics; it charged that in the past the government had discriminated against Catholics in allocating grants-in-aid and spread the rumor that a handful of European freemasons in the Department of Education were really responsible for the government's educational policy." [18] At the height of the U.P.E. debate in 1956–1957, branches of the ENCC were formed throughout the Region—including Port Harcourt, where Deputy Mayor Alagoa assumed the local branch chairmanship.[19] When the interdenominational conflict subsided after the 1957 regional elections, the Port Harcourt branch dissolved. Regionally, however, the Onitsha-centered ENCC remained intact and continued to spearhead the Catholic opposition to the government's educational policy.

In May 1963, a group of local Catholic leaders met to consider the rejuvenation of the Port Harcourt branch of the ENCC. Especially prominent among the approximately twenty persons who gathered for this meeting were the following: M. D. Okechukwu, the shopkeeper from Onitsha Division who was president of the Port Harcourt Town Council from 1951 to 1954, a former treasurer of the Onitsha Divisional Union, and in 1963, the regional first vice-president of the ENCC; Dennis Ndudo, a production assistant for an expatriate firm, a former teacher, a former administrative secretary of the Orlu Federal Union, and in 1963, the regional secretary of the ENCC; B. E. Mbanu, a primary school teacher and contractor, a former secretary of Port Harcourt's Owerri Divisional Union and, between 1961 and 1964, the sole Action Group member of the Port Harcourt Municipal Council; Mathias Obidiaso, a prominent Mile 2 Diobu politician and former municipal councillor from Orlu Division, a trader and former teacher; and Bishop Okoye of the Port Harcourt Diocese. With the exception of the bishop, these men were distinguished by certain shared characteristics. First, they were all involved in the activities of their respective ethnic and geo-ethnic associations. This point assumes particular significance when it is noted that these latter invariably embraced religiously heterogeneous communities; the fact of these overlapping loyalties is a reminder of Port Harcourt's social pluralism and the multiple group affilia-

tions of the town's inhabitants. Second, none were currently occupying positions within the party's local hierarchy. Mbanu and
Okechukwu, in fact, were openly opposed to the ruling NCNC
Executive; and Obidiaso had been passed over during the party
nominations for the 1961 Municipal Council. It is perhaps also
significant that Ndudo, Mbanu, and Okechukwu no longer held
prominent positions within their respective divisional unions. Finally, all were, of course, ardent Catholics who shared a common
distaste for the government's educational policy.

Early in February, an ENCC delegation including the ENCC's regional president, Hon. J. M. Nwosu, a prominent contractor and
independent member of the Eastern House of Assembly, and barrister Mbaegbu, secretary of the Owerri Diocesan branch of the
ENCC, visited Port Harcourt to organize a Port Harcourt demonstration protesting the ban on voluntary agency expansion.[20] They
contacted W. K. Anufuro, the vice-principal of Stella Maris College and the chairman of the advisory (but seldom listened-to)
Regional Board of Education. Anufuro refused to join in organizing a local demonstration, arguing that the minister of education
and premier should first be confronted privately. Both Anufuro
and Bishop Okoye, with whom Anufuro was close, enjoyed easy
access to Premier Okpara. They viewed the premier as reasonable
and politically flexible, and did not wish to endanger their access
to or to unnecessarily antagonize the regional government at a
time of political crisis. The federal elections were rapidly ap-
proaching, and the NCNC was busily engaged in preparations for
the elections and in its struggle with the Northern People's Congress. Moreover, at the very time that plans were underway for a
Port Harcourt demonstration, Bishop Okoye was in Enugu dis-
cussing with the premier a memorandum that he and three other
African bishops had prepared concerning the proposed common
religious syllabus. The premier was sympathetic to the bishop's
position that any such syllabus should be worked out by the religious authorities and not imposed by the government, and had
promised to convene a meeting of church leaders as soon as the
election crisis had concluded.

Failing to enlist Anufuro's support, the organization of the
Port Harcourt demonstration was entrusted to the newly recon-
stituted local ENCC branch, which decided to ask local Catholic

women to play the leading role in the planned demonstration. Women were often more heavily involved in church activities than men, and often assumed responsibility for the payment of their children's school fees. Moreover, a large number of Catholic women could be mobilized on very short notice. As one local ENCC leader explained, "It needed only an announcement in the churches that Catholic women should go and meet the Commissioner with such and such a complaint at such and such an hour. Also, the women have their own 'party' in the Christian Mothers Association."

The demonstration of February 12, 1964, triggered a largely unanticipated political chain reaction that, in the end, extended far beyond the boundaries of the local municipality. The first link in the chain was an emergency meeting of key local officials, including the provincial commissioner (who acted as convener), the provincial secretary, the deputy mayor (and local NCNC president), and the inspector of education (the only Catholic among those named). The principal outcome of this session was a decision to ignore the Catholic demand that the ban on voluntary agency school expansion be lifted and to press the regional government, instead, for the immediate allocation of funds to enable the Municipal Council schools to accommodate the overflow of both Catholic and Protestant children.

The last building grants the Ministry of Education had made available to local councils were authorized during the inaugural period of U.P.E. in 1956. The U.P.E. financial crisis of 1957–1958 had precluded the award of additional building grants, and the local councils had been compelled to assume the costs of new construction. But in 1961 Dr. Imoke assumed the portfolio of minister of education, determined to make the U.P.E. schools succeed. He and the professional educators within his ministry were especially concerned with the fate of the schools in the urban areas. As one ministry official noted in 1964, not only were these schools critically overcrowded, but U.P.E. success in the cities was likely to make nondenominational, council-operated schools more acceptable in the countryside and, it was hoped, more acceptable to the Region's Catholics.[21] Just prior to the February Port Harcourt crisis, Dr. Imoke had in fact succeeded in convincing the Executive Council to allocate an additional £100,000 to the Ministry of Education for the purpose of much needed school construction. Thus, when Port Harcourt Provincial Commissioner E. D. Sigalo suddenly appeared in Enugu, Minister Imoke was in a position to act and to act decisively.

Within twenty-four hours, a telegram was issued from the Ministry of Education authorizing the Port Harcourt Municipal Council "to provide additional accommodation either by additions to existing schools or construction of one for surplus children seeking admission to schools." [22] Simultaneously, the inspector of education in Port Harcourt and the education officer in the Ministry of Local Government in Enugu were directed to survey the situation and make recommendations on measures the council should take to accommodate the overflow school population. The Municipal Council, acting upon its telegrammed authorization, quickly rented five school buildings (two of these from prominent councillor-landlords) and within days temporary classrooms and teachers were serving 1,047 additional school-children. [23]

However, when Provincial Commissioner Sigalo returned from Enugu with the news that the minister of education had agreed to an expansion of the *Municipal Council* schools, the Catholic women and the leaders of the ENCC were furious. They felt that the commissioner on his trip to Enugu had misrepresented their pleading of February 12 to permit the *Catholic* schools to expand. A second demonstration was quickly arranged for February 14, and that day an enlarged delegation (estimated at two thousand in the local press) carried a second petition to the commissioner, the mayor, Catholic Board of Education member W. K. Anufuro, the town's two eastern assemblymen, and even Port Harcourt's member in the federal Parliament. [24] The petition, signed by five women representing the Christian Mothers Association of five local parishes, expressed in no uncertain terms the rising impatience of local Catholic residents:

> We the Catholic women of Port Harcourt hereby representing the entire Catholic Christian Mothers maintain that the Eastern Government has a definite plan against education and the Catholics in this Region. . . . We maintain that we have a right under our constitution to send our children to the school of our own choice, we also maintain that there can be no question of choice where there is no alternative. . . . We therefore demand that

Catholic schools be granted permission to expand their existing schools by addition of streams without further delay. As Catholics we are opposed to the training of our children in non-Catholic schools against our wish. We also demand eight years school period for our children.

This time Provincial Commissioner Sigalo was somewhat less receptive to their entreaties: "Commissioner Mr. E. D. Sigalo warned the demonstrators against giving the impression that they loved their church more than their Government. He advised them not to allow themselves to be used as instruments to oppose and destroy the Government they had contributed so much to build." [25]

Two weeks later, the Port Harcourt Diocesan branch of the ENCC reported to its parent body meeting at Onitsha that they had received no satisfaction from any of the officials who had been contacted and against whom demonstrations had been led. An ENCC delegation of women was despatched to Enugu on behalf of "the entire Catholic Christian Mothers of the region." Their petition reiterated the demand for the abolition of the ban on voluntary agency primary school construction, called for a return to an eight-year primary school course, and asked for the removal of Minister of Education Imoke. It concluded with this ultimatum:

We hope our Hon. Premier will give our grievances his urgent favourable attention and immediate response within a fortnight of delivery of this memorandum in order to avert a resort to a wide public demonstration of all Catholic women of the region now being suspended on the advice and intervention of our Catholic Authorities and in order not to give the impression of being unconcerned with the present political tension in the country. Please take note that we shall be forced to ignore the above restraints if no favourable response is forthcoming with the above limit of time.[26]

Two more weeks passed. ENCC regional president, Assemblyman J. M. Nwosu, returned to Port Harcourt with word that women from Owerri and from Onitsha Town had decided to demonstrate in Enugu. The Port Harcourt ENCC decided that Port Harcourt would send eighty representatives for the demonstration sched-

uled on March 24. Bishop Okoye, however, voiced his strong objections to the demonstration, noting that the premier had already
been contacted and had promised to consider Catholic grievances in the near future. In response to the bishop's plea, the local
ENCC reconsidered its earlier decision, concluding finally that since
"other delegations couldn't be restrained" (as one leader put it),
the Port Harcourt branch could not withdraw entirely but that
only nominal representation of four Port Harcourt women would
be provided.

The "march on Enugu" had a somewhat inglorious conclusion.
Several hundred women, assembled from communities throughout the Region, advanced peacefully to the Eastern House of Assembly. ("The women had palm leaves in their mouths, for si-
lence," an ENCC leader reported.) The police refused to let the
women or their leaders enter the house to deliver a letter to the
premier. Tear gas was fired to disperse the gathering, and seven
women and one man were arrested on charges of unlawful assembly. On April 26, 1964, the ENCC met again at Onitsha and
arranged for defense counsel for the pending trial; on April 29,
the arrested demonstrators were acquitted and discharged.

THE IMPACT OF RELIGIOUS POLITICS

The politics of religious protest in Port Harcourt held much in
common with the politics of militant trade unionism. First, like
the trade union identities activated at the time of the general
strike, religious identities intersected those based upon community of origin or occupational role, resulting in a crisscrossing
pattern of urban group memberships. The Executive Committee
of the local ENCC branch, for example, included persons from diverse sections of Iboland (table 21), and, in 1956, Ibo Catholics
followed the lead of Port Harcourt's non-Ibo deputy mayor in
protesting the ban on voluntary school expansion. Similarly, persons of diverse occupations (and, though the reported data do not
reveal this, of diverse educational backgrounds) were numbered
among the leaders of the Catholic protests in 1956 and in 1963–
1964. It seems likely that the overlapping group affiliations of
Port Harcourt's political actors helped to moderate the intensity
of conflict along any single axis.[27]

Second, while religious groupings transcended those based

TABLE 21

MEMBERSHIP OF THE EXECUTIVE COMMITTEE OF THE
PORT HARCOURT BRANCH OF THE ENCC (1963)

1. *M. D. Okechukwu:* Onitsha Division; shopkeeper.
2. *D. Ndudo:* Orlu Division; production assistant and former teacher.
3. *B. Mbanu:* Owerri Division; teacher and contractor.
4. *M. Obidiaso:* Orlu Division; trader and former teacher.
5. *C. Nwako:* Onitsha Division; foreman, mechanical workshop, Nigerian Ports Authority.
6. *Nwakile:* Onitsha Division; mechanic.
7. *M. O. Marizu:* Orlu Division; barrister.
8. *J. Eleony:* Owerri Division; contractor.
9. *P. Mgbobukwa:* Orlu Division; contractor.
10. *Mrs. F. Iwuorah:* Onitsha Division; teacher.
11. *Mrs. A. Nsolibe:* Owerri Division; teacher.
12. *Mrs. S. Akwiwu:* Orlu Division; teacher.
13. *Mrs. M. Ohedoro:* Owerri Division; housewife.

upon community of origin and occupational role, they simultaneously reflected—as did the division between the trade unionists and the employers—a broad socioeconomic cleavage between the better-educated and occupationally advantaged, on the one hand, and the less-educated and occupationally subordinate, on the other. These educational and occupational imbalances, a product of the relatively greater emphasis that had been placed by early Protestant missionaries upon the development of secondary schools, were closing in the early sixties, but Protestants continued to occupy the dominant positions in the occupational and political hierarchies. Thus, of Port Harcourt's forty-six municipal councillors who served between 1961 and 1964, 58.7 percent reported affiliation with one or another Protestant denomination, 37.0 percent reported they were Catholic, and 4.3 percent reported membership in the National Church of Nigeria. Prior to the merger of the predominantly Catholic stranger community of Mile 2 Diobu with the main township, the Protestant percentage was even higher, exceeding 80.0 percent prior to 1955 (see table 19, chapter 7). Moreover, Protestants continued to dominate the Municipal Council's most influential positions, in 1964 holding five of the six council committee chairmanships.

Third, the leadership of the Catholic protest movement in the 1960s, like that of the militant labor movement, was quite distinct from the leadership of the regional party and the dominant ethnic community. None of the members of the local Catholic Council Executive Committee held office within the NCNC Executive, and at least three Catholic leaders were openly at odds with the local party organization. Indeed, for some Catholic activists, participation in the ENCC may have been motivated by the same kind of antiestablishment protest that led radical Ibos and non-Ibos to involve themselves in the labor movement.

Fourth, religious identities, like trade union identities, were issue-specific. Whereas trade union identities were activated by worker confrontations with employers, religious identities were activated by issues of educational policy. When educational issues were not in the political foreground, the salience of religious identities and the effectiveness of religious protest activity were greatly inhibited. Thus, the approach of the 1964 federal elections and the all-important confrontation between North and South completely overshadowed Eastern Nigeria's lower-order, interdenominational conflict and reduced the political significance of an antigovernment Catholic protest. By the same token, when Catholics or Protestants attempted to use religious issues to advance their political ambitions, they met with no more success than had the politically ambitious trade unionists. One such effort occurred during the 1956 U.P.E. crisis in Port Harcourt, when a Protestant clique within the NCNC Executive Committee unsuccessfully sought to discredit Catholic party leaders for their statements in opposition to the government's educational policy. At the regional level, similarly, despite much talk of a Catholic political rebellion in the bitterly contested 1957 elections, only one independent candidate who was clearly supported by the Eastern Nigerian Catholic Council succeeded against the NCNC.[28] This fact does not mean that the religious activists did not have any impact on governmental policy. To the contrary, the shake-up of the Executive Council following this election attested to the seriousness with which the governmental establishment viewed religious discontent. It is noteworthy, too, that while the government severely restricted the expansion of voluntary agency schools, no attempt was made to assume control of those schools already being operated by the voluntary agencies. Premier Michael Okpara's reluctance to impose a common religious syllabus was still further indication of the political respect that the Catho-

lic activists in particular commanded. Nevertheless, religious political action, while influencing governmental policy, did not
threaten the communal bases of the urban and regional structures
of power. When election time rolled around, communal identities
reasserted themselves and "the establishment" (i.e., Ibo-speaking,
NCNC) politicians remained firmly in control.

Finally, as in the case of the general strike, the key political decisions in the local U.P.E. schools crisis were made not in Port
Harcourt but in distant administrative centers. This fact was not
unusual. Actually, the most crucial policy decisions affecting the
city's economic and social development almost invariably were
made by officials of the regional and federal governments. Local
leaders were often involved in the decision-making sequence, but
their participation was more often at the level of policy execution
than of policy formation. The controls exercised by the regional
ministry of local government, for example, extended far beyond
the relatively narrow confines of expenditures on school construction, to encompass review of contracts entered into by the Municipal Council, approval of local bylaws, supervision of the council's personnel practices, and so on. Similarly, moving into other
governmental areas, the operation of the all-important Nigerian
Ports Authority and Nigerian railway were federal subjects,
within the control of federal officials.

This concentration of power at the center had the important
consequence of directing the political attention of the city's largest commercial and industrial concerns, especially of the critical
petroleum industry, to the regional and federal governments,
rather than to the Municipal Council or the local Planning Authority. This point is important, for it highlights the interrelated-
ness of a local community and the wider political and administrative systems in which it is embedded. Nowhere is this interrelated-
ness manifested more clearly than in the protracted struggle
between Eastern Nigeria's Ibo majority and Ijaw minority over
the creation of a separate Ijaw-dominated Rivers State in which
Port Harcourt was to become the administrative center. It is to
this subject that we now turn.

CHAPTER 10
Oil, War, and Nationality

Communalism, we have seen, manifested itself in Port Harcourt on several levels. Inasmuch as Ibos comprised eighty percent or more of the total population and held a virtual monopoly of political power, local communal conflict usually centered on intra-Ibo cleavages—especially those between geo-ethnic groups—and the wider identities of nationality were generally of less significance. Even in Ibo-dominated Port Harcourt, however, the always latent conflict between Eastern Nigeria's Ibo and non-Ibo nationalities frequently became manifest, forcing at least a temporary closing of ranks at lower levels of the city's communal structure and transforming identities of nationality into viable instruments of political action. Whereas elections were the situational trigger of geo-ethnic conflict, identities of nationality were activated by the persistent demand for the creation of a separate Rivers State inclusive of Port Harcourt. An examination of the confrontation between Ibo and non-Ibo nationalities over "the Port Harcourt question" sheds light not only upon the dynamics of urban communalism but also upon the tragic Nigerian/Biafran conflict and its political aftermath.

IJAW NATIONALISM AND THE MINORITIES COMMISSION

As the date of Nigerian Independence approached, minority ethnic groups within each of Nigeria's three regions grew increasingly apprehensive about their future as permanent regional minorities in a self-governing Nigeria and urged the creation of separate minority states. The London Constitutional Conference

213

of 1957, in response to these concerns, appointed a special Commission of Enquiry to "ascertain the facts about the fears of minorities in any part of Nigeria and to propose means of allaying those fears whether well or ill founded."[1] The minority movements were to be given their day in court.[2]

Within Eastern Nigeria, non-Ibo minorities advanced four proposals for the creation of separate states, two of which—namely, the Calabar-Ogoja-Rivers (COR) State proposal and the Rivers State proposal—directly involved the Port Harcourt municipality.[3] The COR State proposal was the handiwork of Ibibio and Efik separatists who sought to join in a separate state three of Eastern Nigeria's five provinces (excepting the Ibo-speaking Afikpo and Abakaliki Divisions in Ogoja). While Ibos everywhere bitterly opposed the COR State demand, in Port Harcourt this particular proposal received surprisingly little political attention. For one thing, Port Harcourt's Ibibios and Efiks were few in number. Moreover, the proposal lacked the support of the city's largest non-Ibo minority—the Ijaw—who did not view their subordination to Ibibios and Efiks in a COR State as an improvement over their subordination to Ibos within the existing boundaries of the Eastern Region.[4]

The proposed Rivers State, however, was quite another matter —of crucial concern to both the Ibo and Ijaw communities in Port Harcourt. Conceived by Ijaw separatists anxious to break free of Ibo domination and to establish a degree of political autonomy, the proposed Ijaw-dominated state embraced all of the Rivers Province (including the Ibo-speaking Ahoada and Port Harcourt Divisions); the Western Ijaw Division of the Western Region; and the small areas of Opobo, Andoni, and Ndoki which lay within Eastern Nigeria but outside the Rivers Province. For both Ibos and Ijaws, the stakes involved in the contest over the proposed Rivers State were high.

The Ibo Perspective

From the standpoint of the main Owerri-Onitsha body of Eastern Nigeria's Ibo population, to which belonged all but a fraction of Port Harcourt's politically dominant Ibo immigrants, two points were crucial. First, the proposed Port Harcourt-centered Rivers State implied the excision from their Region of the city that served as the administrative headquarters of the Ibo State Union and, more importantly, as the economic center and residence for a large number of Iboland's most prosperous and influential citizens. These Ibo residents had no desire to be the members of a political minority in an Ijaw-dominated region. Nor could they see any logic to the inclusion of what was essentially an Ibo city— both in terms of indigenous land ownership and in terms of immigrant settlement—in a Rivers State controlled by Ijaws.

Second, the projected Rivers State also implied the excision from Ibo-controlled territory of much of Eastern Nigeria's economic potential, as represented by the expanding harbor and industrial facilities of Port Harcourt and by the rich oil palm plantations of the Ibo-speaking (but politically ambivalent) Ikwerre people in Ahoada and Port Harcourt Divisions. It should be noted that in 1958 the full extent and significance of the oil deposits within the Ijaw-speaking Niger Delta were not yet recognized. Consequently, Ijaw separation per se, however, politically distasteful, did not at this time appear to threaten any vital interest of the Ibo people. However, even in 1958, Ijaw separation *involving a claim to Ibo-speaking Ahoada and Port Harcourt* was viewed with considerable alarm.

The Ijaw Perspective

The movement for Ijaw statehood was dictated both by a positive consciousness of cultural nationality and by hatred and fear of Ibo domination. Traditionally, the self-consciousness and political unity of the Ijaw-speaking creek inhabitants was no greater than that which characterized Eastern Nigeria's similarly fragmented Ibo and Ibibio-speaking peoples. But the same forces of change and politicization were at work among the Ijaw as among the Ibo and Ibibio, and in the Ijaw case, geographical isolation from Nigeria's administrative centers and a unique set of economic problems gave particular urgency to a movement toward ethnic political union.[5]

Consciousness of an objective Ijaw nationality manifested itself as early as 1930 in the formation of an Ijaw Rivers Peoples League that had as its objective the removal of the Rivers area from the Owerri Province. And, in November 1943, an Ijaw Tribe Union was inaugurated at Port Harcourt for these expressed purposes:

1. To collect all peoples of Rivers Division into one administrative Division, with the ultimate aim of being formed into an administrative Province of its own.

2. To start with Opobo as the first target, and detach her with all her satellites from the Calabar Province to the Owerri Province, secondly to detach the Forcados District Ijaws from the Warri Province, and then to pursue the final result of being formed into a Province.

3. The advantages will be to boast of adequate manpower which alone can help the peoples of the Rivers Division to pursue any major schemes successfully.

4. To pursue major schemes, in a concerted manner, such as mass and professional education, development of our fishing industry, exploiting the wealth in our mangrove forests, et cetera.

5. To save ourselves from the unenviable status of minority, as we are at present situated in the various provinces into which we are split.

6. To resuscitate and preserve our cultures, and evolve a healthy social order and determine our welfare.

7. To take our stand as a tribe in the progressive evolution of Nigeria.[6]

In January 1944, the Ijaw Tribe Union transformed itself into a more representative Rivers Division Peoples League (renamed the Ijaw Rivers Peoples League a few months later), which continued to press for Ijaw unity and development.[7] Then, in 1954, a new organization known as the Rivers State Congress formally presented the demand for a separate Rivers State to the London Constitutional Conference. It was this congress, subsequently reorganized as the Rivers Chiefs and Peoples Conference, which represented the Ijaw cause before the Minorities Commission in 1958.

If the Ibo could not countenance a Rivers State inclusive of Port Harcourt, the Ijaws could not countenance a Rivers State without Port Harcourt. The municipality, which Ijaws wanted for their state capital, had long been identified, despite the local supremacy of the city's Ibo majority, as the social and political center of Ijaw nationalism. In this sense, Port Harcourt stood in much the same relation to Ijawland as Onitsha Town did to Iboland. The most important Ijaw political initiatives invariably were taken by educated Ijaws resident in Port Harcourt, and the mu-

nicipality, since 1947, had served as the administrative headquarters for the province in which most of Nigeria's Ijaw-speaking
peoples were concentrated. More importantly, Ijaw separatists
recognized that a separate Rivers State without Port Harcourt
would lack geographical contiguity, be economically unviable,
and stand little chance of receiving the Minorities Commission's
sanction.

In support of their claim to Port Harcourt, the Rivers State
advocates pointed to the cultural distinctiveness of the Ibo-speaking groups located in Ahoada and Port Harcourt Divisions which,
it was argued, set these groups apart from the Ibos of the Owerri
and Onitsha heartland. The Ijaw separatists noted, too, the contempt in which the "bush" Ibo to the north were held by the Ibo-
speaking Ikwerres, and the extended contact that the southern-
most Ikwerres (notably, Port Harcourt's indigenous Diobus) had
had with neighboring Ijaw communities, with whom they had
traded and intermarried. In short, in the Ijaw separatist view,
Port Harcourt culturally and historically "belonged" to the proposed Rivers State.

Wooing the Diobus

As the January 1958 date of the Minorities Commission's Port Harcourt hearings neared, both the Rivers State movement and its
Ibo opposition worked feverishly to prepare their cases and to
rally popular support for their respective positions. The especially
well endowed Ibo campaign, reported to have involved expenditures in excess of $11,000 (most of which went toward the pay-
ment of a team of legal advisors), was financed by levies placed
upon the members and wealthy patrons of Port Harcourt's numerous Ibo town and divisional unions, and organized under the institutional auspices of the Ibo State Union. The NCNC adopted an
official hands-off posture, for it did not wish to be cast in the role
of Ibo advocate. However, the local NCNC Youth Association,
which in 1958 was in firm control of the party's local Executive
Committee, used what was in fact an unofficial arm of the party's
youth wing, the Port Harcourt Rate and Taxpayers Association,
to organize a "nonpartisan" community protest during the Port
Harcourt hearings.[8]

The central thrust of the campaign effort of both the Ibos and the Ijaws was directed toward winning Diobu and other Ikwerre adherents to their respective positions. Both sides reasoned that the decision of the Minorities Commission would turn largely upon the wishes of the indigenous inhabitants, and that the testimony of the Ikwerres before the commission would therefore be critical. Each side charged the other with wooing the Ikwerre vote by the expenditure of bribe money and by the rendering of political promises impossible to fulfill.

In point of fact, the pressures exerted upon the Ikwerres, and especially upon the Diobus, were intense. On the one hand, the Ijaws played upon the resentment felt by the Ibo-speaking Ikwerres toward the stranger Ibos in their midst, to whom they had alienated both their land and their traditional position of dominance. Exemplifying the sentiment of many Ikwerres was this testimony of the president of a self-styled Ikwerre Citizens Committee: "The Ikwerre people were not Ibos and their main object was to disassociate themselves completely from the Ibos who violated their tribal customs (1) by attempting sometimes deceitfully to buy from individuals who professed to be owners of land which they knew to be held communally; (2) by competing in the sale of produce in Ikwerre markets; (3) by creating their own markets within the Ikwerre area; (4) by dominating Ikwerre politics and by using the NCNC to assist them in this domination." [9] On the other hand, the Ibo opponents of the proposed Rivers State pointedly warned the Ikwerres that the Rivers State was unlikely to be realized and that their support for the Ijaw separatists consequently entailed considerable political risk.

In the end, the Ikwerres split into two camps. Within Port Harcourt, the late Chief Joseph Wobo, nominally the paramount chief of the seven Diobu sections, declared himself in opposition to the Rivers State, testifying before the Minorities Commission that "The Diobu people were Ikwerres and all the people from there to Onitsha were one. . . . The Ikwerre and Ibo peoples were one and the same." [10] Wobo's claim to the headship of the Diobus, however, was not acknowledged by a large segment of the Diobu population, and his testimony was opposed before the commission by other traditional leaders of the Diobus who were in support of Diobu inclusion within a separate Rivers State.[11]

When the dust had settled, the Ibo viewpoint had prevailed,

the Minorities Commission vetoing the proposed formation of a separate Rivers State:

> There are grave objections to such a state. In the first place, the Ogoni Division is divided from the Brass and Degema Divisions by a broad arm of the sea which runs up to Port Harcourt, and by a long stretch of Ibo territory which culminates in this town. Port Harcourt is an Ibo town; it is growing rapidly and the indigenous branch of the Ibos who were the original inhabitants are already out-numbered by Ibos from the hinterland. Port Harcourt has consistently voted NCNC and has shown a continued attachment to the present Regional Government; the main body of Ibos would be most reluctant to lose it . . . only in the Brass, Degema and Ogoni Divisions was there support for the State, and . . . a state consisting of these three Divisions together with the Western Ijaws would number less than half a million and would besides be divided into two parts by Port Harcourt and the arm of the sea which runs up to it. To create such a state would cut off the inhabitants from their most probable sources of supply. To include within a Rivers State Ahoada and Port Harcourt would, we believe, create a problem as acute as that with which we are asked to deal at present and would be sharply resented by the Ibos of the central plateau.
>
> For these reasons we are unable to recommend any new state in this region.[12]

But the advocates of the Ijaw cause had not failed entirely. They had succeeded in convincing the members of the commission of the peculiar administrative and economic problems with which the fragmented and oftentimes inaccessible riverain area was confronted. The commission recommended that Brass, Degema, Ogoni, and Western Ijaw Divisions be designated a special area and that a federal board be established to formulate and execute a program of economic development.

As for the Diobus, they had little choice but to accept the administrative status quo. The Rivers State controversy, however, gave the Diobus political leverage they had never previously enjoyed, and when the conflict was over, the Eastern Nigerian government sought to assuage injured feelings by making Chief Joseph Wobo a "second class chief" and by according him a seat as traditional ruler on the Port Harcourt Municipal Council. In

219

addition, as we observed in chapter 7, the Port Harcourt NCNC in 1961 selected a Diobu native to stand for one of the municipality's two seats in the Eastern House of Assembly. That native-stranger antipathies still lay beneath the surface was little questioned, but by 1963–1964, Port Harcourt's indigenes had entered into a tolerable political accommodation with the community of strangers.

THE POLITICS OF OIL

With the failure of the Rivers State movement in 1958, the voice of the Delta separatists was temporarily muted. As Kenneth Post has written, "The [Rivers] chiefs were coming to realize their dependence on the favour of the Regional Government, controlled by the NCNC and opposed to new states being created in the East, more especially since two of the most important of them became involved in commissions of inquiry into the legitimacy of their title claims. Many of the younger educated men felt also that their interests would be best served by supporting the government of the day." [13] The dismemberment of the separatist movement was dramatized in the 1959 federal elections by the failure of anti-NCNC candidates in Rivers constituencies. Harold Biriye's newly formed Niger Delta Congress, a party allied with the Northern People's Congress, was successful in only one of nine elections that the NDC contested.[14]

But in the 1960s, two developments stimulated a resurgence of Rivers political agitation: first, the sudden recognition of the vast economic potential contained within the Delta oil fields; second, the political disintegration of the Nigerian Federation. Previously, little attention had been paid by either the national press or the politicians to the fledgling petroleum industry. Virtually no one, including the petroleum engineers themselves, anticipated the richness of Nigeria's petroleum reserves. Nor was there any public awareness of the impact that a sizeable oil industry might have on either the Nigerian economy or the Nigerian political scene. But beginning in 1964, the "oil question" began to filter into the political arena, and in the following year, petroleum emerged as an issue of both regional and national significance: "Any relative disinterest in petroleum that remained in 1965 came to an abrupt halt when the Federal Prime Minister in a statement to the Cham-

ber of Commerce and the Federal Minister of Finance in his annual budget address spoke optimistically about the balance-of-
payments impacts that oil production would have in Nigeria. Political feelings about petroleum changed from apathy to euphoria.
Interest in controlling the newly recognized benefits from oil grew
apace." [15] Interest was especially high in Eastern Nigeria, where
the known petroleum deposits were most extensive—in 1967
yielding two-thirds of Nigeria's total petroleum production.

Even prior to the first military coup of January 1966, Ijaw
leaders had renewed their demands for more favorable treatment
from the Eastern Nigerian and federal governments. It quickly
became evident that the Federal Niger Delta Development Board
would have little impact. Though established at independence,
in October 1960, the board did not convene until March the following year, and two years later it had done little more than as-
semble five expatriate experts, seven launches, and eight powered
dinghies.[16] As Walter Schwarz records, "Its survey and experi-
ments showed that the creeks could support rice growing; but the
experts could hardly ignore the fact that the Rivers area was un-
promising for much in the way of 'development.' " [17] Thus, the
discovery of rich oil fields within the Niger Delta came to have
particular significance for economically impoverished Ijawland.
The one issue on which the otherwise fragmented Ijaw communities could unite was that the oil-producing areas deserved a
greater proportion of the oil revenues than were currently coming
their way.

With the second military coup of July 1966, which saw an Ibo-
dominated military regime replaced by one controlled by Northern military officers, the politics of oil and Ijaw separatism moved
to the center of the political arena. As early as 1964, some members of the Eastern Ibo establishment, despairing of any possibility of reducing the Northern hold on the federal government,
began to talk of Eastern secession. Initially, the voices of moderation were to prevail, and with the ascendancy of an Ibo-led
military regime in January 1966, talk of Eastern secession was
temporarily silenced. But with the July coup, with the series of
massacres that were unleashed against Ibos resident in the North,
and with the resulting massive migration of Ibos abroad, back
to their home region, the secessionist debate was reopened.

The question of Eastern secession, as debated both within Eastern Nigeria and between the Eastern and other regions, involved several issues.[18] But never far from the heart of the debate were the subjects of oil and the minorities. The secession of oil-rich Eastern Nigeria would clearly have major economic consequences for the remainder of the federation. According to one economist's calculations, had Biafra been permitted to secede, Nigerian oil production in 1973 would be between 0.9 and 1.1 million barrels per day, as contrasted to projected 1973 oil production in a united Nigeria of between 1.8 and 2.4 million barrels per day.[19] The economic impact of this reduction would have been enormous: "The prospect of having the loss of Biafra, and especially of Biafran oil, cut total government revenues by 45 percent, reduce foreign exchange availability by nearly 40 percent, and decrease GNP by 30 percent surely provided a strong economic incentive for the leaders of Federal Nigeria to wish to maintain a united Nigeria."[20]

By the same token, oil also provided an important economic rationale to Easterners who felt that their region could and should "go it alone": "an independent Biafra would have had a petroleum-dominated economy, with oil being responsible for as much as two-thirds of government revenues, three-fourths of foreign exchange earnings, and one-fourth of GNP. The potential for growth that petroleum might have imparted to some twelve million Biafrans is enormous."[21] However, oil was not the principal motivating factor behind the Biafran secession or, for that matter, behind the federal decision to resist secession with military force. Far more crucial were the deep-seated communal insecurities and rivalries that existing institutional arrangements could neither contain nor ameliorate. Oil, however, may well have been the "threshold factor" propelling Nigeria toward civil war.

The issue of oil and that of the Eastern minorities were closely linked, because most Eastern oil was centered in non-Ibo areas. This fact quite naturally strengthened the determination of non-Ibo (especially Ijaw) leaders to gain a greater measure of autonomy and control over these important petroleum resources, and just as naturally strengthened the determination of the Eastern Ibo establishment to resist the fragmentation of their Region.

As the East moved toward secession, the federal government

sought to win the support of the Eastern (and other) minorities, first by encouraging Eastern non-Ibo separatist leaders based in Lagos (such as the Niger Delta Congress head, Harold Biriye), and later, just prior to the Biafran secession, by announcing the breakup of Nigeria's regional administrative system and the creation of twelve states. But within Eastern Nigeria, which under the federal decree was divided into an Ibo-dominated East Central State, an Ibibio and Efik-controlled South Eastern State, and an Ijaw-centered Rivers State, open minority support for the federal government was muted.

Several forces appeared to be at work. To begin with, the traditional fragmentation of the non-Ibo groups was continuing to make itself felt: the various cultural subgroups continued to be suspicious of each other, and consensus still had not been reached on the number or the appropriate boundaries of separate minority states. In addition, some Eastern non-Ibos had been caught up in the Northern massacres, and their families and communities were consequently supportive of a move toward regional solidarity with the victimized Ibos. Moreover, the Eastern military astutely had taken steps to establish new lines of communication with non-Ibo leaders. A new system of provincial administration, based upon more culturally homogeneous units, was inaugurated to assuage minority fears and insecurities. The new provinces were to have a greater degree of political autonomy than the previous system of local government had allowed, and the government committed itself to reopening the broader question of minority self-determination at some unspecified point in the future.[22] In addition, ethnic arithmetic was used to maximum advantage, with prominent non-Ibos being appointed to key governmental and military positions. During the September 13, 1966, Lagos Constitutional Conference, for example, only two of the six delegates representing Eastern Nigeria were from core Ibo groups; the remaining four delegates included an Efik, an Ijaw, an Ikom (from the Ogoja area), and an Ikwerre. Similarly, during the 1966–1967 period the head of the civil service was an Ibibio, the chairman of the Eastern Public Service Commission was from Ogoja, and the attorney general was an Ijaw. Finally, when a politics of conciliation did not suffice, the government was not beyond imprisoning the occasionally recalcitrant non-Ibo leader who refused to acquiesce to the government-of-the-day. In short, while anti-Ibo and profederal sentiment remained high within many minority areas (both before and during the military conflict), the separatists—and the federal government—were denied their goal of an united minority movement hostile to the secessionist regime.

PORT HARCOURT'S POSTWAR DISPOSITION

For Eastern Nigeria as a whole, and for Port Harcourt in particular, Biafran collapse and federal victory in January 1970 had a twofold significance. First, Port Harcourt was now firmly in the hands of the federal forces and under the control of the Ijaw-dominated Rivers State administration. In the course of the war, the city had been evacuated by all of its Ibo residents, and it quickly became evident that the newly ascendant Ijaws had no intention of permitting the Ibos to return to Port Harcourt and reassume their historically dominant economic and political position. This point was forcefully driven home when, a few months before the war's end, Dr. Nnamdi Azikiwe visited Port Harcourt and was told by the Rivers State governor, "Port Harcourt is not for the Ibos." [23]

Events since the war's conclusion bear out the firmness of the Ijaw resolve. Through the vehicle of required "security clearance" by the local military authority, Ibos have been discouraged from accepting local employment or taking up residence in Port Harcourt. And, as of this writing, the East Central State is continuing to wage an as yet unsuccessful battle to recover Ibo property in the Rivers State (most of it in Port Harcourt) valued at £56 million. Recently, however, the chairman of the Rivers State Abandoned Property Authority gave verbal assurances that all property in the Rivers State owned by citizens of the East Central State would in fact be returned to its owners.[24]

The second major implication of the federal victory of January 1970 was that, by virtue of the new state boundaries created just prior to the Biafran secession, Ibo hegemony over oil-producing areas was to be greatly reduced; for the Ibo-speaking Port Harcourt and Ahoada Divisions, which were found to be rich in petroleum and natural gas resources, were separated by the federal map makers from the Ibo-dominated East Central State and placed within the Ijaw-dominated Rivers State. As a consequence, Ibo oil areas today account for nearly half of Rivers State total oil production.[25] More importantly, while over one-fourth of the total oil output of the Eastern states is produced in Ibo-inhabited areas, "under the current state system, Ibo leaders can expect to control directly or benefit from only about 14 percent of total Nigerian oil revenues, assuming they govern only the East Central State. This is a far cry from the 67 percent of total oil revenues that would have been controlled by an independent Biafra and from the 43 percent that might have accrued to an Eastern Region within the former federation." [26]

The restraints placed on the mobility of Ibo persons and capital have seriously hindered the economic recovery of the heavily overcrowded and resource-barren East Central State. According to Nigerian economist Sam Aluko, the proposed £50 million expenditure envisaged for the East Central State's 1970–1974 development plan "can only scratch the surface." [27] And, according to Ukpaki Asika, administrator of the East Central State, his government has been able to raise less than a third of even this nominal sum and must depend upon the federal government for the remainder.[28] The East Central State has gone so far as to impose a much resented 25 percent tax surcharge on all government wages and salaries.[29] But the only viable solution to the state's economic difficulties is the acquisition of capital to regenerate local commerce and industry and to provide jobs for the thousands of unemployed. Therefore, the "abandoned property" issue and the Ibo exclusion from Port Harcourt have aroused much bitterness within the East Central State.

Within Port Harcourt itself, the anti-Ibo policies of the Rivers State government have not been without severe economic cost. Shipping has yet to return to prewar levels, despite serious congestion in the Lagos docks and despite calls by the North for reactivation of the Niger Delta port, and the shortage of skilled labor in Port Harcourt has prompted several firms to relocate their operations in the East Central State.[30] All of these problems have been of serious concern not only to the Rivers State government, but also to the federal government that continues to have an important stake in Port Harcourt's development and well-being.

225

Nevertheless, appeals made by General Yakubu Gowon, the head of the federal military government, have been to little avail.[31] The restraints on Ibo mobility remain in force.

What, then, does the future hold for Port Harcourt and the Eastern states? Ibo exclusion from the economically critical city that they once controlled, together with the excision from Ibo control of Ibo lands and important petroleum resources, are constant reminders of defeat and rejection. More immediately, Ibo exclusion and loss of petroleum resources highlight the economic isolation and impoverishment of the East Central State. It is clear that until the related questions of petroleum and Port Harcourt are resolved, the relationships between the three states comprising the former Eastern Region will remain strained, with the resumption of violence—be it only in the form of small-scale border clashes—always imminent.

More than Ibo security is at issue, for the continued inability of federal authorities to guarantee the free mobility of all Nigerian citizens and to settle interstate disputes would call into serious question the political and administrative capabilities of the federal government and the viability of a united Nigeria.

If the will to achieve a political accommodation among the Eastern states can be found—and this point, unfortunately, is problematical—there are at least three kinds of adjustments in the status quo which might be considered. The first potentially negotiable area concerns the formula by which oil and other revenues are distributed among the federal and state governments. Under arrangements in effect prior to the January 1966 military coup, oil royalties and rentals and oil-related customs duties were divided so as to disproportionately benefit the state of origin: state of origin, 50 percent; federal government, 20 percent; and distributable pool (from which the state of origin would again benefit), 30 percent.[32] But this formula has been twice revised, first in 1967 and again in 1970, so as to significantly increase the distributable portion at the expense of the state of origin.[33] Still another provision of the 1970 formula leaves petroleum profits taxes, the future source of more than two-thirds of total petroleum revenue, in the hands of the federal government.[34] And, more recently, a new decree vests ownership of all territorial waters and the continental shelf in the federal government.[35] These developments appear to have significantly reduced the special economic benefits accruing to states that happen to have oil fields located within their boundaries. It is hoped that this will reduce the quarreling among the states over the control of the petroleum resources. However, the ultimate question, concerning the introduction of a new formula for the allocation of revenues between the federal and state governments, still must be resolved.

A second potentially negotiable area of concern is the future administrative status of Port Harcourt. The Ijaws are determined that the Ibos shall never again assume control of this vital port city, but the exclusionary policies of the Ijaws have proven costly to the Rivers State as well as to the East Central State. We have already noted the problems created in Port Harcourt by a shortage of skilled labor. The economic recovery of the city would be even more seriously hampered if East Central State threats to export palm oil via the Mid-West rather than via Port Harcourt were acted upon, or if—as has been threatened—Ibo railwaymen were to refuse to take trains into territory where Ibos were not welcome.[36]

It would appear that the mutual economic interest of both Ibos and Ijaws would indicate the possibility—if not the necessity—for some kind of accommodation. One solution, which received speculative consideration by Nigerian decision-makers even before the January military coup, would constitute Port Harcourt a federal territory, in the manner of Lagos. Ibos would be given assurance that Port Harcourt would always be open to them; the Rivers State would participate in the federal revenue generated by local economic activity; and the federal government would acquire another major source of direct revenue. Alternatively, it has also been suggested that Port Harcourt be controlled by a joint authority representing the three states that most depend on the city. This alternative, too, would appear to meet both the Ibo requirement of access to the port city, and the Ijaw objective that the city not again fall subject to Ibo domination.

Finally, the federal government has indicated that the existing state boundary lines are negotiable. A formal review of demands for new states and for boundary revisions has been delayed, but the possibility of reform of the existing state system has been kept open. Moreover, a commission has been appointed by the

227

federal government to resolve current disputes concerning the precise location of present boundaries; in the case of the Eastern states, the possession of certain oil fields will turn on the commission's findings.[37]

Whether or not major boundary revisions or the creation of more states will be seriously entertained by the federal military government, and whether or not the government will be able to enforce any permanent settlement of these questions, remains to be seen; but a boundary revision would correct what are, from the standpoint of the Ibos, clear inequities in the present state system. Of course, any change that would remove petroleum resources from the control of the Rivers or South Eastern states would be strongly resisted by the ruling non-Ibo minorities. However, these minorities—the Ijaw, in particular—might well be receptive to a broader boundary revision package that would not only join Port Harcourt and Ahoada Divisions to the East Central State, but that would also unite comparably oil-rich Western Ijaw territory with the Rivers State. It is to be hoped that the desires of the people in the disputed areas would be ultimately decisive in any such boundary revision.

PART IV
Conclusions

CHAPTER 11
Communalism and Communal Conflict in Port Harcourt

Political conflict in Africa is commonly described as being very largely a matter of tribalism or tribal rivalry. Tribes are spoken of as fixed entities, and tribalism as the expression of primordial sentiments. The implication, not infrequently, is that tribalism—or communalism, which is preferred here as a more inclusive and less ethnocentric term—is the product of cultural diversity and the reassertion of traditional antagonisms. The Port Harcourt experience, however, suggests that communalism may in fact bear little relationship to traditional rivalries, that the boundaries of communal groups are constantly in flux, that communal conflict is generated by the "sameness" of people—in the sense of the similarity of their wants—rather than by their differences, and that explanations of conflict in terms of tribalism tend to mistake symptom for cause.[1]

A typical Port Harcourt resident belonged not to one but to several communal groups. He was, at one and the same time, a member of a family, a village, a village group, a clan court area, a division, a province, a linguistically defined nationality, a group of strangers, and a racial group. The relative political salience of each of these communal reference points was not fixed, but shifted according to a constantly changing political situation. A stranger in one situation could well be a political ally in another. Thus, the same Ibos who were competing with one another for political position within the municipality could close ranks when threatened by the imposition of an Ijaw-dominated Rivers State. Overnight, as it were, dormant identities of nationality were transformed into potent instruments of political action. The moment the outside threat passed, however, as when the 1958 Minorities Commission denied the Ijaw separatist demands, the narrower identities reasserted their political primacy: the Onitshans and Owerris renewed their political feud, and the Ijaws similarly divided into rival factions.

Of the various levels of communal identity, only the lowest—that of family, village, and village group—could be considered traditional. Occasionally, traditional rivalries within the rural homeland did affect the political fortunes of Port Harcourt politicians, but the small scale of traditional units in Eastern Nigeria meant that traditional groupings in Port Harcourt were essentially powerless. Consequently, communal conflict almost invariably was organized around nontraditional racial, ethnic, and geo-ethnic identities. It bears repeating that even the presumed "tribal" identities of Ibo, Ibibio, Ijaw, and Efik were the expression of a very new consciousness of nationality; they did not refer to traditional social or political entities.

Communalism in Port Harcourt was rooted not in the traditional order, but in the conditions of urban life. The impersonality and strangeness of the city led new urban dwellers to seek out the companionship of persons who shared a common culture and dialect and with whom they would have a sense of "belonging." At the same time, the city's competitiveness, with jobs, political offices, and social status all in short supply, heightened the insecurities and frustrations of urban life, thereby creating the kind of environment in which the rhetoric of communalism was permitted to flourish.

Those who sparked the communalization of competition in Port Harcourt were neither the traditionalists nor the illiterate. Rather, they were the members of the emerging social class of Western-educated clerks, educators, traders, and contractors. It was from the ranks of these men that the leadership of the communal associatons and of the local NCNC organization was drawn. Communalism became for them a weapon in their struggle for personal and political advancement.

In Port Harcourt's heterogeneous and competitive society,

communal appeals struck a responsive chord—especially among the frustrated and disadvantaged. Most residents—of whatever social and economic status—perceived their world through a communal prism, and persons who could most effectively exploit communal fears and perceptions stood to gain, both in personal and political terms. The flexibility and impermanence of communal alliances in Port Harcourt, which were facilitated by the artificiality of the geo-ethnic units around which most competition revolved, reflected the communal pragmatism of the politicians and their often consciously manipulative approach to communal politics. In this respect, the Port Harcourt experience corroborates Richard Sklar's observation that "tribal movements may be created and instigated to action by the new men of power in furtherance of their own special interests which are, time and again, the constitutive interests of emerging social classes. Tribalism then becomes a mask for class privilege." [2]

From this perspective, communalism appears not as an independent political force in its own right, as tribalist explanations of African political phenomena would have it, but rather the channel through which other interests are directed and made manifest. This is so not only in the sense that the opportunistic may manipulate communal symbols so as to advance their own personal interests, but also in the sense that virtually all communal conflicts are rooted in the competition between individuals for the scarce resources of wealth, status, and power. Thus, the conflict between the Diobu indigenes and the Ibo strangers reflected, at base, the alienation of Diobu lands to the commercial entrepreneurs in their midst. Similarly, the geo-ethnic conflict between Owerri and Onitsha Ibos expressed the long-standing educational and occupational inequalities between these two groups. Likewise, the very bitter and continuing conflict between Port Harcourt's Ibo and non-Ibo nationalities was traceable not to linguistic and cultural differences, but rather to a struggle for control of Port Harcourt and the city's important economic resources.

To state that communal conflict in Port Harcourt was generated not by the cultural differences of people but by their competition for the same scarce resources is not to suggest that cultural diversity did not affect the intensity of conflict that resulted from the competitive milieu. People who spoke different languages or who possessed different cultural idioms inevitably encountered greater difficulty in communicating with one another and in developing the empathic bonds necessary for cooperative activity. Mutual understanding is inhibited by cultural and linguistic diversity, and people are suspicious of that which they cannot understand. Moreover, people of different cultural perspectives find it difficult to establish mutually agreeable "rules of the game." In short, pronounced cultural and linguistic differences, such as those that separated Ibos and non-Ibos in Port Harcourt, may well have exacerbated conflict and made more difficult its management or resolution, but they were not its cause or catalyst.

MODERNIZATION AND COMMUNALISM

One implication of the Port Harcourt experience is that economic modernization in a communal setting, to the extent that it accelerates competitive interaction and intensifies personal insecurities, tends to encourage communal modes of organization and to intensify communal conflict. These tendencies are especially pronounced where the rates of economic and educational development proceed unevenly, so that communal cleavages are reenforced by social, economic, and political inequalities. Yet, a common assumption is that economic modernization must inevitably erode communal loyalties. Implicit in such a view is the presumption that communal and noncommunal loyalties are inherently incompatible, and that as people move into the new kinds of socioeconomic roles associated with industrialization and a modern economy, their communal attachments will become of increasingly less political significance.

Turning again to Port Harcourt, we have seen that in the early sixties the city's residents related themselves to the rapidly changing exigencies of urban life through a variety of modes of political organization. Four illustrations of organizational variability in Port Harcourt have been cited: the organization of Ibos *qua* Ibos when their political position was threatened by the creation of a separate Rivers State, the activation of socioeconomic identities and institutions during the general strike, the mobilization of religious groupings to confront the government's educational policies, and the geo-ethnic structure of electoral politics.

234

Port Harcourt residents appeared to move easily among different institutional structures. Their communal loyalties did not preclude their participation in noncommunal modes of political organization, for these latter were operative in situations in which communal identities were relatively less salient. Conversely, their involvement in trade union or church activities did not lessen the significance of their communal identities as social and political reference points at other times. They were, in effect, able to "compartmentalize" their various urban identities and thereby respond flexibly to changing social and political circumstances. It was possible for the same person to join a trade union to advance his occupational interests, a communal association to promote his social or electoral objectives, and a religious interest group to lobby for educational reform. In short, the same individual could be both a communal and noncommunal political actor.

It would seem, then, that there is no necessary incompatibility between functioning as a modern economic man, on the one hand, and performing as a communal political actor, on the other. To the contrary, the retention of compartmentalized communal points of reference enables industrial man to receive the best of two worlds: the collectivism inherent in the functionally diffuse ties of language and community or origin, and the individuation requisite to effective performance in the modern commercial and industrial setting. Indeed, the essence of modernity may lie not in the transition from particularistic to universalistic forms, but in their compartmentalization.

EQUALITY AND COMMUNAL CONFLICT

One implication of the Port Harcourt experience is that the relationship between communal inequalities and communal conflict may be more complicated than is frequently assumed. While it seems clear that in a competitive environment communal imbalances in wealth, status, and power exacerbate communal tensions, it does not follow that progress toward the elimination of such imbalances will be accompanied by communal accommodation. It is evident that intergroup equalization is a necessary condition for the emergence of cross-cutting socioeconomic linkages. That equalization does not mean, however, that the members of different communal groups will in fact perceive the commonality of their socioeconomic interests or that, if they do perceive this commonality, that they will act upon it. In the short term, at least, there are two factors that may link progress toward inter-group equalization with the intensification rather than the amelioration of communal antagonisms.

First, upward mobility typically leads to the alteration of reference groups on the part of the communal participants and, hence, to the alteration of their perceptions of their relative status vis-à-vis their communal competitors.[3] This alteration is what appears to have been involved both in the 1930s, when well-educated Ibos, resentful of their subordination to non-Ibo elements, attempted to unite and politicize the Ibo community, and in the 1950s, when educated and ambitious Owerri politicians moved to displace the historically dominant Onitshans. In both cases, the leaders held much greater prestige and were far more prosperous than the rank and file, and yet felt relatively more deprived vis-à-vis the members of the higher-positioned group with whom they compared themselves. It was this sense of relative deprivation on the part of the upwardly mobile that generated, first, the new Ibo militancy and, subsequently, the Owerri ascendancy. Thus, mobility, rather than producing a sense of competitive gain and satisfaction, may lead to a deepening sense of relative deprivation and communal insecurity. The actual intensity of these feelings of communal deprivation and insecurity will depend very largely upon the responsiveness of the wider society to the new communal assertiveness. The blocking of new communal aspirations to wealth, status, and power will tend to intensify group frustrations and to radicalize political response.

Second, mobility may intensify communal dissatisfaction by producing increased impatience with whatever imbalances remain. The closer the members of a formerly disadvantaged group approach equality on one of the dimensions of wealth, status, and power, the more intolerable becomes inequality on the other two dimensions. It is to this phenomenon that the "revolution of rising aspirations and frustrations" refers. Seldom are the very poorest the most militant. Again, the rising Ibo consciousness of the 1930s and the Owerri ascendancy of the 1950s would appear to be cases in point.

CONTROLLING COMMUNALISM

We have argued that communal conflict—in any country—is symptomatic of the frustrations and insecurities of people caught up in the impersonality and competitiveness of modern technological society. It follows that the control of communalism, be it in Nigeria or India or the United States, hinges ultimately on altering the institutional conditions giving rise to the underlying frustrations and insecurities.

Insuring Institutional Autonomy

In any society, the degree of intensity of communal conflict will be determined very largely by what Huntington has termed the "autonomy" of the society's political institutions. To quote Huntington, "Political institutionalization, in the sense of autonomy, means the development of political organizations and procedures that are not simply expressions of the interests of particular social groups. A political organization that is the instrument of a social group—family, clan, class—lacks autonomy and institutionalization." [4] If political institutions do not possess institutional integrity and appear to be in the control of particular communal interests, those communal groups lacking power and position will tend to question the legitimacy of the institutional order and will be encouraged politically to go it alone. This is precisely the situation that confronted Port Harcourt's non-Ibos who found themselves excluded entirely from the NCNC party establishment and who, as a result, turned to antiestablishment trade unionism and the Rivers State separatist movement as the organizational vehicles for the expression of their political concerns.

It should be noted that it is not the nature of primary institutions and primary group interaction that is at issue; people may in fact live their private lives within their communal compartments without jeopardizing the political viability or stability of the wider society. What *is* at issue is the character of those secondary institutions of any society—such as political parties and governmental bureaucracies—through which the members of communally discrete subsocieties may relate to one another in a systematic and orderly fashion. Thus, in the United States, communal separatism at the primary group level—that is, with re-

237

spect to marriage, friendship cliques, and the like—has characterized intrawhite as well as black/white relationships. However, in the case of white Americans, the secondary institutions of the national society were sufficiently flexible and autonomous to be relevant and legitimate for virtually all communal elements. Only in the case of nonwhites—most notably, of course, of black Americans—were the secondary institutions unresponsive and exclusionary. In effect, from the perspective of the wider society inclusive of both blacks and whites, the political institutions of the society have never possessed autonomy but, rather, have been historically subordinated to the interests of the majority social group. It is not surprising therefore that the most determined separatist sentiment in the United States has been voiced by the members of that group that has been least participant—in the sense of sharing in responsible decision-making power—in the secondary institutions of the society.[5]

In Nigeria, both national and regional political institutions came to be identified with the interests of particular communal groups, thereby impairing their legitimacy in the eyes of minority communal interests at both the national and the regional levels. With the creation of Nigeria's federal constitutional system and, in particular, with the creation of regional sources of wealth and power, it became clear that political parties that controlled the machinery of government could control the political and economic fate of the region.[6] Since Nigeria's administrative boundaries were so drawn as to give clear numerical superiority to a single nationality within each region, political parties on appealing to majority communal interests quickly came to dominate the regions. Much the same dynamics were operative at the national level, wherein the major communal groups competed for marginal advantages and sought to form opportune communal coalitions. It became evident, however, that no coalition was stable and that no group could feel secure in the federal system.

In the course of this communal competition for control of regional and national governmental institutions, communal minorities rapidly became disenchanted with the prevailing institutional structures. Significantly, in the light of the Biafran secession, even communal groups that were dominant at the regional level (such as the Ibo in Eastern Nigeria) were in a minority position with respect to the national institutions and hence shared the same sense of communal insecurity as was characteristic of the regional minority groups. The important point is that at both the federal and the regional levels, governmental institutions became identified with the interests of particular communal groups, thereby losing their legitimacy and institutional effectiveness for crucial elements of the wider society.

The achievement of institutional autonomy in any society depends in large measure upon two factors. First, institutional development will be influenced by the pattern of communal formation characteristic of the society. In particular it would appear that the greater the number of equally powerful communal groups, the greater the likelihood that institutional coherence and impartiality will be retained. The dispersion of power among a number of communal competitors makes less likely the identification of political institutions with a particular communal group or a coalition of such groups. At the same time, as our analysis of the politics of geo-ethnicity illustrates, the dispersion of power among a number of communal competitors helps not only to maintain a stable communal balance, but also to encourage the development of a system of shifting communal coalitions that, in turn, lessens the intensity of communal conflict. In a society in which no communal group is sufficiently large or powerful to stand alone, it becomes necessary to form communal alliances. The greater the number of the communal competitors, the less the likelihood that the same communal groups will join together on all issues. As issues change, so do communal alliances. The resulting pattern of shifting and intersecting communal alliances will tend to mitigate the intensity of communal conflict on any particular issue.

It is the recognition of this relationship that has prompted Nigerian decision-makers, belatedly, to create a greater number of states. The tragic structural flaw of the Nigerian federal system was that there were always enough states to ensure conflict along communal dimensions, and too few states to ensure competitive stability. The new twelve-state system attempts to correct this structural defect by breaking up the administrative—and political—cohesiveness of the historically dominant North and by ensuring to Nigeria's minorities a modicum of self-determination.

Conclusions

The second factor upon which the achievement of institutional autonomy turns is the willingness of the society's national leadership to guarantee the representation of all significant communal elements in the highest reaches of the national government. This representation means, in the case of political institutions, that majoritarian principles may have to be sacrificed and, where communal educational imbalances are present, the government must be willing, at least in the short term, to accept quota arrangements for the staffing of key bureaucracies and to implement programs of compensatory education and job-training in areas of greatest need.

Correcting Communal Imbalances

The origins of communal conflict, we have suggested, lie not in the existence of inequalities between communal groups, but in the nature of the competitive system that brings men into conflict. Even in a culturally plural society of perfectly equal communal groups, competition for the scarce resources of wealth, status, and power would very likely be structured on communal lines. Nevertheless, while the issue of equality does not bear upon the *structure* of communal conflict, it does affect the *intensity* with which that conflict is waged. The greater the imbalances between communities in conflict, the fewer the ties that bind the members of these communities together; therefore, governments that seek to maintain communal peace must take steps to equalize the distribution of resources within their societies. Admittedly, in democratic systems wherein the political survival of leaders rests upon their ability to maintain the support of their communities of origin, policies aimed at the development of "alien" communities entail considerable short-term political risk. In the long term, however, all stand to gain from the amelioration of communal antagonisms.

Transforming Competition

Correcting communal imbalances as a strategy for controlling communalism is at best a stop-gap measure that treats symptoms rather than causes. It leaves the competitive system that underlies all communal conflict in tact, and does little more than mitigate the effects of that system. If we are ever truly to come to grips

with communalism, our goal must be nothing less than the transformation of the competitive systems by which we live. That this
is a monumental task goes without saying. It requires that there
be developed a much greater awareness of how competitive social,
economic, and political processes in fact operate, and a determination to seek viable institutional alternatives. It requires that
communal competitors begin to redefine "the enemy" not as their
immediate rivals but as the dehumanizing competitive systems
that force men to become rivals in the first place. It requires,
finally, the emergence of leaders of courage and foresight who
will appeal to our hopes and aspirations rather than to our fears,
and who will seek to reduce communal insecurities by confronting directly their underlying causes and by insuring to all who
feel threatened an important measure of control over their own
destinies.

The Nigerian/Biafran war was a graphic demonstration of the
destructive potential of uncontrolled communal conflict, but the
real tragedy is that the war and the human suffering that it entailed were avoidable.

Methods and Data

GENERAL

My original intention, early in 1963, was to execute a straight-forward study of the community power structure of Port Harcourt at different points in time. The central problem of data collection, then, was the identification of Port Harcourt's "influentials," and four methods were selected to guide this search: first, a modified form of the reputational technique, in which Port Harcourt's municipal councillors were asked to identify those persons who were "the most influential individuals or groups" involved in making decisions in selected issue areas (roads and drains, health and sanitation, schools, NCNC party nominations); second, a panel technique, in which a number of selected "judges" were asked to group 294 names [compiled from a six-month canvass of the local newspapers, membership lists of the executive bodies of select institutions (such as the NCNC and the Ibo State Union), and personal interviews] into categories of high, moderate, and slight influence with respect to (a) Port Harcourt's physical development, and (b) NCNC party nominations; third, analyses of decision-making in selected issue areas (education, town planning, industrial investment, the general hospital, public works, building of a juvenile remand home, the general strike, party nominations, public housing); and fourth, social background analysis of public officeholders.

But as the interviewing of Port Harcourt's municipal councillors commenced, it quickly became evident that coverage of the universe of councillors, as the first phase of the research design re-

quired, would, in itself, yield very little in the way of an understanding of the dynamics of urban community power. A few
councillors were excellent informants, but many were either not
that well acquainted with the workings of power in the community or were not articulate enough in English to provide the
kind of background material I sought. Moreover, my attention was
increasingly drawn to broader questions relating to the dynamics
of social and political change and the impact of communalism
upon the urban political system. I therefore began to "follow my
leads," and to interview persons who were identified either as participants in making the decisions in which I was interested, or as
officials of present and past governmental institutions (e.g., the
Town Council, the Township Advisory Board, the Planning Authority, the provincial secretariat) and nongovernmental organizations (e.g., the NCNC, the African Community League, the divisional unions, the Ibo State Union, the Council of Labor). In
all, 191 persons (including 43 of the 46 municipal councillors who
served between 1961 and 1964) were formally interviewed, some
on several occasions. The total length of interview time per re-
spondent varied from fifteen minutes to over sixteen hours. The
average length of a single interview was two hours. Almost all interviews were conducted in the homes of the respondents; notes
were taken, verbatim where possible. Except in the case of the
municipal councillors and the influence judges, interviews were
open-ended and loosely structured. All interviews were conducted
by the writer; with a single exception, all were conducted in English.

Interviews provided only one of the principal sources of data
concerning Port Harcourt community power and political development. Once the limitations of the "list" approach to the
study of community power were recognized, I placed greater
emphasis upon the participant-observer techniques of the anthro-
pologist than I had originally intended. The openness of Ibo
society, combined with my clearly established political neutrality
vis-à-vis the competitive urban groups, eliminated virtually all
problems of "access," and I was quickly welcomed into Port
Harcourt homes, community association meetings, NCNC party
caucuses, trade union rallies, and Municipal Council sessions.
The many, many hours spent in these situations provided invalu-

able insight into the informal and more subtle aspects of Port Harcourt political life. All but the community association meetings were conducted in English, but the lack of any competence in Ibo was nevertheless deeply regrettable.

The third principal source of data consisted of six types of written documents: newspapers, government files, party records, archival materials, private files of informants, and the minute books of associations. The latter presented an unexpectedly rich source of historical data. Again, access was never a research problem. Indeed, the reverse was true: after several months had elapsed and rapport had been established with party leaders, so much was made available it was simply impossible to process it all.

OCCUPATIONAL CODE

The occupational categories used in this study were adapted, with certain modifications, from those employed by Richard Sklar in *Nigerian Political Parties*. Attention should be drawn to certain features of this coding scheme as applied to the Port Harcourt data. First, "petty trader" and "petty contractor" are colloquial Nigerian terms that refer to a host of urban income-earning activities. Many petty traders were also petty contractors, i.e., persons who would perform almost any kind of entrepreneurial function that yielded the slightest profit. We have, accordingly, subsumed within these categories debt collectors, market traders, small shop owners, and suppliers of small quantities of construction materials. The classification of one man as "petty trader or petty contractor" and another man as "businessman or big trader" was in a few instances rather arbitrary, and the distinction is not intended to reflect any precise empirical differentiation. As a rule of thumb, a person with an estimated annual income of £500 ($1,400) or less was placed in the "petty" occupational category.

Second, many urban residents held several occupations. Teachers, for example, might also have engaged in petty trade or contract work on the side; a businessman might also have been a journalist. In such instances we have classified that occupation that accounts (or appears to account) for the greatest part of the individual's annual income.

Third, urban residents, over time, frequently changed their occupations and their financial position. We have attempted to relate a person's occupation to the various historical periods in terms of which the analysis of Port Harcourt's political development is organized. Consequently, the same individual may have received different occupational designations at different points in time, meaning that apparent changes in the occupational composition of the Municipal Council, for example, do not always reflect changes in personnel. One exception to this coding is that retired pensioners were identified in terms of their lifetime principal occupation, on the assumption that a person's political status more likely reflected his previous occupational and educational situation than the fact of his retirement.

Fourth, the social background data for several organizations referred to in this study were derived secondhand from interviews with selected officials of these bodies. Wherever possible, their responses were checked and double-checked by asking several individuals to provide the same information. This technique had the obvious advantage of economy, especially in a situation in which the distribution of questionnaires was not feasible and both financial resources and time were in short supply. The limitations of this secondhand method of data solicitation, however, must be recognized. That the social background data reported in this study possess a high degree of reliability we are quite certain; that their accuracy matches that which would have been obtained through personal interviews with the entire organizational membership is unlikely.

RANKING OF PORT HARCOURT'S ECONOMIC NOTABLES

To determine Port Harcourt's African "economic elite," a list of names of "possible economic notables" was prepared on the basis of interviews with Port Harcourt's municipal councillors, a canvass of local newspapers, and the listing of party "patrons" provided by the local NCNC. The names (totaling seventy-four) were then placed on index cards and presented to six "judges": two local bank managers, a local bank accountant, a local internal revenue official, a director of the African Continental Bank, and an officer of the local Kingsway Department Stores (U.A.C.). The judges were asked to classify the name cards into categories of persons "roughly equal in wealth." The weighted ranks received by each of these potential members of the financial elite were totaled, and a rank order of the entire group established.

APPENDIX 2

Port Harcourt Parliamentarians (1945–1966)

1. Rev. L. R. Potts-Johnson: member, Eastern House of Assembly, 1949; Sierra Leonian; pastor, school proprietor, printer, publisher; president, African Community League; Protestant.
2. G. C. Nonyelu: member, Eastern House of Assembly, 1949–1951; Ibo; Awka Division; barrister; president, Port Harcourt Town Council, 1949–1951; Protestant.
3. V. K. Onyeri: member, Eastern House of Assembly, 1951–1961; Aro-Ibo; Awka Division; trader; Catholic.
4. A. C. Nwapa: central minister, Commerce and Industry, 1951–1953; Ibo; Owerri Division; barrister; Protestant.
5. J. O. Umolu: member, Eastern House of Assembly, 1954–1961; Edo; Mid-Western Nigeria; trade unionist; Catholic.
6. D. K. Onwenu: member, Federal House of Representatives, 1954–1957; Aro-Ibo; Orlu Division; secondary school vice-principal; Protestant.
7. D. D. Okay: member, Federal House of Representatives, 1957–1966; Ibo; Mbaise, Owerri Division; trader; National Church.
8. J. N. Amaechi: member, Eastern House of Assembly, 1961–1966; Ibo; Bende Division; printing press proprietor; Protestant.
9. E. Aguma: member, Eastern House of Assembly, 1961–1966; Diobu Ibo; Port Harcourt Division; secondary school principal; Protestant.

APPENDIX 3
Port Harcourt Municipal Councillors
(1955–1958)

1. E. I. Abanah: Ibo; Awka Division; Protestant; electrical contractor.
2. M. Abu: Nupe; Northern Nigeria; Moslem; trader and contractor.
3. D. S. Adoki: Ijaw; Degema Division; Protestant; contractor and engineer.
4. G. I. Aginah: Ibo; Onitsha Division; Protestant; transporter.
5. G. C. N. Akomas: Ibo; Bende Division; Protestant; U.A.C. manager.
6. C. Akuchie: Ibo; Owerri Division; Protestant; contractor.
7. S. O. Akwiwu: Ibo; Orlu Division; Protestant; trader.
8. A. E. Allagoa: Ijaw; Brass Division; Catholic; barrister.
9. J. Amaechi: Ibo; Bende Division; Protestant; printer.
10. F. U. Ihekwoaba: Ibo; Orlu Division; Protestant; trader.
11. A. E. C. Jumbo: Ijaw; Degema Division; Protestant; contractor.
12. D. D. "Diobu" Nsiegbe: Ikwerre Ibo; Port Harcourt Division; Protestant; farmer.
13. E. A. Nwaebele: Ibo; Okigwi Division; Protestant; contractor.
14. R. O. Nzimiro: Ibo; Owerri Division; Protestant; trader.
15. I. E. Obasi: Ibo; Bende Division; Protestant; trader.
16. J. W. Ogbondah: Ikwerre Ibo; Diobu, Port Harcourt Division; Protestant; clerk, contractor.
17. D. D. Okay: Ibo; Mbaise, Owerri Division; National Church; trader.

18. J. O. Okeke: Ibo; Mbaise, Owerri Division; Catholic; trader.
19. D. K. Onwenu: Ibo; Orlu Division; Protestant; vice-principal.
20. D. I. Onyeiwu: Ibo; Okigwi Division; Catholic; baker.
21. A. Opia: Ibo; Mid-Western Nigeria; Protestant; trader.
22. I. M. Uchendu: Ibo; Onitsha Division; National Church; carpenter.
23. Mrs. A. N. Wogu: Ibo; Bende Division; Protestant; teacher.

APPENDIX 4
Port Harcourt Municipal Councillors
(1958–1961)

1. E. I. Abanah: Ibo; Awka Division; Protestant; electrical contractor.
2. M. Abu: Nupe; Northern Nigeria; Moslem; trader and contractor.
3. O. Agba: Ibo; Bende Division; National Church; contractor.
4. G. I. Aginah: Ibo; Onitsha Division; Protestant; transporter, businessman.
5. E. Aguma: Ikwerre Ibo; Diobu, Port Harcourt Division; Protestant; secondary school principal.
6. M. I. Ajieren: Ibo; Aba Division; Protestant; clerk.
7. G. C. N. Akomas: Ibo; Bende Division; Protestant; U.A.C. manager.
8. A. E. Allagoa: Ijaw; Brass Division; Catholic; barrister.
9. E. Anozie: Ibo; Mbaise, Owerri Division; Catholic; contractor.
10. S. D. Arundu: Ibo; Okigwi Division; Protestant; contractor, letter writer, and debt collector.
11. M. W. Dickson: Ikwerre Ibo; Diobu, Port Harcourt Division; Protestant; clerk.
12. J. R. Echue: Ibo; Okigwi Division; Protestant; transporter and landlord.
13. G. I. Egbunine: Ibo; Owerri Division; Protestant; contractor.
14. G. I. Elugwaornu: Ibo; Mbaise, Owerri Division; Catholic; public relations officer.
15. L. E. Emah: Efik; Calabar Division; Protestant; contractor.

16. J. I. Emenike: Ibo; Okigwi Division; Protestant; transporter and landlord.
17. O. Emole: Ibo; Bende Division; Protestant; trader.
18. A. U. Igbokwe: Ibo; Orlu Division; Catholic; trader.
19. U. Ihediohamma: Ibo; Okigwi Division; Protestant; contractor and trader.
20. F. U. Ihekwoaba: Ibo; Orlu Division; Protestant; trader.
21. E. I. Ihute: Ibo; Aba Division; Protestant; journalist.
22. A. D. W. Jumbo: Ijaw; Degema Division; Protestant; businessman.
23. A. E. C. Jumbo: Ijaw; Degema Division; Protestant; contractor.
24. J. U. Mbonu: Ibo; Onitsha Division; Catholic; contractor.
25. Mrs. G. N. Nduka: Ibo; Okigwi Division; Protestant; contractor.
26. G. Ngbemeneh: Ibo; Mbaise, Owerri Division; Catholic; clerk and accountant.
27. G. P. A. Nwagwu: Ikwerre Ibo; Diobu, Port Harcourt Division; Protestant; contractor.
28. R. O. Nzimiro: Ibo; Owerri Division; Protestant; trader.
29. I. E. Obasi: Ibo; Bende Division; Protestant; trader.
30. V. Obi: Ibo; Orlu Division; Catholic; trader.
31. M. O. Obidiaso: Ibo; Orlu Division; Catholic.
32. J. Odunze: Ibo; Orlu Division; Catholic; trader.
33. D. Ohaeto: Ibo; Orlu Division; Protestant; trader.
34. A. Okoro: Ibo; Bende Division; Protestant; clerk.
35. V. Onyewuchi: Ibo; Owerri Division; Catholic; petrol station manager and land owner.
36. A. Opia: Ibo; Mid-Western Nigeria; Protestant; trader.
37. J. O. Otuonye: Ikwerre Ibo; Diobu, Port Harcourt Division; Protestant; contractor.
38. R. N. Owo: Ikwerre Ibo; Diobu, Port Harcourt Division; Protestant; clerk.
39. N. O. Owuru: Ikwerre Ibo; Diobu, Port Harcourt Division; Protestant; clerk.
40. I. M. Uchendu: Ibo; Onitsha Division; National Church; carpenter, contractor.
41. M. Ugboaja: Ibo; Okigwi Division; Protestant; contractor.
42. Mrs. A. N. Wogu: Ibo; Bende Division; Protestant; teacher.

APPENDIX 5
Port Harcourt Municipal Councillors
(1961-1964)

1. E. I. Abanah: Ibo; Awka Division; Protestant; electrical contractor.
2. G. I. Aginah: Ibo; Onitsha Division; Protestant; transporter, businessman.
3. G. C. N. Akomas: Ibo; Bende Division; Protestant; U.A.C. manager.
4. D. O. Aneke: Ibo; Udi Division; Catholic; contractor.
5. J. Anokwuru: Ibo; Orlu Division; Catholic; stevedoring contractor.
6. S. D. Arundu: Ibo; Okigwi Division; Protestant; contractor, letter writer; and debt collector.
7. M. I. Ashiri: Ibo; Mid-Western Nigeria; Protestant; clerk.
8. S. W. Atako: Ikwerre Ibo; Port Harcourt Division; Protestant; sales supervisor.
9. R. Chikere: Ikwerre Ibo; Port Harcourt Division; Protestant; tailor.
10. E. Chukwu: Ikwerre Ibo; Port Harcourt Division; Protestant; printer.
11. T. U. Chukwueke: Ibo; Owerri Division; Catholic; teacher.
12. E. Echeghe: Ibo; Bende Division; Protestant; contractor.
13. J. P. Echue: Ibo; Okigwi Division; Protestant; transporter and landlord.
14. G. I. Elugwaornu: Ibo; Owerri Division; Catholic; public relations officer.
15. J. I. Emenike: Ibo; Okigwi Division; Protestant; transporter and landlord.

16. O. Emole: Ibo; Bende Division; Protestant; trader.
17. T. E. Enwerem: Ibo; Orlu Division; Catholic; trader.
18. A. U. Igbokwe: Ibo; Orlu Division; Catholic; trader.
19. U. Ihediohamma: Ibo; Okigwi Division; Protestant; contractor and trader.
20. F. U. Ihekwoaba: Ibo; Orlu Division; Protestant; trader.
21. J. Iloabuchi: Ibo; Onitsha Division; Catholic; trader.
22. A. D. W. Jumbo: Ijaw; Degema Division; Protestant; businessman.
23. P. O. Maduabum: Ibo; Onitsha Division; Catholic; trader and hotel proprietor.
24. R. O. Madueme: Ibo; Onitsha Division; Protestant; trader.
25. B. E. Mbanu: Ibo; Owerri Division; Catholic; teacher and contractor.
26. B. Muogboh: Ibo; Onitsha Division; Protestant; contractor.
27. Mrs. G. N. Nduka: Ibo; Okigwi Division; Protestant; contractor.
28. G. Ngbemeneh: Ibo; Owerri Division; Catholic; clerk, accountant.
29. B. O. Nnopuechi: Ibo; Orlu Division; Catholic; trader.
30. L. E. Nwachukwu: Ibo; Owerri Division; Catholic; trader and contractor.
31. J. Nwajuaku: Ibo; Onitsha Division; Protestant; trader.
32. I. E. Obasi: Ibo; Bende Division; Protestant; trader.
33. A. K. Odu: Ibo; Bende Division; National Church; contractor and trader.
34. J. Odunze: Ibo; Orlu Division; Catholic; trader.
35. D. Ohaeto: Ibo; Orlu Division; Protestant; trader.
36. E. Ohiri: Ibo; Owerri Division; Catholic; radio repairman.
37. J. O. Okeke: Ibo; Owerri Division; Catholic; trader.
38. A. Okoroji: Ibo; Bende Division; Protestant; secretary-typist.
39. V. Onyewuchi: Ibo; Owerri Division; Catholic; petrol station manager and land owner.
40. R. O. Osuikpa: Ibo; Owerri Division; Protestant; trader and contractor.
41. J. O. Otuonye: Ikwerre Ibo; Port Harcourt Division; Protestant; contractor.
42. R. N. Owo: Ikwerre Ibo; Port Harcourt Division; Protestant; clerk.

43. I. N. Uchendu: Ibo; Onitsha Division; National Church; carpenter, contractor.
44. Y. Ufere: Ibo; Orlu Division; Catholic; transporter.
45. M. I. Ugboaja: Ibo; Okigwi Division; Protestant; contractor.
46. Chief Joseph Wobo: Ikwerre Ibo; Port Harcourt Division; Protestant; farmer.
47. Mrs. A. N. Wogu; Ibo; Bende Division; Protestant; teacher.

Excerpts from the Floyer Report

A Memorandum on the Proposed Municipality for Port Harcourt by R. K. FLOYER, *Local Authority (1946)*

"I have throughout taken the standpoint that my function was to present their aspirations in a form which was likely to be both practicable and acceptable to Government, and that Government and people should collaborate to work out a suitable scheme. I suggest, with all deference, that Government should now be asked to consider these proposals and return them with an indication of policy, showing which points are regarded as fundamental, and leaving others open to adjustment. Port Harcourt cannot expect to get all it wants at once, and it has a pill to swallow in the shape of trebled rates. Both Europeans and Africans are still far from familiar with the practice or the principles of local Government either in Lagos or in England. It is not easy for them to follow the reasoning behind what is, after all, a complicated set of proposals, and it is desirable that they should see the complete picture and get to understand it in the course of discussion and explanation. They may wish to make further representations, and these should be received with patience and sympathy; it is not fully realised yet how far Government has already expressed willingness to go towards acceding to their wishes. It is characteristic of peoples who have not yet reached full development to regard anything new with suspicion, and they have been subjected to propaganda tending to suggest that all proposals emanating from Government should be so regarded."

"Many Europeans and some Africans, express freely their view that the people of this country will not in twenty years, in a generation, or ever, be fit for any form of self government, and some Europeans are apt to see in the sometimes ill-advised pretensions of the semi-educated a character fundamentally little removed from savagery, overlaid by a caricature of themselves and their own habits, which they find revolting. They see the case for political progress put forward by persons whom they rightly judge to lack self respect, consistency and honesty and they are apt to overlook the fact that these aspirations, however far from realisation, are in themselves legitimate, and that there does exist a small but influential class of African who in education, manners and common-sense compare favourably with some of their own number. Few of us are free at all times from these prejudices.

"For different and better reasons, Government while encouraging and sometimes insisting upon the fullest consultation with the people, and trying honestly to fulfill their material and to some extent their political wishes, has been slow, even in local and minor matters, to take the final step of leaving Africans to decide for themselves and stand or fall by their own decisions. No Native Authority in the Eastern Provinces can spend a penny or take executive action without the District Officer's consent, and few Committees have an African majority unless the European chairman is fairly confident that his influence will carry the day. Thus apart from his private life an African seldom finds himself in a position when he must take a decision with a full sense of responsibility, knowing that it will result in executive action, the consequences of which will be publicly and immediately attributable to his decision. Secure in the knowledge that what he says will have no consequence to himself or anyone else, he expresses his sense of frustration in intemperate language, and his importance is measured, in his own eyes and those of his followers, by the amount of abuse which he heaps upon Government. Having built up his personal position on intransigence, he is bound to continue on the same road since as soon as he abandons it his influence will collapse. The propaganda is the more dangerous in that it is not confined to Government but is directed against every established institution, and in immature minds tends to inculcate contempt for all forms of authority—an attitude which if its authors were suddenly to achieve the positions of authority, which they demand, no one would regret more than themselves.

"As a result of this irresponsible conduct Government has to some extent been forced into an attitude of opposition to the very class which has come into existence as a result of its rule and in some degree of its avowed policy. The danger lies, not in the fact that Government is compelled to defend itself against ill-informed criticism—this is the common lot of all Governments—but that this very criticism appeals to the sense of frustration which is felt by even the most sensible of the educated class, and more strongly still to a much larger class of the semi-educated who are in process of reaching that level. These have not the experience nor the knowledge to evaluate such criticism, and their understanding of the principles involved and the terms used is incomplete, but they are accustomed, both in towns and in their own villages to form societies and hold meetings to further a common purpose. These meetings are apt to fall short of their intentions; they are often noisy and inconclusive, and the treasurer not infrequently runs away with the funds; but the fact remains that in the Eastern Provinces they do succeed between them in raising and administering sums larger than the direct tax, and devoting the major part of it to worthy causes dear to their hearts, such as education and the assistance of their fellow townsmen in distress. All this, moreover, is done on their own initiative and without assistance from Government."

". . . when he [the villager] comes to live in a cosmopolitan township, which offers no basis for development on Native Administrative lines, he finds nothing to replace the part to which he is accustomed to take in the local affairs of his village."

". . . this sense of futility [resulting from the policy of Government always superseding the wishes of the Africans] is, I submit, one of the root causes of the present political discontent even among sensible and loyal intelligentsia and of the apathy and irresponsibility of unofficial members of Advisory Boards and Councils. The danger of the situation is that the screams of the Press and professional demagogues do provide an outlet for this sense of futility, which is also felt by their more sensible brethren, and so long as their moderate representations for more responsibility and power are not met, they provide the only outlet."

"[The Town Council proposal originated with the African Community League] . . . a body which includes the element of sensible men of some education, most of whom have a material stake in the prosperity of the Town."

"High standards of efficiency and integrity were not regarded as a condition precedent to the assumption of local responsibilities in England, and it is at least questionable why it should be so when these institutions are transplanted elsewhere. . . . African unofficials in particular are fond of making exceptions to rules and 'giving consideration' to individual pleas, when the interests of themselves or their friends are concerned or from a reluctance to face unpopularity; nor can the possibility of corruption be disregarded. Apart from these weaknesses, it has almost the force of custom that where a 'big man' is appealed to by one of his 'clients,' even though self-styled, he must do what he can to assist—by no means an unpleasant trait of character."

". . . the effect of being in, or being represented by, an unofficial minority is of little educative value (except as to procedure). It may be argued that it tends to produce an irresponsible frame of mind; that it offers temptation to place private interests above those of the community (the official majority will look after this community). It is irritating to be told that one should be satisfied with the opportunity of expressing views, when it is known that such views have little or no chance of acceptance, even when they are representative of sensible public opinion. Official majorities are singularly unsympathetic to oratory and they are apt to be rendered impervious to argument by the dictates of official policy, and by the sheer physical difficulties of influencing it. The most potent weapon of an unofficial minority is its nuisance value, and this it is apt to exploit to the full."

"It is not always fully realised that to the African mind nominated members are not representatives. They regard themselves as the advisers of Government. . . . It is interesting to note that though the racial issue sometimes raises an ugly head when questions of staff are considered, the Community League representatives recognise a need for European technical and commercial assistance, but have little use for African nominated members."

". . . African women are accustomed to manage their own societies in the same way as men, and just as efficiently, and are by no means lacking in public spirit. . . . It may be suggested that on the whole African women are comparatively less educated and have a narrower outlook than African men, but it is doubtful how far this will apply to those who will qualify as electors."

Notes

CHAPTER 1: *Introduction*

1. The dichotomous formulation has a long and classical history, involving Maine, Morgan, Weber, Tonnies, and Durkheim. More recently, it has been reflected in the pattern variable paradigm developed by Talcott Parsons and Edward A. Shils in their edited volume, *Toward a General Theory of Action* (Cambridge: Harvard University Press, 1959), pp. 53–109, and in the work of a number of contemporary scholars concerned with processes of social change and political development. See, for example, Frank X. Sutton, "Social Theory and Comparative Politics," in *Comparative Politics: A Reader,* ed. Harry Eckstein and David Apter (New York: Free Press of Glencoe, 1963), pp. 67–81; Fred W. Riggs, "Agraria and Industria—Toward a Typology of Comparative Administration," in *Toward the Comparative Study of Public Administration,* ed. William J. Siffen (Bloomington: Indiana University, Department of Government, 1957), pp. 23–116; Marion J. Levy, *Modernization and the Structure of Societies: A Setting for International Affairs,* 2 vols. (Princeton: Princeton University Press, 1966); and Max F. Milliken and Donald K. M. Blackmer, eds., *The Emerging Nations* (Boston: Little, Brown, 1961). A useful collection of quotations from these and other works that illustrate the continuity of the dichotomous formulation is offered by C. S. Whitaker, Jr., *The Politics of Tradition. Continuity and Change in Northern Nigeria, 1946–1966* (Princeton: Princeton University Press, 1970), pp. 5–6.

2. Especially useful critiques of the relevant literature appear in Samuel P. Huntington, "The Change to Change: Modernization, Development, and Politics," *Comparative Politics* 3, no. 3 (April 1971): 283–322, and Whitaker, *Politics of Tradition,* pp. 3–15 and "A Dysrhythmic Process of Political Change," *World Politics* 19, no. 2 (January 1967): 190–217. See also the following works: Abner Cohen, *Custom and Politics in Urban Africa. A Study of Hausa Migrants in Urban Towns* (Berkeley and Los Angeles: University of California Press, 1969); James S. Coleman, *Nigeria: Background to Nationalism* (Berkeley and Los Angeles: University of California Press, 1958); S. N. Eisenstadt, "Reflections on a Theory of Modernization," in *Nations by Design,* ed. Arnold Rivkin (Garden City, N.Y.: Doubleday, 1968), pp. 35–61; Joseph R. Gusfield, "Tradition and Modernity: Misplaced Polarities in the Study of Social Change," *American Journal of Sociology* 72 (January 1966): 351–62; Samuel P. Huntington, *Political Order in Changing Societies* (New Haven, Conn.: Yale University Press, 1968); Lloyd I. Rudolph and Susanne Hoeber Rudolph, *The Modernity of Tradition: Political Development in India* (Chicago: University of Chicago Press, 1967); Richard L. Sklar, "The Contribution of Tribalism to Nationalism in Western Nigeria," *Journal of Human Relations* 8 (Spring–Summer 1960): 407–15; Myron Weiner, *The Politics of Scarcity:*

Notes

Public Pressure and Political Response in India (Chicago: University of Chicago Press, 1962); W. Howard Wriggins, "Impediments to Unity in New Nations: The Case of Ceylon," *American Political Science Review* 55 (June 1961): 313–20; Crawford Young, *Politics in the Congo* (Princeton: Princeton University Press, 1965); and Aristide Zolberg, *One Party Government in the Ivory Coast* (Princeton: Princeton University Press, 1964).

3. Coleman, *Nigeria: Background to Nationalism*, p. 335.

4. The theoretical orientation of this study is the product of a collaborative effort between the present writer and Robert Melson. For a more complete and systematic exposition of the relationship between modernization and communalism in the Nigerian setting, see Robert Melson and Howard Wolpe, "Modernization and the Politics of Communalism: A Theoretical Perspective," *American Political Science Review* 64, no. 4 (December 1970): 1112–30. I have borrowed freely from this paper at many points; in this and subsequent chapters several passages are reproduced verbatim. See also Robert Melson and Howard Wolpe, eds., *Nigeria: Modernization and the Politics of Communalism* (East Lansing: Michigan State University Press, 1971).

5. According to Deutsch, complementarity of communication in a group "consists in the ability to communicate more effectively and over a wider range of subjects with members of one large group than with outsiders." See his path-breaking *Nationalism and Social Communication* (Cambridge: M.I.T. Press, 1953), p. 71.

6. Milton Gordon, *Assimilation in American Life* (New York: Oxford University Press, 1964), p. 39.

7. It should be noted that communal groups are not alone in sharing culture, identity, and complementarity. An age-group among the Masai, for example, share in these characteristics, as does the upper class in Britain. But age-grades and social classes are not to be thought of as communal groups, because they do not encompass the full range of demographic divisions within a society, and they are not socioeconomically heterogeneous. It is these latter characteristics that give to communal groups their distinctive political significance in that they are, to use Clifford Geertz's term, "candidates for nationhood." See Clifford Geertz, "The Integrative Revolution," in *Old Societies and New States*, ed. Clifford Geertz (Glencoe, Ill.: Free Press, 1963), p. 111.

8. This argument is elaborated in Charles W. Anderson, Fred R. von der Mehden, and Crawford Young, *Issues of Political Development* (Englewood Cliffs, N.J.: Prentice-Hall, 1967), pp. 15–83, and in the work of scholars associated with the Rhodes-Livingston Institute. See, for example, Max Gluckman, "Tribalism in Modern British Central Afica," *Cahiers d'Etudes Africaines* 1 (January 1960): 55–70; A. L. Epstein, *Politics in an Urban African Community* (Manchester: Manchester University Press, 1958); and Clyde Mitchell, *The Kalela Dance* (Manchester: Manchester University Press, 1956). For a recent application of the situational mode of analysis to the Nigerian scene, see Leonard Plotnicov, *Strangers to the City: Urban Man in Jos, Nigeria* (Pittsburgh: University of Pittsburgh Press, 1967).

CHAPTER 2: *An Introduction to Port Harcourt*

1. Dr. Nnamdi Azikiwe, former president of the Federal Republic of Nigeria, speaking on the occasion of the official opening of the $3.4 million Port Harcourt Hotel Presidential, November 14, 1964, reported in the *Nigerian Outlook*, November 17, 1964.

2. Enugu was founded following the discovery of rich coal deposits, and subsequently became the administrative headquarters of the Eastern Region; Aba and Umuahia were situated on the Eastern Nigeria Railway line and developed from

sprawling rural communities into thriving commercial centers; Port Harcourt was established to permit the evacuation of the Enugu coal.

3. For the history of this coal exploration and of the urban community of Enugu, which was organized around the new coal industry, see P. E. H. Hair, "Enugu: An Industrial and Urban Community in East Nigeria, 1914–1953," *Proceedings of the Second Annual Conference of the West African Institute of Social and Economic Research*, March 1953, pp. 143–69.

4. Accounts of the actual discovery differ. According to one rather romanticized version, rendered by Margery Perham, Nigeria's great colonial administrator Lord Lugard was personally responsible for the port's discovery:

> Lugard now sailed eastward [during a 1912 tour of southern Nigeria], past the Niger mouths and along the coast. One of the main purposes of this tour was to explore the southeast coast for a site at which he could build a port. This would be the outlet for the projected eastern railway. In a canoe, drenched with sweat, Lugard and his staff probed the steamy hot creeks and mud flats, over which the canoe had at times to be hauled. A fringe of uncanny looking mangrove trees stood in the water, while behind rose the densely forested banks. Lugard and Eaglesome found the head of an inlet near Okrika which seemed suitable and which Lugard afterwards named Port Harcourt in honour of a Colonial Secretary towards whom, at that date, he still felt extremely friendly.

See Margery Perham, *Lugard: The Years of Authority, 1898–1945* (London: Collins, 1960), p. 395.

A Nigerian Ports Authority account, however, based upon Ports Authority archives, makes no reference to Lugard's personal involvement in the discovery, and attributes the siting of the port, rather more credibly, to members of a railway and marine department survey team. (Text of a Port Harcourt radio address presented by E. O. Uruakpa, manager for the Eastern ports, n.d., typewritten.)

5. Eastern Nigeria Water Planning and Construction, Ltd., *Report on Roads, Drainage and Sewerage in Port Harcourt* (Enugu: Ministry of Works, September 1961), pp. vi–vii. Dollar equivalences are based on the 1965 valuation: £1 = $2.80.

6. *Eastern Nigerian Local Government Estimates: 1964–65* (mimeographed, 1965).

7. R. K. Floyer, D. O. Ibekwe, and J. O. Njemanze, *Report of the Commission of Enquiry into the Working of the Port Harcourt Town Council* (Enugu: Government Printer, February 1955), pp 10–11.

8. Port Harcourt residents tended to think of the area immediately adjacent to Mile 2 Diobu, known as Mile 1 Diobu, as socially and politically linked with the Mile 2 complex. A similar practice is followed in later sections of this study, but here we are concerned only with Mile 2 Diobu. The inhabitants of the two areas were indeed very similar in their socioeconomic characteristics and their political behavior. However, a massive slum clearance program was executed in Mile 1 some years back and, consequently, Mile 1 Diobu for the most part had been freed of the massive slum still characteristic of a large portion of Mile 2. Within Mile 1, small industrial establishments had taken the place of the former mud-wattle and thatch houses.

9. Data pertaining to Mile 2 Diobu are drawn from Donald Ostrum, "Housing in Diobu Mile 2," report of a sample survey of Mile 2 Diobu presented to the Eastern Nigeria Housing Corporation, 1964 (mimeographed). While the statistical accuracy of the sample is somewhat uncertain—a one percent sample of an underestimated total population was taken—Ostrum's report nonetheless contains useful data and represents the first attempt to systematically study social conditions in this area. With respect to the rental figures, it should be noted that the vast majority

of Port Harcourt residents earned less than $24.00 a month. Rent for a single room, therefore, normally represented at least one-fourth of an individual's monthly income.

10. Ibid. These percentages are similar to those recorded for the main township in the 1953 census. However, it is almost certain (though more recent statistics are not available) that the population of the main township had aged more during the last decade than the less stable population of Mile 2 Diobu.

11. Port Harcourt—Obia Planning Authority File, "Mile Two Diobu Planning Area," Volume I.

12. Frank Kennedy, "An Outline Sketch of the History and Problems of Town Planning in Port Harcourt." Lecture delivered before the Conference on Town Planning and Urbanization held in Port Harcourt, March 12, 1963.

13. Mile 2 Diobu Planning Scheme, presented in the Annual Report of the Eastern Nigerian Ministry of Town Planning, 1958–59 (Enugu: Government Printer, 1962), p. 23.

14. Ibid.

15. In 1962–63, the port handled 876,000 tons, as contrasted with the 1930 figure of 88,000 tons. Data on Port Harcourt shipping operations were extracted from two sources: (1) Nigerian Ports Authority, *Eighth Annual Report for the Year Ended 31st March 1963* (Lagos: Nigerian Ports Authority, July 1963), pp. 32–41, 95; and (2) text of a Port Harcourt radio address presented by E. O. Uruakpa, manager for the Eastern ports, n.d., typewritten.

16. Shell-BP, "Shell-BP in the Nigerian Economy," Port Harcourt, 1964, mimeographed.

17. Sayre P. Schatz, "Look at the Balance Sheet," *Africa Report* 15, no. 1 (January 1970): 18.

18. Ibid., p. 19.

19. Scott R. Pearson and Sandra C. Pearson, "Oil Boom Reshapes Nigeria's Future," *Africa Report* 16, no. 2 (February 1971): 14.

20. Ibid. Next to the British and Dutch, American oil companies have the largest interest in the exploration and production of Nigerian petroleum; however, French and Italian companies are also heavily involved, and more recently, a Japanese group, a West German company, and a private Nigerian company obtained concessions.

21. Scott R. Pearson, *Petroleum and the Nigerian Economy* (Stanford: Stanford University Press, 1970), pp. 93–94.

22. See *West Africa*, February 27, 1965.

23. The Trans-Amadi Industrial Estate was one result of a survey of Port Harcourt's industrial and social requirements executed in 1957 by Mr. A. G. Saville, an administrative officer of the Eastern Region government. The Saville Report, still not a public document, provided a blueprint for planned urban and industrial development; the government in the 1960s continued to be guided by many of its recommendations.

24. These data on Port Harcourt's industries are drawn from personal interviews, from the Annual Reports of the Regional Ministry of Commerce, and from *Distribution of Amenities in Eastern Nigeria* (Enugu: Government Printer, 1963), pp. 50–52.

25. See Peter Kilby, *Development of Small Industries in Eastern Nigeria* (Enugu: Ministry of Information, 1963), pp. 2–3. According to this report, Port Harcourt's 2,258 small firms employed 6,017 workers.

26. Computations are based upon the revenue figures presented in *Distribution of Amenities*, p. 73, and upon the results of the controversial 1963 census. For a useful discussion of this census controversy, see Walter Schwarz, *Nigeria* (New York: Praeger, 1968), pp. 157–64. For an assessment of the validity of the official census figures, see Chukuka Okonjo, "A Preliminary Medium Estimate of the 1962 Mid-Year Population of Nigeria," in *The Population of Tropical Africa*, ed. J. C.

Caldwell and C. Okonjo (New York: Columbia University Press, 1968), pp. 78–96.

27. *Eastern Nigeria Industrial Enquiry 1961–62* (Enugu: Ministry of Economic Planning, 1964), and International Bank for Reconstruction and Development, *The Economic Development of Nigeria* (Baltimore: Johns Hopkins Press, 1955), p. 616. The regional per capita product probably increased after 1953, but more recent statistics are unavailable.

28. Inasmuch as the census classified Port Harcourt's Diobu indigenes simply as "Ibos" the precise ratio of natives to strangers within the city cannot be determined. The "less than 7%" estimate is based upon population figures for those wards that were predominantly indigenous in composition. Since some strangers lived within these predominantly indigenous wards, the actual indigenous population may have been significantly smaller than that suggested by the 7% figure. The 1963 census figures for Port Harcourt were drawn from the official Census Report for Census District 309201 (Lagos, mimeographed).

29. Estimates vary, but Port Harcourt's prewar expatriate population was probably in the range of three to four thousand. Most Europeans and Americans were in Port Harcourt on short, two-year contracts, and had little contact with the city's African population outside of working hours. Expatriate social life centered around Shell-BP's Umuokoroshe Club and the Port Harcourt Club. The latter was formerly the municipality's "European Club" and was still referred to as such by most of the city's African residents. In 1963, a hundred of the Club's twelve hundred members were reported to be African. See Canon R. S. O. Stevens, *The Church in Urban Nigeria* (publication of the Church Missionary Society, 1963).

30. Ostrum, "Housing in Diobu Mile 2."

31. James S. Coleman, *Nigeria: Background to Nationalism* (Berkeley and Los Angeles: University of California Press, 1958), pp. 75–76.

32. A prewar population projection, based upon an underestimated 1960 population, forecast that by 1990 Port Harcourt's population would rise to 390,000 and, "at the ultimate stage of development, it may grow further and even exceed half a million." Eastern Nigeria Water Planning and Construction, *Roads, Drainage and Sewerage in Port Harcourt*, pp. 1, 16–18.

33. The unemployment figure is derived from data supplied by Dr. Archibald Callaway. I am indebted to Dr. Callaway for these and other data pertaining to Port Harcourt's labor force.

34. These data on property ownership were distilled from the building assessment records of the Port Harcourt Municipal Council. These records were poorly kept, and the precise figures reported above must be handled with considerable caution. Plot registrations were frequently incorrect, buildings were often underassessed, and many recorded assessments were out of date. Nonetheless, in the absence of other data the council assessment records do present what impressionistically appears to be a generally valid picture of property distribution in Port Harcourt. It should be noted, also, that sixteen of the fifty Africans with the highest recorded assessments are found within the writer's list of Port Harcourt's twenty-five wealthiest Africans, overall financial rankings having been determined by a modified reputational mode of analysis. The technique by which this rank ordering was obtained is described in appendix 1 at the conclusion of this study.

35. The term, "indivisible benefits," is borrowed from Robert Dahl. Writing of politics in New Haven, Connecticut, Dahl observes that "Certain benefits are *divisible* in such a way that they can be allocated to specific individuals; jobs, contracts, and welfare payments are examples of divisible benefits. Other benefits are more nearly *indivisible*: parks, playgrounds, schools, national defense and foreign policies, for example, either cannot be or ordinarily are not allocated by dividing the benefits piecemeal and allocating various pieces to specific individuals." Robert Dahl, *Who Governs?* (New Haven, Conn.: Yale University Press, 1961), p. 52.

36. Another factor reducing the salience of the ward as a reference point for municipal councillors was the strength of the local NCNC party organization. Gen-

erally, nomination by the NCNC tended to insure election to public office; most councillors, therefore, owed their office to their supporters within the local NCNC divisional executive rather than to their ward constituencies. See chapter 7.

37. Sylvia Leith-Ross, *African Women: A Study of the Ibo of Nigeria* (London: Faber, 1939), p. 247.

38. Illustrative of this divided orientation, the personal letterheads of Port Harcourt's African businessmen often included not only the address of their city residence but also that of their rural residence.

39. Thirty-four of the forty-one strangers who served on Port Harcourt's Municipal Council between 1961 and 1964 were queried on the frequency of their visits to their home towns. Seventeen of these thirty-four councillors (fifty percent) indicated that they averaged a trip home at least every two or three weeks. (Seven reported weekly visits to their home towns.) For many, it should be noted, "home" was over a hundred miles away.

40. Ostrum found that despite the youthfulness of the population of Mile 2 Diobu, thirty percent of the household heads interviewed already owned a house in their village, "with many more planning to build as soon as they acquire a little money." See his "Housing in Diobu Mile 2."

41. Ninety-six percent of the Mile 2 Diobu sample indicated they intended to retire in their home village; forty-one percent of this sample reported that their wives and/or children remained at home. Ibid. Leonard Plotnicov has suggested that often times urban immigrants tend to present to interviewers an idyllic view of their home area, and that a number of countervailing pressures—such as a lack of economic success in the urban area, or social hostility from the more traditionally minded "stay-at-homes"—prevent urban dwellers from returning home. See Leonard Plotnicov, *Strangers to the City: Urban Man in Jos, Nigeria* (Pittsburgh: University of Pittsburgh Press, 1967), especially pp. 296–99. It cannot be denied, however, that even those urban dwellers who do not act upon their declared intention of returning home retain emotional and economic ties with their home communities. It should be noted, too, that Port Harcourt's relative proximity to the rural homeland of most of the city's residents, both Ibo and non-Ibo, facilitated contact with their communities of origin.

CHAPTER 3: *The Regional Backdrop*

1. Following James Coleman, *Nigeria: Background to Nationalism* (Berkeley and Los Angeles: University of California Press, 1958), p. 423, a "nationality" is defined as "the largest traditional African group above a tribe which can be distinguished from other groups by one or more objective criteria (normally language)." Thus, the Ibo (taken as a whole to mean all Ibo-speaking tribes), the Efik, the Ibibio, and the Ijaw are all termed nationalities. According to one count, there are seventeen major languages and some three hundred of lesser importance in Eastern Nigeria. See Colonial Office, *Commission Appointed to Enquire into the Fears of Minorities and the Means of Allaying Them* (cmnd. 505, London, 1958), p. 34 (hereafter cited as the *Minorities Report*).

2. For general materials on the Ibo see Daryll Forde and G. I. Jones, *The Ibo and Ibibio-speaking Peoples of South-Eastern Nigeria* (London: Oxford University Press, 1950); C. K. Meek, *Law and Authority in a Nigerian Tribe* (London: Oxford University Press, 1937); V. C. Uchendu, *The Igbo of Southeast Nigeria* (New York: Holt, Rinehart and Winston, 1965); G. I. Jones, *Report of the Position, Status, and Influence of Chiefs and Natural Rulers in the Eastern Region of Nigeria* (Enugu: Government Printer, 1956) (hereafter cited as the *Jones Report*).

3. A "house" was a localized kin group that, during the era of the slave trade, developed into a broader-based competitive trading and fighting corporation. The outstanding works on Delta social and political organization are G. I. Jones, *The Trading States of the Oil Rivers* (London: Oxford University Press, 1963); K.

Onwuka Dike, *Trade and Politics in the Niger Delta, 1830–1885* (London: Oxford University Press, 1959); and E. J. Alagoa, *The Small Brave City State* (Madison: University of Wisconsin Press, 1964).

4. Simon Ottenberg, "Ibo Oracles and Intergroup Relations," *Southwestern Journal of Anthropology* 14, no. 3 (Autumn 1958): 296.

5. Jones, *Trading States of the Oil Rivers*, p. 13.

6. Dike, *Trade and Politics*, p. 28.

7. Even these specialist communities, it should be noted, contained many persons who were engaged in more conventional agrarian occupations, such as fishing or farming, the proportion thus employed depending on the capacity of their specialist relatives to develop and extend their specialization. See Jones, *Trading States of the Oil Rivers*, p. 15. To this list of communities producing migrant nonagriculturalists must be added Onitsha Town and the large Mbieri and Mbaise groups in Owerri Division.

8. M. M. Green, *Ibo Village Affairs*, 2nd ed. (London: Frank Cass, 1964), pp. 216, 232. The effectiveness of the women's rural communications system explains, in part, the prominent role women have played in rural protest movements—such as the Aba Women's Riots of 1929 protesting anticipated new taxes and the discredited warranted chief system of native administration, and the Regionwide 1958 riots protesting the imposition of new school fees. Concerning the Aba Riots, see Margery Perham's synopsis in her *Native Administration in Nigeria* (London: Oxford University Press, 1937), pp. 206–20. The background to the 1958 disturbances is presented in David B. Abernethy, *The Political Dilemma of Popular Education* (Stanford: Stanford University Press, 1969), pp. 161–87.

9. Ottenberg, "Ibo Oracles and Intergroup Relations," p. 299. "Aro colonies became the divinely ordained trade centers in the interior; Aro middlemen the economic dictators of the hinterland . . . with wealth came great political influence." Dike, *Trade and Politics*, p. 38. This discussion of the Aro oracle system draws primarily upon these studies of Ottenberg and Dike.

10. *Bende District Annual Report, 1912* (National Archives File E 1917/12; Riv Prof; 1/6/137). All National Archives citations refer to Enugu holdings.

11. *Okigwi District Annual Report, 1912* (National Archives File E 1917/12; Riv Prof; 1/6/137).

12. *Owerri District Quarterly Report, June 1914* (National Archives File OW 508/14; Riv Prof; 1/12/377).

13. Despite the oracle's surreptitious slave dealings, its judicial wisdom was greatly respected and its advice invariably taken. Writing in 1937, C. K. Meek observed that "the oracles could hardly have attained and retained their enormous influence unless they had been administered with a considerable degree of impartiality and very considerable skill in the sifting of evidence. Their decisions can seldom have run counter to the weight of local opinion. At the present time many elders of the Awgu Division regard the destruction of the oracle at Aro in 1901 as an abominable outrage which has caused Chuku [the Supreme Spirit] to withdraw his presence and protection from Iboland." C. K. Meek, *Law and Authority in a Nigerian Tribe* (London: Oxford University Press, 1937), p. 48.

14. I do not mean to say that the oracle systems did not also have significant divisive characteristics. As Simon Ottenberg notes, "The oracle system also contained serious disruptive patterns. . . . Families were broken up and communities disrupted by the loss of members who did not return from the oracles or who were waylaid into slavery. Communities were looted and their members dispersed by the mercenaries. Individuals suffered extreme hardships. While persons were fearful of being seized by anybody if they went far from their home area, they were also fearful of being captured by oracle agents, and this was an important factor in keeping communities and individuals localized and isolated." See Ottenberg, "Ibo Oracles and Intergroup Relations," p. 313.

15. Coleman, *Nigeria: Background to Nationalism*, p. 30.

16. *Jones Report*, p. 11.

17. "An *age set* consists of persons living in one village born within approximately three years of one another. . . . An *age grade* is a grouping in which several contiguous age sets combine to form a larger body having recognized functions." Phoebe Ottenberg, "The Afikpo Ibo of Eastern Nigeria," in *Peoples of Africa*, ed. James L. Gibbs, Jr. (New York: Holt, Rinehart and Winston, 1965), p. 15. See also G. I. Jones, "Ibo Age Organization, with Special Reference to the Cross River and North-Eastern Ibo," *Journal of the Royal Anthropological Institute* 92, part 2 (1962): 191–211; and the *Jones Report*, p. 11.

18. Commenting upon the political function of these societies, G. I. Jones observes that "quite apart from the work of its members at public meetings, the title or secret society had other equally important political functions. It brought together the leading men of all the segments of the community, and it provided them with a forum for the discussion of community affairs privately and in a noncontroversial atmosphere free from sectional disputes and sectional loyalties." *Jones Report*, p. 18.

19. See Simon Ottenberg, "Ibo Receptivity to Change," in *Continuity and Change in African Cultures*, ed. William R. Bascom and Melville J. Herskovits (Chicago: Phoenix Books, 1959), p. 140. See also L. T. Chubb, *Ibo Land Tenure*, 2nd ed. (Ibadan: Ibadan University Press, 1961), p. 30, where he observes, "Ibos everywhere are prepared to give land to strangers of whom they approve provided they will live within the confines of the village dwelling-lands and identify themselves with the local customs and taboos."

20. James S. Coleman, "The Politics of Sub-Saharan Africa," in *The Politics of the Developing Areas*, ed. Gabriel Almond and James S. Coleman (Princeton: Princeton University Press, 1960), p. 256.

21. G. I. Jones, "From Direct to Indirect Rule in Eastern Nigeria," *Odu* 2, no. 2 (1966): 72–80.

22. Ibid.

23. It has been suggested that wealth became more important as a means to political power following the great increase in both domestic and external trade in the late eighteenth and nineteenth centuries. As a result of this trade expansion, many Rivers, Ibo, and Ibibio communities "became more dependent on a money and less on a subsistence economy. . . . The development of the House system in the Rivers ports, of the Title Societies of the Northern Riverain and Central Ibo and the Secret Societies of the Calabar and Cross River area . . . can be seen as a response to these changed conditions." *Jones Report*, p. 13.

24. Ibid.

25. Phoebe Ottenberg, "Afikpo Ibo of Eastern Nigeria," p. 27. Some Niger River Ibo communities—such as Onitsha Town and Oguta—did develop fairly elaborate chieftaincy institutions, apparently patterned after those of the Benin Kingdom to the west. Even in these cases, however, royal prerogatives were carefully circumscribed.

26. The designation of these governing bodies as councils of elders was something of a misnomer, inasmuch as they were made up not only of the senior ritual heads of the component villages and village subsections, but also of the community's natural leaders. Moreover, even the traditionally designated elders sat on the councils as the representatives of their respective social units, and not as the members of a homogeneous age group. The use of the age-grade terminology, however, helped to disguise the fragility of the segmentary political system. To quote G. I. Jones, "Ibo Age Organization," p. 196:

> To refer to these councillors as the heads and leaders of their respective segments emphasized the weakness of the political system, for their authority as head or leader was limited to the members of the segment which they represented, and while representing it their loyalty belonged primarily to the

segment and only secondarily to the whole community. But as elders they were collectively the heads of another segmentary system of a different kind, a vertical one which cut right across the horizontal one of politically equal territorial and patrilineal segments (villages), and which divided the men of the community on a basis of age into segments (age-grades) which were ranked in a hierarchy with the elders at the top. They were a grade to which all other grades were subordinate.

27. In practice, persons "who were poor and without descendants and other supporters" tended to stay away from these meetings. Ibid., p. 197.

28. See Robert A. Le Vine, *Dreams and Deeds: Achievement Motivation in Nigeria* (Chicago and London: University of Chicago Press, 1965), and Simon Ottenberg, "Ibo Receptivity to Change," in *Continuity and Change in African Cultures*, ed. William R. Bascom and Melville J. Herskovits (Chicago and London: University of Chicago Press, 1962), pp. 130–43. The precise role and significance of such cultural predispositions in the development process is as yet uncertain. For a critical analysis of the Ibo "receptivity to change" hypothesis, see Richard Henderson, " 'Generalized Cultures' and 'Evolutionary Adaptability': The Comparison of Urban Efik and Ibo in Nigeria," *Ethnology* 5 (October 1966): 365–91.

29. Karl W. Deutsch, "Social Mobilization and Political Development," *American Political Science Review* 55 (September 1961): 493.

30. Coleman, *Nigeria: Background to Nationalism*, p. 40.

31. Richard L. Sklar, *Nigerian Political Parties: Power in an Emergent African Nation* (Princeton: Princeton University Press, 1963), p. 16.

32. *Jones Report*, p. v.

33. Henderson, " 'Generalized Cultures,' " p. 377.

34. The translation of the Bible by European missionaries into Onitsha and Owerri dialects added linguistic substance to the administrative division. However, the Owerri and Onitsha dialect groups did not coincide perfectly with the provincial boundaries, the latter being affected by considerations of geography and administrative convenience as well as by cultural and linguistic homogeneity.

35. *Minorities Report*, p. 36.

36. See Abernethy, *Political Dilemma*, pp. 52, 258.

37. Owerri Provincial Estimates, 1917 (National Archives File OW 274/16; Riv Prof; 1/14/240).

38. When the terms, Owerri Province and Onitsha Province, are employed in this study, reference is made to the pre-1959 administrative boundaries.

CHAPTER 4: *The Formative Years: Land Acquisition and the Colonial Presence (1913–1919)*

1. With the victory of the federal forces in the Nigerian/Biafran war, and the subsequent local political ascendancy of the previously subordinated Ijaws, Port Harcourt entered a new historical phase touched upon in chapter 10 below. This recent history, however, falls largely outside the scope of the present study.

2. Robert A. Dahl, *Who Governs?* (New Haven, Conn.: Yale University Press, 1960).

3. Ibid., p. 11.

4. Kenneth Little, "The West African Town: Its Social Basis," *Diogenes* 29 (Spring 1960): 17. See also Simon Ottenberg, "The Social and Administrative History of a Nigerian Township," *International Journal of Comparative Sociology* 7, nos. 1/2 (1966).

5. Memorandum, dated October 4, 1914, addressed to the Owerri provincial commissioner from District Officer Hargrove. National Archives File OW 1/13, Riv Prof; S/1/1.

Notes

6. Ibid.

7. Ibid.

8. It should be noted that not all of the seven sections of Diobu were converted into Crown land under the original acquisition. Specifically, Oroabali Village was permitted to retain its land.

Many years of complaint and petition by the Diobus followed the 1913 acquisition. By the "Penny Stamp" agreement of 1927, the government promised the villagers of Orogbum-Diobu and Orominike-Diobu compensation if their houses were subsequently demolished and twelve months' notice of the government's intent to execute the demolition order (Port Harcourt-Obia Planning Authority, File No. 6883). Then, in 1928, a government enquiry into the land dispute resulted in the formulation of a new land agreement. The government now undertook to pay to the Diobus a lump sum of £7,500, to pay an annual rent of £500 in perpetuity, and to surrender approximately three square miles of the original acquisition. (According to an expatriate officer with long experience in Port Harcourt Division, the government returned a large portion of the three-mile area to the wrong people. According to this informant, it was actually the Umuemes, rather than the Diobus, who were the original owners of this land.) Still dissatisfied, however, the Diobus continued to petition the government, charging that the original acquisition was illegal and that, in any event, the payment of £500 per annum was inadequate compensation for their loss. The matter eventually went to the courts, and a protracted period of litigation ensued. Finally, in 1956, the Privy Council of Great Britain rendered the final decision in the Diobu land case, upholding the legality and the terms of the 1913 and 1928 land agreements.

9. Excerpts from an address delivered by the Owerri provincial commissioner to the chiefs and people of Owerri on the occasion of the amalgamation of Northern and Southern Nigeria, January 1, 1914. National Archives File OW 1/13; Riv Prof; S/1/1.

10. Memorandum directed to the Calabar provincial commissioner. National Archives File OW 1/13; Riv Prof; S/1/1.

11. Memorandum, dated June 28, 1914, addressed to the Port Harcourt district officer from the Uyo district officer. National Archives File OW 1/13; Riv Prof; S/1/1.

12. Ibid.

13. Frank Kennedy, "An Outline Sketch of the History and Problems of Town Planning in Port Harcourt," mimeographed (Paper delivered before the Conference on Town Planning and Urbanization held in Port Harcourt, March 12, 1963).

14. Sanitary Report on Port Harcourt, 1917. National Archives File OW 432/17; Riv Prof; 1/15/404.

15. Personal interview.

16. Kennedy, "Outline Sketch of Town Planning," p. 4.

17. Sylvia Leith-Ross, African Women: A Study of the Ibo of Nigeria (London: Faber, 1939), p. 238.

18. Dahl, Who Governs?, p. 15.

19. Memorandum, dated December 9, 1913, from the colonial secretary to the Owerri assistant provincial commissioner. National Archives File OW 1/13; Riv Prof; 1/12/2.

20. National Archives File OW 680/16; Riv Prof; 1/14/660.

21. Ibid.

22. Township Advisory Board Minutes, 1918–1919. National Archives File OW 104/18.

23. Simon Ottenberg, "The Development of Local Government in a Nigerian Township," Anthropologica 4, no. 1 (1963): 122.

24. Memorandum, dated October 12, 1918, addressed to the Owerri Provincial Resident from Governor-General Lugard. National Archives File OW 104/18.

25. Memorandum, dated March 21, 1924, addressed to the Port Harcourt Local

Notes

Authority from the Owerri Provincial Resident. National Archives File OW 72/24; Riv Prof; 1/22/63.

26. In 1922 or 1923, Port Harcourt became the administrative headquarters for the vast Owerri Province. The administrative significance of the railway-port was thereby substantially increased.

27. National Archives File OW 632/17; Riv Prof; 1/15/667 and Port Harcourt Municipal Council Estimates (mimeographed).

28. Annual Report of the Port Harcourt Station Magistrate, January 28, 1921. National Archives File OW 134/21; Riv Prof; 1/19/118.

29. The writer's own tabulation, based upon the "Proposed Establishment 1964/65" figures approved by the Eastern Nigerian Ministry of Local Government (mimeographed).

30. Township Advisory Board Minutes, August 26, 1920. National Archives File OW 104/18.

31. Township Advisory Board Minutes, November 3, 1919. National Archives File OW 104/18.

CHAPTER 5: *The Political Coalescence of the African Community (1920–1943)*

1. Charles W. Anderson, Fred R. von der Mehden and Crawford Young, *Issues of Political Development* (Englewood Cliffs, N.J.: Prentice-Hall, 1967), p. 30.

2. Crawford Young, *Politics in the Congo* (Princeton: Princeton University Press, 1965), pp. 242–46.

3. Lloyd I. Rudolph and Susanne Hoeber Rudolph, *The Modernity of Tradition: Political Development in India* (Chicago: University of Chicago Press, 1967), p. 100.

4. Minute Book of the Owerri Progressive Union, 1932–33.

5. *Nigerian Observer*, March 29, 1930.

6. Dr. Onwu's return to Nigeria was also the occasion for the formation of the Lagos Ibo Union. In this connection, it would appear that Coleman and Sklar are mistaken when they indicate that Dr. Francis Ibiam, who returned to Nigeria in 1935, was Nigeria's first Ibo doctor and that it was Dr. Ibiam's return that inspired the formation of the Lagos Ibo Union. See James Coleman, *Nigeria: Background to Nationalism* (Berkeley and Los Angeles: University of California Press, 1958), p. 340, and Richard L. Sklar, *Nigerian Political Parties: Power in an Emergent African Nation* (Princeton: Princeton University Press, 1963), pp. 54–55.

7. This was but the local extension of the pattern established in the Owerri provincial administration. See chapter 3. In the 1930s the highest African position in the township, that of chief clerk in the Resident's office, was held by one Ajakwa, an immigrant from the Gold Coast.

8. These data were drawn from the National Archives and from personal interviews. Occupationally, civil servants dominated the African Club's membership lists. In 1938, the earliest year for which occupational data were available, two of the club's ten officers were customs officials, two were government clerks, one was a senior sanitary inspector, one was a senior inspector of police, one was a former railway official, and one was a chargehand in the public works department. The remaining two club officials were both clerks in the United African Company. It should be noted that the transfer of the Owerri provincial headquarters from Owerri Town to Port Harcourt in 1927 increased the railway-port's administrative significance and drew to the new township an unusual number of administrative personnel.

9. The concept of geo-ethnicity has much the same meaning as that of ethnicity, as used by Immanuel Wallerstein, "Ethnicity and National Integration in West Africa," in *Cahiers d'Etudes Africaines*, 7 no. 3 (October 1960): 129–39. The

269

Notes

former term is preferred here for two reasons. First, it offers a sharper conceptual tool than does ethnicity to descibe the new kinds of urban groupings that were based upon nontraditional or neo-traditional communities of origin. The differences between Orlu Division and Okigwi Division (two Ibo-speaking administrative units around which communal groups in Port Harcourt organized), for example, were no more ethnic in character than are the differences between Kansas and Nebraska. The new administrative units were differentiated primarily by the arbitrary placement of colonial boundaries and only secondarily by cultural variations. Second, the use of the geo-ethnicity term to describe urban groupings based upon new, artificial entities enables us to reserve the concept of ethnicity for urban groupings based more strictly on kinship, cultural, and linguistic ties.

10. The largest area in Owerri Division, Mbaise was also the poorest and the most densely crowded. Mbaise complaints that their area had not received its legitimate share of amenities from the regional government go back several years, and Mbaises have long contended that the size of their community—which is comprised of a collection of numerous, traditionally autonomous, village groups—justified the creation of a separate Mbaise administrative division. Port Harcourt Mbaises, well organized and politically articulate, dramatized their demand for divisional autonomy by refusing, as from 1954, to take an active part in the affairs of the local Owerri Divisional Union. Politically, Mbaises tended to act independently of their Owerri brethren, except in instances where the Owerri provincial community was challenged by the candidacy of an Onitsha or other non-Owerri person. In effect, then, Mbaise was the political equivalent of any of the geo-ethnic divisional units around which Ibo politics in Port Harcourt normally revolved.

11. The educational and occupational distributions of these executive committees did not necessarily parallel the distributions that were to be found among the rank and file of Port Harcourt's Onitsha, Orlu, and Mbaise communities. Executive committees, especially at the divisional level of the union structure, tended to be composed of high status individuals, and it is certain that the rank and file *of all three communities* included a far larger number of uneducated persons and of petty traders and unskilled laborers than the composition of the executive committees would suggest. It is the *relative* proportions, however, in which we are interested, and these should hold for the larger populations as well.

12. The term, economic notables, is Robert Dahl's; the method by which Port Harcourt's economic notables were identified, however, differs from that employed by Dahl. See Robert Dahl, *Who Governs?* (New Haven, Conn.: Yale University Press, 1960), pp. 63–86, and the methodological description in appendix 1 at the conclusion of this study.

13. It would be desirable to know the relative proportions of Onitsha and Owerri Ibos in the population at large. Unfortunately, these statistics are not available. It is certain, however, that Owerris greatly outnumbered Onitshans. Consequently, we must assume that the Owerri preponderance among Port Harcourt's leading businessmen was due, at least partially, to the Owerri numerical advantage within the larger community. By the same token, it is equally certain that despite their numerical disadvantage, Onitsha Ibos contributed disproportionately to the highest posts within Port Harcourt's commercial and governmental establishment.

14. Sylvia Leith-Ross, *African Women: A Study of the Ibo of Nigeria* (London: Faber, 1939), p. 251.

15. Banham Church, Port Harcourt's first Methodist Church, was built by Elijah Henshaw, a Calabar Efik who worked as a private contractor, supplying food to the local prison. According to one report, Henshaw intended to hand over the church to the Presbyterians, but when they failed to appear, he handed it over instead to Banham, a Methodist missionary. As a consequence, all normally Presbyterian Calabar Efiks and Uyo Ibibios became Methodist—at least for the duration of their stay in Port Harcourt. In 1964, of the seventeen members of the Banham Church Committee, seven were from Uyo or Calabar, nine were Bende Ibos, and

270

one was an Ibo from Ovim (a community in Okigwi Division with close historical
ties with Ibos in Bende Division).

16. Petition of March 9, 1925. National Archives File OW 203/25; Riv Prof;
1/23/137.

17. Kenneth Little, *West African Urbanization: A Study of Voluntary Associations in Social Change* (Cambridge: Cambridge University Press, 1965), pp. 101–
02.

18. Following Little, voluntary associations refer to "institutionalized groups in
which membership is attained by joining," i.e., by an act of volition rather than by
the involuntary fact of birth. Ibid., p. 1. Little's short study offers an excellent
synthesis of the literature on African voluntary associations. See also Immanuel
Wallerstein, "Voluntary Associations," in *Political Parties and National Integration
in Tropical Africa,* ed. James Coleman and Carl Rosberg, Jr. (Berkeley and Los
Angeles: University of California Press, 1964), pp. 318–39, and Coleman, *Nigeria:
Background to Nationalism,* pp. 211–20.

19. Clan court area was simply an administrative designation; it seldom referred
to genealogically defined clan units.

20. Little, *West African Urbanization,* p. 24.

21. See William Kornhauser, *The Politics of Mass Society* (Glencoe, Ill.: Free
Press, 1959), especially pp. 119–28 and 142–58.

22. Coleman, *Nigeria: Background to Nationalism,* p. 215, has drawn attention
to the political impact of these urban associations on rural life and institutions, noting that they "exercised a powerful influence in the democratization of native authority councils." For a study of an improvement union operating in a rural
environment, see Simon Ottenberg, "Improvement Associations Among the Afikpo
Ibo," *Africa* 25, no. 1 (January 1955): 1–28.

23. In its first issue, the *Observer* made an oblique reference to an earlier newspaper that failed shortly after its introduction; its impact appears to have been as
abbreviated as its tenure.

24. These quotations are drawn from personal interviews with political figures
who were Potts-Johnson's contemporaries.

25. African Methodist Episcopal Zion Church, *Memorial Booklet,* 1949; *Nigerian Observer,* January 1949.

26. *Nigerian Observer,* January 4, 1930.

27. *Nigerian Observer,* March 29, 1930. For a brief mention of Garvey's impact
on Nigerian political thought, see Coleman, *Nigeria: Background to Nationalism,*
pp. 189–91; Aggrey is mentioned in passing on page 223 of the same work.

28. *Nigerian Observer,* March 22, 1930.

29. *Nigerian Observer,* June 21, 1930.

30. *Nigerian Observer,* February 22, 1930.

31. Leith-Ross, *African Women,* p. 239.

32. Letter, dated October 1, 1935, from the African Community League to the
Local Authority. National Archives File RP 2807; Riv Prof; 1/46/30.

33. Letter, dated September 26, 1936, from the African Community League to
the Owerri Provincial Resident. National Archives File RP 2807; Riv Prof; 1/46/30.

34. Memorandum, dated December 2, 1936, from the Local Authority to the
Owerri Provincial Resident. National Archives File RP 2807; Riv Prof; 1/46/30.

35. This meeting is recalled in a welcome address presented by the Ibo Union
to the Owerri Provincial Resident, January 28, 1944. National Archives File RP
11/22, Vol. II; Riv Prof; 1/45/2.

36. These are excerpts from the league's statement of its "Aims and Objects,"
presented in a letter, dated October 1, 1935, from the African Community League
to the Local Authority. National Archives File RP 2807; Riv Prof; 1/46/30.

37. James Coleman makes a like observation in connection with the Lagos political leadership during these same years. In Lagos, as in Port Harcourt, many of the
early leaders of thought were non-Nigerian Africans for whom the notion of a

territorially defined Nigerian nation held little significance. Coleman, *Nigeria: Background to Nationalism,* pp. 210–11.

CHAPTER 6: *The Transfer of Power (1944–1954)*

1. This terminology is borrowed from Robert K. Merton, *Social Theory and Social Structure* (Glencoe, Ill.: Free Press, 1957), pp. 387–420.

2. Excerpts from the report of the medical officer of health, as quoted in Local Authority Palmer's Annual Report, 1943. National Archives File OW 5389/7; Riv Prof; 1/29/1101.

3. Ibid.

4. Memorandum, dated December 22, 1943, from Local Authority Palmer to the Owerri Provincial Resident. National Archives File RP 2807; Riv Prof; 1/46/30.

5. Minutes of the meeting of the chief commissioner for the eastern provinces with a delegation of the African Community League, February 21, 1944. National Archives File 2807; Riv Prof; 1/46/30.

6. L. Gray Cowan, *Local Government in West Africa* (New York: Columbia University Press, 1958), p. 85.

7. At the request of the chief commissioner for the eastern provinces, the league dropped its demand for Legislative Council representation, pending the completion of a review of the Nigerian Constitution then in process.

8. Floyer presided at the Town Council's inaugural session, but was replaced at the council's second meeting by H. N. Harcourt.

9. Memorandum of the African Community League, forwarded by the Local Authority to the Owerri Provincial Resident on March 8, 1945. National Archives File RP 5744, Vol. I; Riv Prof; 1/46/119.

10. R. K. Floyer, *Memorandum on Proposed Municipality for Port Harcourt, 1946.* Port Harcourt Provincial Office Archives (hereafter cited as *The Floyer Report*).

11. Commentary appended to the league memorandum calling for local self-government, forwarded by the Local Authority to the Owerri Provincial Resident on March 8, 1945. National Archives File RP 5744, Vol. I; Riv Prof; 1/46/119.

12. Actually, the approval of council estimates by the central government constituted a departure from the British model. See Ronald Wraith, *Local Government in West Africa* (London: Allen and Unwin, 1964), p. 98.

13. Circular letter issued in June 1949. Port Harcourt Provincial Office Archives, File No. 4744, Vol. II.

14. These resolutions were reported by Chairman Floyer to a meeting of the Township Advisory Board, September 23, 1947. In response, Floyer observed, "If these resolutions were upheld, it probably means that there would be no municipality for Port Harcourt, since they at any rate claimed to represent the majority of the inhabitants." Township Advisory Board Minutes of September 23, 1947. National Archives File RP 5744; Vol. I; Riv Prof; 1/46/119.

15. This article appeared in the *Eastern Nigerian Guardian* early in September 1947.

16. Township Advisory Board Minutes, September 23, 1947. National Archives File RP 5744; Vol. I; Riv Prof; 1/46/119.

17. Privately, Floyer was not unsympathetic to the African desire for a lower general rate. He noted, in his policy memorandum, that a general rate had never before been paid in Port Harcourt and that a proposal to introduce such a rate had in fact been dropped in 1938 "owing to public opposition." "It is perhaps asking a good deal from the infant Council to expect it to enter upon office with the odium of a 2/ rate all at once. The argument that Port Harcourt must pay for what it gets does not take into account the fact that any community takes some time to get used to a new idea, particularly a new tax, and a rate at this level may have the effect of increasing still higher the extortionate rents now charged by the local landlords." *The Floyer Report.*

18. *The Floyer Report.*
19. Memorandum, dated January 23, 1946, from Local Authority Floyer to the Owerri Provincial Resident. National Archives File RP 5744, Vol. I; Riv Prof; 1/46/119.
20. *The Floyer Report.*
21. Memorandum on the "Revised Floyer Report," addressed from the secretary to the commissioner for the eastern provinces, September 2, 1946. National Archives File RP 5744, Vol. I; Riv Prof; 1/46/119. In a marginal note, the commissioner replied: ". . . I do not think that we should be over apprehensive. It is part of the experiment."
22. *The Floyer Report.*
23. Township Advisory Board Minutes, September 10, 1947. National Archives File RP 5744, Vol. I; Riv Prof; 1/46/119.
24. *The Floyer Report.*
25. Memorandum, dated October 21, 1947, from Local Authority Floyer to the Owerri Provincial Resident. National Archives File RP 5744, Vol. I; Riv Prof; 1/46/119.
26. Township Advisory Board Minutes, September 30, 1947. National Archives File RP 5744, Vol. I; Riv Prof; 1/46/119.
27. District Officer Harcourt reporting to the Owerri Provincial Resident, March 8, 1950. Port Harcourt Municipal Council Archives.
28. Memorandum, dated October 21, 1947, from Local Authority Floyer to the Owerri Provincial Resident. National Archives File RP 5744, Vol. I; Riv Prof; 1/46/119.
29. Proposals of G. Beresford Stook, the officer administering the government, presented to Arthur Creech Jones, secretary of state for the colonies, on February 25, 1948. Port Harcourt Provincial Office Archives.
30. Minutes of a meeting between Eastern Commissioner Carr and the representatives of various interests in Port Harcourt, September 21, 1947. Township Advisory Board Minutes, September 30, 1947. National Archives File RP 5744, Vol. I; Riv Prof; 1/46/119.
31. *The Floyer Report.*
32. Memorandum, dated October 1, 1945, from Local Authority Floyer to the Owerri Provincial Resident. National Archives File RP 5744, Vol. I; Riv Prof; 1/46/119.
33. Town Council Archives File 675; National Archives File RP 5744, Vol. II; Riv Prof; 1/46/119.
34. Mrs. E. Adesigbin, the only woman councillor during this period, a prosperous trader and the wife of a Yoruba magistrate, held a few committee headships during the council's first months. Her influence declined, however, as the Ibo members grew accustomed to their new powers and responsibilities.
35. Onyeri entered the Eastern House of Assembly in 1951 and did not contest the 1952 council election; Nonyelu was reelected to the council but failed in his attempt to recapture the council presidency.
36. See Margaret Green, *Igbo Village Affairs*, 2nd ed. (London: Frank Cass, 1964), and Francis Ikenna Nzimiro, "Oguta," *Nigeria Magazine*, no. 80 (March 1964): 30–43.
37. Port Harcourt Town Council File No. 675.
38. Ibid.
39. For the background and history of the nationalist movement, see James S. Coleman, *Nigeria: Background to Nationalism* (Berkeley and Los Angeles: University of California Press, 1958), and Richard L. Sklar, *Nigerian Political Parties: Power in an Emergent African Nation* (Princeton: Princeton University Press, 1963), pp. 1–86.
40. Sklar, *Nigerian Political Parties*, p. 149.
41. Coleman, *Nigeria: Background to Nationalism*, p. 295.
42. This fact was still largely true in 1964. Occupational data were tabulated for

67 of the 101 members of the Port Harcourt Ibo Union Executive Committee. Of these 67 members, 48 (or 71.6%) were engaged in some form of private enterprise (trading, contracting, transporting, and the like). Comparable data for the Lagos Ibo Union were not available.

43. See Margaret Katzin, "The Role of the Small Enterpreneur," in *Economic Transition in Africa*, ed. Melville J. Herskovits and Mitchell Harwitz (Evanston, Ill.: Northwestern University Press, 1964), pp. 179–98.

44. A special comment is in order concerning the first named of the three City Fathers cited above. Chief M. I. Asinobi was one of Port Harcourt's oldest residents, having arrived in the new township in 1914 while the Eastern Nigeria railway line was still under construction. (For a brief period, Chief Asinobi served as a labor headman on the railway gang.) A native of Mbieri village group (Owerri Division), Chief Asinobi in the early sixties was often referred to as the city's first citizen, and a special place of honor was not infrequently reserved for him on public occasions. Despite his lack of formal education, he commanded the respect of all segments of the community and played a critical role in the township's social and political development. His home often served as the meeting place for forums of national as well as local significance. He was the outstanding exception to the general conservatism of Port Harcourt's commercial and propertied interests, having supported Nnamdi Azikiwe and the NCNC from the outset of their campaign and having assisted the party financially on a number of occasions. He was the president of the Port Harcourt Ibo Union for seventeen years, the president of the Owerri Divisional Union for eighteen years, the first president of the Mbieri Improvement Union, and a long-term president of his village union, the Obazu Welfare Union. A former member of the Port Harcourt Town Council, Chief Asinobi in 1964 was the trustee of the Ibo State Union, a member of the Eastern House of Chiefs, a patron of the local branch of the NCNC, and a patron of the Port Harcourt Ibo Union. His chieftaincy title, it should be noted, like that of so many Ibo notables, was honorific rather than traditional; it celebrated his personal achievement rather than his position of birth.

45. Coleman, *Nigeria: Background to Nationalism*, p. 223.

46. Ibid., p. 143.

47. Sklar, *Nigerian Political Parties*, p. 55.

48. Coleman, *Nigeria: Background to Nationalism*, p. 341.

49. Ibid., pp. 332–43.

50. Ibid., p. 250.

51. Prince A. A. Nwafor Orizu, a son of the Obi of Nnewi (Onitsha Division) and the former president of the precoup Nigerian Senate, is the author of *Without Bitterness, Western Nations in Post-War Africa* (New York: Creative Age Press, 1944). For an assessment of his writings and their impact, see Sklar, *Nigerian Political Parties*, pp. 72–83. For a brief period in the early 1950s Orizu was a resident of Port Harcourt and an active participant in the then-declining African Community League.

52. This incident and trial are detailed in Sklar, *Nigerian Political Parties*, pp. 74–76.

53. See Sklar, *Nigerian Political Parties*, pp. 80–81.

54. National Archives File ADS 1358 Ahoada District 1/8/1259. Of the political significance of the Enugu shooting, Sklar writes: "Historians may conclude that the slaying of coal miners by police at Enugu first proved the subjective reality of a Nigerian nation. No previous event ever evoked a manifestation of national consciousness comparable to the indignation generated by this tragedy." *Nigerian Political Parties*, pp. 76–77.

55. As compensation for the loss of his Port Harcourt seat, the national NCNC leadership appointed Umolu (who, following his 1957 reelection to the House of Assembly, had become parliamentary secretary to the premier) to the Eastern House of Chiefs, and he was subsequently made a provincial commissioner. When

the new region of Mid-Western Nigeria was created in 1963, Umolu returned home and became the region's first minister of establishments.

56. Nwapa had come to local political prominence through his opposition to the government's allocation of three highly commercial plots of land to local Lebanese traders. It was felt by some elements of the African community that members of the Town Council had accepted money in exchange for their support of the Lebanese allocation. Thus, Nwapa became at one and the same time, the champion of "African rights" and of "good government."

57. While the validity of these particular allegations is not known, bribery has always been a fairly common feature of Nigerian electioneering. Richard Sklar quotes the observations of one candidate to the Eastern House of Assembly in 1953 on the meeting of a final electoral college: "On the morning of the election some leaders of the clan of agents would wear special large overflowing native robes with specially designed large pockets. These pockets would be filled with folded currency notes and the carrier (sic) rolled luxuriously to the polling station. He would take a stand directly opposite the voters but on the side of the fence which was built to keep off the intruders. He would take a fixed glance at a voter and signal him off to see him. He would greet him by shaking one of the folded notes into his hands and bidding him good-bye and, naming the candidate, would ask him to call out the next on his bench. That process repeated until the whole people were met and instructed . . . the last minute (bribes) . . . usually carried more weight than thousands of pounds already spent." *Nigerian Political Parties*, p. 29. In the 1951 Port Harcourt elections it was alleged, in addition, that at least one candidate had his bribe recipients swear oaths over a local ju-ju shrine to guarantee their pledge of loyalty.

58. Sklar, *Nigerian Political Parties*, p. 116.

59. Ibid., pp. 118–25.

60. For an analysis of the financial bases of regional power in precoup Nigeria, see Richard L. Sklar, "Nigerian Politics: The Ordeal of Chief Awolowo," in *Politics in Africa*, ed. Gwendolen Carter and Alan Westin (New York: Harcourt, Brace and World, 1966), pp. 119–65; see also Sklar, *Nigerian Political Parties*, pp. 143–89, 446–53.

61. "After the Zikist Movement was declared unlawful in April 1950, radical youth sought alternative channels of expression. Neither the revolutionary Freedom Movement nor its successor, the Convention People's Party of Nigeria and the Cameroons, were able to survive the constitutional and electoral surges of 1951, and the former Zikists decided to return to the fold of the NCNC. They organized the NCNC Youth Association on January 28, 1952." Sklar, *Nigerian Political Parties*, p. 403.

62. The NCNC leaders involved in this meeting were Nnamdi Azikiwe and two prominent Aro-Ibo nationalists, Mbonu Ojike and K. O. Mbadiwe. Ironically, in a few years time Onyeri was to join with his two Aro kinsmen in bitter, though unsuccessful, opposition to Azikiwe. See Sklar's account of this conflict in *Nigerian Political Parties*, pp. 216–30. For biographical sketches of Ojike and Mbadiwe, see pp. 112–13 in the same volume.

63. See R. K. Floyer, D. O. Ibekwe, and J. O. Njemanze, *Report of the Commission of Enquiry into the Working of the Port Harcourt Town Council* (Enugu: Government Printer, February 1955).

64. Ibid., p. 11.

65. Ibid., p. 18. The Commission of Enquiry found against the council on nine separate counts, ranging from the acceptance of bribes to methods of staff recruitment. In this respect, however, Port Harcourt's experience was not unique in the history of Nigerian local government. See Ronald Wraith and Edgar Simpkins, *Corruption in Developing Countries* (London: Allen and Unwin, 1963).

66. Minutes of the Port Harcourt NCNC Executive Committee meeting, March 27, 1953.

67. Minutes of the Port Harcourt NCNC Executive Committee meeting, May 11, 1953, personal interviews.

68. Minutes of the Port Harcourt NCNC Executive Committee meeting, October 5, 1953.

69. National Archives File RP 5744, Vol. II; Riv Prof; 1/46/119.

70. *Eastern Outlook* and *Cameroons Star*, February 25, 1954.

71. Floyer, Ibekwe, and Njemanze, *Report of the Commission of Enquiry*, pp. 22–28.

72. National Archives File RP 5744, Vol. II; Riv Prof; 1/46/119.

73. Minutes of the Port Harcourt NCNC Executive Committee meeting, March 16, 1955.

74. Sklar, *Nigerian Political Parties*, p. 135.

75. Ibid., pp. 447–50. By 1964, the number of political appointees to public boards and statutory and industrial corporations exceeded two hundred. If to this number there is added the sixty-three members of the Eastern Nigerian House of Chiefs, the significance of the government's power over public appointments—which were often construed as appointments to communities rather than to individuals—becomes clear. See *Distribution of Amenities* (Enugu: Government Printer, 1963), pp. 149–96, and *Know Your Legislators* (Enugu: Ministry of Information, 1963), pp. 83–103.

76. The origins of the Ibo State Union are described by Coleman, *Nigeria: Background to Nationalism*, pp. 339–41, 346–58. See also Sklar, *Nigerian Political Parties*, pp. 64, 70, 460–64, and Audrey Chapman Smock, *Ibo Politics: The Role of Ethnic Unions in Eastern Nigeria* (Cambridge: Harvard University Press, 1971).

77. See, for example, Sklar's discussions, "The Struggle for the Onitsha Instrument," and "The Enugu Tangle," in *Nigerian Political Parties*, pp. 151–57, 207–16. At one point in the late 1950s, the president of the Ibo State Union, the secretary of the Ibo State Union, and the president of the Port Harcourt Ibo Union were all under suspension from the NCNC for local antiparty activities having little to do with national issues. The suspension of the Ibo State Union secretary, for example, was the product of a struggle for control of the Executive Committee of the Port Harcourt NCNC. Similarly, the suspension of the two presidents stemmed from their refusal to give obedience to the local party executive: in 1954, Ibo State Union President Z. C. Obi had rejected his party's directive that he resign from the Port Harcourt Town Council; and in 1955, as we have seen, he and Port Harcourt Ibo Union President S. O. Akwiwu both stood against the party as independent candidates for the reorganized Municipal Council.

78. Ibid., p. 463.

79. For the pamphlets in question, see Ibo State Union, *Nigerian Disunity: The Guilty Ones* (Enugu: Ibo State Union, 1964) and *One North or One Nigeria* (Enugu: Ibo State Union, 1964). Ibo State Union leaders disclaimed any and all involvement in political affairs. To quote from the first of the above pamphlets: "Unlike cultural Unions founded and managed by politicians to achieve certain political objectives, Ibo State Union from its debut, has never identified itself with politics. It concentrates on cultural and social activities. The leaders of the Ibo State Union have always resisted any attempt to use the Union as a political instrument with the result that it has no support from active politicians and political parties." The disclaimer notwithstanding, the Ibo State Union was one of the organizations outlawed by the military regime that assumed power in January 1966.

CHAPTER 7: *Democracy, Opportunism, and Geo-ethnicity*

1. Robert Dahl, *Who Governs?* (New Haven, Conn.: Yale University Press, 1960), p. 11.

2. Statistical breakdowns of the Owerri and Onitsha Ibo populations are not available. In 1964, however, most estimates of informants indicated that the Owerris outnumbered the Onitshans by two to one or three to one.

3. Barrister E. C. Akwiwu, destined in later years to become deputy speaker of the federal House of Representatives (representing his Orlu constituency in the federal Parliament), assumed the chairmanship of the Union's Caretaker Committee. The committee's secretary was C. C. Udom, a former trade unionist and secretary of the NCNC divisional Executive. Other officers included Francis Ihekwoaba, a prominent Nkwerre-Orlu merchant who was to become mayor of Port Harcourt in 1961 and A. Ihejiotoh, a member of the Town Council's administrative staff.

4. The new mayor and his wife were two of Port Harcourt's most celebrated personalities. By 1955, Richard Nzimiro had retired from the United Africa Company, which he had served for twenty-three years. His high standing within the U.A.C., his reputation for straightforwardness and personal integrity, and a sizeable family fortune accumulated through an extremely profitable trading relationship that he and his wife had established with the U.A.C.—these were all factors underlying the immense prestige of Nzimiro within both the African and the European sectors of the local community.

A. E. Alagoa's father was the Amanyanabo of Nembe (Brass Division). For a history of Nembe written by a member of the Alagoa family, see Joe Ebiegberi Alagoa, *The Small Brave City-State: A History of Nembe Brass in the Niger Delta* (Madison: University of Wisconsin Press, 1964). Alagoa succeeded Nzimiro as mayor upon the latter's death in 1959. Two years later a quarrel with the local NCNC Executive led to Alagoa's resignation. The barrister was subsequently appointed to the high court.

5. Data concerning the composition of the Executive Committee in the intervening years are incomplete. The Owerri increase may have been more gradual than that suggested by the 1951–1956 comparison.

6. See Richard L. Sklar, *Nigerian Political Parties: Power in an Emergent African Nation* (Princeton: Princeton University Press, 1963), p. 403.

7. Senator Chief Z. C. Obi was the only Onitsha personage to hold high public office after 1955. However, he was appointed rather than elected to his position in the federal Senate; moreover, the appointment was in recognition of Obi's position as president of the Ibo State Union, and did not derive from his local political standing.

8. For a more extended discussion of the relationship between segregation and communal conflict, see Robert Melson and Howard Wolpe, "Modernization and the Politics of Communalism: A Theoretical Perspective," *American Political Science Review* 64, no. 4 (December 1970): 1118–19.

9. For analyses of the Constitutional crisis of 1964–1965, see Richard L. Sklar, "Contradictions in the Nigerian Political System," *Journal of Modern African Studies* 3, no. 2 (August 1965): 201–13, reprinted in Robert Melson and Howard Wolpe, eds., *Nigeria: Modernization and the Politics of Communalism* (East Lansing: Michigan State University Press, 1971), pp. 514–29; Walter Schwarz, *Nigeria* (New York: Praeger, 1968), pp. 152–90; Douglas G. Anglin, "Brinkmanship in Nigeria," *International Journal* 20, no. 2 (Spring 1965): 173–88; Frederick A. O. Schwarz, Jr., *Nigeria: The Tribe, the Nation, or the Race* (Cambridge: M.I.T. Press, 1965), pp. 101–48; and John P. Mackintosh, *Nigerian Government and Politics* (Evanston, Ill.: Northwestern University Press, 1966), pp. 545–609.

10. The 1957 dissolution of the Eastern House of Assembly was intended as an indication of support for Premier Nnamdi Azikiwe who was the subject of a government enquiry into certain of his financial activities. It was only after the personal intervention of Azikiwe and other party leaders that Okay and the Port Harcourt Executive agreed to abide by the national party directive.

11. NCNC registration fees for new members were two shillings; annual dues were six shillings. Candidates allocated a substantial portion of their campaign funds to the registration and annual fees of party supporters. As finally constituted, Port Harcourt's nominating committee consisted of ninety-five to ninety-seven persons, slightly over twice the size of the local Executive Committee.

12. Personal interview with a local party activist.

13. This account is based upon the writer's notes of the meeting, which he was privileged to attend.

14. Obienu's initiative was taken outside the institutional framework of the Onitsha Divisional Union, possibly because the president of the O.D.U., Senator Chief Z. C. Obi, was thought to be opposed to Obienu's candidacy. At the Obienu-initiated gathering there were present, in addition to several prominent Onitsha businessmen, four of Port Harcourt's young Onitsha barristers and one doctor. The subsequent involvement of these professionals in the election, however, appears to have been extremely limited.

15. When the Enugu disclaimer was issued, a number of Councillor Jumbo's supporters protested vehemently, and it was necessary for Dr. Mbanugo, the Eastern Working Committee chairman, to travel to Port Harcourt on a peace mission.

16. For the background of these anti-NCNC candidates, see chapter 8.

17. *Eastern Nigerian Guardian*, March 19, 1965. In the 1964–1965 election, all persons over twenty-one years of age who had been counted in the 1963 census were automatically registered to vote. The writer departed from Nigeria in February and did not have the opportunity to observe the election. According to the *Guardian* article, 13,472 votes were cast in the 1959 federal election. In that election, Okay's margin of victory over an Action Group candidate was 12,301.

18. Eastern Nigeria Ministry of Town Planning, *Annual Report, 1958–59* (Enugu: Government Printer, 1963), pp. 5, 22–23.

19. Of the sixteen landowners who served in the Cabinet between 1948 and 1955, all but two were from either Orlu or Okigwi Divisions. The Cabinet members were of diverse occupational, educational, and religious backgrounds. Occupationally, they included two former police constables, several skilled artisans, traders, and farmers. One Cabinet member had received some secondary education, three had completed their elementary schooling, and at least six had not attended school. They included nine Catholics, two Protestants, and two animists. These data are based upon interviews with Mile 2 Diobu informants.

20. This analysis is based upon interviews with British administrative officers who served in Port Harcourt and Ahoada Divisions and upon a study of the minutes book of the Port Harcourt-Obia Planning Authority. For a more general discussion of Eastern Nigeria's tiered system of local government, see L. Gray Cowan, *Local Government in West Africa* (New York: Columbia University Press, 1958), pp. 66–75.

21. The conflict between the administrators and the landlords is described in fascinating detail in the records of the Port Harcourt-Obia Planning Authority.

22. Mile 2 Diobu's Onitsha politicians tended to support the more cosmopolitan Mbaise and Bende wing of the party; this support was in contrast to the dominant pattern of alliances within the main township.

23. Chief Emenike eventually stood as an independent and lost to the official NCNC candidate.

24. Report of the Okafor Commission of Enquiry, December 19, 1960, mimeographed.

25. With less than 30 percent of the registered electorate voting, Nwanodi received 13,289 votes to Elugwaornu's 12,898. Two other candidates between them collected 2,526 votes. It should be noted that Mile 2 Diobu's population of 83,795 represented only 39.86 percent of the total population of the Ahoada Central constituency (210,763). *Eastern Star*, March 22, 1965, and Eastern Nigeria Census Report for District No. 309301, mimeographed.

26. The apparent relative decline in private enterprise occupations in 1957 is probably due to the omission of the 1957 party patrons from the data on which table 15 is based.

27. Kenneth Post, *The Nigerian Federal Election of 1959* (London: Oxford University Press, 1963), p. 49.

28. Three men who stood election for well-salaried positions in the Regional

House of Assembly reported campaign expenses of £1,200, £3,000, and £4,950, respectively. In 1964, the total annual remuneration for a regional assemblyman (salary plus allowances) was £888. If an assemblyman received an appointment as parliamentary secretary, he could expect an additional £817 over a five-year term. Moreover, parliamentarians of all but the highest rank were able to pursue their regular occupation through most of the year. Port Harcourt's municipal councillors, by contrast, worked long hours throughout the year for only a nominal sitting allowance. This inequity did not go unnoticed by the local officeholders.

29. The council in 1964 conducted the bulk of its business by means of seven standing committees: finance, markets, works, medical and health, staff, commerce and industry, and education and library. The first two of these committees comprised the entire council membership and were chaired by the mayor. Committee and plenary meetings of the council were held monthly. The day-to-day business of the council was conducted by the staff, whose executive members (the town clerk, town engineer, deputy town clerk, and municipal treasurer) consulted regularly with the mayor and deputy mayor and, when the occasion required, with the committee chairmen. The deputy mayor was also, in 1964, the local NCNC president; pointedly, the chairmanship of the Works Committee was in his hands.

30. The notoriety attached to public office was a matter of some concern to several Port Harcourt councillors, as indicated by the following interview excerpts:

> Mostly what I dislike about being a Councillor is that no Councillor has a good name in Nigeria. They regard you as a bribe-eater. These accusations of bribery and corruption—there are times when you know nothing. But if you are a member of the Committee, you are accused and you cannot deny it. And all troubles go to the Council (bad roads, maladministration, bribery and corruption), and give the Council a bad name and the public hates you. If someone loses his job, he will blame the council. If a car drives over a child, the Council will be blamed because the Council did not pay the Electricity Corporation. And the other day, a £14,000 contract was awarded to twelve people, and some who were not favored portrayed the Council in a bad light.

> If you don't want to be called a rogue, don't be a Councillor. People believe anyone who is a Councillor lives by foul means.

31. The quotations in this passage are drawn from the writer's notes of the meeting of the Port Harcourt NCNC Divisional Executive Committee, August 1, 1963.

32. Memorandum of the Port Harcourt Welfare Society, mimeographed.

CHAPTER 8: *Proletarian Protest*

1. The events recorded in this section were either witnessed firsthand or reported by direct participants. However, the writer was not present during strategy meetings of either the Council of Labor or the Nigerian Employers Consultative Association. An attempt has been made to handle admittedly fragmentary data as conservatively as possible; the anonymity of respondents, of course, must be preserved. The writer would like to acknowledge his indebtedness to Robert Melson whose own analysis of the general strike from the perspective of Lagos helped to clarify its meaning for Port Harcourt. See Robert Melson, "Nigerian Politics and the General Strike of 1964," in *Protest and Power in Black Africa*, ed. Robert C. Rotberg and Ali A. Mazrui (New York: Oxford University Press, 1970), pp. 771–87; "Ideology and Inconsistency: The Cross-Pressured Nigerian Worker," *American Political Science Review* 65, no. 1 (March 1971): 161–71, reprinted in Robert Melson and Howard Wolpe, eds., *Nigeria: Modernization and the Politics of Communalism* (East Lansing: Michigan State University Press, 1971), pp. 581–605; and "Marxists in the Nigerian Labor Movement: A Case Study in the Failure of

Ideology," (Ph.D. diss., M.I.T., 1967). An account of the general strike is presented in William H. Friedland, "Paradoxes of African Trade Unionism: Organizational and Political Potential," *Africa Report* 10, no. 6 (June 1965): 6–13. Use has also been made of the chronological summary of the strike's development in *Africa Report* 9, no. 7 (July 1964): 28–29, and of a summary article in *West Africa*, July 4, 1964.

2. Friedland, "Paradoxes of African Trade Unionism," p. 7.

3. Ibid., p. 8.

4. *Report of the Commission on the Review of Wages, Salaries and Conditions of Service of the Junior Employees of the Governments of the Federation and in Private Establishments, 1963–64* (Lagos: Federal Ministry of Information, 1964), p. 2 (hereafter cited as the *Morgan Report*).

5. See "Conclusions" of the *Federal Government on the Report of the Morgan Commission on the Review of Wages, Salaries and Conditions of Service of the Junior Employees of the Governments in the Federation and Private Establishments, 1963–64,* Sessional Paper No. 5 of 1964 (Lagos: Federal Ministry of Information, 1964). For a discussion of the living-wage concept, see the *Morgan Report*, pp. 8–21.

6. David B. Abernethy, *The Political Dilemma of Popular Education* (Stanford: Stanford University Press, 1969), p. 251.

7. For a discussion of the origins and history of the Dynamic party, see Richard L. Sklar, *Nigerian Political Parties: Power in an Emergent African Nation* (Princeton: Princeton University Press, 1963), pp. 406–08.

8. See A. L. Epstein, *Politics in an Urban African Community* (Manchester: Manchester University Press, 1958), pp. 232–35.

9. The provincial commissioner was an administrative innovation introduced by then-Premier Dr. Nnamdi Azikiwe in 1959 as part of an administrative reorganization designed to meet the demands of minorities for more culturally homogeneous administrative units. The commissioner was to serve "as the eyes and ears" of the Regional government, to represent the wishes of the local community to the government, and more especially, to insure that minority interests were safeguarded. In actuality, he more often functioned simply as an overseer of party affairs in the area of his jurisdiction. In Port Harcourt, the commissioner's responsibilities were almost entirely ceremonial in nature. On occasion, however, as during the Catholic protests of 1964 described in chapter 9, he served as an important intermediary between the Regional government and the local community.

The provincial secretary was the modern counterpart of the colonial resident. He was the leading government official in the province, charged with the coordination of all government activities in the area and with the mediation of communications between the Regional ministries and their outlying provincial offices. In 1964, Port Harcourt's provincial secretary was one of very few expatriate officers still with the Eastern Nigerian government. When the term of his predecessor (also an expatriate) expired in 1963, there had been some discussion as to whether a Nigerian should be appointed. One factor reported to have entered into the final decision to appoint another Englishman was Port Harcourt's large expatriate business community. The provincial secretary was the principal intermediary between most businessmen and the Regional government, and it was apparently felt that the expatriate investor would be more at ease in dealing with another European.

10. At the end of August 1964, Shell-BP directly employed 2,650 persons. Many more workers were employed by Shell-BP subcontractors. Shell-BP, "Summary of Activities," Port Harcourt, 1964, mimeographed.

11. The document concerning negotiating strategy was reported to have been written in twenty-five minutes and to include only such basic principles of bargaining as "leave major agreements for the last to avoid a walk-out over trivial matters," "to create a climate of agreement," "not to negotiate management prerogatives."

12. At a meeting of the Lagos NECA during the strike's second week, the

tax rate (then pegged at four shillings per pound of taxable value), on the assumption that more property owners would then be willing to pay their taxes. Other sources of municipal revenue were Regional government block grants, a local capitation tax of fifteen shillings per annum, school fees, and miscellaneous license fees. Statistical sources include Port Harcourt Municipal Council, Comparative Statement for Revenue Abstract Ledger, 1962/63 (mimeographed); Minutes of the special meeting of the Municipal Council Finance Committee, April 27, 1964 (mimeographed); and a personal memorandum of the Port Harcourt town clerk.

16. The provincial education office had threatened to prohibit council schools from offering Standard VI instruction in 1964 if additional classrooms were not constructed. In January, Mayor Ihekwoaba asked the provincial secretary to use his good offices to insure the necessary approval, observing that if children in Standard V classes were not permitted to continue there would be "serious political upheaval which might get out of hand and cause untold harm to my Council." Letter dated January 10, 1964, from Mayor Francis Ihekwoaba to the Port Harcourt provincial secretary, Municipal Council File 26911.

17. The *Eastern Star* of February 12, 1964, reported that "about 1000 Roman Catholic women" were involved in the demonstration; by the writer's own estimate, between a hundred and two hundred women were actually present. The demonstration was peaceful, and the commissioner, E. D. Sigalo, spoke with the leaders of the women in his office.

18. Abernethy, *Political Dilemma*, p. 174.

19. The deputy mayor created a national stir at the time by his public observation that most local councils had not the experience to run markets efficiently, let alone schools, and by speaking at a mass rally of Catholic parents in support of a resolution calling upon the Regional government to remove the restrictions on voluntary agency school expansion. *Eastern Nigerian Guardian*, September 27, 1965.

20. Outside of the formal officeholders, considerable secrecy was attached to an alleged leadership nucleus of the ENCC; reportedly, other members of this nucleus whose names could not be disclosed were members of the delegation to Port Harcourt.

21. In the rural areas in the 1960s, the problem was still too many schools rather than too few: "there is no doubt whatever that in many areas the enrollment in classes falls below the economical level of thirty. . . . Many villages support two and three small schools of differing denominations in circumstances where one large school would be financially a more viable proposition and where the burden of a shortfall in Assumed Local Contribution would be considerably reduced or even eliminated." Eastern Nigeria Ministry of Education, *1961 Annual Report* (Enugu: Government Printer, 1963), p. 14.

22. Telegram dated February 13, 1964, from the ministry of education to the inspector of education (Rivers Division), the Port Harcourt provincial commissioner, and the mayor. Provincial Education Office (Rivers Division), File No. 1979. Minister Imoke also spoke with the mayor by phone, stating that the council should do everything it could to remedy the situation quickly.

23. Letter dated March 19, 1964, from the town clerk to the permanent secretary, ministry of education. Provincial Education Office (Rivers Division), File No. 1679. Some weeks later, Minister Imoke made a personal visit to Port Harcourt for a consultation with the mayor. The town clerk had previously estimated the cost of construction of permanent facilities at £22,000. But the mayor, a shrewd businessman, upon hearing that the ministry of education had £100,000 to spend, asked for £30,000. In the perfect bargaining solution, £25,000 was finally agreed upon.

24. During the women's U.P.E. riots of 1958, which were sparked by the reintroduction of school fees, demonstrators similarly failed to draw distinctions between regional and federal NCNC representatives (the latter having nothing to do with the formation of Regional educational policy). David Abernethy, *Political Dilemma*, p. 182, records these 1958 incidents: "The home of Chief Jackson Mpi,

a member of the House of Representatives from Ahoada was demolished. Another member of the federal House, Mr. A. E. Ukatah, was besieged in his home by angry women, who replied in answer to his plea that he was in the federal legislature: 'The federal government should have told the regional government what to do.'"

25. *Eastern Star,* February 15, 1964.

26. Petition to the Eastern Nigerian premier, typewritten.

27. For theoretical statements concerning the effect of multiple group affiliations upon intergroup conflict, see George Simmel, *Conflict,* trans. Kurt H. Wolff (Glencoe, Ill.: Free Press, 1955), and Lewis Coser, *The Function of Social Conflict* (Glencoe, Ill.: Free Press, 1956). Also in point is the literature on cross-pressures. For the original formulation of this concept, see B. Berelson, P. F. Lazarsfeld, and W. N. McPhee, *Voting* (Chicago: University of Chicago Press, 1954).

28. Sklar, *Nigerian Political Parties,* p. 188.

CHAPTER 10: *Oil, War, and Nationality*

1. *Minorities Report.*

2. Despite the numerous separatist proposals that the commission entertained during over four months of both public and private hearings, there is some question as to whether the commission ever seriously considered the creation of separate states as a solution to Nigeria's minorities problem. As Frederick Schwarz has noted, the United Kingdom made it clear "that it was very reluctant to agree to the creation of new regions. It was concerned lest the Federation break up, worried about the economic and administrative viability of new regions, and anxious to disengage itself from Nigeria without beginning all over again the process of constitution making." Frederick A. O. Schwartz, *Nigeria: The Tribes, the Nation, or the Race* (Cambridge: M.I.T., 1965), p. 92. Schwarz points out that the Minorities Commission's terms of reference reflected the British government's opposition to new administrative gerrymandering and that the commission's final report revealed, in its reasoning and in its conclusions, the same fundamental bias.

Whatever the reality of the commission's alleged bias, it did not diminish the commission's significance as a political catalyst. The fact is that both majority and minority groups throughout Nigeria anticipated that their own political interests would be directly affected by the Minorities Commission and organized themselves so as to make the most effective representations. We are concerned here neither with the functioning of the Commission nor with its recommendations, but with the local confrontation between Port Harcourt's Ibo and Ijaw residents which was generated by the commission's presence.

3. The other two proposals, one advocating the creation of a separate Ogoja State and the other the creation of a separate Cross Rivers State were of no immediate concern to Port Harcourt and, in any event, were quickly dismissed by the Minorities Commission as lacking popular support within the areas concerned.

4. One Ijaw leader testified before the Minorities Commission that his people "feared the Ibibios as much as the Ibibios feared the Ibos." Testimony of Harold Biriye, offered on behalf of the Rivers Chiefs and Peoples Conference, in the *Record of the Proceedings of the Minorities Commission,* n.d., mimeographed.

5. This movement, however, did not diminish the emotional significance of lower-level Ijaw village and "House" loyalties, and Ijaw politicians have always been confronted with the same problems of subculture competition as have plagued Ibo leaders. In 1964, there were no less than three different Rivers State organizations operating in Port Harcourt, each attempting to maximize the political strength of a different cultural subgroup by drawing the boundaries of the proposed Rivers State in such a way as to give that subgroup a numerical advantage.

6. Minutes of the inaugural meeting of the Ijaw Tribe Union, Port Harcourt, November 13, 1943.

7. The Ijaw Rivers Peoples League was a federated body comprised of the following unions: Ijaw Tribal Union, Forcados; Ijaw Tribe Union, Port Harcourt;

Ijaw Tribe Union, Aba; Kalabari Central Union; Okrika Progress Union; Opobo Improvement Union; Bonny Central Union. It is interesting to note that the first meeting of the league was chaired by R. T. E. Wilcox, subsequently an important Bonny chief, Port Harcourt barrister and magistrate, and the father of Harold Biriye, the leading proponent of Ijaw nationalism in the 1950s and the president of the separatist Niger Delta Congress party in 1964.

8. Richard L. Sklar, *Nigerian Political Parties: Power in an Emergent African Nation* (Princeton: Princeton University Press, 1963), p. 403.

9. Testimony of E. A. D. Alikor. *Record of the Proceedings of the Minorities Commission,* n.d., mimeographed.

10. Ibid.

11. Wobo's testimony was supplemented by that offered by Hon. J. M. Mpi and E. J. Oriji, non-Diobu Ikwerre leaders who, in 1958 were, respectively, chairman and vice-chairman of the Ikwerre Rural District Council, and by Chief J. H. E. Nwuke of Etche-Ikwerre in Ahoada Division, chairman of the Ahoada County Council and destined to become Port Harcourt provincial commissioner and minister of state in the Eastern Nigerian Ministry of Works.

Among those testifying on behalf of Port Harcourt's stranger Ibos were Chief J. O. Njemanze, a former police inspector who served in Port Harcourt from 1916 to 1932 and who, in 1958, was chairman of the Owerri Urban District Council, and Chief Z. C. Obi, the president of the Ibo State Union. The latter declared that "the people of Port Harcourt . . . were 80% Ibo and apart from Government buildings and commercial buildings owned by foreign companies 90% of the buildings in Port Harcourt belonged to Ibos. They had not been consulted about the proposal to include Port Harcourt in a COR State and they feared that it might result in their being expropriated."

12. *Minorities Report,* p. 51.

13. K. W. J. Post, *The Nigerian Federal Election of 1959* (London: Oxford University Press, 1963), p. 95.

14. Even where the NDC was successful, Ijaw separatists had little cause for rejoicing, for it was evident that the NDC candidate's electoral success was more a personal than a party victory. As Kenneth Post records: "In 1954 a clergyman had been elected as an Independent, and had then declared for NCNC. In 1959 he was renominated and defeated in a five-cornered contest, being beaten into third place by an Independent. In such a constituency, and with so many candidates, a man's reputation and size of his local following counted for more than party organization, and the NDC had been lucky (or skillful) enough to pick the right man." Post, *The Nigerian Federal Election of 1959,* p. 366. In addition to this contest, the NCNC was narrowly defeated in one other contest in the Rivers area by an Action Group candidate.

15. Scott Pearson, *Petroleum and the Nigerian Economy* (Stanford: Stanford University Press, 1970), p. 137.

16. Walter Schwarz, *Nigeria* (New York: Praeger, 1968), p. 259.

17. Ibid.

18. For incisive analyses of the factors underlying Biafran secession and the Nigerian/Biafran conflict, see Richard L. Sklar, "Contradictions in the Nigerian Political System," *The Journal of Modern African Studies* 3 (1965): 201–13, and "Nigerian Politics in Perspective," *Government and Opposition* 2 (July–October 1967): 524–39; also, James O'Connell, "Nigerian Politics: The Complexity of Dissent," in *Nigeria: Modernization and the Politics of Communalism,* ed. Robert Melson and Howard Wolpe (East Lansing: Michigan State University Press, 1971), pp. 629–72.

19. Pearson, *Petroleum and the Nigerian Economy,* p. 151.

20. Ibid., p. 152.

21. Ibid., p. 151.

22. Walter Schwarz, *Nigeria,* pp. 260–61. See also C. Odumegwu Ojukwu, *Biafra. Selected Speeches with Journal of Events* (New York: Harper and Row,

1969), pp. 94–101, and *Biafra. Random Thoughts of C. Odumegwu Ojukwu* (New York: Harper and Row, 1969), pp. 122–23, 129–35.

23. "Nigeria: Federal Victory," *Africa Confidential* 11, no. 2 (January 16, 1970): 3.

24. *West Africa*, April 21, 1972.

25. Pearson, *Petroleum and the Nigerian Economy*, p. 141.

26. Ibid., p. 145.

27. "Nigeria: Political Uncertainties," *Africa Confidential* 12, no. 3 (February 5, 1971): 4.

28. Pauline H. Baker, "The Politics of Nigerian Military Rule," *Africa Report* 16, no. 2 (February 1971): 19.

29. "Nigeria: Political Uncertainties," p. 4.

30. "Nigeria: The Troublesome East," *Africa Confidential* 11, no. 20 (October 2, 1970): 4.

31. Baker, "Politics of Nigerian Military Rule," pp. 18–19.

32. The revenues of the distributable pool were reallocated on the following basis: North, 42 percent; East, 30 percent; West, 20 percent; and Mid-West, 8 percent.

33. The 1970 formula called for the following distribution of revenues accruing from petroleum royalties and rentals: state of origin, 45 percent; federal government, 5 percent; and distributable pool, 50 percent. Half of the revenues within the distributable pool are to be distributed equally among the twelve states and half is to be allocated to the states according to population. See Pearson, *Petroleum and the Nigerian Economy*, p. 143.

34. Scott R. Pearson and Sandra C. Pearson, "Oil Boom Reshapes Nigeria's Future," *Africa Report* 16, no. 2 (February 1971): 15.

35. *West Africa*, April 16, 1971.

36. "Nigeria: The Troublesome East," p. 4.

37. "Nigeria: So Many Soldiers," *Africa Confidential* 12, no. 12 (June 11, 1970): 4.

CHAPTER 11: *Communalism and Communal Conflict in Port Harcourt*

1. The theoretical statement developed in this chapter borrows extensively from the paper coauthored by Robert Melson and the present writer, "Modernization and the Politics of Communalism: A Theoretical Perspective," *American Political Science Review* 64, no. 4 (December 1970): 1112–30.

2. Richard L. Sklar, "Political Science and National Integration—A Radical Approach," *The Journal of Modern African Studies* 5, no. 1 (1967): 6.

3. Daniel Lerner, for example, has suggested that "a person with high achievement may still be dissatisfied if his aspirations far exceed his accomplishments. Relative deprivation . . . is the effective measure of satisfaction among individuals and groups." See his "Toward a Communication Theory of Modernization," in *Communications and Political Development*, ed. Lucian W. Pye (Princeton: Princeton University Press, 1963), p. 333. For a parallel treatment of the problem of relative deprivation, see Ulf Himmelstrand's application of rank-equilibration theory to Yoruba-Ibo competition in "Tribalism and Nationalism in Nigeria," in *Nigeria: Modernization and the Politics of Communalism*, ed. Robert Melson and Howard Wolpe (East Lansing: Michigan State University Press, 1970), pp. 254–83.

4. Samuel P. Huntington, *Political Order in Changing Societies* (New Haven, Conn.: Yale University Press, 1968), p. 20.

5. See Stokely Carmichael and Charles V. Hamilton, *Black Power: The Politics of Liberation in America* (New York: Vintage, 1967).

6. See Richard L. Sklar, "The Ordeal of Chief Awolowo," in *Politics in Africa: 7 Cases*, ed. Gwendolen M. Carter and Alan Westin (New York: Harcourt, Brace and World, 1966), pp. 119–66.

Bibliography

I. BOOKS AND PAMPHLETS

Abernethy, David B. *The Political Dilemma of Popular Education.* Stanford: Stanford University Press, 1969.

Aboyade, Ojetunji. *Foundations of an African Economy, A Study of Investment and Growth in Nigeria.* New York: Praeger, 1966.

———. *Arrow of God.* London: William Heinemann, 1964.

Achebe, Chinua. *Things Fall Apart.* London: William Heinemann, 1958.

———. *No Longer At Ease.* London: William Heinemann, 1964.

———. *A Man of the People.* New York: John Day, 1966.

African Methodist Episcopal Zion Church. *Memorial Booklet.* Port Harcourt: Privately printed, 1949.

Akpan, N. U. *The Struggle for Secession, 1966–1970.* London: Frank Cass, 1971.

Alagoa, Ebiegberi Joe. *The Small Brave City-State: A History of Nembe Brass in the Niger Delta.* Madison: University of Wisconsin Press, 1964.

Allport, Gordon W. *The Nature of Prejudice.* Garden City, N.Y.: Doubleday, 1958.

Almond, Gabriel A., and Verba, Sidney. *The Civic Culture: Political Attitudes and Democracy in Five Nations.* Boston and Toronto: Little, Brown, 1965.

Anderson, Charles W.; von der Mehden, Fred R.; and Young, Crawford. *Issues of Political Development.* Englewood Cliffs, N.J.: Prentice-Hall, 1967.

Apter, David E. *Ghana in Transition.* New York: Atheneum Press, 1963.

Awolowo, Chief Obafemi. *Awo: The Autobiography of Chief Obafemi Awolowo.* Cambridge, Eng.: Cambridge University Press, 1960.

———. *Path to Nigerian Freedom.* London: Faber, 1966.

———. *Thoughts on the Nigerian Constitution.* London and New York: Oxford University Press, 1966.

———. *The People's Republic.* Ibadan: Oxford University Press, 1968.

———. *The Strategy and Tactics of the People's Republic of Nigeria.* London: Macmillan, 1970.

———. *Tribalism: A Pragmatic Instrument for National Unity.* Enugu: Eastern Nigeria Printing, May 1964.

Azikiwe, Nnamdi. *Zik: A Selection from the Speeches of Nnamdi Azikiwe.* Cambridge, Eng.: Cambridge University Press, 1961.

———. *Origins of the Nigerian Civil War.* Lagos: Nigerian National Press, 1968.

———. *My Odyssey.* New York: Praeger, 1970.

287

Bibliography

Banfield, Edward C. *Political Influence.* Glencoe, Ill.: Free Press, 1962.

Banton, Michael. *West African City: A Study of Tribal Life in Freetown.* London: Oxford University Press, 1957.

Bauer, P. T. *West African Trade: A Study of Competition, Oligopoly and Monopoly in a Changing Economy.* Cambridge, Eng.: Cambridge University Press, 1954.

Bello, Sir Ahmadu. *My Life.* Cambridge, Eng.: Cambridge University Press, 1962.

Biobaku, Saburi O. *The Egba and their Neighbors, 1842–1872.* Oxford: Clarendon Press, 1957.

Blitz, Franklin, ed. *The Politics and Administration of Nigerian Government.* New York: Praeger, 1965.

Bohannan, Laura, and Bohannan, Paul. *The Tiv of Central Nigeria.* London: International African Institute, 1953.

Bohannan, Paul. "The Tiv of Nigeria." In *Peoples of Nigeria,* edited by James L. Gibbs, Jr. New York: Holt, Rinehart and Winston, 1965.

Bradbury, R. E. *The Benin Kingdom and the Edo-Speaking Peoples of Southwestern Nigeria,* together with a section on the Itsekeri by P. C. Lloyd. London: International Africa Institute, 1957.

Bretton, Henry L. *Power and Stability in Nigeria: The Politics of Decolonization.* New York: Praeger, 1962.

Brewin, Andrew, and MacDonald, David. *Canada and the Biafran Tragedy.* Toronto: James Lewis & Sameul, 1970.

Buchanan, K. M., and Pugh, J. C. *Land and People in Nigeria.* London: University of London Press, 1955.

Burns, Alan C. *History of Nigeria.* 5th ed. London: Allen and Unwin, 1955.

Carmichael, Stokely, and Hamilton, Charles V. *Black Power: The Politics of Liberation in America.* New York: Vintage, 1967.

Cervenka, Zdenek. *The Nigerian War, 1967–1970.* Frankfurt am Main: Bernard & Graefe Verlag fur Wehrwesen, 1971.

Chubb, L. T. *Ibo Land Tenure.* 2nd ed. Ibadan: Ibadan University Press, 1961.

Cohen, Abner. *Custom and Politics in Urban Africa: A Study of Hausa Migrants in Yoruba Towns.* Berkeley and Los Angeles: University of California Press, 1969.

Cole, Taylor, and Tilman, Robert O., eds. *The Nigerian Political Scene.* Durham, N.C.: Duke University Press, 1962.

Coleman, James S. *Nigeria: Background to Nationalism.* Berkeley and Los Angeles: University of California Press, 1958.

Collis, Robert. *Nigeria in Conflict.* London: Secker & Warburg, 1970.

Coser, Lewis. *The Functions of Social Conflict.* Glencoe, Ill.: Free Press, 1956.

Cowan, L. Gray. *Local Government in West Africa.* New York: Columbia University Press, 1958.

Crowder, Michael. *A Short History of Nigeria.* New York: Praeger, 1962.

Dahl, Robert A. *Who Governs?* New Haven, Conn.: Yale University Press, 1961.

Davidson, Basil. *Black Mother: The Years of the African Slave Trade.* Boston: Little, Brown, 1961.

de Blij, Harm J. *A Geography of Subsaharan Africa.* Chicago: Rand McNally, 1961.

de St. Jorre, John. *The Nigerian Civil War.* London: Hodder and Staughton, 1972.

Deutsch, Karl W. *Nationalism and Social Communication.* Cambridge, Mass.: M.I.T. Press, John Wiley, 1953.

Dike, K. Onwuka. *Trade and Politics in the Niger Delta, 1830–1885.* Oxford: Clarendon Press, 1956.

Duverger, Maurice. *Political Parties: Their Organization and Activity in the Modern State.* London: Methuen, 1955.

Eicher, Carl K., and Liedholm, Carl, eds. *Growth and Development of the Nigerian Economy.* East Lansing: Michigan State University Press, 1970.

Ekwensi, Cyprian. *People of the City.* London: William Heinemann, 1963.

———. *Jagua Nana.* Evanston, Ill.: Northwestern University Press, 1963.

Elias, Taslim Olawale. *Nigeria: The Development of Its Laws and Constitution.* London: Stevens, 1967.

Emerson, Rupert. *From Empire to Nation.* Cambridge, Mass.: Harvard University Press, 1960.

Epstein, A. L. *Politics in an Urban African Community.* Manchester: Manchester University Press, 1958.

Ezera, Kalu. *Constitutional Developments in Nigeria.* Cambridge, Eng.: Cambridge University Press, 1960.

Fage, J. D. *An Introduction to the History of West Africa,* 2nd ed. Cambridge, Eng.: Cambridge University Press, 1961.

Flint, J. E. *Sir George Goldie and the Making of Nigeria.* London: Oxford University Press, 1960.

———. *Efik Traders of Old Calabar.* London: Oxford University Press, 1956.

Forde, Daryll. *The Yoruba-Speaking Peoples of South-Western Nigeria.* London: International African Institute, 1951.

——— and Jones, G. I. *The Ibo and Ibibio-Speaking Peoples of South-Eastern Nigeria.* London: International African Institute, 1950.

Frey, Frederick W. *The Turkish Political Elite.* Cambridge, Mass.: M.I.T. Press, 1965.

Gerth, H. H., and Mills, C. Wright, eds. *From Max Weber: Essays in Sociology.* New York: Oxford University Press, 1958.

Gluckman, Max. *Custom and Conflict in Africa.* Oxford: Basil Blackwell and Mott, 1956.

Green, M. M. *Igbo Village Affairs.* 2nd ed. London: Frank Cass, 1964.

Gutteridge, W. F. *The Military in African Politics.* London: Methuen, 1969.

Hagen, Everett. *On the Theory of Social Change.* Homewood, Ill.: Dorsey Press, 1962.

Hance, William. *The Geography of Modern Africa.* New York: Columbia University Press, 1964.

Harris, Philip J. *Local Government in Southern Nigeria.* Cambridge, Eng.: Cambridge University Press, 1957.

Hatch, John. *Nigeria: The Seeds of Disaster.* Chicago: Henry Regnery, 1970.

Helleiner, Gerald K. *Peasant Agriculture, Government, and Economic Growth in Nigeria.* Homewood, Ill.: Irwin, 1966.

———. *African Political Parties.* Harmondsworth: Penguin Books, 1961.

Hodgkin, Thomas. *Nigerian Perspectives, An Historical Anthology.* London: Oxford University Press, 1960.

Hunter, Floyd. *Community Power Structure.* Chapel Hill: University of North Carolina Press, 1953.

Huntington, Samuel P. *Political Order in Changing Societies.* New Haven, Conn.: Yale University Press, 1968.

Ibo State Union, *Nigerian Disunity: The Guilty Ones.* Enugu: Ibo State Union, 1964.

———. *One North or One Nigeria.* Enugu: Ibo State Union, 1964.

International Bank for Reconstruction and Development. *The Economic Development of Nigeria.* Baltimore: Johns Hopkins Press, 1956.

Jennings, Sir W. Ivor. *The Approach to Self Government.* Cambridge, Eng.: Cambridge University Press, 1956.

Jones, G. I. *The Trading States of the Oil Rivers.* London: Oxford University Press, 1963.

Jones-Quartey, K. A. B. *A Life of Azikiwe.* Baltimore: Penguin Books, 1965.

Bibliography

Kirk-Green, A. H. M. *Adamawa: Past and Present*. London: Oxford University Press, 1958.
——. *Crisis and Conflict in Nigeria: A Documentary Sourcebook*. 2 vols. London: Oxford University Press, 1971.
Kopytoff, Jean Herskovitz. *A Preface to Modern Nigeria: The "Sierra Leoneans" in Yoruba, 1830–1890*. Madison: University of Wisconsin Press, 1965.
Kornhauser, William. *The Politics of Mass Society*. New York: Free Press, 1959.
Leith-Ross, Sylvia. *African Women: A Study of the Ibo of Nigeria*. London: Faber, 1939.
Lerner, Daniel. *The Passing of Traditional Society: Modernizing the Middle East*. Glencoe, Ill.: Free Press, 1958.
Levy, Marion J. *Modernization and the Structure of Societies: A Setting for International Affairs*. 2 vols. Princeton: Princeton University Press, 1966.
Lipset, Seymour Martin. *Political Man*. New York: Doubleday, 1960.
Little, Kenneth. *West African Urbanization: A Study of Voluntary Associations in Social Change*. Cambridge, Eng.: Cambridge University Press, 1956.
Lloyd, Peter C. *Yoruba Land Law*. London: Oxford University Press, 1962.
——; Mabogunje, A. L.; and Awe, B., eds. *The City of Ibadan*. Cambridge, Eng.: Cambridge University Press, 1967.
Luckham, Alexander Robin. *The Nigerian Military: A Sociological Analysis of Authority and Revolt, 1960–67*. Cambridge, Eng.: Cambridge University Press, 1971.
Mabogunje, Akin. *Yoruba Towns*. Ibadan: Ibadan University Press, 1962.
McClelland, David C. *The Achieving Society*. Princeton: Van Nostrand, 1961.
Mackintosh, John P. *Nigerian Government and Politics*. Evanston, Ill.: Northwestern University Press, 1966.
Marris, Peter. *Family and Social Change in an African City*. London: Routledge & Kegan Paul, 1962.
Martin, Anne. *The Oil Palm Economy of the Ibibio Farmer*. Ibadan: University College Press, 1956.
Matthews, Donald R. *The Social Background of Political Decision-Makers*. Garden City, N.Y.: Doubleday, 1954.
Meek, C. K. *Law and Authority in a Nigerian Tribe*. London: Oxford University Press, 1937.
Melson, Robert, and Wolpe, Howard, eds. *Nigeria: Modernization and the Politics of Communalism*. East Lansing: Michigan State University Press, 1971.
Merton, Robert K. *Social Theory and Social Structure*. Glencoe, Ill.: Free Press, 1957.
Milliken, Max F., and Blackmer, Donald K. M., eds. *The Emerging Nations*. Boston: Little, Brown, 1961.
Mills, C. Wright. *The Power Elite*. New York: Oxford University Press, 1957.
Miners, N. *The Nigerian Army, 1956–1966*. London: Methuen, 1971.
Ndem, Eyo. *Ibos in Contemporary Nigerian Politics: A Study in Group Conflict*. Onitsha: Etudo Limited, 1961.
Niven, C. R. *A Short History of Nigeria*. 2nd ed. London: Longmans, Green, 1940.
——. *The War of Nigerian Unity, 1967–1970*. Totowa, N.J.: Rowman and Littlefield, 1971.
Nordlinger, Eric. *Conflict Regulation in Divided Societies*. Cambridge, Mass.: Harvard University Center for International Affairs, 1972.
Nwankwo, Arthur Agwuncha, and Ifejika, Samuel Udochukwu. *Biafra: The Making of a Nation*. New York: Praeger, 1970.

Odumosu, Oluwole I. *The Nigerian Constitution: History and Development.* London: Sweet and Maxwell, 1963.
Ojukwu, C. Odumegwu. *Biafra: Selected Speeches with Journal of Events.* New York: Harper and Row, 1969.
——. *Biafra: Random Thoughts of C. Odumegwu Ojukwu.* New York: Harper and Row, 1969.
Okigbo, Pius. *Nigerian Public Finance.* Evanston, Ill.: Northwestern University Press, 1965.
Okpaku, Joseph, ed. *Nigeria: Dilemma of Nationhood.* New York: Third Press, 1972.
Okpara, M. I. *Presidential Address at the NCNC Convention, February 21, 1964.* Enugu: Government Printer, 1964.
Oyinbo, John. *Nigeria: Crisis and Beyond.* London: Knight, 1971.
Panter-Brick, S. K., ed. *Nigerian Politics and Military Rule: Prelude to the Civil War.* London: University of London, 1970.
Parrinder, E. Geoffrey. *Religion in an African City.* London: Oxford University Press, 1953.
——. *The Story of Ketu, an Ancient Yoruba Kingdom.* Ibadan: University College Press, 1956.
Parsons, Talcott, and Shils, Edward A., eds. *Toward a General Theory of Action.* Cambridge, Mass.: Harvard University Press, 1959.
Pearson, Scott R. *Petroleum and the Nigerian Economy.* Stanford: Stanford University Press, 1970.
Perham, Margery. *Native Administration in Nigeria.* London: Oxford University Press, 1937.
——. *Lugard: The Years of Authority, 1898–1945.* London: Collins, 1960.
——. *The Colonial Reckoning.* London: Cox and Wyman, 1963.
Phillips, Claude S. *The Development of Nigerian Foreign Policy.* Evanston, Ill.: Northwestern University Press, 1964.
Plotnicov, Leonard. *Strangers to the City. Urban Man in Jos, Nigeria.* Pittsburgh: University of Pittsburgh Press, 1967.
Polsby, Nelson W. *Community Power and Political Theory.* New Haven, Conn.: Yale University Press, 1963.
Port Harcourt Chamber of Commerce. *Port Harcourt.* Port Harcourt: C.M.S. (Nigeria) Press, n.d.
——. *The New States of West Africa.* Harmondsworth: Penguin Books, 1964.
Post, K. W. J. *The Nigerian Federal Election of 1959.* London: Oxford University Press, 1963.
Powdermaker, Hortense. *Copper Town: Changing Africa.* New York: Harper and Row, 1965.
Pye, Lucian. *Politics, Personality, and Nation Building.* New Haven, Conn.: Yale University Press, 1962.
——. *Aspects of Political Development.* Boston: Little, Brown, 1966.
——, ed. *Communications and Political Development.* Princeton: Princeton University Press, 1963.
Roper, J. I. *Labour Problems in West Africa.* London: Penguin Books, 1958.
Royal Institute of International Affairs. *Nigeria: The Political and Economic Background.* London: Oxford University Press, 1960.
Rudolph, Lloyd I., and Hoeber, Susanne. *The Modernity of Tradition: Political Development in India.* Chicago: University of Chicago Press, 1967.
Samuels, Michael A., ed. *The Nigeria-Biafra Conflict: Report of a One-Day Conference.* Washington, D.C.: Georgetown University Center for Strategic and International Studies, 1969.
Schatz, Sayre P. *Development of Bank Lending in Nigeria.* London and New York: Oxford University Press, 1965.

Bibliography

Schermerhorn, Richard A. *Society and Power*. New York: Random House, 1961.
Schwarz, Frederick A. O., Jr. *Nigeria: The Tribes, the Nation, or the Race*. Cambridge, Mass.: M.I.T. Press, 1965.
Schwarz, Walter. *Nigeria*. New York: Praeger, 1968.
Simms, Ruth P. *Urbanization in West Africa: A Review of Current Literature*. Evanston, Ill.: Northwestern University Press, 1965.
Simpkins, Edgar, and Wraith, Ronald. *Corruption in Developing Countries*. London: Allen and Unwin, 1963.
Skinner, G. William. *Leadership and Power in the Chinese Community of Thailand*. Ithaca: Cornell University Press, 1958.
Sklar, Richard. *Nigerian Political Parties: Power in an Emergent African Nation*. Princeton: Princeton University Press, 1963.
Smith, M. G. *Government in Zazzau, 1800–1950*. London: Oxford University Press, 1960.
Smock, Audrey C. *Ibo Politics: The Role of Ethnic Unions in Eastern Nigeria*. Cambridge, Mass.: Harvard University Press, 1971.
Smock, David R. *Conflict and Control in an African Trade Union*. Stanford: Hoover Institution Press, 1969.
Smythe, Hugh H., and Smythe, Mabel M. *The New Nigerian Elite*. Stanford: Stanford University Press, 1960.
Southall, Aiden, ed. *Social Change in Modern Africa*. London: Oxford University Press, 1961.
Stevens, Canon R. S. O. *The Church in Urban Nigeria*. Lagos: Church Missionary Society, 1963.
Stolper, Wolfgang. *Planning Without Facts: Lessons in Resource Allocation from Nigeria's Development*. Cambridge, Mass.: Harvard University Press, 1966.
Talbot, P. Amaury. *The Peoples of Southern Nigeria*. London: Oxford University Press, 1926.
Tilman, Robert O., and Cole, Taylor, eds. *The Nigerian Political Scene*. Durham, N.C.: Duke University Press, 1962.
Tonnies, Ferdinand. *Community and Society* [Gemeinschaft und Gesellschaft]. Translated and edited by Charles P. Loomis. East Lansing: Michigan State University Press, 1957.
Truman, David. *The Governmental Process*. New York: Knopf, 1953.
Tukur, Mahmud, ed. *Administrative and Political Developments: Prospects of Nigeria*. Zaria: Ahmadu Bello University Bookshop, 1972.
Uchendu, Victor. *The Igbo of Southeast Nigeria*. New York: Holt, Rinehart and Winston, 1965.
Uwechue, Raph. *Reflections on the Nigerian Civil War*. 2nd ed. London: Meier Holmes, 1971.
Wallerstein, Immanuel. *Africa: The Politics of Independence*. New York: Vintage, 1961.
Weiler, Hans N., ed. *Education and Politics in Nigeria*. Freiburg im Breisgau: Verlag Rombach, 1964.
Weiner, Myron. *The Politics of Scarcity: Public Pressure and Political Response in India*. Chicago: University of Chicago Press, 1962.
Wheare, Joan. *The Nigerian Legislative Council*. London: Faber, 1950.
Whitaker, C. S., Jr. *The Politics of Tradition: Continuity and Change in Northern Nigeria, 1946–1966*. Princeton: Princeton University Press, 1970.
Wolpe, Howard. *A Study Guide for Nigeria*. Boston: Boston University African Studies Center (Development Program), 1966.
Wraith, Ronald. *Local Government in West Africa*. London: Allen and Unwin, 1964.
———, and Simpkins, Edgar. *Corruption in Developing Countries*. London: Allen and Unwin, 1963.

Yesufu, T. M. *An Introduction to Industrial Relations in Nigeria.* London: Oxford University Press, 1962.

Young, Crawford. *Politics in the Congo.* Princeton: Princeton University Press, 1965.

———. *Creating Political Order: The Party-States of West Africa.* Chicago: Rand McNally, 1966.

Zolberg, Aristide R. *One-Party Government in the Ivory Coast.* Princeton: Princeton University Press, 1964.

II. ARTICLES AND PERIODICALS

African Urban Notes 1, no. 2 (May 1966): 3–7.

Agger, R. E. "Power Attributions in the Local Community: Theoretical and Research Consideration." *Social Forces* 34 (May 1956): 322–31.

Akinyemi, A. B. "Viewpoint: What Should Replace Military Rule?" *Africa Report* 16, no. 2 (February 1971): 22–23.

Akpan, E. E. "The Development of Local Government in Eastern Nigeria." *Journal of Local Administration Overseas* 4, no. 2 (April 1965): 118–27.

Almond, Gabriel A. "Comparative Political Systems." *Journal of Politics* 18 (August 1956): 391–409.

———. "Introduction: A Functional Approach to Comparative Politics." In *The Politics of the Developing Areas,* edited by Gabriel A. Almond and James S. Coleman. Princeton: Princeton University Press, 1960, pp. 3–64.

Aloba, Abiodun. "Tribal Unions in Party Politics." *West Africa,* July 10, 1954.

Anber, Paul. "Modernization and Political Disintegration: Nigeria and the Ibos." *Journal of Modern African Studies* 5, no. 2 (1967): 163–79.

Anglin, Douglas G. "Brinkmanship in Nigeria." *International Journal* 20, no. 2 (Spring 1965): 173–88.

Anton, Thomas J. "Power, Pluralism, and Local Politics." *Administrative Science Quarterly* 7 (March 1963): 453.

Ardener, Shirley G. "The Social and Economic Significance of the Contribution Club Among a Section of the Southern Ibo." *Proceedings of the Second Annual Conference of the West African Institute of Social and Economic Research* (March 1953): 128–43.

Arikpo, Okoi. "Future of Nigerian Federalism." *West Africa,* May 28–June 2, 1955.

Azikiwe, Nnamdi. "Essentials for Nigerian Survival." *Foreign Affairs* 43, no. 3 (April 1965): 447–61.

Bachrach, Peter, and Baratz, Morton. "Two Faces of Power." *American Political Science Review* 56 (December 1962): 947–52.

Baker, Pauline. "Nigeria: The Politics of Military Rule." *Africa Report* 16, no. 2 (February 1971): 18–21.

Banton, Michael. "Role Congruence and Social Differentiation Under Urban Conditions." *Proceedings of the Pan American Union Seminar on Social Structure, Stratification and Mobility* (Rio de Janeiro), June 6–15, 1962.

———. "Social Alignment and Identity in a West African City." In *Urbanization and Migration in West Africa,* edited by Hilda Kuper. Berkeley and Los Angeles: University of California Press, 1965, pp. 131–47.

Bascom, William. "Urbanization among the Yoruba." *American Journal of Sociology* 60, no. 5 (March 1955): 446–54.

Bierstedt, R. "An Analysis of Social Power." *American Sociological Review* 15 (December 1950): 730–38.

Bose, Nirmal Kumar. "Calcutta: A Premature Metropolis." In *Cities,* edited by Scientific American. New York: Knopf, 1965, pp. 59–74.

Callaway, Dr. Archibald. "School Leavers and the Developing Economy of Nigeria." In *The Nigerian Political Scene,* edited by Robert O. Tilman and Taylor Cole. Durham, N.C.: Duke University Press, 1962.

Bibliography

————. "Nigeria's Indigenous Education: The Apprentice System." *ODU* (University of Ife Journal) 1, no. 1 (July 1964).

Coleman, James S. "The Politics of Sub-Saharan Africa." In *The Politics of the Developing Areas,* edited by Gabriel A. Almond and James S. Coleman. Princeton: Princeton University Press, 1960, pp. 247–368.

Dahl, R. A. "The Concept of Power." *Behavioral Science* 2 (July 1957): 201–15.

————. "A Critique of the Ruling Elite Model." *American Political Science Review* 52 (June 1958): 463–69.

Davis, Kingsley, and Golden, Hilda H. "Urbanization and the Development of Pre-Industrial Areas." *Economic Development and Cultural Change* 3, no. 1 (October 1954): 6–24.

Deutsch, Karl W. "Social Mobilization and Political Development." *American Political Science Review* 55 (September 1961): 493–514.

————. "Nation-Building and National Development: Some Issues for Political Research." In *Nation-Building,* edited by Karl W. Deutsch and William J. Foltz. New York: Atherton Press, 1963, pp. 1–16.

Easton, David. "An Approach to the Analysis of Political Systems." *World Politics* 9 (April 1957): 383–400.

Eisenstadt, S. N. "Breakdowns of Modernization." *Economic Development and Cultural Change* 12, no. 4 (July 1964): 345–67.

————. "Reflections on a Theory of Modernization." In *Nations by Design,* edited by Arnold Rivkin. Garden City, N.Y.: Doubleday, 1968, pp. 35–61.

Emerson, Rupert. "Nation-Building in Africa." In *Nation-Building,* edited by Karl W. Deutsch and William J. Foltz. New York: Atherton Press, 1963, pp. 1–16.

Erlich, Howard J. "The Reputational Approach to the Study of Community Power." *American Sociological Review* 26 (December 1961): 926–27.

Evans-Pritchard, E. E. "The Nuer of the Southern Sudan." In *African Political Systems,* edited by M. Fortes and E. E. Evans-Pritchard. London: Oxford University Press, 1940, pp. 272–96.

————, and Fortes, M. "Introduction." In *African Political Systems,* edited by M. Fortes and E. E. Evans-Pritchard. London: Oxford University Press, 1940, pp. 1–23.

Frazier, E. Franklin. "Urbanization and Its Effects Upon the Task of Nation-Building in Africa South of the Sahara." *Journal of Negro Education* 30, no. 3 (Summer 1961): 214–22.

Frey, Frederick W. "Political Development, Power, and Communications in Turkey." In *Communications and Political Development,* edited by Lucian W. Pye. Princeton: Princeton University Press, 1963, pp. 298–326.

Friedland, William H. "Paradoxes of African Trade Unionism: Organizational Chaos and Political Potential." *Africa Report* 10, no. 6 (June 1965): 6–13.

Garrison, Lloyd. "Nigeria: Wounds Too Deep?" *New York Times,* August 14, 1966.

Geertz, Clifford. "The Integrative Revolution." In *Old Societies and New States,* edited by Clifford Geertz. Glencoe, N.Y.: Free Press, 1963, pp. 105–57.

Gluckman, M. "Tribalism in Modern British Central Africa." *Cahiers D'Etudes Africaines,* January 1960, pp. 55–70.

Gusfield, Joseph R. "Tradition and Modernity: Misplaced Polarities in the Study of Social Change." *American Journal of Sociology* 72 (January 1966): 351–62.

Hair, P. E. H. "Enugu: An Industrial and Urban Community in East Nigeria 1914–1953." *West African Institute of Social and Economic Research* 2, no. 1 (March 1953): 143–69.

Harris, Richard. "Nigeria: Crisis and Compromise." *Africa Report* 10, no. 3 (March 1965): 25–31.

Hart, Henry. "Bombay Politics: Pluralism or Polarization." *Journal of Asian Studies* 20, no. 3 (May 1961): 265–66.

Herson, Lawrence I. R. "The Lost World of Municipal Government." *American Political Science Review* 51 (June 1957): 330–45.

Horowitz, Donald. "Three Dimensions of Ethnic Politics." *World Politics* 23, no. 2 (January 1971): 232–44.

Huntington, Samuel P. "The Change to Change: Modernization, Development and Politics." *Comparative Politics* 3, no. 3 (April 1967): 283–322.

Hyman, Herman. "Mass Media and Political Socialization: The Role of Patterns of Communication." In *Communications and Political Development*, edited by Lucian W. Pye. Princeton: Princeton University Press, 1963, pp. 128–48.

"Industrial Production, 1962–63." *Nigerian Trade Journal* 2, no. 3 (July/September 1963).

Jacob, Philip E., and Teune, Henry. "The Integrative Process: Guidelines for Analysis of the Bases of Political Community." In *The Integration of Political Communities*, edited by Philip E. Jacob and James V. Toscano. Philadelphia: J. B. Lippincott, 1964, pp. 1–45.

Jones, G. I. "Ibo Age Organization, with Special Reference to the Cross River and North-Eastern Ibo." *Journal of the Royal Anthropological Institute* 92, part 2 (1962): 191–211.

————. "Political Boycott—Eastern Tradition." *Nigerian Opinion*, February 1965, pp. 6–7.

Kahl, Joseph A. "Some Social Concomitants of Industrialization and Urbanization." Reprinted in *Independent Black Africa*, edited by William Hanna. Chicago: Rand McNally, 1964, pp. 86–136.

Katzin, Margaret. "The Role of the Small Entrepreneur." In *Economic Transition in Africa*, edited by Melville J. Herskovits and Mitchell Harwitz. Evanston, Ill.: Northwestern University Press, 1964, pp. 179–98.

Kolb, William L. "The Social Structure and Functions of Cities." *Economic Development and Cultural Change* 3, no. 1 (October 1954): 30–46.

Kuper, Hilda. "Introduction." In *Urbanization and Migration in West Africa*, edited by Hilda Kuper. Berkeley and Los Angeles: University of California Press, 1965, pp. 1–22.

Legum, Colin. "New Hope for Nigeria. The Search for National Unity." *Round Table* 230 (April 1968): 127–36.

"Leopoldville and Lagos: Comparative Study of Urban Conditions in 1960." *United Nations Economic Bulletin for Africa* 1, no. 2 (June 1961): 50–65.

Lerner, Daniel. "Toward a Communication Theory of Modernization." In *Communications and Political Development*, edited by Lucian W. Pye. Princeton: Princeton University Press, 1963.

Lindsay, Kenneth. "Dialog: Nigerian Peace Settlement?" *Africa Report* 15, no. 1 (January 1970): 14–15.

Little, Kenneth. "The West African Town: Its Social Basis." *Diogenes* 29 (Spring 1960): 16–31.

————. "Studies of Urbanization in Sierra Leone." *Conference Proceedings of the Nigerian Institute of Social and Economic Research*, March 1962, pp. 73–77.

————. "West African Urbanization as a Social Process." In *Independent Black Africa*, edited by William Hanna. Chicago: Rand McNally, 1964, pp. 137–48.

————, ed. "Urbanism in West Africa." *Sociological Review*, July 1959.

Lloyd, P. C. "Cocoa Politics and Yoruba Middle Class." *West Africa*, January 17, 1953.

————. "Some Modern Changes in the Government of Yoruba Towns." *Proceedings of the Second Annual Conference of the West African Institute of Social and Economic Research*, March 1953, pp. 7–21.

Bibliography

————. "Organization Among the Yoruba." *American Journal of Sociology* 60, 5 (March 1955): 446–54.

————. "Traditional Authorities." In *Political Parties and National Integration in Tropical Africa,* edited by James Coleman and Carl Rosberg, Jr. Berkeley and Los Angeles: University of California Press, 1964.

————. "The Yoruba of Nigeria." In *Peoples of Africa,* edited by James L. Gibbs. New York: Holt, Rinehart and Winston, 1965, pp. 547–82.

McCall, Daniel F. "Dynamics of Urbanization in Africa." *Annals of the American Academy of Political and Social Science* 298 (March 1955): 151–60.

Maduegbuna, B. A. "Oil in the Nigerian Economy." *Morning Post,* September 24, 1964.

Meisler, Stanley. "The Nigeria which is not at War." *Africa Report* 15, no. 1 (January 1970): 16–17.

Melson, Robert. "Politics and the Nigerian General Strike of 1964." In *Protest and Power in Black Africa,* edited by Robert Rotberg and Ali Mazrui. New York and London: Oxford University Press, 1970.

————, and Wolpe, Howard. "Modernization and the Politics of Communalism: A Theoretical Perspective." *American Political Science Review* 64, no. 4 (December 1970): 1112–30.

————. "Ideology and Inconsistency: The Politics of the 'Cross-Pressured' Nigerian Worker." *American Political Science Review* 65, no. 1 (March 1971): 161–71.

Messenger, John C., Jr. "Religious Acculturation Among the Annang Ibibio." In *Continuity and Change in African Cultures,* edited by William R. Bascom and Melville J. Herskovits. Chicago: University of Chicago Press, 1959, pp. 279–99.

Miner, Horace M. "Urban Influences on the Rural Hausa." In *Urbanization and Migration in West Africa,* edited by Hilda Kuper. Berkeley and Los Angeles: University of California Press, 1965, pp. 110–30.

Morgenthau, Ruth Schachter. "Single-Party Systems in West Africa." In *Independent Black Africa,* edited by William Hanna. Chicago: Rand McNally, 1964, pp. 419–43.

Morrill, W. T. "Immigrants and Associations: The Ibo in Twentieth Century Calabar." *Comparative Studies in Society and History* 5, no. 4 (July 1963): 424–48.

"Nigeria: Political Uncertainties." *Africa Confidential* 12, no. 3 (February 5, 1971): 4–5.

"Nigeria: So Many Soldiers." *Africa Confidential* 12, no. 12 (June 11, 1971): 1–3.

"Nigeria: The Troublesome East." *Africa Confidential* 11, no. 20 (October 2, 1970): 4–5.

Nzimiro, Francis Ikenna. "Oguta." *Nigeria Magazine,* no. 80 (March 1964): 30–43.

O'Connell, James. "The State and the Organization of Education in Nigeria: 1945–1960." In *Education and Politics in Nigeria,* edited by Hans N. Weiler. Freiburg: Verlag Rombach, 1964, pp. 113–37.

Offonry, H. Kanu. "The Strength of Ibo Clan Feeling." *West Africa,* May 26–June 2, 1951.

Okonjo, Chukka. "A Preliminary Medium Estimate of the 1962 Mid-Year Population of Nigeria." In *The Population of Tropical Africa,* edited by J. C. Caldwell and C. Okonjo. London: Longmans, 1968, pp. 78–96.

Ottah, Nelson. "Why Hate the Ibos." *Nigeria Drum Magazine,* February 1964.

Ottenberg, Phoebe. "The Changing Economic Position of Women Among the Afikpo Ibo." In *Continuity and Change in African Cultures,* edited by William R. Bascom and Melville J. Herskovits. Chicago: University of Chicago Press, 1959, pp. 205–23.

————. "The Afikpo Ibo of Eastern Nigeria." In *Peoples of Africa,* edited by James L. Gibbs, Jr. New York: Holt, Rinehart and Winston, 1965, pp. 1–39.

Ottenberg, Simon. "Improvement Associations Among the Afikpo Ibo." *Africa* 25, no. 1 (January 1955): 1–28.

————. "Ibo Oracles and Intergroup Relations." *Southwestern Journal of Anthropology* 14, no. 3 (Autumn 1958).

————. "Ibo Receptivity to Change." In *Continuity and Change in African Cultures,* edited by William R. Bascom and Melville J. Herskovits. Chicago: University of Chicago Press, 1959, pp. 130–43.

————. "The Development of Local Government in a Nigerian Township." *Anthropologica* 4, no. 1 (1962): 121–62.

————, and Ottenberg, Phoebe. "Afikpo Markets: 1900–1960." In *Markets in Africa,* edited by Paul Bohannan and George Dalton. Evanston, Ill.: Northwestern University Press, 1962, pp. 118–69.

Pearson, Scott, and Pearson, Sandra. "Nigeria: Oil Boom Reshapes the Future." *Africa Report* 16, no. 2 (February 1971): 14–17.

Polsby, N. "Three Problems in the Analysis of Community Power." *American Sociological Review* 24 (December 1959): 786–803.

Price, J. H. "The Eastern Region of Nigeria, March 1957." In *Five Elections in Africa,* edited by W. J. M. Mackenzie and Kenneth E. Robinson. Oxford: Clarendon Press, 1960, pp. 106–67.

Pye, Lucian. "The Politics of Southeast Asia." In *The Politics of Developing Areas,* edited by Gabriel A. Almond and James S. Coleman. Princeton: Princeton University Press, 1960, pp. 65–152.

————. "Introduction." In *Communications and Political Development,* edited by Lucian W. Pye. Princeton: Princeton University Press, 1963, pp. 3–23.

————. "Introduction: Political Culture and Political Development." In *Political Culture and Political Development,* edited by Lucian W. Pye and Sidney Verba. Princeton: Princeton University Press, 1965, pp. 3–26.

Riggs, Fred W. "Agraria and Industria—Toward a Typology of Comparative Administration." In *Toward a Comparative Study of Public Administration,* edited by William J. Siffen. Bloomington: Indiana University Department of Government, 1957, pp. 23–116.

Robinson, M. S. "Nigerian Oil: Prospects and Perspectives." *Nigerian Journal of Economic and Social Studies,* 6, no. 2 (July 1964): 219–29.

Rossi, Peter H. "Power and Community Structure." *Midwest Journal of Political Science* 4 (November 1960): 390–401.

Rudolph, Lloyd. "Urban Life and Political Radicalism." *Journal of Asian Studies* 20, no. 3 (May 1961): 283–97.

Schachter, Ruth. "Single Party Systems in West Africa." *American Political Science Review* 55, no. 3 (June 1961): 294–307.

Schulze, R. O. "The Role of Economic Dominants in Community Power Structure." *American Sociological Review* 23 (February 1958): 3–9.

————, and Blumberg, L. U. "The Determination of Local Power Elites." *American Journal of Sociology* 63 (December 1957): 290–96.

Schwab, William B. "An Experiment in Methodology in a West African Urban Community." *Human Organization* 13, no. 1 (Spring 1954): 13–19.

————. "Oshogbo—An Urban Community?" In *Urbanization and Migration in West Africa,* edited by Hilda Kuper. Berkeley and Los Angeles: University of California Press, 1965, pp. 85–109.

Singer, Milton. "Urban Politics in a Plural Society: A Symposium—Introduction." *Journal of Asian Studies* 20, no. 3 (May 1961): 265–66.

Sklar, Richard L. "The Contribution of Tribalism to Nationalism in Western Nigeria." *Journal of Human Relations* 8 (Spring and Summer 1960): 407–18.

Bibliography

———. "Contradictions in the Nigerian Political System." *Journal of Modern African Studies* 3, no. 2 (1965): 201–13.

———. "Nigerian Politics: The Ordeal of Chief Awolowo." In *Politics in Africa: 7 Cases*, edited by Gwendolen M. Carter and Alan Westin. New York: Harcourt, Brace and World, 1966, pp. 119–65.

———. "Nigerian Politics in Perspective." *Government and Opposition* 2 (July–October 1967): 524–39.

———. "Political Science and National Integration—A Radical Approach." *Journal of Modern African Studies* 5, no. 1 (1967): 1–11.

———, and Whitaker, C. S., Jr. "Nigeria." In *Political Parties and National Integration in Tropical Africa*, edited by James Coleman and Carl Rosberg, Jr. Berkeley and Los Angeles: University of California Press, 1964, pp. 597–654.

———. "The Federal Republic of Nigeria." In *National Unity and Regionalism in Eight African States*, edited by Gwendolen M. Carter. Ithaca: Cornell University Press, 1966, pp. 7–150.

Smith, M. G. "The Hausa of Northern Nigeria." In *Peoples of Africa*, edited by James L. Gibbs, Jr. New York: Holt, Rinehart and Winston, 1965, pp. 119–55.

Smock, Audrey. "The Politics of Relief." *Africa Report* 15, no. 1 (January 1970): 24–26.

Smythe, Hugh H. "Social Stratification in Nigeria." *Social Forces* 37, no. 2 (December 1958): 168–71.

———. "Urbanization in Nigeria." *Anthropology Quarterly* 33, no. 3 (July 1960): 143–48.

Sutton, Frank X. "Social Theory and Comparative Politics." In *Comparative Politics: A Reader*, edited by Harry Eckstein and David Apter. New York: Free Press, 1957, pp. 67–81.

Tugbiyele, E. A. "Problems of Local Government in Nigeria." *Conference Proceedings, the Nigerian Institute of Social and Economic Research*, March 1962, pp. 54–65.

Van de Walle, Etienne. "Who's Who and Where." *Africa Report* 15, no. 1 (January 1970): 22–23.

Wallerstein, Immanuel. "Ethnicity and National Integration in West Africa." *Cahiers D'Etudes Africaines*, no. 3 (October 1960): 129–39.

———. "Voluntary Associations." In *Political Parties and National Integration in Tropical Africa*, edited by James Coleman and Carl Rosberg, Jr. Berkeley and Los Angeles: University of California Press, 1964.

Wallis, C. A. G. "Urgent Local Government Problems in Africa." *Journal of Local Administrations Overseas* 2, no. 2 (April 1963): 61–75.

Ward, Barbara. "Uses of Prosperity." *Saturday Review*, August 29, 1964.

Weiner, Myron. "Violence and Politics in Calcutta." *Journal of Asian Studies* 20, no. 3 (May 1961): 275–81.

———. "Political Integration and Political Development." *Annals of the American Academy of Political and Social Science* 358 (March 1965): 52–64.

Whitaker, C. S., Jr. "Three Perspectives on Hierarchy: Political Thought and Leadership in Northern Nigeria." *Journal of Commonwealth Political Studies* 2, no. 4 (March 1965): 1–19.

———. "A Dysrhythmic Process of Political Change." *World Politics* 19, no. 2 (January 1967): 190–217.

Wirth, Louis. "Urbanism as a Way of Life." Reprinted in *Cities and Society: The Revised Reader in Urban Sociology*, edited by Paul K. Hatt and Albert J. Reiss. Glencoe, Ill.: Free Press, 1951, pp. 46–63.

Wolfinger, Raymond E. "Reputation and Reality in the Study of Community Power." *American Sociological Review* 25 (October 1960): 636–44.

Wolpe, Howard. "Port Harcourt: Ibo Politics in Microcosm." *Journal of Modern African Studies* 7, no. 3 (1969): 469–93.
Wriggins, W. Howard. "Impediments to Unity in New Nations: The Case of Ceylon." *American Political Science Review* 55 (June 1961): 313–20.

III. GOVERNMENT DOCUMENTS

A. *Great Britain, Colonial Office*

Report of the Commission Appointed to Enquire into the Fears of the Minorities and the Means of Allaying Them. Cmnd. 505. London, 1958.
Report of the Commission of Enquiry into the Disorders in the Eastern Provinces of Nigeria. Col. No. 256. London, 1950.

B. *Nigeria. Printed in Lagos by the Government Printer unless otherwise noted.*

Annual Report and Accounts, 1960–1961 of the Lagos Executive Development Board. Lagos: C.M.S. (Nigeria) Press, n.d.
Census Report for Census District 309201. Lagos, 1963, mimeographed.
Conclusion of the Federal Government on the Report of the Morgan Commission on the Review of Wages, Salaries and Conditions of Service of the Junior Employees of the Governments in the Federation and Private Establishments, 1963–64. Sessional Paper No. 5 of 1964.
Federal Electoral Commission. *Report on the Nigeria Federal Elections, December, 1959*.
Industrial Directory, 1964.
Investment in Education: Report of the Commission on Post-School Certificate and Higher Education in Nigeria.
National Development Plan, 1962–68. Apapa: Nigerian National Press Limited, n.d.
National Economic Council. *Economic Survey of Nigeria, 1959*.
Nigerian Ports Authority, *Eighth Annual Report for the Year Ended 31st March 1963*. Lagos: Nigerian Ports Authority, 1963.
Okotie-Eboh, Chief the Hon. F. S., *The National Budget*. Budget Speech delivered March 18, 1964.
Population Census of the Eastern Region of Nigeria, 1953. Lagos: Government Statistician, 1953–54.
Report of Coker Commission of Inquiry into the affairs of certain Statutory Corporations in Western Nigeria. 4 vols.
Report of the Commission on the Review of Wages, Salary, and Conditions of Service of the Junior Employees of the Governments of the Federation and in Private Establishments, 1963–64.
The Constitution of the Federal Republic of Nigeria.
This Is Nigeria: Port Harcourt.
Story, Bernard. *Report of the Commission of Inquiry into the Administration of the Lagos Town Council*.

C. *Eastern Nigeria. Printed in Enugu by the Government Printer unless otherwise noted.*

Annual Report of Heavy Industries, 1957–58.
Annual Report of the Internal Revenue Division, 1957–58. Official Document No. 19 of 1960.

Bibliography

Annual Report of the Ministry of Commerce, 1958–59. Official Document No. 17 of 1960.

Annual Report of the Ministry of Commerce, 1959–60. Official Document No. 13 of 1961.

Annual Report of the Ministry of Commerce, 1960–61. Official Document No. 11 of 1962.

Annual Report of the Ministry of Education, 1961. Official Document No. 30 of 1963.

Annual Report of the Ministry of Local Government, 1960–61. Official Document No. 2 of 1962.

Annual Report of the Ministry of Local Government, 1961–62. Official Document No. 15 of 1963.

Annual Report of the Ministry of Town Planning. 1958–59. Official Document No. 18 of 1962.

Approved Estimates of Eastern Nigeria, 1964–65. Official Document No. 13 of 1964.

Coatswith, R., Esq., M. C. *Report of an Inquiry into a Proposal to Excise the Aba District from the Aba-Ngwa County.*

Constitution of Eastern Nigeria Law, The, n.d.

Directory of Teachers' Colleges, Secondary Schools, Commercial Schools, Trade and Technical Schools, 1962. Official Document No. 1 of 1963.

Distribution of Amenities in Eastern Nigeria, 1963.

Eastern Nigeria Industrial Enquiry 1961–62. Official Document No. 6 of 1964.

Eastern Nigeria Local Government Estimates: Port Harcourt, 1964–65, mimeographed.

Eastern Nigeria (Local Government) Regulations, Orders, etc., 1956.

Eastern Nigerian Development Plan, 1962–68. Official Document No. 8 of 1962.

Eastern Nigeria Public Service. *Policy Paper.* Official Document No. 5 of 1963.

Eastern Nigeria Water Planning and Construction, Ltd. *Report on Roads, Drainage and Sewerage in Port Harcourt.* Enugu: Ministry of Works, September 1961.

"Eastern Region Local Government Law 1960, The." In *Supplement to the Eastern Regional Gazette* 9, no. 28 (May 26, 1960).

Education Graphs and Statistics, 1952–59. Extracted from The Ministry of Education Annual Report, 1959.

"First Three Years: A Report of the Eastern Nigeria Six Year Development Plan, The," n.d.

Floyer, R. K. *Memorandum on Proposed Municipality for Port Harcourt, 1946.* Port Harcourt Provincial Office Archives, 1946, mimeographed.

————, Ibekwe, D. O., and Njemanze, J. O. *Commission of Inquiry into the Working of the Port Harcourt Town Council,* 1955.

Goldway, Michael. *Report on Investigation of Vocational Education in Eastern Nigeria.* Official Document No. 13 of 1962.

Grant, P. F., U. B. E. *Report of the Inquiry into the Allocation of Market Stalls at Aba,* 1955.

Gunning, O. P. *Report of the Inquiry into the Administration of the Affairs of the Onitsha Urban District Council,* 1955.

Harding, R. W. *Report of the Enquiry of the Dispute Over the Obiship of Onitsha, 1961–63.* Official Document No. 6 of 1963.

Industrial Directory. Official Document No. 29 of 1963.

Investment Opportunities in Eastern Nigeria, 1962.

Investment Possibilities in the Eastern Region of the Federation of Nigeria. Official Document No. 11 of 1960.

Jones, G. I. *Report of the Position, Status, and Influence of Chiefs and Natural Rulers in the Eastern Region of Nigeria*, 1956.
Kilby, Peter. *Development of Small Industries in Eastern Nigeria*, 1963.
Kingsley, Dr. J. D. *Staff Development*. Official Document No. 7 of 1961.
Know Your Legislators, 1963.
Local Government, n.d.
Memorandum on Local Government Estimates, 1962–63.
Parliamentary Debates, Eastern House of Chiefs. Official Report, Third Session, 1963–64.
Parliamentary Debates of the Eastern House of Assembly. Official Report of the Third Session, 1963–64.
Perkins, N. C. *Report of the Inquiry into the Administration of the Affairs of the Enugu Municipal Council*, 1960.
Policy for Education. Sessional Paper No. 6 of 1953.
Policy for Local Government. Official Document No. 13 of 1963.
Progress Report of the Eastern Region Development Plan, 1962–68. Official Document No. 15 of 1964.
Report of the Commission of Inquiry into the Nembe Chieftaincy Dispute. Official Document No. 24 of 1960.
Report on Eastern Nigerian Election, November 1961.
Report on the General Election to the Eastern House of Assembly 1957. Sessional Paper No. 1 of 1957.
Report on the Review of the Educational System in Eastern Nigeria. Official Document No. 19 of 1962.
Self Government in the Eastern Region, Part I: Policy Statements. Sessional Paper No. 2 of 1957.
Self Government in the Eastern Region, Part II: Data and Statistics. Official Document No. 1 of 1958.
Statistical Digest of Eastern Nigeria, 1963.

IV. UNPUBLISHED MATERIAL

Frey, Frederick W. Paper on problems in the analysis of power. Cambridge, n.d., mimeographed.
Hanna, William John, and Hanna, Judith Lynne. "The Political Structure of Urban-Centered African Communities," mimeographed.
Henderson, Richard N. " 'Generalized Cultures' and 'Evolutionary Adaptability': The Comparison of Urban Efik and Ibo in Nigeria." Paper read before the meeting of the American Anthropological Association, November 1964.
———. "Onitsha Kingship Succession: Traditional and Contemporary Patterns in Ibo Politics." Paper read before the African Studies Association Conference, 1965.
Jenkins, George, and Post, Kenneth. "Alhaji Adegoke Adelabu: Africa in Transition." Paper presented to the Annual Meeting of the African Studies Association, October 30, 1965.
Jones, G. I. "From Direct to Indirect Rule in Eastern Nigeria." Paper presented to the Institute of African Studies, University of Ife, November 1964.
Kennedy, Frank. "An Outline Sketch of the History and Problems of Town Planning in Port Harcourt." Paper presented to the Conference on Town Planning and Urbanization held in Port Harcourt, March 12, 1963, mimeographed.
Laguian, Aprodicio A. "The City in Nation-Building: Politics in Metropolitan Manila." Ph.D. dissertation. Department of Political Science, M.I.T., 1965.

Bibliography

Ostrum, Donald. "Housing in Diobu Mile 2." Report of a sample survey of Mile 2 Diobu presented to the Eastern Nigeria Housing Corporation, 1964, mimeographed.

Radio address on the Nigerian Ports Authority delivered by E. O. Uruakpa, manager for the Eastern ports, n.d., typewritten.

Shell-BP. "Shell-BP in the Nigerian Economy." Port Harcourt, 1964, mimeographed.

Sklar, Richard. "A Note on the Study of Community Power in Nigeria." Paper presented before the Annual Conference of the African Studies Association, October 13, 1962.

U.A.C. Associated Companies African Worker Union. "Our Case for Salaries Revision." Memorandum submitted to the Morgan Commission, Lagos, 1963.

Weiner, Myron. "Urbanization and Political Extremism: An Hypothesis Tested." Cambridge, n.d.

V. NEWSPAPERS AND JOURNALS

Africa Confidential. Africa Confidential, London.

Africa Report. African-American Institute, Washington, D.C.

Daily Express. Amalgamated Press of Nigeria, Ltd., Lagos.

Daily Times. Nigerian Printing and Publishing Company, Lagos.

Eastern Nigerian Guardian. Associated Newspapers of Nigeria, Ltd., Port Harcourt (Zik Group).

Eastern Outlook, Eastern Nigeria Information, Enugu.

Eastern Star. Goodwill Press, Port Harcourt.

Journal of Modern African Studies, The. Cambridge University Press, Cambridge.

Nigerian Morning Post. Nigerian National Press Limited, Lagos.

Nigerian Observer. Enitonna Press, Port Harcourt.

Nigerian Opinion. Nigerian Current Affairs Society, Ibadan.

Nigeria Trade Journal. Federal Ministry of Information, Lagos.

Port Harcourt This Week. Goodwill Press, Port Harcourt.

West Africa. West Africa Publishing Company, Ltd., London.

VI. OTHER SOURCES

Files of the Archives of the Port Harcourt Provincial Secretariat, Port Harcourt.

Files of the Eastern Nigerian Ministry of Education, Enugu.

Files of the Nigerian National Archives, Enugu and Ibadan.

Files of the Port Harcourt Municipal Council.

Files of the Port Harcourt-Obia Planning Authority.

Files of the Rivers Province Education Office of the Eastern Nigerian Ministry of Education, Port Harcourt.

Files of the secretariat of the Eastern Nigerian Headquarters of the National Convention of Nigerian Citizens (NCNC), Enugu.

Minutes and memoranda of various town and divisional unions, Port Harcourt.

Minutes of General and Committee Meetings of the Port Harcourt Municipal Council, 1949–1965. National Archives and Port Harcourt Municipal Offices.

Minutes of Meetings of the Executive Committee of the Port Harcourt Branch of the United Africa Company and Associated Companies African Workers Union, 1962–1964.

Minutes of Meetings of the Executive Committee of the Shell-BP and Allied
  Workers Union of Nigeria, Port Harcourt, 1963–1965.
Minutes of Meetings of the Port Harcourt Divisional Executive Committee
  of the National Convention of Nigerian Citizens (NCNC), 1952–1964.
Minutes of Meetings of the Port Harcourt Township Advisory Board, 1918–
  1949. National Archives, Enugu.
Personal File of G. I. Egbunine, Port Harcourt.
Personal Files of V. K. Onyeri, Port Harcourt.

Index

Aba, 14, 24
Aba Division, 38
Abana, 38
Abecheta, 121
Abeokuta, 13
Abernethy, David, 13, 181, 196, 201
Abiribans, 35, 38, 74
Abu, Mallam, 155
Action Group, 131, 204
Afenmai Union, 165
Afikpo, 42
African Club: early non-Ibo dominance of, 71, 96; and emergent African elite, 80; Onitsha Ibo membership in, 74
African Community League: and bifurcation of local leadership, 127–128; declining influence of, 113; and drive for local self-government, 102–112 *passim;* formation of, 70, 72, 90–91; increasing militancy of, 98; leadership of, 86–87, 120; non-Ibo dominance of, 95; and Palmer affair, 100–102; role of "locals" in, 99; social composition of, 94; structure and functions of, 91–94; and Zikists, 125
African Continental Bank, 138, 155
African Progress Union, 79
Age organizations, functions of, 39–40
Aggrey, J. E. K., 87
Agulefo, Dr. N. T. C., 174, 175
Aguma, Emmanuel, 155
Aguta, Margaret, 163
Ahoada County Council, 166
Ahoada District Office, 164
Ajibade, Dr. O., 96, 127–129
Akokwa Town, 73–74
Akomas, G. C. N., 133, 162
Akpulu, 73–74
Alagoa, A. E.: as deputy mayor, 148;

as local ENCC chairman, 204; resignation of as Mayor, 174
Alajo, Jones, 183, 184, 193
Aluko, Sam, 225
Amalgamated Union of the United African Company Workers Union (UNMAG), 126
Americans, in Port Harcourt, 25
Anene, V. C. I., 139, 140, 151, 173
Anglican Church: establishment by of industrial mission in Onitsha Division, 46; penetration into Ijaw country by, 55
Anufuro, W. K., 149, 205, 207
Anyanwu, F. U., 160
Aro Chuku, 36, 37; commercial and political preeminence of, 45; oracle of, 36–39
Aros, 35; absorption within non-Ibo communities of, 36–37, 40; as relatively advantaged among Ibos, 44–45; control of slave trades by, 37–39; postslave trade adaptability of, 45
Asika, Ukpabi, 225
Asinobi, M. I., 120
Azikiwe, Nnamdi: and Ibo State Union, 139, 140; and market stall dispute, 135; as NCNC leader, 99, 120, 133; as Onitshan, 45; and Port Harcourt, 122–125; on Port Harcourt, 13; and Rivers State, 224; and 1953 sit-tight crisis, 131–133

Bakongo, 69
Bangala, 69
Bende Divisional Union, 162
Biafran secession, 221; and Eastern minorities, 223–224; and Federal victory, 224–228; and oil, 222, 224–225

Index

Bille, E. I., 183, 184
Biriye, Harold, 220, 223
Bonny, as administrative center, 47
Business elite, 74–77. *See also* Traders

Cabinet of Mile 2 Diobu, 165–168
Calabar, 46; as administrative center, 47; as location of Hope Waddell Institute, 47
Calabar-Ogoja-Rivers State, 214
Caretaker Council, appointment of, 136–137; dissolution of, 147, 148, 149; Ikokwu as president of, 115; Onitsha dominance of, 146–147
Christian Mothers Association, 206, 207
Churches: and comity agreements, 197; conflict between Catholic and Protestant, 48–49, 78, 195–212; as integrative force, 78–79; and voluntary agency schools, 196–200
Class differentiation and conflict, between Eastern Nigerian "haves" and "have-nots," 5; within communal groups in Port Harcourt, 79–80; and general strike of 1964, 177–194; between Mile 2 Diobu and main township, 21–22, 169–170; in Mile 2 Diobu, 164–166, 168; and NCNC Ibo State Union cleavage, 140–141; as manifested in Zikist clash with African Community League, 125
Climate, 15
Coleman, James, 4, 45, 120, 122
Colonial government, 14, 16–17; centralization of power under, 65–66; and direct rule in Port Harcourt, 63; and drive for self-government in Port Harcourt, 102–112; and educational policy, 196–197; new communal identities generated by administrative structure of, 49–50; and 1913 land acquisition, 19, 54–56, 164; and Port Harcourt Local Authority, 62–63, 66–67
Commercialization of politics, 171–174. *See also* Traders; Business elite
Communal associations: and Bende Divisional Union, 162; electoral involvement of, 82, 113–114, 159–160, 162; formation of, 80–84; leadership of, 232; and Mbaise Federal Union, 75–77; and NCNC, 120, 123, 129; and Onitsha Divisional Union, 75–77, 114; and Orlu Divisional Union, 75–77, 162; and Owerri Progressive Union,

70, 84; and Rivers State Movement, 217; and Sierra Leone Union, 87; Zikists as members of, 125
Communal differentiation, 7, 77–80; by occupation, 79–80; by religion, 48–49, 77–79, 195; by social stratification, 80
Communal divisions and conflict; between Diobus indigenes and strangers, 77; between Diobus and Okrikans, 54–56; between Diobus and Owerri Ibos, 55; between Europeans and Africans, 67, 69–70, 98; between geo-ethnic groups, 73–77, 234; between Ibos and non-Ibos, 5, 41–47, 71–73, 113–115; between Ibos and Yorubas, 122–123; between Ijaws and Ibos, 213–228, 232, 234; between Mbaises and Onitshas, 160–161; between Okrikans and Owerri Ibos, 55; between Onitshan Ibos and Owerri Ibos, 5, 45, 74–77, 99, 100, 145–170, 232; between Orlu-Okigwi and Bende-Mbaise, 164–170
Communal expansion: defined, 69; as manifested in cleavage between indigenes and strangers, 77; as manifested in growing racial consciousness, 69; as manifested in new geo-ethnic identities, 73–77, 232; as manifested in new identities of nationality, 70–73, 232; and the multiplication of communal reference points, 69
Communal identities: among Ibos, 42–43, 69–77 *passim*; based upon administrative units of colonial system, 49–50; intensified by democratization, 98, 99, 113–114; in interaction with noncommunal identities, 7–8, 28–29, 42–43, 77–80, 178–179, 185–186, 193–194, 204–205, 209, 234–235; and political recruitment, 155–156, 164–176; as political weapon, 146–147, 171, 232–233; primacy of, 29, 97, 140, 195, 212
Communalism: compatible with individualism among Ibos, 42–43; and competition, 6–7, 70–73, 232–233, 240–241; contrasted with ethnicity, 6; contrasted with tribalism, 6–7, 231; controlling of, 237–241; and cultural pluralism, 6–7, 231; defined, 6; and democratization, 98–99, 112–119; and equality, 235–236; and institutional autonomy, 237–240; moderated by overlapping affiliations, 209, 239; as modern urban phenomenon, 6–7, 73,

Index

4, 6, 14–15, 22, 215; as industrial center, 4, 5, 6, 23, 215; and natural gas, 22, 23; and oil, 6, 22–23, 215; and oil refinery, 23; as railway terminus, 15, 22; as regional economic center, 24; and Rivers State, 215–217, 224–227; and local salary and wage levels, 24; and Shell-BP, 22–23; and small industry, 23–24; Trans-Amadi Industrial Estate, 23
Edos, in Port Harcourt, 24, 124–128, 184
Edo Union, 125
Education. *See* Universal primary education; Churches; Religious conflict; Missionaries
Efiks: and COR State, 214; as early graduates of Hope Waddell Institute, 47; ethnography of, 32–33; mobilization of, 44, 46–48; in Port Harcourt, 25, 26, 28; sense of superiority vis-à-vis less educated Ibos, 46–47
Elections: 1949 Town Council, 112–119, 127–128, 129, 150–151; 1951 Regional House of Assembly, 129, 131–132; 1953 Regional House of Assembly, 127, 132–133, 138; 1954 Federal elections, 132; 1955 Municipal Council, 148–151; 1957 Regional House of Assembly, 127, 159, 166–168, 199, 204, 211; 1958 Municipal Council, 150–151; 1959 Federal elections, 220; 1961 Municipal Council, 150–151, 184; 1961 Regional House of Assembly, 141, 168–169, 175, 220; 1964–65 Federal elections, 157–163, 169, 193–194, 211
Elugwaornu, G. I., 165, 166, 167, 168, 169
Emenike, J. I., 166, 167
Enugu, 14
Enugu shooting, 126–127
Equality, and commercial conflict, 235–236
Ethnicity, 6, 97. *See also* Communalism; Communal identities; Geo-ethnicity
Ethnography. *See* Eastern Nigeria
Europeans: African response to domination by, 96–112; and expatriate business firms, 186–189, 191–192; and franchise, 111; in Port Harcourt, 25; as Port Harcourt's political elite, 62–67

Federal victory, 224–228

Floyer, Commission of Enquiry, 147
Floyer Report, 102–112
Foot, Sir Hugh, 125–126
Franchise: and communal strategies, 171; debated, 108–112; and exclusion of non-Ibos, 114–115; and first election, 112–113; intensifies intra-African commercial conflict, 113–114; and new politicans, 118–119; and Owerri ascendancy, 145–170; and patterns of political recruitment, 98–99
Friedland, William, 178-179
Fulani, 26

Gabriel, Watson, 183
Garvey, Marcus, 87
General strike of 1945, 124
General strike of 1964, 177–194; and communalism, 184–186; highlights of, 188–193; and International Christian Federation of Trade Unions, 181, 182; and Joint Action Committee, 180, 181, 187, 188, 190, 191, 192, 193; and Labor Unity Front, 182; and Morgan Commission, 179–181, 187, 192; and Nigerian Employers Consultative Association, 186, 187, 188, 189, 191, 193; and Port Harcourt Council of Labor, 182–183, 184, 186, 187, 188–192, 193; and reemergence of non-Ibos, 181–186; as socioeconomic protest, 177–178, 190–191; and United Labor Congress, 181
Geo-ethnicity: and alienation of intelligentsia, 174–175; and commercialization, 171–174; and electoral politics in Mile 2 Diobu, 164–169; as example of communal expansion, 73–77; impact on local electoral politics, 145–176; and 1964–65 Federal elections, 157–163; and Owerri ascendancy, 145–155; particular importance of in Port Harcourt, 73; political assessment of, 170–176; and political recruitment, 157–176; as political weapon, 171; and pragmatism, 170–171, 239; socioeconomic roots of, 168
Ghanaians: as early graduates of Hope Waddell Institute, 47; and sense of superiority vis-à-vis less educated Ibos, 47
Gowon, Kakubu, 226

Harcourt, H. N., 118, 119
Harcourt, Lewis, 15

Index

Kano, 13
Kanuri, in Port Harcourt, 26
Katsina, 13
Kornhauser, William, 82

Labor movement: *See* General strike of 1945; General strike of 1964; Trade unionists
Lagos, 14, 15, 86, 102, 103, 110, 119, 120, 123, 139, 181, 186, 187, 190, 191, 193, 223, 225, 227
Lagos Constitutional Conference of 1966, 223
Leadership. *See* Political leadership
Leith-Ross, Sylvia, 62, 91–92
Little, Kenneth, 54, 81, 82
Local authority: and African Community League, 92–93; limited powers of, 66; and Palmer Affair, 100–102; and Port Harcourt Station magistrate, 63
Locals, as leadership type, 99, 127–128, 175
Local self-government, drive for, 100–112
London Constitutional Conference of 1957, 213–214, 216
Lugard, Lord, 57, 65

MacPherson Constitution, 131
Main Township, 15
Marketing Board, Eastern Nigeria, 132, 138
Market Traders Association, 92
Mbaegbu, 205
Mbaise, 158, 163
Mbaise Federal Union: composition of executive committee, 75–77; and 1964–65 Federal election, 159–160
Mbakwe, S. O., 161–163
Mbanefo, Louis, 122
Mbanesa Clan, 73–74
Mbanu, B. E., 204, 205
Mbonu, J. U., 149, 155, 158, 161, 163
Mercantile Workers Union, 126
Mile 1 Diobu, 166–167
Mile 2 Diobu, 15, 18; brought under jurisdiction of Port Harcourt Municipal Council, 21; cabinet, 164–165; Catholics predominant in, 210; electoral politics and ethnicity in, 164–170; health problems in, 20–21; lack of planning in, 19–20, 61, 164, 166; Local Council of, 166; and main township, 21–22, 169–170; NCNC

in, 165–170; overcrowding of, 20–21; political style of, 21–22; and regional election of 1957, 166–168; Stranger Elements Association of, 165; young population of, 20
Minorities Commission, 214, 216, 217, 218, 219, 232
Missionaries: establish Anglican industrial mission in Onitsha Division, 46; locate first schools in riverain communities, 45, 47; and secular education, 196–200. *See also* Churches, Roman Catholic missions, Church Missionary Society, Educational policy
Mobilization. *See* Social mobilization; Differential mobilization
Modernization: and communal conflict, 6–7, 73, 231, 232–235; and communal transformation, 7; compatible with communalism, 7–8, 42–43, 77–78; and competition, 6, 232–233; as sociological concept, 3–4
Morgan, Justice Adeyinka, 180
Morgan Commission, 179–181, 187, 192
Moslems, in Port Harcourt, 28
Municipal Committee, 134, 136
Municipal Council: Action Group member of, 204; corruption in, 173, 202; and Diobus, 219; elections of 1955, 148, 150–151; elections of 1958, 150–151; elections of 1961, 150–151; established, 148; and general strike of 1964, 191; and Owerri ascendancy, 148; and Port Harcourt Welfare Society, 174; Protestant domination of, 210; subject to control by regional government, 212; and U.P.E. schools, 201, 212. *See also* Councillors; Town Council
Municipal Councillors. *See* Councillors

National awakening, 99, 119–128; and Azikiwe, 122–123; and bifurcation of local leadership, 127–128; delayed in Port Harcourt, 120–121; and "Enugu shooting," 126–127; and NCNC, 119–120; and Umolu, 126; and Zikists, 123–126
National Church of Nigeria, 210
Nationality identities: in conflict, 213–228, 232; as example of communal expansion, 70–73; as product of competition, 70–73
Nationalities of Port Harcourt: American, 25; Edo, 24, 92, 125; Efik, 24,

Index

Trade unionists: and communalism, 184–186; and Mercantile Workers Union, 126; and 1945 general strike, 120, 124; and 1964 general strike, 177–194; and non-Ibo leadership, 181–186; opposed to property-based franchise, 110; and SWAFP, 163; and UNAMAG, 126. *See also* General strike of 1945; General strike of 1964

Tradition: as applied to Ibo culture, 39–43, 232; as sociological concept, 3–4; versus modernity, 3–4, 42–43, 77–78, 232–235

Trans-Amadi Industrial Estate, 23, 188

Transformation. *See* Communal transformation

Tribalism, 6; as political weapon, 146–147, 171, 232–233; as product of modernity, 6–7, 73, 231, 232–233. *See also* Communalism

Tribal union. *See* Communal associations

Umolu, John: and dissolution of Town Council, 135; and election to Regional House of Assembly, 127–128; and ethnic arithmetic, 155; as involved in communal association, 165; 1953 reelection of, 133; and 1961 ouster, 128; as organizer of Port Harcourt Zikist Movement, 124; and UNAMAG, 126

Umuahia, 14

UNAMAG. *See* Amalgamated Union of the United African Company Workers Union

Unemployment in Port Harcourt, 26–27

United African Company, 94, 112, 121, 124, 126, 188

United Labor Congress, 181

United Progressive Grand Alliance, 193

Universal primary education, 198, 201–212

Urbanism: and agriculturally oriented urban centers, 13–14; and ancient trade centers, 13; and communal associations, 80–84; and communalism, 232; and new towns, 14; and overlapping group affiliations, 209

Voluntary agencies. *See* Churches

Voluntary associations. *See* Communal associations

West African Pilot, 122, 124

Western-educated elite, 80, 85, 95–97, 232–233

Western impact, 4, 14; as altering previous subordination of Ibos, 46; and communal identities, 44–50; and education, 196–197; on rates of mobilization, 44–48

Williams, Rev. E. K., 79, 86, 91, 94, 97

Wobo, Joseph, 218, 219

Women: and Catholic protests, 203, 205–209; and Ibo system of exogamy, 35; and 1964–65 Federal election, 163; and Owerri Provincial Union, 147; as Town Councillors, 111, 146

Yellowe, Sonny, 184

Yorubas: and colonial administration system, 171; in competition with Ibos, 47, 122–123, 131, 139; as early graduates of Hope Waddell Institute, 47; in Port Harcourt, 24, 83, 111, 127, 129, 163, 183, 184, 193

Yoruba towns, 13–14

Young, Crawford, 69

Zikist Movement, 99, 110, 112, 123–127, 133, 149, 155, 161

Zikist National Vanguard, 146

314